THE BUILDINGS OF ENGLAND

BERKSHIRE

NIKOLAUS PEVSNER

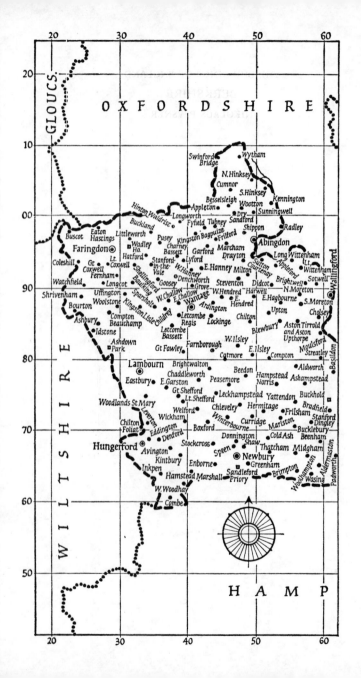

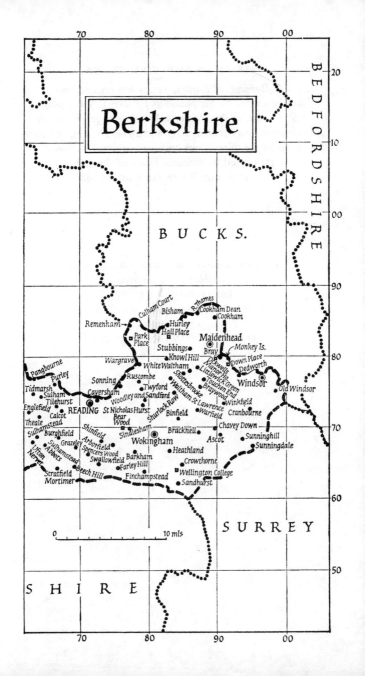

PEVSNER ARCHITECTURAL GUIDES

The Buildings of England series was created and
largely written by Sir Nikolaus Pevsner (1901–1983).
First editions of the county volumes were published by
Penguin Books between 1951 and 1974. The continuing
programme of revisions and new volumes has been
supported by research financed through
the Buildings Books Trust since 1994

*The publication of this volume has been made
possible by a grant from*
THE LEVERHULME TRUST
*to cover all the necessary research work
and by a generous contribution from*
ARTHUR GUINNESS, SON & CO. LTD

Berkshire

BY

NIKOLAUS PEVSNER

★

YALE UNIVERSITY PRESS
NEW HAVEN AND LONDON

YALE UNIVERSITY PRESS
NEW HAVEN AND LONDON
302 Temple Street, New Haven CT 06511
23 Pond Street, London NW3 2PN
www.yale.edu/yup
www.yaleup.co.uk
www.pevsner.co.uk

—

Published by Penguin Books 1966
First published by Yale University Press 2002
2 4 6 8 10 9 7 5 3 1

—

ISBN 0 300 09582 1

—

—

Printed in China
through World Print
Set in Monotype Plantin

—

CHI NON FA, NON SBAGLIA

This volume is dedicated to
STEPHEN, MARTIN, AND RUTH
all born while this volume
was under way

CONTENTS

★

Map References

*

The numbers printed in italic type in the margin against the place names in the gazetteer of the book indicate the position of the place in question on the index map (pages 2–3), which is divided into sections by the 10–kilometre reference lines of the National Grid. The reference given here omits the two initial letters (formerly numbers) which in a full grid reference refer to the 100–kilometre squares into which the country is divided. The first two numbers indicate the *western* boundary, and the last two the *southern* boundary, of the 10-kilometre square in which the place in question is situated. For example Abingdon (reference 4090) will be found in the 10-kilometre square bounded by grid lines 40 and 50 on the *west* and 90 and 00 on the *south*; Pangbourne (reference 6070) in the square bounded by grid lines 60 and 70 on the *west* and 70 and 80 on the *south*.

The map contains all those places, whether towns, villages, or isolated buildings, which are the subject of separate entries in the text.

FOREWORD

Berkshire is the first county I had to travel and describe after my wife had died. She had driven me through nearly all the preceding counties, had done all the day-to-day planning, and more and more also visited the buildings. Four eyes see more than two, and her eyes were quicker than mine. I fear this volume will have suffered from that private circumstance. The journey could not have the zest, the fun, the cursing in common which all belonged to so well tried a partnership. I am all the more grateful to those who offered their help and thus made the book possible. My son Dieter drove me for two weeks, my senior assistant Mrs Judy Nairn for one, and Mr John Newman for another. Where would I have been without them?

And where would I have been without Mrs Helen Braham (then Miss Helen Butterworth) and Mrs Sonya Wood (then Miss Sonya Hopkins), who shared the tedious job of extracting all the information which has to be available before I can take over? To them also I express my gratitude. Then there are those good friends Mrs Camilla Israel and Sir Allen Lane and Lady Lane who made it possible for us to exchange for more than a week the pub or hotel for a temporary home, The Old Kennels, Bucklebury Slade, and Priory Farm, Beech Hill.

But the number of those to whom I owe a debt of gratitude is much greater. The cases grow where recognition is needed so often that initials are used to indicate indebtedness. To the familiar NBR for the National Buildings Record, MHLG for the Ministry of Housing and Local Government, GR for the Goodhart-Rendel index of Victorian churches, TK for Sir Thomas Kendrick's lists of Victorian stained glass, PF for Mr Peter Ferriday's index of Victorian restorations, I have now to add GS for Mr Geoffrey Spain's invaluable and rapidly growing lists of tenders from the architectural magazines, and BC for the Rev. Basil Clarke's extracts from Berkshire ecclesiastical papers which he most kindly offered me for use.

Basil Clarke in addition examined the whole of the galleys for Victorian accuracy, Mr Neville Hadcock examined the Newbury galleys, and Messrs Maurice Bond, the Hon. Custodian of the Muniments of St George's Chapel, and Robert Mackworth-Young, the Windsor Castle Librarian, after having conducted me in the greatest detail over *Windsor Castle* and answered any number of tedious questions, finally read the galley proofs as well and commented on them. I also wish to thank Mr S. H. Horrocks, the Reading Borough Librarian, Mr W. J. Smith, the Berkshire County Archivist, Mr J. C. Powell, the Maidenhead Borough Librarian, and Mr M. Hocking, the Abingdon Librarian. Mr S. E. Rigold of the Ancient Monuments Department, Ministry of Public Building and Works, helped me on timber roofs, Denis Evinson on Catholic building in the C19, Stuart Smith on Alfred Waterhouse, John Hills on Bradfield College, the Rev. and Mrs H. F. D. Sparke on Wytham.

Mr Derek Simpson, in addition to the introduction on prehistory, did the gazetteer on prehistoric and Roman antiquities. Mr Terence Miller's notes on Berkshire geology will be found on p. 47.

After these I must thank more generally all those rectors and vicars who have helped me by answering letters about their churches and by examining proofs, and those owners or occupiers of houses who have allowed me entry and also replied to inquiries. I owe it to the latter to state here that description of a house in my gazetteer does not necessarily mean its being open to the public.

The principles on which the following gazetteer is founded are the same as in the twenty-nine volumes of the *Buildings of England* which precede it. I have myself seen everything that I describe. Where this is not the case the information obtained by other means is placed in brackets. Information ought to be as complete as the space of the volume permits for churches prior to c.1830 and all town houses, manor houses, and country houses of more than purely local interest. Movable furnishings are not included in secular buildings, though they are in churches. Exceptions to the latter rule are bells, hatchments, chests, chairs, plain fonts, and altar tables. Royal arms, coffin lids with foliate crosses, and brasses of post-Reformation date are mentioned occasionally, church plate of after 1830 only rarely. Village crosses are omitted where only a plain base or stump of the shaft survives. As for churches and chapels of after 1830, I had to make a selection, and this is dictated by architectural value or by significance otherwise in the light of architectural history. The same applies to secular buildings of the C19 and C20.

Finally, as in all previous volumes, it is necessary to end the foreword to this with an appeal to all users to draw my attention to errors and omissions.

INTRODUCTION

PREHISTORY AND ROMAN ANTIQUITIES
BY DEREK SIMPSON

The earliest evidence for human settlement in Berkshire is the numerous flint tools – hand axes – of the Old Stone Age (Palaeolithic), abundant both in public museums and private collections. Unfortunately many of them are unlocated, but the comparatively small number whose contexts are known all come from gravel deposits (e.g. Abingdon, Earley, Reading), indicating settlement in river valleys. Most of the axes are of Acheulean type and belong to the second of the three major periods which came between those of intense cold during the Ice Age. A few rare finds of implements and flakes of Mousterian type probably belong to the last interglacial phase and might indicate the presence of Neanderthal man, as this industry is associated with the physical type on the Continent, although no fossil human remains have been found in Berkshire.

The gradual retreat of the ice and increasingly warm conditions at the end of the last glaciation produced a considerable change in the environment in which prehistoric man lived, notably in the encroachment of forests, first of birch and pine and later of oak. To meet these changes technological improvements and a new pattern of settlement were evolved. The Mesolithic groups, like their Palaeolithic predecessors, were hunters, but now their quarry were the roe and red deer and wild pig, which they pursued through the forests with the aid of dogs, their only domesticated species. Evidence for these hunters comes from numerous sites in the county. Their flint axes, the so-called Thames Picks, are recorded, chiefly as surface finds, from the Thames Valley, with a particular concentration below the Goring Gap. These tools reflect the forested conditions in which their makers lived and represent a positive reaction to the spread of forests and the problem of forest clearance. The settlement sites so far discovered all lie in the tributaries of the Thames, possibly because in the main valley the sites have been covered by later alluvium. The most important group is in the Kennet Valley (e.g. Newbury, Thatcham, Speen). At Thatcham, on the shores of a small lake, Mesolithic hunters had cleared the pine and birch to provide living space. No structures other than hearths were found during the excavation of the site, and presumably the group lived in tents which have left no trace. The lakeside was first settled c. 8000 B.C. and was occupied intermittently by hunters over a period of about a thousand years.

The first farming communities settled in Britain in the middle of the fourth millennium. The primary areas of settlement were the lightly forested downs of Wessex and Sussex, and the Berkshire Downs, the N extension of the former province, appear to have been included in this primary area, although the characteristic monuments of this first farming culture – the Windmill Hill Culture – are not so numerous in the county as in the chalk lands to the S. These first farmers practised a mixed economy of cereal production and stock breeding, and it is with the latter activity that the causewayed camps are to be associated. The majority of these camps occupy hill-top situations on the chalk, but the only Berkshire example of the type, at Abingdon, is a low-lying site on the Thames gravels. The interrupted construction of its ditches with numerous causeways is typical, but here use has been made of the natural barriers of the two rivers, the ditches blocking access to the spur which they form. Occupation of causewayed camps appears to have been intermittent and primarily in the autumn, when herds would be rounded up within the confines of the camp for identification, barter, and slaughter. The camps contain little in their interiors to suggest use as permanent settlements, the most consistently recurring features being storage pits, as at Abingdon. The axes of stone from Great Langdale, Westmorland, found at Abingdon also indicate that these periodic gatherings within the camps provided opportunities for trade, and probably too for religious activities. Elsewhere in the county the former presence of these farming communities is attested by flint axes, ranging from roughly flaked, unfinished specimens to the carefully ground and polished final products. Most of these axes occur as stray finds, but in some cases they are associated with a considerable quantity of knapping debris and other flint tools (e.g. Uffington, West Woodhay).

Another category of monument characteristic of the culture is the earthen long barrow, represented by the sites of Wayland's Smithy, Ashbury and Gallows Hill, Combe. The long barrow is an elongated earthen mound, generally wedge-shaped in plan, the material being obtained from flanking quarry ditches. Beneath the broader, generally E, end of the mound are found multiple inhumation burials. The thirteen partially articulated skeletons beneath the Wayland's Smithy barrow lay in a ridged-roofed mortuary enclosure of wood and stone and similar mortuary buildings have been noted under long barrows elsewhere in Britain. At this site too the relative chronological relationship between the earthen long barrow and the stone-built chambered tomb was established. After the construction of the long barrow the mound was enlarged by the digging of two new flanking ditches and a megalithic tomb and façade added to its s end. The material of this enlarged mound was revetted with a series of large sarsen slabs set along its flanks. This structure, and a probable second monument at Lambourn, are N outliers of a distinctive group of megalithic tombs centred on the Cotswold region and lands bordering the estuary of the Severn. The material from them suggests that they overlap chronologically with the causewayed camps and earthen long barrows and that many features of their material culture and economy are common to both groups.

Later Neolithic groups, characterized by coarse, poorly fired pottery richly ornamented with cord, bird-bone, and fingernail impressions and by a series of flint types which appear to owe much to Mesolithic flint-knapping traditions, have left no distinctive monuments in the county. Their economy appears to have been based on stock raising, perhaps supplemented by hunting, both dictating a semi-nomadic existence. Traces of their occupation have been found in the upper filling of the ditches of the Abingdon causewayed camp, and their characteristic flint equipment, including scrapers, knives, and arrowheads, was associated with flint-knapping debris in several parts of the county marking the sites of temporary encampments. The distribution of axes from the axe factories of Craig Llwyd in North Wales, Langdale in Westmorland, and from several outcrops in Cornwall is probably the work of these groups, whose nomadic existence would make them familiar with the natural routes across Britain along which these and less durable trade goods passed.

From c. 2000 B.C. the last stone-using peoples, the Beaker Folk, began to settle in Berkshire, penetrating the county by way of the Thames valley from landfalls in East Britain. A number of the earthen round barrows on the downs (e.g. The Seven Barrows, Lambourn) covered inhumation burials accompanied by their characteristic drinking cups. Two cultural groups are represented in the finds from the region: one is marked by Bell Beakers with smooth, S-shaped profile, the second by pots with tall necks separated from a globular body by a marked constriction.

Each group has its own characteristic ornaments and weapons, but the latter are largely represented as stray finds in the county, such as the stone battle-axes from Aston Upthorpe and North Hinksey. The battle-axes are part of the equipment of the Long-Necked-Beaker groups, which also includes beautifully flaked flint daggers (an example comes from one of the Lambourn Seven Barrows), copies of the rarer riveted bronze forms, and finely worked barb-and-tang arrowheads of flint. The distribution of finds shows a concentration on the chalk downs and valley gravels, and many of the ring ditches, representing the ditches of ploughed-out barrows, are probably to be attributed to these Late Neolithic settlers.

In the Early Bronze Age (c.1650–1400 B.C.), Berkshire marks the N limits of the brilliant Wessex Culture with its centre in South Wiltshire and Dorset. None of the many round barrows have so far produced examples of the exotic material which characterizes the culture, but the forms of the monuments themselves – bell, disc, and saucer barrows – indicate that the Berkshire Downs are to be included within its province. The finds from the few excavated sites suggest a more impoverished society than that at the heart of the culture in the s. Collared urns containing cremations embody, both in their form and in the rite itself, the continuing Neolithic ceramic and funerary traditions overlain by the foreign-derived culture of the Wessex chieftains. Graves provide almost all the material evidence although a small ditched enclosure on Rams Hill, Kingston Lisle, has produced collared-urn sherds. The site is probably a stock enclosure.

The later phases of the Bronze Age are even less well represented by structures and finds. Admittedly one can perceive the increasing proficiency of the bronze smith in the growing variety and complexity of his products, although these are largely represented in the county by stray finds. Occasional hoards like that from Yattendon Court indicate that the area benefited incidentally from the reorganization of the bronze industry in the Later Bronze Age. Most of the bronzes come from near the Thames, however, lost by merchants plying their trade along this great natural route. Some of the groups of small rectangular fields termed Celtic Fields which occur on the downs may be the work of Late Bronze Age groups, as has been demonstrated elsewhere, but most probably belong to the Early Iron Age, when evidence suggests a considerable increase in population.

In the middle of the C4 a village of small, circular, timber-built houses was constructed on Blewburton Hill (Aston Tirrold), with their associated grain storage pits defended by a palisade. Similar open village settlements are known from the area, e.g. Frilford (*see* Garford). These first iron-using peoples appear to have been peasants subsisting on mixed farming but capable of purchasing the fine haematite-coated pottery of the Wessex Iron Age A Culture. The threat of invasion from the s by more war-like Iron Age B groups must have prompted the construction of the first fortifications on hilltops *c.*300 B.C. (e.g. Blewburton Hill). The evidence from Blewburton points to the abandonment of these hilltop sites after their initial fortification, and the mixed A/B Culture must have lived in comparative security until the end of the C2, when a threat of invasion again produced a wave of hill-fort building. The relationship of these new forts – e.g. Grimsbury Tower (Hermitage), Bussock Wood (Winterbourne), Caesar's Camp (Bracknell) – is with the sw in Sussex and Kent and suggests a movement of peoples from that area reacting to the threat of Belgic, Iron Age C, invasion.

For the C1 the evidence of archaeology can be supplemented by that of the native coinage and classical references, and something of the politics and personalities of the period can now be discerned. About 50 B.C., after the great revolt in Gaul, one of the Belgic tribes, the Atrebates, under their leader Commius, fled to Britain, where their territory embraced the modern county of Berkshire. The material remains of these newcomers are scantily represented in the county. The Atrebates settled in Britain as a tribal unit, and, like other Belgic peoples in the se, appear to have been better organized both socially and economically than the Iron Age groups to the n and w. The most striking economic change was the introduction of a native gold and silver coinage, although the economic unit appears still to be the isolated farmstead defined by a rectilinear ditched enclosure, e.g. Robin Hood's Arbour, Maidenhead and Windmill Hill, Hinton Waldrist. The most famous monument of the latter part of the prehistoric Iron Age in the region is the great chalk-cut figure of a stylized horse at Uffington, whose form can be matched on the[3b] contemporary coinage. Hillfort building was not a major aspect of Belgic culture, and the changing settlement pattern is marked by occupation of the heavier clay soils of the valleys which had previously been shunned. Tribal centres, too, tend to occur in low-lying areas associated with natural routes and rivers (a quirk of modern political geography has detached from the county the Atrebatic tribal centre at Silchester). The re-fortification of some of the Berkshire hillforts however (Blewburton) was probably in response to a new threat from their powerful neighbours to the N of the Thames, the Catuvellauni. The suzerainty of the Commian dynasty over Berkshire was brought to a close *c.* A.D. 25, when the Catuvellauni under their great king Cunobelin crossed the Thames to annex the N part of the kingdom. Their conquest was short-lived, and within two decades the area had been incorporated in the Roman Empire.

The impact of Roman life and Roman culture has left no outstanding monuments. There are no towns in the area, although lesser settlements existed at Thatcham and Reading, the latter probably serving as the river port of Silchester (Calleva Atrebatum), the cantonal capital. Villas – e.g. Hampstead Norris (*see* Hermitage) and Letcombe Regis (*see* Wantage) – are again few, in part perhaps because of the absence of any major population centres which would provide a market for their produce. The only modern excavation of one of these sites is that at Cox Green, Maidenhead, built in the C2 and subject to a number of structural alterations and additions which continued until the late C4. The commoner form of rural unit was the native farmstead, e.g. Uffington and Ashbury (*see* Ashdown Park), which differed little in form from its prehistoric antecedents and was romanized only to the extent that its inhabitants now used industrially produced pottery and metal tools and trinkets of Roman character. This same continuity from prehistoric to Roman times is also reflected in religious ideas. At Frilford (*see* Garford) a Romano-British temple was built on the site of an earlier Iron Age shrine, emphasizing the continuing sanctity of the site.

As elsewhere, the history of the last decades of Roman rule in Berkshire is obscure, but the Saxon penetration by way of the Thames must have been achieved early in the C5. Their presence is marked by a series of flat cemeteries (e.g. Frilford, Abingdon) and indirectly by the great linear earthworks known as Grim's Bank (*see* Aldermaston), built by the Britons, centred on Silchester, as a bulwark against Saxon incursions. Apart from cemeteries, the only contemporary sites of note are the villages at Radley and Sutton Courtenay. At the latter site over forty small rectangular huts were excavated. Some of these squalid buildings may have been dwellings, but others produced evidence of weaving and pottery manufacture.

THE BUILDINGS OF BERKSHIRE
BY NIKOLAUS PEVSNER

Berkshire is half home county, half West Country. Even the

way people speak leaves no doubt about that. The E as far as Reading is now commuters' or weekenders' territory. The W is what it is in its own right. The Downs link it to Wiltshire. The sense of remoteness which they create, of being alone with nature, is something one can never experience nearer London. And Berkshire landscape has more variety even than this; for there are also the sandy heath and pinewoods bordering on Bagshot Heath and the military areas, the well wooded hilly country between Newbury and the Thames, a country of commons and prep schools, and the Thames-side estates of the mansions of nobility and the rich and the villas of the affluent and more and more of bungalows and flats.

As varied as the landscape are the building materials. A note on Berkshire geology is appended on p. 47. Here it is enough to say that the county does not participate in the oolitic limestone, England's best stone. Instead stones had to be used qualitatively so indifferent as the chalk and the sarsen stones of the Downs, the ragstone available locally or near by, the rare, dark brown conglomerate from the Bagshot sands, and the ubiquitous flint.

Reading Abbey, by far the most important monastic establishment of Berkshire, is of flint. It was founded for Cluniacs – the most powerful and active order of the time – by Henry I in 1121 and was his favourite abbey. But Abingdon Abbey had the most venerable history, having been founded in the C7 and refounded by St Aethelwold. Of Abingdon we have only a gatehouse and a minor administrative range left, of Reading also a gatehouse and dramatic but uneloquent ruins.* Of other [34a] monastic houses no more survives. The county anyway was never rich in them. Besides Reading and Abingdon there were only three other Benedictine houses, Hurley, where the Norman nave of the church and the refectory range exist, Steventon, a cell of Bec-Hellouin, where a timber-framed hall range is supposed to have belonged to the guest quarters, and Wallingford, where nothing has remained. The house of Benedictine nuns at Broomhall also is completely gone. The Augustinian Canons had three houses: Bisham, Poughley, and Sandleford. At Bisham, taken over in 1337 from the Templars, whose great hall, porch, and solar can still be seen, the Augustinians added a cloister, highly irregular in site and appearance. At Poughley near Chaddleworth there is just a bit of walling, at Sandleford

* Fragments from Reading Abbey, or said to be from Reading Abbey, are at St James Reading, St Giles Reading, and Park Place.

one C14 roof. Otherwise nothing is left, except for a substantial part of the Greyfriars church of Reading. This was the only Franciscan house in the county, and the Dominicans did not have even one.

And if Berkshire is poor in major monastic remains (and has no cathedral), it is in the secular field as poor in major towns. Reading is the only one with more than 100,000 inhabitants (1961: 120,000), and Reading is a town for which one can safely predict fast growth. Otherwise there are Maidenhead with only 35,000, Windsor with 27,000, Newbury with 20,000, Abingdon with 14,000, and Wokingham with 11,000, and heaven preserve Berkshire from a 200,000 new town between Newbury and Hungerford.

For it will be seen that altogether Berkshire is a moderate county, a county which offers to the traveller, whether he looks at nature or buildings, plenty of enjoyment, but few great thrills – none in fact in architecture except for Windsor Castle.

These introductory pages are bound to reflect that situation. For ANGLO-SAXON art and architecture, to start with, there is hardly anything to summarize: the W tower of Wickham, the lower parts of the crossing tower of Cholsey, a doorway *ex situ* at Aston Tirrold, a large coffin lid inscribed to Aegelwardus who died in 1017 at Stratfield Mortimer, and – the only visually 13rewarding item – a tympanum, also early C11, at Strattenborough Castle Farm Coleshill which is of the Viking style called by the archaeologists Ringerike.

Of NORMAN there is quantitatively of course more, but qualitatively also not much: the wide early C12 nave of Buckland, the rare plan of Cholsey with transepts provided with apsed E chapels and probably a major E apse as well, nave, aisles, and crossing at Lambourn, the rib-vaulted crossing and rib-vaulted chancel of Blewbury, the complete village church of Avington, including a formerly rib-vaulted chancel – the ribs carrying beakhead decoration – the splendid (if over-restored) apse arch and chancel arch of St Leonard Wallingford, a fragmentary W façade at St Nicholas Abingdon, and just one round tower at Great Shefford. Of doorways there are plenty, but really richly decorated ones are confined to Bucklebury, Lambourn, and Tidmarsh. The most interesting tympanum is that with a scene 14adoubtfully connected with the Alexander romance at Charney Bassett. Nearly all these are Late Norman jobs. PILLAR PISCINAS have been preserved oddly often. As for FONTS, one is used to finding Norman ones everywhere, many completely plain (and in that case not even listed in my gazetteer), many also decorated. Of these the majority have just blind arcading, straightforward or intersecting; in some cases the space under the arches is used for stylized leaf motifs or the space in the spandrels. At Avington there are instead eleven figures. At 14b Childrey is a Norman lead font of c.1200 with little figures of bishops, at Long Wittenham another, with rosettes, wheels, and also little bishops.* The standard Purbeck 'table-top' type with shallow blank arches curiously enough is preserved only once, in spite of the relative proximity of the Isle of Purbeck (Shrivenham). Of other church furnishings only a few Late Norman DOORS with iron hinge-enrichments can be referred to (Buckland, Sparsholt, Kingston Lisle).

But the finest door is mid C13 and led into the galilee of 16b Henry III's EARLY ENGLISH Royal Chapel at Windsor Castle. It is covered in scroll-work all over.‡ Unfortunately nearly all has been swept away of that major job, begun just a few years before Westminster Abbey, about 1240. We have no more than the doorway to which this door belongs, two blank arches l. and r., and one range of blank arches with a sumptuous doorway of the cloister adjoining the chapel to the N. On the walls of the galilee and the cloister two exquisite painted heads have been uncovered, mid C13, and as good as any C13 PAINTING anywhere in England. But of the SECULAR BUILDINGS of Henry III at Windsor Castle we can see no more than one plain N window of a N–S hall range in the Lower Ward. Windsor Castle was built by William the Conqueror, but it was then a motte-and-bailey castle of a standard type – lower bailey – motte – upper bailey – and had no stone buildings. It was Henry II who built the first stone walls, of which quite something can still be 35 recognized by the expert, in spite of a hundred and fifty years of sweeping restorations, and he built the shell keep, i.e. the Round Tower, as well. Of the royal dwelling in the Upper Ward there are again only mute walls. Henry III's towers are recognizable by their semicircular or nearly semicircular form. Of all he provided for the royal apartment in the Upper Ward we have nothing telling. But this scanty evidence can be strengthened by looking round the MANOR HOUSES. Looking round castles, other than Windsor, would not pay. Only at Donnington is the late C14 gatehouse of a once oblong castle with angle towers, 37

* Woolstone has a lead font as late as C14.

‡ Other scrolled iron door-hinges at Blewbury (C13 ?), Buckland, Faring- 16a don (C13• of splendid quality), Frilsham, Lockinge, Uffington (C13).

licensed in 1386, and at Wallingford some fragments of towers and of the collegiate church on the castle. Other castles need not engage our attention at all. So to the manor houses. Norman Hall at Sutton Courtenay has its main range with a doorway and lancets of *c.*1200, Appleton Manor a sumptuous doorway with stiff-leaf capitals of about the same date or a little later, Bisham Abbey, then a preceptory of the Templars, a big, rib-vaulted late C13 porch, the s wall of the substantial great hall, and a solar window, the Chequer Room of Abingdon Abbey its

34b late C13 chimneystack with tiny lancet openings, and Charney Bassett the solar wing with chapel of *c.*1280. Fyfield Manor with hall, porch, and service wing takes us out of the C13 into the early C14.

This is more of a harvest than the EARLY ENGLISH CHURCHES can yield. Admittedly, if one includes minor things in one's study, one can build up a nice sequence of transition from Late Norman to mature Early English, watching how the square abacus of round piers becomes octagonal and then round, the round arch becomes pointed, the moulded or heavily roll-moulded arch is replaced by the slightly and then the fully chamfered or double-chamfered arch, and so on. However, one must be careful. In Berkshire the square abacus still appears with waterleaf capitals, i.e. capitals of *c.*1170–80, and even with pointed arches (e.g. Appleton). Stiff-leaf is complete before 1200 – that is proved by the date 1196 at St Laurence Reading. Early stiff-leaf is easily distinguished from mature stiff-leaf, the former having much of the bell of the capital visible, the latter rich and varied in directions. The time after 1250 is recognizable by plate tracery and then bar tracery and finally by the arrival of intersecting and Y-tracery and the pointed-trefoiled lights and their grouping in three stepped ones under one arch, as they liked it especially in Berkshire. All this belongs to the end of the C13, and all this is general considerations. Individual buildings worth including in a summary are few. The most interesting church and one highly idiosyncratic is Uffington.* It has a grand porch and a crossing tower, and the chancel was meant to be vaulted. Uffington is of *c.*1250, Wantage, also cruciform, is a little later. Several villages have earlier C13 chancels with lancet windows and groups of three in the E wall (e.g. Chieveley, Cholsey). Tidmarsh has a polygonal apse which is a great rarity in England, Abingdon a proud N tower, Little Cox-

* Even if one assigns the windows of the transept chapels to the C17.

well a double bellcote, Baulking a very plain stone rood screen, Sparsholt – again something rare – an E.E. wooden rood screen, St George's Chapel Windsor a fragment of a beautiful Purbeck marble font with a head and stiff-leaf, and several churches have WALL PAINTING of the C13, some of it – e.g. the Virgin at Hampstead Norris – very beautiful, some – especially the scenes at Ashampstead – very interesting. Of masonry patterns and tendril patterns there are also examples. An initial examination of funerary monuments can still be delayed; for they link up with the Dec rather than the E.E. phase.

For the DECORATED we are a little better provided with dates. This is the story they tell. A chantry was founded at North Moreton in 1299. The E and W windows of the chapel have the characteristic motif of arches upon arches, the motif familiar from the Wells Lady Chapel, and not yet any ogees.* Money was left to the building of the Greyfriars at Reading in 1311. What remains of the church has reticulated side by side with intersecting tracery. At Shottesbrooke in 1337 a college was established, and the (still cruciform) church has exuberant flowing tracery. The only tracery which can compare with this is that of the chancel of Warfield, which is very rich inside as 4a well. Another richly appointed chancel is that of Sparsholt. Stanford-in-the-Vale has Kentish tracery, Cumnor and North Hinksey wilful tracery of straight-sided lozenges under a straight-sided arch. Finally, to conclude with another date, the N chapel at East Hagbourne is entirely Dec, yet was founded by a husband and wife who died in 1403 and 1414. 1375 is the earliest date one would permit oneself to suggest, and that is a late date for Dec, especially since Perp had certainly entered the county by 1350.

Edward III created the Order of the Garter in 1348. In 1350–4 he built at Windsor the chapter house and possibly the chapel for his order, the latter as a replacement of Henry III's chapel. He also built a lavish porch from the NW into Henry 4b III's cloister, and nearly rebuilt the cloister. The porch with a lierne-vault and blank wall decoration is a demonstrative piece of the transition from Dec to Perp, but in the cloister with its tracery and the one remaining window of the chapter house the PERPENDICULAR style is complete, just about fifteen to twenty years after it had been introduced at St Paul's and Gloucester. Mr Harvey has recently made out a case for attributing the

* The same motif occurs at Chilton and Cholsey.

chapel (i.e. what is now the Albert Memorial Chapel), always assigned to Henry VII, also to Edward III, with the tracery of its tall windows and its polygonal apse inspired by Lichfield Cathedral.

If this chapel is the major monument of the Early Perp in Berkshire, St George's Chapel is the major monument of the Late Perp, and of course one of the major monuments of the style in all England. It is one of the four royal chapels of *c.*1440 to *c.*1520 which epitomize the best in late medieval English architecture. Henry VI started with Eton and King's in the 1440s. They were not continued while he was in eclipse. Only when he was firmly established did Edward IV return to them; but his own enterprise was St George's Chapel, begun in 1475. It was completed only by Henry VII towards the end of his reign, and he also probably completed or remodelled Edward III's chapel. St George's Chapel is visually as thrilling outside as inside. Outside what makes it unique is the position of the transept exactly halfway between w end and e end, a demonstration of balance which shows that England was getting ready for the Renaissance, and the polygonal closing of the transept, taken over perhaps from the polygonal apse of Edward III's chapel and done now with so much conviction that it was re-echoed in the e chapel and the w chapels. These features combine to make of St George's a building to be taken in at one go and broadwise and not in the w–e way of medieval progress. Internally St George's is emphatically Late Perp in its stress on depressed arches and a vault of the same depressed section. The vault is in fact almost a coved ceiling, with lierne stars in the *plafond* and palm-frond ribs up the coving. Fan-vaulting, which was to culminate in Bath Abbey and King's College Chapel, occurs only in the aisles. Vaulting in the aisles apparently started about 1480, but the main vaults are by *William Vertue* and belong only to 1506 etc.

Anything after St George's Chapel is of course an anti-climax, but the Newbury parish church is a substantial, prosperous building, all of a piece, which would hold its own among parish churches anywhere. No wonder, if one remembers Jack of Newbury (*see* p. 179). The church is of *c.*1500–32. Abingdon rebuilt its parish church too, very spacious, with double aisles, but architecturally unenterprising. The piers are octagonal throughout, with concave sides – a motif familiar from Campden and North Leach. Octagonal piers with straight sides and double-chamfered arches are the standard elements of Perp, and indeed of Dec, arcades. In the gazetteer they will be called just that and left alone. Another general remark may here come in. Roofs are usually of the tie-beam and kingpost type, and they also are often not mentioned in the gazetteer. Otherwise no generalization can be made, except that village churches often have the timber bell-turrets with shingled broach spires so frequent in Surrey and Sussex too,* and that in large parts of the county the Victorian restorers had enough money available to replace most external features which would have given interest to the buildings. After this a brief catalogue of worthwhile Perp items: the complete Perp crossing tower of Shrivenham, the Waynflete Chantry transported from Magdalen Chapel Oxford to Theale (its arches are straight-sided, its tracery of the lozenge kind which the Dec style had invented), the timber arcade of Radley,‡ and the two detached chapels with priest's house at East Hendred and Fyfield.§

FURNISHINGS of course are more frequent now, and MONUMENTS must take their place with them. DECORATED first, i.e. from the late C13 to the mid C14. As regards monuments, Berkshire has first and foremost the series of eight at Aldworth, six of them under ornate (if drastically restored) canopies. One of 25a the ladies is in the arrangement of the drapery still in the C13 cathedral tradition, one of the men is in a posture of which one 25b might not have considered even the Dec style capable. Not only are his legs crossed – this convention is universal in England, even if wholly absent on the Continent – but his whole body writhes and twists. Yet some stiff-leaf on the slab itself makes a very early Dec date a necessity. At Childrey is a cross-legged knight in a recess with ballflower, that characteristic early C14 motif, at Sparsholt are three oaken effigies (and others at Bark- 26a ham and Burghfield). Cross-legged stone effigies also at Burghfield and Sparsholt. Didcot has a late C13 mitred abbot of Purbeck marble, Long Wittenham an amazing late C13 miniature 17b stone effigy built into a piscina. In Hampstead Norris church is a mysterious relief, over 2 ft high, of a man on horseback, also 15 late C13, and very accomplished. What did it belong to? Of the late C13 fragment at Ardington we also do not know what it belonged to. Then PAINTING and the beautiful early C14 Annunciation at Enborne and some C14 figures at Aldermaston

* Stone spires are not lacking, but Berkshire is not a spire county. The most prominent example is perhaps Abingdon.
‡ Another, of 1592, at Winkfield.
§ Detached Perp chapels also at Newbury and Thatcham.

and Kingston Lisle, and STAINED GLASS with the s chapel E
18a window of North Moreton of c.1300–10, and one of the two
fairly complete windows in the county. The other is the great W
21 window of St George's Chapel, and that of course is long past
the end of Dec.

So to the PERPENDICULAR in the matters of FURNISHINGS
and monuments. St George's Chapel has also interesting
heraldic GLASS of the late C15, and it has the finest WOODWORK
19 by far in the stalls with their misericords, made by *William
Berkeley* and others in 1478–85, and extremely skilfully restored
and supplemented by *Henry Emlyn* in 1787–90. The stalls have
high canopies, exceptional poppyheads with whole scenes carved
in relief, relief carvings in the tympana and spandrels of the
traceried desk fronts, and innumerable misericords. The carving
is naïve and not at all courtly. But set against the stall backs are
the Garter Plates, ENAMEL plaques with the arms of the
Knights of the Garter, a unique set stretching in time from the
C14 to the C20. The quality of some of them is exquisite. Stalls
with misericords, though minor ones, are also at Wantage. The
18b best of the Perp wooden screens is at Warfield, Perp stone
screens are in the transept chapels of St George's (with the hemp-
bray of Sir Reginald Bray), and a great part of the exquisite
iron screen of Edward IV's chantry (by the Cornish blacksmith
John Tresilian) is again in St George's Chapel. This is without
doubt the finest piece of C15 smith's work in England. Of iron
also the eminently curious almsbox in St George's with the
initial h repeated on it, a sign that it was meant for donations to
the cult of Henry VI, when this had established itself for a short
time after the king's body had been brought from Chertsey in
1484. The best late medieval GLASS is that of c.1460 at Ockwells
Manor, all armorial, the best late medieval PAINTING the ceiling
20a of one of the chancel chapels at Abingdon which dates from the
late C14. The two bishops from the Urswick Chantry at Windsor
are early C16 and good too, the paintings in the Hastings
Chantry of 1503 are thoroughly bad, those in the Oxenbridge
Chantry of 1522 are indifferent and certainly the work of a
Fleming.

Chantries really ought to be listed as MONUMENTS. St
George's Chapel has two more, the Beaufort Chapel being the
counterpart to the Urswick Chapel, i.e. early C16, and that odd
little excrescence in the angle between s transept and s chancel
aisle, Bishop King's Chantry of 1492–6. Why he, a canon like
others and apparently no special benefactor, should have been

allowed this one addition to the superb unity of the chapel remains a mystery. The only effigies to go with any of these chapels are those of the Earl of Worcester †1526 in the Beaufort Chapel. They are of alabaster, and Berkshire has quite a good series of alabaster monuments, from that at Wantage †1361 to Sir Thomas Fettiplace †c.1442 at Little Shefford and Lord Roos †1513 at Windsor and Sir George Forster (his wife died 27 in 1526) at Aldermaston, both the last-named ones with mourners. But the most moving monument is that of Sir John Golafre †1442 at Fyfield with the cadaver on a tier below the 26b effigy, the type introduced in France c.1400 and established in England by Bishop Fleming's Monument at Lincoln Cathedral of c.1435.* BRASSES need no special mention in the county, although there are about eighty-five effigies of before 1550.‡ But one other type of Perp monument may in conclusion be referred to, although it is also a national rather than local type: the tomb recess of Purbeck marble, made no doubt on the isle and exported to whoever paid for them. They have a tomb-chest, angle shafts, and a canopy with pendant arches or a plain, very depressed and almost straight horizontal arch, vaulting inside, and the effigies of brass on the lid of the tomb-chest or against the back wall. Such monuments survive in Berkshire at Bisham, Childrey, St Nicholas Hurst, Englefield (c.1500), Cookham (†1517), Little Shefford (†1524), and also Faringdon (†1547), St George's Chapel Windsor (†1551), and Cumnor (c.1572). These are amazingly late dates, and they may be explained by the pirating of an existing tomb or Easter Sepulchre. But it remains a fact that Berkshire did not accept the Italian Renaissance with enthusiasm.

SECULAR BUILDINGS show that too. In that field we have not looked round for anything yet after the C13. What is worth recording? It is rather a *mixtum compositum*. First at Windsor Castle more work on the fortifications by Edward III, including 35 the heightening of the Round Tower, and by Henry VIII, including the Great Gate. The College meanwhile built a high hall for the Vicars Choral in 1415–16, but otherwise nothing in stone. Timber-framed are the Horseshoe Cloister w of the chapel (which is now so thoroughly by *Sir George Gilbert Scott*) and a canon's house now called Merbeck and which has a good

---

* Almost as moving in its own strange way is the Throkmorton Monument 28a (†1535) at Shottesbrooke with the deceased appearing as if he were lying in a stone coffin.

‡ Counting couples etc. as one.

hall roof. Both have the infilling of brick, but brick otherwise did not establish itself in Berkshire as early as, say, in London and at Hampton Court. Altogether timber-framing remained a widespread technique, even occasionally for so major a house as 38 Ockwells Manor of 1446/66, a courtyard house of interesting and unusual planning features and with a delightful (if also much restored) façade. As a rule the interest of timber-framed buildings does not show externally, and so my gazetteer may not always do justice to the most deserving ones. The NBR for instance has a list of cruck houses and cottages in Berkshire. Only a few of them have been taken over here (e.g. two at Long Wittenham). Some of the best roofs must however be listed: the C14 roof of the hall at Middle Farm Harwell, the C15 roof of the great hall of the so-called guest house of Steventon Priory, and the C14 roof of the hall at The Abbey, Sutton Courtenay. The Abbey is a C14 courtyard house and preserves e.g. one major window with flowing tracery. Compton Beauchamp is a courtyard house too, but has no more of our period now than one early C16 window. Wytham Abbey is early C16 and had originally two courtyards. Of the surviving details the best is an oriel window. Hendred House East Hendred has a big C15 chimneypiece in the hall (apart from a C13 chapel, of which two lancets are evidence).

36b   That leaves as a postscript Christ's Hospital Abingdon, founded in 1446, with a wooden cloister in front of its one long range, such as those of the Canons' Cloister and the Horseshoe at Windsor and, even more similar, the courtyard of Ockwells Manor of the same years as Christ's Hospital. A second postscript must be two BARNS, one internally perhaps the finest in England – the Great Coxwell barn of the C14 – the other only a 36a shadow of its former self, the Cholsey barn which was built about 1200, pulled down in 1815, and later partly and not satisfactorily re-erected. It was the largest barn in Europe, 303 ft long (Reading Abbey Church was 375 ft long), and had stone piers to divide nave from aisles. The mighty roof went down from a height of 51 to a mere 8 ft.

Where is the dividing line between Gothic and RENAISSANCE in Berkshire? Its importance can be exaggerated. The Italian Renaissance was introduced by the Court as a fashion of ornament rather than a new conception of art and architecture. When that began to form, in the Elizabethan Age, it was more indebted to the Perpendicular, to English tradition, and to the Netherlands, than to the Mediterranean. Even so, it is worth investigating where and when the Italian Renaissance made its first appearance. For Berkshire the answer is clear. In the N transept of St George's Chapel remains a fragment of a decorative frame of a wall panel which is of coloured glazed maiolica or fayence, i.e. the della Robbia technique introduced in England by *Giovanni da Majano* in the roundels of Roman Emperors on the gateways of Hampton Court in 1521. He must have done this frame – one probably of several – as well, and so the date we are looking for is presumably about 1520–5.* The next monument is Henry VIII's oriel inside St George's Chapel with Gothic arches but Renaissance balusters, undated but probably of *c*.1530. The next actual date is 1533, the date of the death of Sir Thomas Unton, whose alabaster monument at Faringdon has colonnettes, wreaths, and shell-niches, i.e. typical Early Renaissance elements. But after that nothing followed immediately. In monuments the Essex Monument at Lambourn – date of death 1558 – is, if anything, less Renaissance than that at Faringdon. But from 1560 onwards the EARLY ELIZABETHAN style began to spread, and this included Quattrocento motifs on pilasters and friezes. The examples are the surviving frieze of the Perkyns Monument at Ufton Nervet – date of death 1560 – and a chimneypiece at Bisham Abbey of about 1560. The house, 39a converted from the Templars' preceptory and Augustinian abbey, has stepped brick gables, and windows with mullions and a transom or a mullion-and-transom cross and a shallow pediment.

Berkshire has little to offer of ELIZABETHAN AND JACOBEAN ARCHITECTURE AND ART. Englefield House, much enlarged and internally completely changed in the C19, and Shaw House, completed in 1581, are really the only major houses. Shaw House is of brick, and designed on the E-plan. On 40a the same plan, but timber-framed, is the substantial Ufton Court of the same years. Of brick again, but smaller, are Hinton House of before 1589, Stanlake Park, Haines Hill,‡ and High Chimneys, all in the parish of St Nicholas Hurst, and all of Elizabethan type, though High Chimneys is dated as amazingly late as 1661.§ At Windsor Queen Elizabeth's Gallery dates 39b

---

* We must of course exclude from this chronology the North Italian Adoration of the Magi (Verona?) of the early C15 at Littlewick Green, a 20b panel, 10 ft long, because it was not made in or for Berkshire.

‡ Haines Hill, which I have not been able to enter, has, according to the VCH, an original long gallery.

§ The Almshouses at St Nicholas Hurst are still later and yet entirely pre-classical. They were founded in 1682.

probably from 1583, the date on the ornate chimneypiece. South
Fawley Manor House, Great Fawley, has a date 1614, the Jesus
Hospital at Bray, one of the largest almshouse foundations in
the county, a date 1627. Small's House, Mackney, Sotwell is undated, which is a pity, as it is an extremely interesting house on a
quite exceptional plan: two oblong ranges (of which one contained the hall), kept close together and connected by a square
link in which the staircase is placed.

This exhausts secular building qualifying for inclusion here.
Of CHURCH ARCHITECTURE no one would expect much. It was
a rare age for new church buildings, or even parts of buildings.
7 Foremost in Berkshire is Bishop Jewel's w porch of Sunningwell church of c.1560–70, polygonal with incorrectly shaped
columns and originally a steep-pitched polygonal roof. Equally
interesting is the internal remodelling of Winkfield church in
1592. The church, probably formerly of nave and aisles, was
made two-naved with a dividing timber arcade. The w tower of
Lockinge is dated 1564, but of no interest. Otherwise, where
towers were rebuilt, they were made of brick. There are no
fixed early dates, but those of Bradfield and Wargrave are
assigned to the C16. St Nicholas Hurst is of 1612, Purley of
8a 1626, Winkfield of 1629, and Ruscombe of 1638–9 – the latter
two with mullioned-and-transomed windows entirely of brick –
and the lower part of Easthampstead (Bracknell) looks Jacobean
too.*

In CHURCH FURNISHINGS also Berkshire simply follows the
national rule that little was done afresh in the late C16, and much
only in the Laudian period. Proof is an examination of Pulpits.
There may well be undated Elizabethan ones – e.g. the exceptionally fine one with Floris motifs at Aldworth – but as for
dates, this is the tally: Newbury 1607 (quite splendid), Waltham
St Lawrence 1619 (fragmentary), Binfield 1628, Easthampstead
(Bracknell) 1631, St Peter Didcot 1634, St Helen Abingdon
1636, Ruscombe c.1639, West Hanney 1649. The Font Case of
Long Wittenham (an unusual object) is undated; so is that of
22a Stanford-in-the-Vale, but the wrought-iron Hourglass Stand at
St Nicholas Hurst has a date 1636,‡ and the completely Perp Font
at Bray is, according to accounts, of 1647 (unless they refer to a
font which has disappeared). Only in MONUMENTS – and this

---

* Later dated Berkshire brick towers are as follows: Boxford c.1692,
Pangbourne 1718, Finchampstead 1720, Basildon 1734, Peasemore 1737,
Tilehurst 1737, Brimpton 1748, Winterbourne 1759.

22b   ‡ Another hourglass stand is at Binfield.

is the national situation again – are quantity and quality higher.
Indeed one is hard put to it to select for such a summary as this.
The types are well known: the recumbent effigy on a tomb-chest
remains from the Middle Ages, the kneeling figure or figures
(two facing one another across a prayer desk) is the most usual
new type, a Flemish type. Material is stone or preferably, and
almost without exception with aesthetically better results, alabaster. Decoration is Flemish rather than Italian: strapwork
often handled very successfully, columns of touch, coffered
arches shallow or deeper. So here is a catalogue of major
examples. Recumbent effigies of alabaster: Sir Philip and Sir
Thomas Hoby, Bisham, †1558 and †1566, Earl of Lincoln, St 28b
George's Chapel, †1585, Appleton 1593, Speen †1597, Tilehurst
†1627, Arborfield †1639, and Radley a few years before (†1631
and †1632). The last-named is by *Nicholas Stone.* The county has
nothing typologically more interesting by him. Recumbent effigies of stone: Pangbourne †1625. Semi-reclining effigies, laid
stiffly on one side: Little Wittenham †1611, Uffington †1638.
Kneeling figures: Bisham †1609, Sonning †1630, St Nicholas 30a
Hurst †1631 (three groups framed by columns). That leaves
the exceptions. There is an Early Elizabethan type without
any figures, just with a framed inscription, ornament, and a
decorative coat of arms. This in Berkshire is represented by a
monument at Hurley (†1558 and †1579 – which date is valid?).
Frontal demi-figures were usual for scholars and divines: John
Blagrave, the mathematician, †1611 at St Laurence Reading (with 30b
Mannerist surrounding allegorical figures) and Giles Tomson,
Bishop of Gloucester, †1612, at Windsor Chapel. Small brass
plates appear in the county, not only with upright or kneeling
figures, but also in a less standard way. They are often framed in
stone, perhaps with a guilloche or an egg-and-dart motif. But the
finest, most delightedly remembered Jacobean monument in
Berkshire is that of Margaret Hoby at Bisham (†1605), which is 29
an obelisk carried by four swans with a heart on top.*

In a history of art and architecture on a European scale, England
in the fifty years between 1615 and 1665 would be represented
by the work of Inigo Jones, Webb, Pratt, May, and so on to
Wren, i.e. by the introduction and the spread of Palladianism
and then the French and Dutch classical style of the C17, and
by the work of Rubens and van Dyck in and for England and

---

* As an appendix a STATUE of Queen Elizabeth I must be recorded. It is
now in Cumnor church, but is said to come from the Earl of Leicester's
house, Dean Court. It is not a masterpiece.

their effect on the country. The fascinating thing about any provincial survey is the mixture between the contribution of the central, London, events to the region or county and the cross-currents in opposition to them, or in misunderstanding or half-understanding of them. As for Berkshire, Coleshill by *Pratt* of the 1650s was central, London, stuff, but it has alas gone completely. Hamstead Marshall of the 1660s by *Gerbier*, completed by *Winde*, looks in engravings of the same type as Coleshill, but not so pure. It disappeared after only about fifty years. Aldermaston Court also is no longer in existence. If one can trust the date 1636, the house was one of the very earliest of the brick-box type which became so characteristic of the English smaller-scale country house for two hundred years to come. The next in date are Chevening in Kent, perhaps by Inigo Jones, and built before 1638, and a house certainly by Jones of which we have his drawing dated 1639.* Ashdown, that adorable doll's

40b house, five by five bays, with a hipped roof and a belvedere cupola and two symmetrical detached ranges delineating the forecourt, remains as the early representation of the type in Berkshire. Its architect and its date are unrecorded. Its style is decidedly Dutch. The 1660s are the most likely date.

Sir John Summerson has christened the provincial version of this style, with its quirks and its resistance to classicity, Artisan Mannerism. It is interestingly and enjoyably represented in Berkshire. Semi-classical is West Woodhay House, which carries the date 1635 more than once. Can it be so early? It is the brick-box type entirely, with hipped roof. Only its raised brick window surrounds and raised brick quoins join it to the group with which we are now dealing. Semi-classical also is one canon's house inside Windsor Castle dated 1660. It has giant pilasters along its front, and the Ionic capitals are made of cut brick. Semi-classical again, and really only departing from the correct line in a steep gable-like instead of a correct pediment, is the

44 Lucas Hospital at Wokingham, dated 1665. It is a big composition with projecting wings and a cupola. More Artisan Mannerism are Milton House, Welford Park, and Hall's Farmhouse Farley Hill, all three undated, and all three of course of brick.

41   * The only surviving part of Aldermaston Court is the staircase, and this is also of great importance as being one of the earliest where the balustrade of banisters is replaced by a pierced parapet. The details are on the way from strapwork to the gristle and the leaves of the second third of the century. Other early examples of the pierced parapet are Radclive in Buckinghamshire of 1621 and Cromwell House, Highgate, London, of c.1637–40.

The first has giant pilasters with waistbands which turn out to be fleurs-de-lis and a typical sub-Inigo chimneypiece. It also has an Inigo plaster ceiling. The second has raised brick window surrounds like West Woodhay but a raised vertical strip to connect the windows vertically. The third has not only raised brick angle quoins but crazy brick quoins framing every bay of windows. At The Priory, Beech Hill, dated 1648 are two specially characteristic chimneypieces, and at Newbury is a house, dated 1669 (8 Northbrook Street), which, instead of giant pilasters, has superimposed short pilasters, a special fashion of the mid c17. Another fashionable motif, only a little later, say of *c*.1660–75, is the so-called Ipswich window, a three-light window with a wider centre light, a transom in each side light, and an arch instead in the middle light. The *locus classicus* is Sparrowe's House at Ipswich of *c*.1670. It occurs a number of times at Abingdon, and also at Sutton Courtenay, especially in the Manor House. The Manor House has also the charming and uncommon motif of a colonnade with Tuscan columns forming a loggia below one wing of the house. The gatepiers of the Manor House 42c are typical of the years *c*.1660, and Berkshire has indeed a fine collection of later c17 gatepiers, including one at Besselsleigh, several at Coleshill, and a whole minuet of them alone on 42a, a lawn where the mansion of Hamstead Marshall had once e,f stood. One step forward from these and one has *Talman*'s former doorway (now garden gateway) of Swallowfield Park. 43 Talman worked here for the Earl of Clarendon in 1689–91, and his may indeed be the H-shaped house that now exists, even if devoid of other telling external features. But it has inside a spectacular if small oval vestibule with lush stucco. The outbuildings are interesting too, of brick, extensive, and with giant pilasters and heavy loggias or arcades, looking decidedly 1700 and Late Wren in character, i.e. Office of Works style of the turn of the century (Talman was Comptroller under Wren from 1689 to 1702). At Windsor Castle *Hugh May* did an extensive remodelling and rebuilding job from 1675 onwards. It included the most spectacular staircase in England and one of the most Baroque interiors, the chapel, but all of it was swept 12 away by Wyatville and we have nothing left but two round-arched giant windows in Henry III's Tower. May was Surveyor of Windsor from 1673 to his death in 1684, i.e. came under Wren as Surveyor General. Of all May's interior work only three rooms remain. The woodwork by *Grinling Gibbons* and *Henry* 46 *Phillips* is superb, the painting by *Verrio* pedestrian.

With these buildings the first PUBLIC BUILDINGS must be
45b named, and especially the splendid Town Hall of Abingdon of
1678–82, built and perhaps designed by *Christopher Kempster*,
one of Wren's City masons. It has the usual open ground floor,
long, slender giant pilasters above, a hipped roof, and a cupola.
45a The Windsor Town Hall of *c*.1687–90 was designed by *Sir
Thomas Fitch* and is less correct, with its giant pilasters on the
upper floor (above the open ground floor) set in, i.e. away from,
quoins. *Wren* supervised the completion of the building. The
late C17 Town Hall at Faringdon is smaller and more provincial.
The Town Hall at Wallingford with the date 1670 is the earliest
of the group. It has much sturdier, more Jacobean, columns,
but a Venetian window and a hipped roof.*

No interior decoration of these years needs recording apart
from Talman's stucco work at Swallowfield, nor any CHURCH
FURNISHINGS apart from the remains of *Grinling Gibbons*'s
gorgeous wooden railing round the former Royal Pew at
Windsor Castle now in the parish church and perhaps one or
the other brass Chandelier on the Dutch pattern. That at
Sonning is dated 1675, two at St Helen Abingdon are 1710 and
1713, that at Wantage 1711, and then the type continued un-
changed right into the C19.‡

In MONUMENTS the interesting development is the loosening
of the stiffness of Jacobean attitudes and also of Jacobean typo-
logical conventions. The former is illustrated in a recumbent
effigy at St Nicholas Hurst (†1651) and a semi-reclining effigy at
Coleshill (†1647), followed by the Bishop Brideoake at Windsor
Castle (†1678), also semi-reclining but now quite at ease, the
latter by Katherine Thomas at Waltham St Lawrence †1658,
which is just a short stubby column in a niche with an urn on
top of an oddly organic shape, and no figures at all. A few years
later the Rich monument at Sonning (†1667 and 1663) consists
of two white urns on a black slab held up by four white putti.
Of new motifs the bust in an oval recess appears at Sonning

* Yet earlier and a job out of the ordinary is the Cloth Hall (now Museum)
at Newbury of 1626–7, timber-framed and perhaps also originally open
below, and the longer attached range with an upper wooden balcony or
gallery which was a store house and lay close to the former wharf. It is
supposed to date from *c*.1660–80. The Cloth Hall was, it seems, an early
municipal weaving workshop. At Denchworth is a small house known as
the Wool Store. This is dated 1708 and still pre-classical, with mullioned-
and-transomed windows, even if they are now composed symmetrically.

‡ Little Coxwell 1729, Buckland given 1733, Caversham 1743, Harwell
1766, Aldermaston C18, Wootton C18 ?, Sutton Courtenay 1821 – a survival
or revival.

with a date of death 1653, thick compact garlands of the Inigo Jones kind (apart from the chimneypiece at Milton House) at St Mary Reading with a date of death 1635 and at Buckland c.1648, the open curly pediment at Buckland with a date of death 1658, and twisted columns at Sonning with a date of death 1665 (or 1656). Add to this the two frontal demi-figures perfectly at ease at Wantage (†1684) and the two lively kneelers with a third figure upright behind at St Nicholas Hurst (†1683), and we are ready for the c18. The former is by *William Bird* of Oxford, the latter by *William Stanton*.*

But our survey has so far omitted any reference to CHURCHES after 1600. There are few, and of what there is little need detain us. For the first half of the c17 there is just one major building: Shrivenham of 1638. It is large, and it is complete. It has a plain oblong plan built round the Perp crossing tower, a W porch and two symmetrically placed E entrances, and large, even, straight-headed Perp windows of three to five lights, but Tuscan columns inside – a general impression totally different from that 11b of any medieval church and curiously Protestant, in spite of its Laudian date. For the second half of the century only the riddle of Uffington and Buckland comes in here, that is, the date of the windows with mullions just pushing up without any compromise into the two-centred arch or (at Uffington) into a hard 8b triangular top. The VCH calls them c13. They can hardly be. At Uffington we know of repairs in 1677–9. This seems a more convincing date.‡ For the c18 there is pretty well nothing, that is of before the Gothic Revival. The church at Pusey, St Peter Wallingford, and the church at Kingston Bagpuize are the only ones to mention, the first of c.1745–50, the third of 1799–1800, the second of 1760–9. *Sir Robert Taylor*'s spire of St Peter belongs in 9a another context. The scarcity is the same in church furnishings.

MONUMENTS of value are more frequent and illustrate, as do the mansions, the growing acceptance of a Berkshire country place by Londoners or half-Londoners. At the beginning stand two types: White Waltham, †1723, by *W. Palmer*, large and competent and purely architectural with no figures,§ and

---

* By *Edward Stanton* a minor monument at Faringdon (†1706), and another, in partnership with *Horsnaile*, at St Mary Wallingford (†1722).

‡ Egglestone Abbey in the North Riding of Yorkshire has windows just like those of Uffington, and there it is admittedly more difficult to argue for a c17 date.

§ Of the same year, most elegantly done and anonymous, Theodore Randue in St George's Chapel Windsor, and of 1719, more Vanbrughian and also anonymous, a monument at Shellingford.

Kintbury, †1711, with two free-standing busts and an urn on a pedestal. *Peter Scheemakers* took this up for a monument also at Kintbury, †1754, and *Thomas Scheemakers* for yet another at Kintbury, †1767. A much better *Peter Scheemakers* is at Pusey church, †1742 and †1753 – a seated woman by a bust – a weak one again with busts in Windsor parish church, †1735. But the *nec plus ultra* of manipulating busts is *Hickey*'s *chef d'œuvre* at St Helen Abingdon, 1782, with six busts ingeniously arranged. There is no Roubiliac in Berkshire, and the only *Rysbrack* (Coleshill †1751) is comparatively insignificant. In fact the most impressive monument of the mid-century is surprising by name 31a of sculptor and by style. It is *Thomas Carter*'s Mrs Benyon †1777 at Englefield, a fully Berninesque relief.

When it comes to EIGHTEENTH-CENTURY HOUSES numbers and variety grow at once beyond what we have so far found in Berkshire. Yet, before the Victorian Age, the county had few really grand mansions. Only three of the c18 can be called grand, and even they more for reasons strictly architectural than for reasons of sheer size. They are Buckland House 50a by the younger *Wood* of Bath, Benham Park Speen by *Capability* 50b *Brown*, and Basildon Park by *John Carr* of York. The first is of 1757 etc. and was doubled in size at the beginning of the c20, the second is of 1772–5, the third of 1776. Buckland House has some splendid interiors too, especially the so-called chapel, all exposed stone, Basildon Park a curious recessed portico within which by two small staircases one reaches the *piano nobile*.

Of medium-size however there is a great deal. The first third of the century in particular is very rich, in the towns as well as the country. The series starts just before 1700 with the Old House Hotel at Windsor, connected hypothetically with *Wren*, a quiet, dignified brick house near the river. Also hypothetically connected with *Wren* and also at Windsor is the Masonic Hall, but this represents rather the style of Hawksmoor and in any case is as late as 1725–6. The typical early c18 or rather Early Georgian house in Berkshire is faced with blue vitrified or, in some areas, pale grey vitrified brick and has red-brick or rubbed-red-brick dressings. Often the blue brick is used as headers only. Windows are segment-headed, and roofs disappear behind parapets. Kirby House, Inkpen, of 1733 is a typical example. A group of such houses have the centre raised and also introduce some other means of dramatization. Vanbrugh inspiration is likely. To this group belong Kingston House 47b at Kingston Bagpuize, West Hanney House of 1727, a house in

Church Street Faringdon, Manor Farm at West Challow, Coxe's Hall at Stanford-in-the-Vale of 1733, and also the specially swagger Ardington House of 1721, where it is the side elevation rather than the front that exhibits Vanbrughian features. To the same group belong the very individual Brick Alley Alms- 47a houses at Abingdon of 1718 and their arched giant recesses, inside which the upper floors of the dwellings have balconies.* No. 24 Northbrook Street at Newbury of 1724 is small but particularly ornate. The old, original house of Radley College is of 1721–7 and has as part of its door surround pilasters disappearing part of the way up in the pattern of the rustication – a Lutyens motif which also occurs at Kingston House. An interior in this English Baroque is the entrance hall and staircase of Purley Hall, dated 1719. The wall paintings covering even the underside of the staircase are *Thornhill* school. Fine slightly &49 later interiors are at Hall Place near Hurley. But the most splendid interior of the first third of the century is the entrance 48b hall of Farley Hill, a house in its exterior still Queen Anne rather than Palladian.‡

Once Baroque drama had been discarded, the county settled down to the standard five-bay or seven-bay brick or stone houses, mostly with a centre pediment as one knows them in all counties of England. Hall Place near Hurley of the thirties has already been mentioned, Pusey House is of 1753, Calcot House near Reading (rather grander) of 1755, Ascot Place – like Buckland and Basildon with linked pavilions – probably of the 1760s, Culham Court of 1770, Faringdon House of *c.*1780–90, and so on to *Wyatt*'s Purley Park and *Wyatville*'s Woolley Park, Brightwalton, with a semicircle of Tuscan columns round an ample bow window. This is dated 1799.

But the county was not entirely classical and columnar. The GOTHIC REVIVAL and the Picturesque made their appearance early and left their mark. The earliest date seems to be the two pretty churchyard gateways of Newbury parish church, i.e. if they are by *Fuller White* and of 1770. Immediately after follows Donnington Grove just outside Newbury. The dates here are before 1772 and about 1785. The first designer was *John Chute* of The Vyne. At Milton House in 1776 *Stephen Wright* added

* Twitty's Almshouses at Abingdon are of 1707 and Tomkins' Almshouses of 1733.

‡ One public interior must find its place here too: the Abingdon Council Chamber of 1759, built in an addition of 1731–3 on top of the Perp St John's Hospital just across the Market Place from the Town Hall.

52a two wings, Gothic internally, and the library is the most
charming Gothicist interior in Berkshire. In 1777 *Sir Robert*
9a *Taylor* gave to the church of St Peter at Wallingford its delightful fancy spire, undecided as to whether it should be considered
classical or Gothic. Sandleford Priory is one of *Wyatt's* first
essays in the Gothic: 1780–1 (with the two finest and largest
rooms in a wing attached to the back and treated entirely classi-
cally). At Buckland House about 1790 the stables were given a
Gothic façade as an eye-catcher from the house. A much more
effective eye-catcher was Strattenborough Castle Farm from
Coleshill. The former buildings here, in 1792, were not only
51a made to appear a medieval ruin but a medieval ruin repaired –
a piece of ingenuity and sophistication worth recording. Binfield
House has nice Gothic trim too, and Farley Castle, Farley Hill,
of 1809–10. In St George's Chapel, Windsor, *Henry Emlyn*
designed the charming Gothic monument to Edward IV in 1789
and the perfectly convincing *Coade*-stone screen between
crossing and chancel with its pretty fan-vault in 1790–2. He also
19 added and repaired the stalls equally convincingly. The same
can alas not be said of his contribution to the classical style. His
English Order, as demonstrated at Beaumont Lodge (now Beaumont College), Old Windsor, in 1790 is terrible, the way a pair
of columns coalesces at bottom and top into one quite inexcus-
able.

THE PICTURESQUE was given a field-day in Windsor Park.
It is the ensemble one must try to visualize – difficult now that
so much of it is inaccessible to the public. If a few items have to
be singled out, Fort Belvedere or Shrub Hill Tower, a triangular
medievalizing tower of *c.*1750, much imitated later, is one,
Cranbourne Tower of 1808 another, the wonderful ruins of
52b Lepcis Magna presented to the Regent in 1816 and re-erected
by Virginia Water a third. Virginia Water of *c.*1750 is the largest
of the made lakes of Berkshire, but most of the country houses
had their lakes, small or large, and the Thames was also called
in for picturesque siting. The Temple on the island between
Fawley Court in Bucks and Remenham, designed by *Wyatt* and
built in 1771, is not easily forgotten, and the third Duke of
Marlborough's fishing lodge and banqueting house on Monkey
Island of *c.*1744 must originally also have been a delight. It
derives its name from the monkey paintings by *Clermont* inside.
Again at Windsor, Frogmore House, given a classical remodelling by *Wyatt* in 1792, has a room with pretty decoration of
53 flowers and garlands by *Mary Moser*. At Park Place, General

Conway's estate, the cyclopean bridge at the foot of the grotto valley is placed so that coming from the grotto one sees the water of the Thames through it, although the river is not all that near. But the climax of the picturesque apparatus of Park Place is of course 'little master Stonehenge', as Horace Walpole called it, the stone circle given by the inhabitants of Jersey to General Conway in 1787 and re-erected accurately. Buckland House has a fair number of picturesque objects in its grounds as well, including an Ice House with a portico to the lake. The portico has a kind of intermittent vermiculated grotto rustication, a treatment which also occurs in the quadrant walls of Pusey House and the porch of the rectory of Kingston Bagpuize, which is dated 1723. To these large-scale ornaments two on a small scale must be added: Halfway House, that enlarged piece of Staffordshire ware, halfway between Newbury 51b and Hungerford, and Hop Castle near Winterbourne, with an octagonal centre and ogee cap, walls of whole flints and bones, and at least partly a grotto treatment of the interior.

The Medieval Revival started Rococo, turned Romantic, and finished Archaeological. The story is familiar, but that Windsor Castle, the major architectural monument of Berkshire, is more 35 than anything a monument to the transition from Romantic to Archaeological is less familiar and, as far as the layman is concerned, hardly realized at all. Yet it is true that the Windsor we see today and which remains in the memories of Continental visitors as one of the most spectacular castle ensembles anywhere is essentially the work of *Sir Jeffry Wyatville* in the eighteen-twenties. Had he not heightened the Round Tower by 33 ft, had he not heightened many of the other towers, had he not created the s front with its central gateway and recast the E front, Windsor from a distance or Windsor from within the Lower and Upper Wards would not be half as impressive as it is. The naïvety with which the early C19 believed in the possibility of making a better medieval castle out of an existing and faulty one may amaze us now. Yet this attitude – which is of course the same that has given us better picturesque landscape than nature could provide – set off Windsor on the greatest period of its social life, which is the Victorian period. The State Apartments were ready for it, their remodelling begun by *Wyatt* about 1800, but principally done by *Wyatville*. Some rooms are classical,* the Grand Reception Room is a remarkably early case of 56

* But the specially fine doors in the Crimson Drawing Room were brought 55 from Carlton House, the Regent's London house, and date from *c*.1810.

neo-Rococo, and most of the rooms are Gothic and tend to be
somewhat gloomy. The scale is remarkable. St George's Hall is
185 ft long, the Waterloo Chamber (re-decorated in 1861) about
90 by 45 ft.

But before we can take our stand in the year 1837 and look
forward over the second and the last third of the C19, we must
see what happened in sculpture and the decorative arts at the
time of Wyatville. It is true, nothing has yet been said about
sculpture and decoration of the second half of the C18 either,
but there is little to be said. In CHURCH FURNISHING only a
little mopping up is needed – i.e. one large head of typical mid-
Georgian Stained Glass by *John Rowell*, 1744, at Arborfield, and
the lovely engraved clear armorial glass of 1792 by *Eginton* at
Great Coxwell,* and in MONUMENTS scarcely more. One *Wilton*
at Padworth (†1776), and several minor works by several other
sculptors whose names the reader can try in the index, *Nollekens*
31b e.g., *Bacon* e.g. *Canova* did an enormously heavy tablet at Speen
(†1806), *Flaxman* a lot of tablets of no special value and one
extremely fine one at Cookham (1810), *Westmacott* a noble one
at Ruscombe (†1799), one to *Wyatt*'s design at Shrivenham
(†1793), and several others, but the sculptural or perhaps rather
scenic sensation of C19 sculpture in Berkshire is without any
32 doubt that snow-white *tableau vivant*, the apotheosis of Princess
Charlotte in Windsor Chapel. This is by *Matthew Cotes Wyatt*
and was executed between 1817 and 1824. The basic conception
is entirely Baroque, the dead body invisible under a heavy cloth
except for the fingers of one hand, the mourning maidens with
their heads all covered by their mantles, the rising young body
in the middle, the front of the tomb-house, the large marble-
carved curtain. But the whiteness and the chaste, motionless
faces of the ascending princess and the two angels counterbalance
that violence and result in a unison of Baroque and Classical
which is typical of Romantic sculpture (and also of the Romantic
cartoon).

The typical CHURCHES of the same years are Gothic, but
also in their composition and their internal space still wedded
to the classical Georgian ideals. Berkshire examples of this type,
known as the type of the Commissioners' Churches, are the Wind-
9b sor parish church of 1820–2, Hungerford of 1816, Sunninghill

---

* Berkshire has an uncommonly complete series of heraldic glass from
Ockwells (*see* above) via Radley (C16) and Lucas Hospital Wokingham
(*c.*1665–70) to Abingdon Town Hall (*c.*1830) and Windsor Chapel (by
Willement).

of 1826–7,* and, after 1837, Holy Trinity Windsor of 1842–4 and Bear Wood of 1846. But Gothic was not the only medieval style admitted for inspiration. Norman had much to recommend it, just because the square, static element of the classical, which they did not want to give up yet, is more easily attained in a *Rundbogen* style than in a pointed style. So there was a brief national fashion for the neo-Norman in the forties. In Berkshire it is heralded remarkably early at Kennington in 1828. Even *Pugin* at St James Reading, in 1837–40, succumbed to the Norman, tempted no doubt by the adjoining abbey ruin.‡ The other examples are Hermitage 1835, Shaw 1840–2 (by *Hansom*), and Burghfield 1843. The Nonconformists during these same years demonstrated their anti-medievalism by keeping away from Gothic altogether and sticking to classical. Windsor has two specially good examples: the Congregationals of 1832 and the Baptists of 1839.

But the most valuable church of the pre-Victorian C19 in Berkshire is no doubt Theale, by the little-known *E. W. Garbett*, and of 1820–32. This, at a moment when Gothic almost without exception meant minimum Perp or indifferent lancets, is in a scholarly and a very ambitious way E.E. It is inspired directly from Salisbury Cathedral and makes a proud show, where it stands outside the village.

Yet how different are its tight verticals from the 'reality', i.e. the substantial, full-blooded VICTORIAN CHURCH BUILDINGS designed by those who came after Pugin. *Scott* is the oldest of these, and his Bradfield parish church of 1847–8 is a first-class example to demonstrate that change. It is Second-Pointed now, as they called it, i.e. with tracery from Geometrical to Early Decorated; it performs feats of variety and picturesqueness internally and externally, but a thicker, heavier picturesqueness now than that of the Rococo Gothic had been.§ Of the slightly younger men of the Victorian Gothic *Butterfield* did much, but nothing special, except the spiky and idiosyncratic St Nicholas' 58b

* This and the Windsor parish church have cast-iron piers.

‡ There is one more *Pugin* church in the county: Tubney, 1844–7, uninteresting architecturally, but interesting in that a Roman Catholic architect in the 1840s could be commissioned to design a Church of England church and could accept. Tubney is close to Oxford. And another Pugin P S. Messrs Betjeman and Piper report that the Presbytery at East Hendred possesses furniture and crockery from Pugin's house at Ramsgate.

§ This is not Scott's first appearance in Berkshire. He started as a designer of workhouses, and that at Old Windsor by the firm *Scott & Moffatt* is of 1835 and yet Tudor, not classical as workhouses used to be.

School at Newbury of 1859 and perhaps the odd neo-Norman nave of Ascot Priory of 1877, *Teulon* did just one duly perverse church – Leckhampstead (1858–60) – but *Street*, who lived for some early years (1850–2) at Wantage, can be studied excellently in the county, and so can *Woodyer*. Boyne Hill, Maidenhead, of 1854–7 is Street at his best, a powerful group of church, gate, parsonage, school, and schoolmaster's house, Great Fawley of 1866 is as serious and almost forbidding, and the Convent of the Wantage Sisterhood of 1855 etc. is at least eminently characteristic of his domestic style. Most attractive of his secular buildings however are the village schools such as Inkpen of 1850, and Eastbury of 1851, where period precedent is waived in favour of commodity. *Woodyer*, who liked ornate interiors, could show this in three major buildings: St Paul Wokingham of 1862–4, ornate externally as well, Christ Church Reading of 1861–2 and 1874 with the curious and wholly successful large tracery area above the chancel arch, and the surprisingly large chapel of the House of Mercy at Windsor of 1881.

Berkshire is a bonanza of High Anglo-Catholic communities. At Wantage the Sisterhood had Street's small chapel replaced by a large rib-vaulted one in 1887. The designer was *Pearson*, who also designed the large, also rib-vaulted parish church of Ascot in 1896–7. Also at Wantage *William White* did the Retreat House of St Michael in 1855. Ascot Priory was begun by *Buckeridge* in 1861 and continued by *Scott*. Other orders built too, but need not be recorded here. On the other hand Douai Abbey at Woolhampton, Roman Catholic, ought perhaps to be remembered, though its architectural record is poor, and also the public schools, like Wellington with a chapel by *Scott*, less memorable by far than the college buildings themselves to which we shall revert presently, Bradfield with a competent and externally well composed chapel by *John Oldrid Scott*, Sir G.G.'s son, and the Catholic Beaumont, Old Windsor, with a chapel most unexpectedly in a Raphaelesque style. The room is tunnel-vaulted and the decoration by *Bentley* is *alla* Loggie or Pompei. Italian also is the exterior of the spectacular Royal Mausoleum in Windsor Park, built in 1862–71 by *A. J. Humbert*, but designed as regards the Raphaelesque interior by *Professor Grüner* of Dresden, in whom Prince Albert had had much confidence. It is one of the most complete and convincing High Victorian interiors in the Italian style. The exterior is rather Romanesque instead, whereas *Humbert*'s Mausoleum for the Duchess of Kent of 1861 is a domed rotunda, of a rather French Dixhuitième flavour. Some fifteen years later the chapel of the Royal Military Academy at Sandhurst was built in a Byzantine-cum-Italian-Romanesque style (consecrated in 1879). It has since been more than doubled in size.

Much of the original CHURCH FURNISHINGS has been kept in the Victorian churches. The round stone Pulpits, the low iron Screens, the carved Fonts are too little noticed and too little appreciated.* The Reredoses are often sculptured, weakly almost without exception. The weakness of Victorian SCULPTURE is altogether a fact hardly to be denied. The monument to the Duchess of Gloucester of 1859 in St George's Chapel, designed by *Scott* and carved by *Theed*, is Victorian sculpture at its best. So is Prince Albert's Monument in the Albert Memorial Chapel by *Baron Trinqueti*, who was responsible for the design of the whole interior of the chapel in 1863–73, by far the most eminent Victorian ecclesiastical interior of Berkshire, with its Latest Classical stories on the walls, engraved in marble, and its small white marble reliefs. The total effect is eclipsed however by the gorgeous monument to the Duke of Clarence by *Alfred Gilbert*, 33 and that, though of 1892, is post-Victorian by any terms of definition one could apply to the Victorian style. It is Arts and Crafts turned Art Nouveau in the hands of a decorator of genius. The lava-like curves of structure and draperies and so much else is Art Nouveau without doubt, and earlier than nearly all Continental Art Nouveau.

The Arts and Crafts component is originally derived from *William Morris*'s patterns. Morris's influence is much greater than such a survey as this can point out. Morris's own work in Berkshire is confined to STAINED GLASS, but there – if we include that designed by *Burne-Jones* before Morris's did their own as a firm – it ranges from 1861 to the years of decline after his death. The glass in the original chapel of Bradfield College by Burne-Jones of 1862 is among the most astonishing of the century, forceful, bold in composition and colouring, and not a bit historicist. Of the same year but tender and intimate the *Morris* glass at Cranbourne. Other Morris glass at Dedworth (1863–87) and Tilehurst (1869) and then, of the seventies, and of mature excellence, at Eaton Hastings and Easthampstead (Bracknell).‡ *Kempe*, the other familiar name in Later Victorian glass, is

* The Font in St Paul Wokingham by *Woodyer* is specially noteworthy. Its freely growing plants all along the drum of the bowl are proto-Art Nouveau in a way not infrequently found in the 1860s.

‡ One major domestic job of *Burne-Jones*'s ought also to be referred to, 61 the series of paintings of Briar Rose at Buscot Park, done in 1890.

ubiquitous in Berkshire. Nowhere can he compare with Morris, either in colouring or in composition or in the use of leading. *Gibbs* among the pre-Morris purveyors of stained glass is the one most intelligently aware of the role of leading. The county is rich in Victorian stained glass, and those who want to train themselves to recognize the handwritings of *Hardman, Wailes, Clayton & Bell,* and others can do so. Here only a few special windows need be annotated: *J. P. Seddon,* the architect and friend of the Pre-Raphaelites, designed one *c.*1877 at Sunningwell, and it is thoroughly successful. *Heywood Sumner*'s E window at Longworth is on the way from the Arts and Crafts to the English variety of Expressionism, and *Brangwyn* did a series of windows at Bucklebury in 1912 and about 1920 in his customary robust and colourful style. No other church furnishings deserve a word, except perhaps the Painting of Christ at Emmaus by *Westlake* at St John Stratfield Mortimer and the Pulpit at St Mary Wallingford by *Onslow Ford.* This is of 1888 and has bronze reliefs of saints in a marble setting.

The contrast between the character and the quality of the churches and of Victorian SECULAR ARCHITECTURE is baffling alike to the layman and the expert. By and large the churches are scholarly, and where they depart from Gothic authority, they are in their heresies thoroughly considered. Their architects knew exactly what they were doing. Licence, even major licence, is not arbitrary: it is taken advisedly. Not so in most secular architecture, especially of the pre-Morris–Webb–Shaw decades. Berkshire illustrates this to perfection. Up to the thirties classical reasonableness still prevailed, and the safeguards of the pattern-book were firm. Typical are such buildings as St George's School at Windsor of 1803, the Abingdon Gaol of 1805–11, a veritable Bastille, the Sandhurst Military Academy of 1807–12 with its monumental Greek Doric portico, and the grandiose Royal Berkshire Hospital at Reading of 1837–9 – all four incidentally public buildings, a sign of the growing importance and range of public architecture in the C19. The concomitant of such large buildings of the first third of the century is the large terraces in towns such as those opposite the Reading hospital in London Road, or those of King's Road Windsor, e.g. Adelaide Terrace, dated 1831. One need only compare this with Queen's Terrace a little further s, which is about twenty years later, to have the full impact of the change from pre-Victorian to Victorian, red brick with blue-brick diapers, shaped gables, recessions and juttings-forward, and a broken skyline.

The first sign of the change, i.e. the first sign of personal power and inventiveness getting the better of the pattern-book, is the astonishing sequence of rooms made about 1825–30 inside Kingston Lisle House. Who can have thought out this coffered-vaulted entrance passage, this groin-vaulted hall, this flying 57 staircase, their scale and their highly individual detail? We do not know. *Basevi* has been suggested, and *Cockerell* too.

But while here the elements are still derived from the Roman and the Grecian, they turned to Italianate-Villa, Tudor, Jacobean, and Frenchy soon, and to mixtures which explain the term Free Renaissance used at the time. At Windsor e.g. the Royal Waiting Room of the Southern Region station is Gothic (and internally very pretty: 1850–1), the Workshops in Great Park by *Teulon* are utilitarian but if anything Gothic too (1858–61), and the Dairy in the Home Park (by *John Thomas*, the sculptor: 1858) is 60 internally Cinquecento with a lot of shiny fayence. But all this is minor work. No major work was needed at Windsor.

On the other hand the securely rich middle class called for houses of a size and especially a number of rooms that easily outdid Georgian sizes in the county. Berkshire, after the railway had come in 1840, was near enough to London to be desirable as a county for wealthy people's country mansions. Aldermaston Court comes first, 1848–51 for D. H. D. Burr, by *P. C. Hard-wick*, totally asymmetrical, with a tower and a generally Tudor appearance. It cost £20,000. Easthampstead Park (Bracknell) is Jacobean, as big, and dates from 1860. At Englefield enlargement and remodelling took place after a fire in 1886. But the climax, and in its brazen way one of the major Victorian monuments of England, is *Robert Kerr*'s Bear Wood, begun in 1865 59b for John Walter, owner of *The Times*. This is again part-Tudor, part-Frenchy, has again an asymmetrically placed tower, and is in volume probably an equivalent of Blenheim. Nor did the pressure for houses on that scale subside. Marlston House was built for the Palmers of Reading by *Edward Burgess* as late as 1895–9, and *Waterhouse* built country houses on that scale or nearly that scale left and right. His own at Yattendon – he was Lord of the Manor of Yattendon – has been replaced, but Buck-hold House of 1884–5 survives, and a whole corpus of others, e.g. round Reading University. He also designed the Reading Town Hall in 1872–5.

But by far the best of these major High Victorian buildings of Berkshire, and the one most disciplined in its layout and most consistent in its stylistic apparatus, is Wellington College 59a by *John Shaw*, begun in 1856. The style chosen is a mystery. It is derived from two sources both equally unfavoured at the time: that of William and Mary's Hampton Court and that of Louis XIII. So here is brick with ample stone dressings, here are segment-headed and oval windows, here are garlands and mansard roofs, and here above all is a firm axiality conducted triumphantly through two courtyards and ultimately punctuated by two identical towers. Did it impress Nesfield, when he turned Queen Anne, and later *Norman Shaw*? It is far from certain. Norman Shaw went over from his delightfully easy Tudor to the so-called Queen Anne only after 1865. In Berkshire he is represented by two of his Tudor houses, both exemplary of the elegance with which he could treat the Home Counties precedent: Greenham Lodge near Newbury of 1875 and Holme Grange, Wokingham, of 1883 are both imaginatively composed and, especially inside, boldly detailed.

Norman Shaw's influence on English domestic architecture was immense. It even reached as far as the Continent and America. It started off Lutyens as well as Stokes as well as Newton as well as *Baillie Scott*. By the latter there is one quite characteristic house dating from 1899 at Wantage, by *Stokes* Shooter's Hill House, Pangbourne, of 1898 and an exceedingly good new range at Ascot Priory of 1901, by *Newton* Luckley,
63 Wokingham, of 1907, but by *Lutyens* two of his best early houses: Deanery Gardens, Sonning, of 1901 and Folly Farm, Sulham-
62 stead, of 1906 and 1912. Folly Farm, however, shows him at the moment of abandoning the Arts and Crafts Tudor at which he was so supremely good and deserting to the William and Mary in which Shaw also had preceded him. Folly Farm is indeed the moment of transition; for here the William and Mary house of 1906 (added to a genuine timber-framed farmhouse) precedes the brilliant Arts and Crafts range by six years. This range, with its enormous roof, its low loggia of short piers, and its pool was Lutyens's last in that style. It was also among the last on that scale; for the First World War brought an end to the commissioning of rich men's country mansions. Berkshire has one of the most uninhibited Edwardian ones, even if designed a few years before Queen Victoria's death: *Sir John Belcher*'s Pangbourne Tower.

And there we can end – or nearly end. For the TWENTIETH CENTURY has not done much yet to the county other than covering large areas with indifferent houses and bungalows and all main roads with cars. New buildings of value which would justify inclusion on the standards so far applied all belong to the last five years: a forceful, somewhat overpowering skyscraper block of flats at Bracknell New Town by *Arup Associates* as 64 the only contribution Bracknell has so far made, a factory at Wokingham by *Yorke, Rosenberg & Mardall*, the Road Research Laboratory at Crowthorne by the Ministry of Public Building and Works (*J. Moss*), and the Army School of Electronic Engineering at Arborfield by *J. A. Ford* of the same Ministry. Add to this the fact that a private art lover has in his garden at Bucklebury two of *Henry Moore*'s reclining figures, and the survey is done.

Those who want to deepen their knowledge of the art and architecture of the county beyond what this Introduction and the following Gazetteer can do are referred to the following books. First and foremost the *Victoria County History* vols 3 and 4 of 1923 and 1924; then the accounts of country houses in *Country Life* and sundry papers in the *Berkshire Archaeological Journal*. The MHLG has completed its survey of the county, and this contains brief descriptions of far more houses than are mentioned in my gazetteer. The *Little Guide* (by F. G. Brabant, largely as written for the first edition in 1911) has just that much of historical enrichment as is missing in my pages, and Messrs Betjeman and Piper's *Berkshire*, 1949, has sensitive descriptions and a galaxy of first-rate photographs selected so as to keep away from the obvious. Having tried to do the same as far as possible, I regret to find that in the end I often chose the same subjects for the photographers as they had done.

APPENDIX: GEOLOGY

BY TERENCE MILLER

Berkshire, like its neighbours Wiltshire and Buckinghamshire, straddles the great chalk ridge of South and East England that runs down from the Wash to Weymouth Bay. The dominant geological feature of the county is thus the chalk, whether visibly present as surface rock, or lying buried beneath newer rocks, or, as in North Berkshire, w of Oxford, only comparatively recently – in the geological sense – stripped away to expose older strata below.

The structure of the chalk as a bed of rock is a sheet, 700 ft thick, dipping gently s, with its exposed upper or N edge forming the ridge which runs from White Horse Hill, by West Ilsley

Downs, down to the Thames N of Goring. This sheet passes s under the valley of the Kennet, and then turns up in a sharp wrinkle to reappear at the surface and form a second scarp face under Inkpen Beacon. In East Berkshire the quadrilateral Sonning–Henley–Farnham–Maidenhead also has chalk bedrock, and Windsor Castle stands on an outlying hump of it.

Only the N part of the chalk area – Lambourn Downs, for example – can be called 'typical chalk country', with bare, rolling grassland and clumps of beech or mixed timber. Elsewhere the pure white limestone is obscured by a jumbled deposit known as 'clay-with-flints'. This is the insoluble residue left after the weathering away of an originally thicker chalk cover. With a veneer of this kind, although the resulting soils are stony, they are capable of carrying good crops and much more extensive woodland than the bare chalk downs.

N of the chalk main scarp, with the ancient Ridgeway running along its crest, and the Icknield Way at its foot, lie the Vale of White Horse, the Berkshire Ridge, and, beyond, the valley of the upper Thames. These three strips are controlled by rock formations older than the chalk.

Immediately at the foot of the downs there is a flat shelf breaking the slope down to the River Ock. On this shelf, which is the outcrop area of a hardish sandstone (Malmstone) in the Upper Greensand formation, are Kingston Lisle, Wantage, Harwell, Didcot, and North Moreton. Parts of it carry notable cherry (and other fruit) orchards. Below this shelf the main part of the Vale of White Horse has been carved out of two adjacent clay formations, the Gault Clay (Cretaceous), and the Kimmeridge Clay (Jurassic). Neither of these is often exposed, as the surface of the bedrock is much covered by sands and gravels deposited by the meanders of river systems, both recent and ancient. The soils are cold and stiff, the fields often prominently marked by 'ridge-and-furrow', the hedges high, with strong oak trees. Much the same kind of clay land, but based on a still older formation, the Oxford Clay, underlies the upper Thames. Here, the flat river-sand and gravel terraces are wider and better defined than in the Vale. Between the two clay belts runs the North Berkshire Ridge, from Coleshill and Shrivenham, by Faringdon and Kingston Bagpuize, to Cothill and Cumnor, just outside Oxford.

This ridge marks the outcrop of relatively resistant mid-Jurassic (Corallian) limestones and sandstones, the same rocks which were formerly quarried enormously for the colleges of

Oxford. As the name suggests, certain of the limestones contain great masses of fossil corals. Parts of the ridge carry an additional capping of the much younger – but still pre-chalk – pebbly Lower Greensand. Badbury Hill and Faringdon Folly are examples of these Lower Greensand hills. Near Faringdon this sandy formation includes the famous Faringdon Sponge Bed, with a remarkable assemblage of fossil sponges, sea-urchins, and other sea creatures. Where the Coral Rag limestone forms the surface the soil is stony and good for wheat; elsewhere there is more loam, which carries orchards and hop-fields, or, in a few places, sandstone weathering down into sand-hills, as at Buckland Warren.

s of the line Hungerford–Reading–Windsor, Berkshire is made, for the most part, of rocks younger than the chalk. These younger rocks are mainly stiff yellow-brown clays and either greenish or red-brown sands, often pebbly. Isolated remnant patches of the same soft rocks also lie out on the chalk surface forward (i.e. N) of their main outcrop, as around Boxford and Hermitage, N of Newbury. There are three divisions: the oldest, the Reading Beds, mainly sandy; the middle, a thick (250 ft) sheet, of London Clay; and the youngest, also sandy, the Bagshot Beds. Of these, the Reading Beds have a relatively narrow outcrop, and the London Clay, like other clay formations, produces a rather dull and featureless landscape. In their own right, therefore, they contribute little to the Berkshire scene. Above them, however, sands and pebble-beds of the Bagshot group are responsible for many of the 'commons', gorse- or heather-covered, and with fine expanses of pine 'forest'. Considerable stretches of South Berkshire are modified – whether on a clay or sand bedrock – by spreads of sand and gravel produced originally by rivers draining off the great ice-sheet which once lay across North Berkshire. Although the main component of these Plateau Gravels and River Gravels is the familiar flint, there are, in addition, variable proportions of other, more exotic rock fragments, brought s by the ice-sheet itself, or by rivers draining from it, from the midland and northern counties. Greenham and Bucklebury Commons, and Aldermaston Park, are examples of the effect of Plateau Gravel patches; Bagshot Heath is a mixture of Bagshot sands and Plateau Gravels; Windsor Great Park, and most of the country from there w almost to Reading, is practically bare London Clay.

Berkshire has no important source of building stone of its own, but is within easy range of some of the most famous of

English freestones – Bath, Headington, and Portland. There has always been a steady flow of stone into the county, and comparatively little 'native' quarrying, with the exception of the Corallian limestones of the N, as at Cothill, near Oxford. On the other hand, as might be expected, both North and South Berkshire have an abundance of clays for brick-making – Oxford, Kimmeridge, and Gault Clays from formations older than the chalk; London Clay from the beds younger than the chalk. The chalk itself has been used, as in churches at Tilehurst, Sonning, and Waltham St Lawrence, but it is too soft for external use unless artificially protected. However, the irregular silica concretions – flints – which are scattered through the middle and upper chalk, and occur in profusion in the clay-with-flints and Plateau Gravels, have been an important building stone at least from Roman times. They were used in the Roman walls at Silchester, and appear, combined in various ways with stone, brick, or timber, in many Berkshire buildings.

The Reading, London, and Bagshot Beds, unmodified, contain no rock suitable for building. But by a natural process of patchy and irregular hardening certain sands of these formations provide isolated 'boulders' of tough sandstone – the famous Berkshire sarsens. These, left lying on the surface after the weathering away of the softer parent sand, may remain in place or be re-incorporated into river sands or gravels, or become embedded in the clay-with-flints. They may be found all over Berkshire, and have often been used as corner-stones, as stepping-stones, or gate-posts, or simply built into walls. Sarsen-built houses can be seen e.g. at Lambourn, Ashbury, and Idstone. Sarsen stones were also used in the chambered barrow 3a of Wayland's Smithy, Ashbury, and, very extensively, in Windsor Castle. Another example of a similar natural hardening process is found around Bagshot Heath, where a pebbly layer has been 'cemented' by ironstone to form a conglomeratic rock. Blocks of this are used at Wokingham church (tower) and the churches of Binfield, Warfield, and Winkfield.*

* Also Byfleet and Chobham in Surrey.

BERKSHIRE

*

INTRODUCTION

Abingdon owes its existence to the abbey founded in 675. The
town grew up in front of the abbey gates with its market place
immediately outside the gatehouse – the same pattern as e.g.
Battle Abbey in Sussex. In Domesday Book no town is yet
mentioned – only 'ten traders before the gates'. The abbey
extended along the Thames. So did the town, with the church
at the far end. It makes a very fine view from the bridge, in
spite of the bloody-minded insistence of the gaol on its own
presence. The prosperity of Abingdon was first that of the
abbey, later of a flourishing woollen trade. There were bitter
struggles between abbey and town throughout the Later Middle
Ages.

CHURCHES

ST HELEN. The steeple rises splendidly at the s end of East St
Helens. It is a C13 steeple, which is surprising considering
the rest of the church. Doorway to the N with shafts with leaf
capitals. Smaller blank arches l. and r. Lancet windows with
continuous roll mouldings above. Pairs of lancets as bell-
openings. Perp parapet with pinnacles. Spire with one set of
lucarnes at the foot and a band above. The steeple has often
been restored. The spire was last rebuilt in 1888. To this
tower, which was always a N tower, a C13 church belonged.
This consisted of nave and N aisle. Part of the E wall still remains, but the rest was remodelled when, in the C15 and C16,
Abingdon built itself an exceedingly spacious new church
with double aisles N and S. One examines the exterior by
entering the churchyard from the tower through an Elizabethan archway. Between steeple and two-storeyed N porch
a formerly two-storeyed structure supposed to have been
the priest's dwelling. The porch has to the front three small
niches. Then (renewed) Dec windows, i.e. in the N wall of the

c 13 N aisle. The w view is all Perp, four large windows, but no regularity. Also a w porch. The s side is Perp and ends on the E in a vestry or treasury, so that to the E there are five gables of different pitch and details. Those of the chancel E window are evidently Victorian. This E side borders immediately on a street. The interior has four arcades all essentially the same, with concave-sided octagonal piers, concave-sided capitals, and moulded depressed arches. The nave has a clerestory. The outer s aisle was built in 1539, according to a preserved will. The chancel details are even more blatantly High Victorian–E.E. internally than externally. They are by *Woodyer*, 1873, and cost £7,000 (PF). By him no doubt also the N doorway from the tower porch.

FURNISHINGS. FONT. By *H. P. Peyman* of Abingdon. Shown in the 1851 Exhibition. Copy in white marble of the font of Sutton Courtenay. – FONT COVER. Dated 1634. – REREDOS. By *Bodley*, 1897. – ALTAR in the inner N aisle. By *Bodley*, c.1897. – PULPIT. Dated 1636. Very good; not over-done. Angle columns, simple arched panels, but with a pedimented feature in each panel with an indicated false perspective (cf. Buckland and Shrivenham). – ORGAN CASE. 1725 by *Abraham Jordan*, with good carving. – MAYOR'S SEAT. 1706, with openwork foliage front, carved lion and unicorn instead of poppy-heads, and a small iron SWORD REST. – PAINTING. The roof of the inner N aisle is panelled, and the panels were painted about 1390. The *ensemble* is unique in England and artistically very valuable. It consists of canted sides painted with figures and a flat top part painted with delightfully traceried interlocked lozenges. The figures are set in narrow cusped panels and each pair under an ogee arch with panelled spandrels. At the foot, disregarding the panels, runs a vine trail. This motif reveals the whole as having been a Tree of Jesse. Prophets and Kings alternate, but at the E end of the N side is Christ crucified framed by the Annunciation. Jesse himself and the other earliest figures were at the w end of the s side and are not preserved. An inscription runs all along the cornice of the canted parts and tells us that the chapel was built by William Reve, and the roof repaired by William Cholsey, and that Boniface IX offered an indulgence to those helping in the repair. Reve belongs to the second half of the c 13, but Boniface IX ruled from 1389 to 1404, and the indulgence dates from 1391. The style of the figures is typical of this date and may be compared with panels from screens in East Anglia or the Despenser Retable in Norwich Cathedral. – STAINED GLASS. In the outer N aisle W window large figures in strident colours, early C19 (TK: c.1819 ?). – By *Kempe* N 1889, inner N aisle W c.1914, outer S aisle 1893. – CHANDE- LIERS. Of brass, three large, one smaller. Two of the large ones are inscribed 1710 and 1713, the third seems C16. – PLATE. Cup of 1567, altered; Almsdish given in 1829. – MONUMENTS. Brass to Geoffrey Barbour † 1417, a merchant, demi-figure (inner S aisle W), 13 in. long. – Brass to William Herward † 1501 (inner S aisle E), 29 in. long. – Edmund Bostock † 1605. Nice small tablet (inner S aisle E). – Mrs Hawkins, by *J. Hickey*, 1782. A major work by a minor sculptor. It was a difficult job to compose a monument so as to display six portraits. Seated woman holding books. She sits in front of a Rococo strigillated object which may mean a sarcophagus. Her arm rests on a medallion with the portrait of her fiancé, the Rev. Mr Hart. L. and r. busts, above the strigillated object two busts and an urn. The busts represent Mrs Hawkins's father and mother, sister and cousin. – Dr John Crossley † 1790 by *Nollekens*. Conventional, with a big putto by an urn. – Very many more tablets.

CHRIST CHURCH, Northcourt Road. Converted by *W. Emil Godfrey* in 1961 from the BARN of Northcourt Farm, a tithe barn of Abingdon Abbey. The transept now has a glazed end wall, and there is an identical window opposite. The barn it- self is of stone and attributed to the C13. The roof has tie- beams and queen-posts, probably C15 or C16.

ST MARY AND ST EDMUND (R. C.), Oxford and Radley Roads. 1857 by *G. Goldie* (GS). Tall, of nave with bellcote and chancel and S aisle and N chapel. Geometrical tracery. The former SCHOOL to the N. (In the churchyard MONUMENT to the 7th Earl of Abingdon † 1928 by *Eric Gill*.)

ST MICHAEL, Park Road. 1864–7 by *Sir G. G. Scott*. Nave and aisles, transepts, chancel, high bellcote. Geometrical tracery. A quiet, dignified design. Round and octagonal piers, quatre- foil clerestory.

ST NICHOLAS, Market Place. An odd W front. Late Norman doorway with three orders of shafts. Arch with roll mouldings, one with a fillet. Though much restored, there seems to be indication of more Norman work here, including blank arcading, and it is not in line with the present church. This church has to the N two lancets and traces of a third, to the S (where the parapet is of 1881) two Dec windows. Otherwise

Perp, including the W tower, built into the older nave, and the odd oriel or shallow chapel to the N. This is said to be of the restoration of 1881, but the window is certainly at least partly old. – FONT. C15. Broad, panelled stem, bowl with quatrefoils. – PULPIT. Jacobean. The book rest is supported by two eagles. – SCULPTURE. Small stone relief of the Crucifixion and two saints. – PLATE. Set of 1786. – MONUMENT. John Blacknall † 1625. Two kneeling figures. Altar front with flat strap decoration. The monument was not erected till 1684 and moved in 1881.

NONCONFORMIST CHAPELS. A most instructive set of four, all of between 1840 and 1875. First BAPTIST, Ock Street, 1841, still purely classical, with an attached portico of Tuscan columns carrying a pediment. Then CONGREGATIONAL, The Square, 1862 by *J. S. Dodd* (BC), classical going Italian, with giant pilasters and a pediment, just a little less disciplined than twenty years before. Then METHODIST, Ock Street, 1845 by *Wilson* of Bath, Gothic in the early, modest lancet way, and finally TRINITY METHODIST, Park Road, by *Woodman*, 1875, full-blown churchy, with a large N steeple and fussy Geometrical tracery, evidently to outdo Scott's St Michael's in the same street of the 'west-end' of Abingdon.

ABINGDON ABBEY

Abingdon Abbey, as has already been said, was founded in 675. The Abingdon Chronicle tells us that the church was only 120 ft long, but had a W as well as an E apse, a custom extant in North Africa (Orléansville) in Early Christian times and in Germany from the C9 onwards (Fulda, plan for St Gall). Further efforts ought to be made to excavate. After all, the church was on ground not now covered by buildings. The Danes wrought destruction. Under Aethelwold in 955 the abbey was re-founded. Under Abbot Fabritius (1100–17) it reached a climax of prosperity. In 1100 there were twenty-eight monks, in 1117 seventy-eight. In the C15 and early C16 the average was about thirty. Nothing of the abbey church is visible *in situ* at all, and little of the monastic buildings. The W boundary of the area extended from the river N, along Stert Street as far as the railway station. The street called The Vineyard was indeed the abbey vineyard. The most impressive monument now is the ABBEY GATEWAY. It is of the late C15 and has three archways, the southern one C19. The archways have depressed pointed arches with traceried spandrels. Above the middle arch a niche with an original statue of the Virgin. Two-light windows, battlements. Three bays of tierceron vaulting across the interior. The E face of the gatehouse is similar to the other. The gatehouse is attached to the church of St Nicholas, which must have been in the same relation to the abbey as was St Lawrence by the gatehouse to Reading Abbey. And as at Reading the *hospitium* of St John Baptist is close to this place, so it was at Abingdon, where the Hospital of St John is now the Municipal Buildings (*see* below). E of the abbey gateway are the Abbey Gardens. It is here, a little to the E, that the church stood. Instead there are now in the gardens a number of salvaged architectural fragments: two window-heads, one late C13, the other Dec, an artificial ruin with three-bay arcades running N–S, piers and arches identical with those of St Helen, and large E and W window frames. Too little seems known about these fragments.

The only consistent range of abbey buildings is a subsidiary one along the river, SE of the gateway and SW of the church. They consist from E to W of the Long Gallery, the Chequer, and then a lower range. The LONG GALLERY dates from about 1500. It is partly of stone, partly timber-framed. It was originally divided into divers rooms, and access to them was by a timber gallery or cloister walk, comparable to that of the Long Alley Almshouses and to the gallery of the Horseshoe Cloister and the older Canons' Cloister at Windsor. The windows are straight-headed and were never glazed. The rooms were separated from the gallery by partition walls. They had a roof with tie-beams on arched braces. To the W of this range is the CHEQUER, a square C13 block of stone *See* with buttresses and a doorway which has a two-centred arch $\frac{p.}{359}$ and continuous mouldings. This leads into an undercroft with one octagonal pier. No capital, single-chamfered ribs in four bays. The room above has another doorway with continuous mouldings and two Dec two-light windows. Tall chimney with a rare and interesting top, the most interesting of its date 34b in England. The vents are three stepped little lancets in a gable. The room inside has to the S also two windows which are blocked. Excellent C13 fireplace with stiff-leaf and other leaf capitals and a projecting hood. The room was divided in two in the C14 and a triangular lobby made with three doorways. One opened towards the river. W of the Chequer is a lower stone range and then a timber-framed gable on a stone

base. Roof with two tiers of wind-braces. This range was
probably the GRANARY.*

PUBLIC BUILDINGS

45b TOWN HALL, Market Square. Built in 1678–82. The 'under-
taker' of the work was *Christopher Kempster* of Burford, one
of Wren's City masons. It is not known whether he also
designed it, or who else did. Of the free-standing town halls
of England with open ground floors this is the grandest –
grander decidedly than Windsor. It is also remarkably high
and monumental for its two storeys. Celia Fiennes called it
the finest town hall in England. Brown stone, four by two
bays. Giant pilasters on very high plinths used consistently.
Open arches below, the windows above of three lights arched
with a transom and the mullions forming a concentric arch
above the transom – Wren's pattern at Trinity Library Cambridge. Hipped roof, top balustrade, and cupola, as was used
for country houses of *c.*1635–75. At the back a staircase tower
ending in bulbous pinnacles. The stair rail is of the dumb-
bell type. The ground floor was of course used as a market,
the upper room as a court room. It is now absolutely plain.
Balcony on four wooden Corinthian columns. – STAINED
GLASS. Heraldic, from St Nicholas. Made by *J. H. Russell,*
*c.*1830. – REGALIA. Small Mace bought in 1584; two Cups,
1639; Tankards of 1651, 1653–4, 1675, and 1681; Great Mace,
silver-gilt, 1660 or earlier; small Mace, *temp.* Charles II;
small Mace, *temp.* James II; large Tankard, 1700; Set of
Casters, pair of Salts, and twelve Spoons, 1721; Plate, 1735;
two Punch-Bowls and Ladles given in 1740; two large Cups
and two Salvers given in 1744; four Salts, 1759–60; two
Punch-Bowls and Ladles, given in 1760–1; four Salts, 1764–5;
two Candlesticks, 1774; large Cup and Cover, 1795–6; Sets
of Spoons of 1798–9, 1799, 1818, 1826–7; Strainer, 1810;
Salt Spoons inscribed 1810; Strainer, 1814–15; Fish Slices,
1827–8; also later C19 plate.

MUNICIPAL BUILDINGS, Market Place. A group of buildings
not originally belonging together. The range towards St
Nicholas and the Abbey Gate has a rubble ground floor with
restored Perp windows and a better preserved s doorway and
belonged to the Hospital of St John. In 1731–3 *John Stevens* of

* The surviving range of abbey building faces THAMES STREET to the
s. At the E end of this is MILL HOUSE, now the vicarage. This has a doorway
with a two-centred arch, and on the attic floor blocked Perp windows.

Wantage raised the building one storey, and in this new part, in 1759, a fine Council Chamber was made. The N front has in the middle a big niche flanked by pairs of Doric pilasters, placed naïvely on brackets. The main doorway inside the Council Chamber has a pediment and is well detailed. Nice coving. Two end chimneypieces. To the W the Municipal Buildings have a successful outer staircase arrangement provided in 1958 and incorporating to the N a curious doorway with Elizabethan caryatids but C18 Gothick top parts. The continuation is of 1811. Behind, towards Bridge Street, is an irregular brick part, also of 1731 etc. This contains the staircase (with turned and twisted balusters) and the so-called Bear Room with a handsome Venetian window. The doorways have odd, rather heavy, still Early Georgian surrounds. There follows part of the former ROYSSE'S GRAMMAR SCHOOL, to which the entrance was the archway mentioned before. It is a timber-framed building which also formed part of the hospital originally. Inside is now a gallery with a stucco tunnel-vault. This dates from 1911.

POLICE, Bridge Street. 1857. Seven bays, two storeys, the windows widely spaced. A plain, honest job.

FREE LIBRARY, High Street. 1896 by *J. G. T. West*. Half-timbered, with gables, and too tall to be either historically credible or suitable within the scale of Abingdon.

GRAMMAR SCHOOL, Park Road. The oldest part is the W part: 1869–70 by *Edwin Dolby*: brick, high, clumsy, and Gothic. The range to the E of this is lighter in brick and style: 1879–80. The Chapel is of 1902, by *West*.

CONVENT SCHOOL OF ST HELEN AND ST KATHERINE, Ferndale Road. 1904–5 by *F. Pearson*, brick; the stone chapel by the same, 1922.

FITZHARRY'S SCHOOL, Northcourt Road. By *J. T. Castle*, the Berkshire County Architect, 1958–60. Good.

PRIMARY SCHOOL, E of the former. By *Bridgwater & Shepheard*, 1949–52. Is this the earliest school in England to use pre-stressed concrete?

GAOL. 1805–11, by *Daniel Harris* of Oxford. This bastille of Berkshire is impressive enough by itself; as a job of siting it is unpardonable. Hexagonal centre and radiating wings, as then usual. Brown stone, small windows.

CORN EXCHANGE, Market Place. 1886 by *Charles Bell*. Brick, and really with no definite style nor alas any personality.

ABINGDON BRIDGE. The medieval bridge, dating from 1416,

was mostly rebuilt in 1927. The first two ribbed, depressed-pointed arches on the Abingdon side were allowed to remain. They were widened with ribs of the older, rebuilt arches. The view towards St Helen's church is lovely, or would be, if it were not for the gaol.

PERAMBULATION

The MARKET PLACE has of course its fair share of fine buildings, but it has also two for which nothing good can be said: the Corn Exchange (*see* above) and the QUEENS HOTEL, red and yellow brick, of 1864, and quite unbelievably joyless. No houses of individual interest otherwise. We must radiate from the Market Place. To the S BRIDGE STREET with the CROWN HOTEL, whose pretty courtyard repays a visit. Also to the S, from behind the TOWN HALL, EAST ST HELENS runs to the church. It is as a street perhaps the best in Abingdon – also because it is not haunted by traffic as badly as the others. The first notable house still belongs to the Market Place: four bays, three storeys, early C18, the top windows with frills to the lintels. No. 19 is timber-framed and has windows of the so-called Ipswich type which are typical of *c.*1665–75 and occur often at Abingdon. They are tripartite and straight-topped, but the middle light has an arch below the top. Then opposite TWICKENHAM HOUSE, built for Joseph Tomkins, mid Georgian, of red brick, five bays, two storeys, with a three-bay pediment. Doorway with Ionic columns and a pediment. In the frieze a Kentian head. Pretty, white Chinese–Chippendale staircase. (Other rewarding interior features, e.g. late C18 Gothic bookcases.) Stables on the l. with a pediment. Nos 31–33 are early C19, Bath stone and perfectly smooth. No. 26 is of the late C15, with overhang and two gables. Inside, a stone chimneypiece with a lintel decorated with cusped panels. The sides of the dormers have trefoil-headed windows, and a similar window of three lights is in the E wall. No. 28 is of *c.*1570, low and long, and originally had gables. The doorway has a segmental pediment on composite pilasters and a frieze running up to a point in the middle – i.e. Early Georgian. To its r. are two small Elizabethan or slightly later windows. Panelling, fireplaces, and original roof timbers inside. No. 30 is Early Georgian too, of five bays, chequer brick with two gables. The doorway similar to the previous one. At the back some C15 evidence. The street then narrows and has a gabled house (Nos 32–34) across the vista. Overhang on brackets. Opposite another house with an oversailing upper floor. Its neighbour is No. 57, dated 1732. Chequer brick, five bays, even brick quoins. The middle bay framed by pilaster strips. Later doorway. So on to the steeple of St Helen, which forms the *point-de-vue* for the later part of the walk along the street. The last house is FELLOWS' CLOSE (formerly Helenstow), two-storeyed with a large, arched entrance to the yard. Several pre-Reformation windows, one of them wooden, another stone, of two lights.

In the CHURCHYARD of St Helen a small square brick box with a pyramid roof, which is the Organ Blowing Chamber, and three sets of Almshouses. No other churchyard anywhere has anything like it. The centre of the three is CHRIST'S HOS-PITAL or the LONG ALLEY ALMSHOUSES. They were built 36b in 1446, though it is doubtful if much of that date is still visible on the front. This front has a wooden pentice or cloister walk. The porch is of 1605 and has pilasters with volutes outside and a gable. The cloister windows with arched lights may well be of the same date. The pretty lantern was put on in 1707. The side to the river is rubble-faced and c15, though it carries a date 1674. In the centre inside is a panelled hall with pilasters and a bay window to the back. To the r. of Christ's Hospital TWITTY'S ALMSHOUSES of 1707. Red brick, also one-storeyed. Hipped roof with gable and lantern. Seven dwellings. To the l. of Christ's Hospital and with their back to the river the BRICK ALLEY ALMSHOUSES of 1718, 47a built for Christ's Hospital by *Samuel Westbrooke*, mason. Chequer brick and rubbed brick. Seven bays, the centre solid and raised with a pediment, the sides giant arches or niches in which are the doors and upper balconies, a very unusual and rather modern conceit. To the river just two storeys, the ground floor with segment-headed windows. Back from here to the church by the s end of East St Helens, with Nos. 58–60, John Tomkins's malthouse, of chequer brick, dated 1748.

Now from the Market Place w, i.e. along HIGH STREET. No. 10 has a charming c18 ground floor with the doorway between two bow windows and a metope frieze running all along. Opposite the LION INN, timber-framed, with two slightly projecting gabled windows. The High Street ends at THE SQUARE, not at all square. On its E side a nice timber-framed group. We shall go on here presently. First OCK STREET, the continuation of High Street. On the r. a deep Doric porch. Then No. 5, with some Gothick window details, and No. 7,

with a nice doorcase with a decorated frieze. After that the
grandest Abingdon house, built probably for one of the
Tomkins family. Early Georgian, nine bays, three full storeys,
panelled parapet. Straight-headed windows. Windows one,
four, six, nine are narrower. Paired doorways (later ?). Good
interior features. To the l. STABLES, a deep open courtyard
with, in the middle of the end range, archway, Venetian
window, and cupola. The wings have giant blank arches and
pediments to the street. Much more of nice houses (notably
No. 28, with a rich mid C18 chimneypiece and a staircase with
stucco panels and alternatingly columnar and twisted balusters). At the corner of CONDUIT ROAD, ELY'S CONDUIT, a
plain brick niche, with a date 1719. This is followed by
TOMKINS' ALMSHOUSES, 1733. Brick. Two rows with a
characteristic frontispiece at the far end. More worthwhile
houses further W: Nos 91–93 of c.1700, Nos 105–109 of the
late C17, Nos 125–129 of c.1700 (three large gables), and No.
143 of c.1600 (overhang of the E wall).

From the Square BATH STREET goes N. The best house here
is STRATTON HOUSE, built by Benjamin Tomkins and dated
1722. Seven bays with bays three and five narrower and
blocked. Red and rubbed red brick. Segment-headed windows
with frills to the lintels. Doorway with Roman Doric pilasters
and a triglyph frieze. The middle window also flanked by
pilasters. Staircase with thin twisted balusters. Then, on the
other side, THE GABLES, timber-framed, mid C16, with three
gables. Turn w from Bath Street to have a look at PARK
ROAD and ALBERT PARK. This is the 'North Abingdon' in
the North Oxford sense, villas and terrace houses in Gothic
varieties. In the park the CONDUIT, a plain C16 stone cube
with a pyramid roof (SE corner), and the MONUMENT to
Prince Albert, a statue on a pedestal so high that it is almost
like a column (total 48 ft). By *Gibbs* of Oxford, 1865.

Back again to the Market Place and now N along STERT
STREET. No. 3 is timber-framed and of pre-Reformation date.
The stone doorway, though, may be *ex situ*. The two projecting gabled upper windows and the two main gables are
probably a C17 alteration. Nos 31–33 are also timber-
framed and have two symmetrical gables. They are structurally C15. Then BROAD STREET on the l. Nos 12–16 with
three gables. No. 32 with Ipswich windows. Stert Street
narrows a little further N and No. 52, THE KNOWL, stands
across, a charming timber-framed house with an oversailing

upper floor and pargetting to the side, but an early C18 front of five bays and a doorway with Roman Doric pilasters, decorated metopes, and a segmental pediment. Staircase with twisted balusters. On into VINEYARD. On the l. BANBURY COURT, flats in a stepped arrangement. 1962 by *Dennis Page & Partners.* Opposite No. 21, five bays, doorway with pilasters and pediment. Then No. 45, late C18, three bays, and the second floor all three as big lunette windows. Opposite ST JOHN'S HOSPITAL, 1801. Two-storeyed, chequer brick, with projecting wings.

Then, to finish with, out along the Radley Road, to the r. into Barton Lane and to BARTON MANOR, where, next to the house, the inarticulate, two-storeyed ruin of the former barn of the abbots of Abingdon.

PAGAN SAXON CEMETERY. The site was discovered during road work in Saxton Road. The cemetery consisted of seventy-nine cremations in urns and one-hundred and twenty-two inhumation burials. Among the grave goods were numerous disc and saucer brooches, miniature toilet instruments of iron, and in male graves knives, javelins, and swords.

ROUND BARROW, s of Gosford. This large, tree-covered barrow is 60 ft in diameter and 4 ft high. Ploughing right up to the perimeter of the mound has obliterated all traces of the surrounding ditch, which is now visible only as a crop mark from the air.

ROUND BARROW, 1½ m. SW, on Sutton Wick Field. This great barrow, 150 ft in diameter and 5 ft high, has been much reduced by ploughing. No surrounding ditch is visible.

ALDERMASTON

ST MARY. Nave and chancel long, under one roof; s transept, w tower with shingled broach spire. The length of the building is explained by the fact that the nave was Norman and that then, early in the C13, the chancel was thrown into the nave (see the break in the width inside), the transept was added, and a new chancel, itself long, was built. In the chancel lancets, the s transept arch pointed with only a slight chamfer. Norman the small N doorway into the former chancel and the re-set w doorway with an order of colonnettes with spiral and zigzag decoration. The capitals have pairs of birds. Inside the church an excellent large Norman head (s wall). Chancel roof with tie-beams and kingposts. – PULPIT. Elizabethan, with tester. Arabesques and blank arches. – PANELLING of the nave walls; C17. – Two CHANDELIERS of the C18. – PAINTING. Much is preserved in the S transept, though not very well. On the l. of the S window large early C14 St Christopher. On the r. C15 scene with luxuriant canopy. Also traces of C13 masonry patterns. – (PAINTING. Triptych, Adoration, Flemish, early C16.) – STAINED GLASS. In two chancel N windows C13 roundels of the Annunciation and the Coronation of the Virgin. – The rest of the chancel by *Kempe*, 1898. – Funeral HELM in the S transept. – PLATE. Cup and Cover, 1576; Silver-gilt Cup and Cover, *c.*1635; two silver-gilt Flagons, 1718; Paten, 1718; Set of 1809. – MONUMENT. Sir George Forster and his wife who died in 1526. Made probably *c.*1530. Alabaster and of the highest quality, especially the small figures. Recumbent effigies. Against the tomb-chest standing sons and standing daughters under canopies. From the same hand probably as the Roos Monument at Windsor.

ALDERMASTON COURT. The house of 1636 was destroyed by fire in 1843. In illustrations it looks, with its hipped roof, rather 1660 than 1636, but 1636 is the date on a preserved tablet, and it fits the preserved woodwork. This consists of the splendid staircase running through two storeys and some additional figures. These figures, all allegorical or mythological, are still as Mannerist as in 1610, besides being very good for their date. The staircase itself is memorable as being one of the earliest to have a pierced parapet instead of banisters. The parapet moreover is no longer strictly strapwork, but in a state of transition from strapwork to broad-leaved foliage and to gristly forms. The staircase is now inside *P. C. Hardwick*'s mansion for Daniel Higford Darvall Burr. He built it in 1848–51, and it cost over £20,000 (GS). Tudor style, completely asymmetrical on the main (entrance) side. Brick with blue diapers. Mullioned and transomed windows, with and without arched lights. Further back, i.e. part of the back elevation, a slender tower with close 'flushwork' of stone and brick and a kind of steep pavilion-roof top. Very spiky chimneystacks. Large rooms inside. The STABLES are C17, see e.g. the doorway with the steep open pediment. Of *c.*1636 also the grand LODGES, two-storeyed with semicircular gables. They were originally the two wings of a house.

The lodges look down the almost straight village street, which is closed visually at the bottom by the C18 inn. L. and r. all brick cottages, varying in date and shape, but none an intrusion. Behind the inn the village LOCK-UP, brick, with a shallow dome.

In the grounds of Aldermaston Court the buildings erected in 1949–61 by the Ministry of Works for the ATOMIC ENERGY AUTHORITY, impressive and architecturally well-designed structures by the *Ministry of Works* architects.

OLD MILL. Nice group of a five-bay brick house and the brick mill.

GRIM'S BANK. This great earthwork begins on Little Heath, 1 m. SE of Aldermaston Court. At this point the bank still stands 8 ft high and the W-facing ditch is clearly visible. The earthwork runs in a straight NE direction for over $\frac{1}{2}$ m. and then changes to a more northerly direction for a further 300 yds to the W edge of Padworth Common. There is then a gap of some 450 yds before the earthwork resumes its course in a NE direction across the common. Presumably the vegetation at the time of the earthwork's construction was sufficiently dense to provide a natural barrier at this point. At the beginning of this second length of earthwork the bank is some 5 ft high, but traces of the ditch have been almost obliterated by infilling and ploughing. In its continuing NE course close to the summit of Raven Hill and through Old Park the bank is a comparatively slight feature, only 3 ft high. Beyond Old Park it alters course to a more northerly direction for 270 yds and then turns again NE for the final 70 yds of its length.

In Old Park and 150 yds SE of Grim's Bank is a second massive earthwork, GRIM'S BANK II. This earthwork has a bank some 8 ft high with a broad, W-facing ditch. It runs in a straight NE direction across flat country for nearly $\frac{3}{4}$ m.

Both these earthworks and the lesser bank and ditch systems associated with them in the Old Park area are regarded as boundary dykes erected in the C5 by the Britons, centred on Silchester, Hants, as a bulwark against the growing pressure of Saxon incursions.

ALDWORTH

5070

ST MARY. The church houses one of the richest collections of C14 effigies in the country. It is in fact partly of the early C14 itself. But the W tower is earlier, broader than deep, with pairs of single small lancets as bell-openings and a recent pyramid roof. The chancel side window probably *c.*1300 (cusped Y-tracery), and the s aisle properly Dec, i.e. with windows of three lights with two big reticulation units, a doorway with a typical moulding, and arcade arches of a typical moulding. The octagonal piers, however, both bases and capitals, look later C14. To the aisle they have two dogs as hood-mould stops who look as if they came straight from a comic of today. The aisle is remarkably wide, a little wider in fact than the nave. The date 1315 recorded for the re-dedication of the high altar probably refers to the chancel, but it could also refer to at least six of the eight MONUMENTS to members of the de la Beche family. The six are arranged three against the N wall under identical canopies, three against the s wall under identical canopies, very similar to the others, but not quite the same, and two under arcade arches. The canopies were alas terribly over-restored by *St Aubyn* in 1871, or rather by (BC) *Earp*, who did the actual carving. They are cusped and subcusped with pierced spandrels and the cusps in a very original way not meeting at a point, but forked. Ogee gables with crockets and finial. The s canopies are divided by two buttress shafts, the N canopies by one broad one. Now the effigies themselves. One of those under the canopies is a Lady. She has an ample mantle falling in chiefly vertical folds. The others are Knights, all cross-legged, one totally defaced. The most interesting are the Lady, the Knight to her E, and the easternmost Knight on the N side, the first two because they are not recumbent but turned slightly but decidedly to one side – which adds something intimate that is unusual in early C14 monuments – the third because he is represented in a most exceptional way, semi-reclining, almost like a Sansovino or an English Jacobean effigy. He leans on one elbow, his knees are pulled up, his feet are crossed, and by his feet sits a page. There is also stiff-leaf foliage to indicate the grass on which the page sits. Stiff-leaf was dead by 1300. How early can this monument be? One would not risk any date earlier than 1290, and even then it is all highly individual. The two monuments under the arcade seem later, mid C14 probably, because the two Knights have their legs no longer crossed. But that argument is not always reliable. The Lady lying next to one of them, however, must be early C14 again, or indeed late C13; for her drapery still falls in the convention of C13 Virgins, i.e. with a rounded fold across and then diagonals down. – PULPIT. Very fine, with decoration

of a Cornelis Floris type not at all common in England.* –
READER'S DESK. Also very Netherlandish, but much busier.
– BENCH ENDS. With large, very summarily shaped poppy-
heads and a nice variety of inhabitants. Three of them are
Perp, the other three Jacobean. – SCULPTURE. Head of
Christ(?). In the vestry. Mid C14 and supposed to have be-
longed to one of the monuments. Originally probably a
bracket. – PLATE. Cup and Cover, 1632. – In the churchyard
a yew-tree of 27 ft girth, called gigantic in the *Gentleman's
Magazine* already in 1760, 1798, and 1799.

ALFRED'S CASTLE *see* ASHDOWN PARK

AMBERROW COURT *see* SANDHURST

APPLEFORD

5090

ST PETER AND ST PAUL. Over-restored, but with a simple
Late Norman s doorway and a C13 chancel s doorway. The
nave was recast by *Ewan Christian*, the w tower, whose buttresses rise in many set-offs and which carries a square spire
with half-hipped lucarnes, by *W. Gillbee Scott*, 1885–6 (BC). –
COMMUNION RAIL. Early C18.

APPLETON

4000

ST LAWRENCE. A Late Norman church, as the four-bay N
arcade shows. Round piers, square abaci, the capitals not high
and two with leaf. The w respond has trumpet scallops.
Pointed arches with one slight chamfer. Perp w tower unbuttressed. – FONT. The base is part of a Norman font with
spiral decoration including beaded bands. – COMMUNION
RAIL. Early C18. – PLATE. Cup, 1659; Almsdish, 1683; Cover
Paten, 1728. – MONUMENTS. Brasses to John Goudrington
† 1518 and wife. 27 in. figures in shrouds. – Sir John Fettiplace, 1593. Stone. Recumbent effigy. Columns l. and r.
Elaborate strapwork on the back wall. – Mrs Southby † 1806.
By *R. Blore*. In the style of Bacon. Two female figures by an
urn.

APPLETON MANOR. An amazing survival. Part of a manor-
house of 1190 or 1200 with a doorway worthy of any major
church. Three orders of colonnettes. Big upright stiff-leaf

---

* In the vestry are two panels, re-used for a cupboard door, which
probably were the doors of the pulpit. The pulpit came from St Laurence at
Reading.

capitals. Round arches with deep mouldings. Through the doorway one entered the hall, and two quite large round-arched doorways to the service rooms have also survived. They have one slight chamfer and rolls as hood-moulds. A small head between the two. The hall outer walls are evident, by one nook-shafted corner. The fireplace is a Tudor insertion, though lengths of roll moulding have been re-used. In front of the main doorway a Tudor porch with timber-framed upper floor. The timbers are exposed on one side. To the N of the Manor a weatherboarded barn and attached to it a gateway.

POST OFFICE. Dated 1690. The porch has a gable or steep tympanum with a symmetrical leaf-trail pattern in pargetting. S of it a brick cottage, probably of the early C18, with windows not segment-headed but half-ellipse-headed.

7060   ARBORFIELD

ST BARTHOLOMEW. 1863 by *J. A. Picton*. Nave, chancel, apse. Flint. Early Dec style. – STAINED GLASS. Head of Aaron by *John Rowell* of Wycombe; 1744. Large head, strong colours, entirely pictorial. – PLATE. Two Patens inscribed 1793. – MONUMENT. William Standen † 1639. Large tomb-chest with black columns and on it the two recumbent effigies, their small child lying across their feet. Alabaster, and feelingly carved.

The OLD CHURCH and ARBORFIELD HALL have both gone. Of the church one flint wall remains, and the shell of a brick addition.

ARBORFIELD COURT, 1 m. S. Neo-Georgian of the early Edwardian type. By *F. B. Wade*, 1906.

BARTLETT'S FARMHOUSE, 1 m. SSW. Red brick, five bays, doorways with Roman Doric pilasters.

R.E.M.E. SCHOOL OF ELECTRONIC ENGINEERING, 1¼ m. SE. By *J. A. Ford* (*Ministry of Public Building and Works*). An excellent group, axial to one side, free to the other, Miesian in style.

4080   ARDINGTON

HOLY TRINITY. The church is dominated externally by the Victorian spire on the N tower and the Victorian N chapel, and internally by the rich Victorian decoration of the chancel with much stencilling. The tower and spire are by *Joseph Clarke*, 1856 (BC), the rest of the Victorian building and enrichment by

Somers Clarke (1887). But when one looks more closely, the church has a long and interesting architectural history. It starts about 1200 or a little later with the N doorway, which has a round arch of many mouldings and some dogtooth enrichment, and a small N lancet, and is continued at once, i.e. *c.*1210 or so, by the four-bay s arcade with round piers, big stiff-leaf capitals of three different varieties (one with two tiers), and pointed arches with one slight chamfer, and then the N tower to its E, whose arch towards the church is double-chamfered and has a hood-mould on stiff-leaf stops, and the chancel arch with three orders of columns, one with stiff-leaf capitals and an arch of three proper chamfers, and the arches to the s and N chapels, the one with two chamfers, the other with two hollow chamfers. There is more work of that date, but it is in confusion. What for instance is original of the two big squints ? One, in the s chapel, has a pointed-trefoiled arch. And are the two responds of the arch from s aisle into s chapel *ex situ* ? One has a stiff-leaf capital, the other a brilliant late C13 capital with naturalistic leaves and a dragon and a lion. The arch they carry is clearly Perp. The s doorway has, in one moulding, the charming motif of ballflowers connected by a trail.* In the aisle is one window with Y-tracery. So that dates the aisle wall as early C14. Perp the nave roof with foliage bosses on lively stone corbels. – FONT. Octagonal, with ballflowers on the base. – PULPIT. Jacobean, with blank arches. The tester is not genuine. – ARCHITECTURAL FRAGMENTS. In the porch a charming late C13 gablet with a king's 17a head, foliage, and two dragons. – Also a Pelican corbel and the canopy of a former image. – PLATE. Cup and Cover of 1573; Flagon of 1633; Paten of 1636. – MONUMENTS. Clarke family, *c.*1635. Tablet with black columns, swags, and angels. – Robert Vernon † 1849. Two memorials, one his bust in a lavish Gothic surround, the other a large white kneeling female figure, amply draped. This is by *Baily*. – In the churchyard CROSS. The shaft is, and the part above with the 'gargoyles' seems to be, original.

ARDINGTON HOUSE. Built in 1721 (VCH). A swagger three-storeyed building of vitrified grey and red brick. Seven bays with a projecting three-bay centre. This carries a decorated pediment. The windows are segment-headed in the centre, normally oblong otherwise. Stone doorway with ears and a complex top. Is this original? The garden side is the same

* Cf. e.g. the St Albans Lady Chapel.

except for the doorway, but it has a later four-column wooden veranda. The sides are perhaps even more remarkable than the main elevation. They are of three bays only, and hence appear very high. This height and the details are decidedly Vanbrughian. The windows are set close together and all are round-arched, except for those of the second floor, which are circular. Pediment right across at the top. Entrance hall with paired fluted pilasters flanking one niche l., one r. The hall is open to the staircase behind, which is spacious and rises in two arms to return in one. Thin twisted balusters.

ASCOT

ALL SOULS, South Ascot. 1896–7 by *Pearson*. Large, red-brick, E.E. Square crossing tower with a rather unexpected pyramid roof.* Equally unexpected the baptistery, which projects to the s at the w end like a porch and has two rounded angle buttresses with solid E.E. pinnacles. Main N porch, small s porch attached to the angle between nave and transept. Brick interior, with four-bay arcades, unemphasized, with a rib-vaulted crossing and sexpartite rib-vaults in the chancel and the lower s chapel. The baptistery is also rib-vaulted. It is octagonal with three open sides projecting into the s aisle. High three-light w window, broader five-light e window.

ALL SAINTS, ⅞ m. NW, on the main Bracknell road. Modest, red brick, by *T. H. Rushforth*, 1864. Varieties of c13 windows. Two-bay aisle arcades. – STAINED GLASS. *Kempe* e window 1907 (Jesse), but the rose window above by *Hardman* (BC). – The PAINTING of chancel and aisles by *Heaton, Butler & Bayne*, 1874 and 1883 (BC).

ST FRANCIS, ½ m. SSE. 1889 by *A. J. C. Scoles* (BC). Red brick, with an apse and no tower. Aisles, octagonal piers, lancet windows and windows with plate tracery.

ASCOT PRIORY, 1½ m. NW. The priory is of the Society of the Holy Trinity, founded by Priscilla Lydia Sellon, a friend of Pusey's. The society started at Devonport in 1848 and built St Dunstan's Abbey, Plymouth, in 1850 etc. The Ascot house was built as a convalescent hospital. The original buildings *See* p. 359 are by *Charles Buckeridge* (BC) and were begun in 1861. He was followed by *Scott*. The chapel is by *Butterfield*, 1877 etc., the fine s wing by *Stokes*, 1901. Scott's is the w end at r. angles to Stokes's wing, with high plate tracery windows and formerly an open timber roof. Scott's also

* A spire was intended.

other rooms and passages in the centre. Stokes's building is at once recognizable as his by the tower in the re-entrant angle. The top part in particular, with its open lantern and the sloping sides of the lantern, is delightful. The broad flat buttresses on the r. side of the front of the range are a sensitively introduced motif too. Mullioned and transomed main windows. Large roof with hipped dormers. The CHAPEL is surprising. It has a short, two-bay nave with aisles in the Norman style, E.E. transepts, and a long, aisleless E.E. chancel. Red and white stone. The shafts in the chancel must imply the intention to vault in stone. – STAINED GLASS. Good side windows by *Gibbs*. – The E windows by *Comper*. – Separate LADY CHAPEL of 1935 by *Mitchell & Bridgewater*, simple, but Expressionist Gothic, all steep arches and no bases or capitals.

RACECOURSE. Ascot horse racing was started by Queen Anne in 1711, but it was only taken up seriously, and indeed revived, by the Duke of Cumberland, who kept his stud at Cumberland Lodge in Windsor Great Park. At the end of the C18 the races were already attended regularly by King and Queen and Prince of Wales. Of the earliest grandstands and royal stand nothing remains. Even the Royal Pavilion as remodelled by *Sir Albert Richardson* in 1936 has disappeared. The present grandstand is a rebuilding of 1961–4, impressive in its length and sweep, but of no structural originality or indeed enterprise. It is by Messrs *Wimpeys* architect's department (*E. V. Collins*).

ASCOT HEATH HOUSE, S of the racecourse, on the Egham road. By *Robert Kerr*, 1868. Red brick, symmetrical, not very big. Two gables with bay windows under. A third gable in the centre, and to the l. and r. a characteristic difference in the fenestration. On the l. the staircase shows by the stepped windows; the same motif Kerr was using at the same time at Bear Wood.

ROYAL ASCOT HOTEL, immediately SW of the racecourse. Seven-bay centre and long lower r. attachments. Brick and stone dressings. Homely, and of no architectural merit.*

BUTTERSTEEP HOUSE, Buttersteep Rise, 1¾ m. SSW. By *Francis Lorne*, for himself, illustrated in 1942. Whitewashed, but originally yellow Dutch brick. Dutch otherwise as well. The operative name is Dudok. Flat roofs. Typical apsidal staircase projection, not with a specially wide or high window.

* Additions by *Clark & Holland*, 1871 (GS).

ASCOT PLACE, 2¼ m. N. Mid Georgian. Yellow brick. A seven-bay centre of two storeys and two three-bay pavilions with square cupolas. The centre block has a three-bay pediment and a deep porch of paired Tuscan columns. This may be a C20 addition. The interior has (or had) many such additions as well, and it is not easy to recognize what is C18 and what is germane to the house. Following the views and knowledge of Mr Frank Scarlett, the Tuscan columns at the back of the entrance hall and the staircase are original. The staircase has thin turned balusters and carved tread-ends. The fireplace in the room to the l. of the entrance hall seems trustworthy too. In the room to the r. of the entrance hall the two columns are all right but not *in situ*. The doorcase is Georgian but comes from another house.

5070

ASHAMPSTEAD

ST CLEMENT. Early C13 nave and chancel – see a few lancet windows. Weatherboarded bell-turret with shingled spire. Good roofs with tie-beams, collar-beams on arched braces, and two tiers of wind-braces. – PAINTING. Important wall paintings in nave as well as chancel. They date from *c.*1230–40. Stiff-leaf trails, scrolls, etc. Also in the nave the Annunciation, the Visitation, the Nativity, and the Annunciation to the Shepherds, all of extremely slender, supple figures under trefoiled arches. The scenes are easily recognizable, even if they are no longer aesthetically enjoyable. Above the tie-beam which separates nave from chancel Christ in Majesty, the Virgin and St John, and six seated figures.

PARSONAGE, E of the church. By *T. H. Wyatt & D. Brandon*, before 1851. Whitewashed, Tudor, with steep gables and dormers.

The house at the cross-roads NNE of the church has a castellated TOWER in the garden.

PYT HOUSE. The centre has a façade which seems Early Georgian. Arched windows between giant pilasters in the middle. Steep broken pediment. Somewhat later additions.

2080

ASHBURY

ST MARY. Of chalk and brown stone. Evidence of a Norman church with aisles is the S doorway (one order of shafts, decorated capitals, zigzag meeting along a ridge) and one shaft of the W respond of the S aisle arcade with its scallop capital and the springing of an arch lower than the present one. The

N aisle has the same shaft, but no capital or arch is left. E.E. the W tower. The bell-openings have tracery with a spherical triangle in the head, i.e. late C13. The situation in the transepts is difficult. They are also C13, but the windows are later (S transept S c.1300, N transept N Dec). However the responds of the arches from the aisles to the transepts give enough E.E. evidence: S aisle S, N aisle N. In the S transept below the S window a tomb recess with a cinquefoiled arch. The chancel late C13 too, or c.1300. So are the intersecting tracery of the E window and the tracery of the S windows. The four-bay arcades in their present form are Perp. Piers of the four-shaft-and-four-hollows section, the arches the easternmost double-chamfered, the other double-hollow-chamfered. Good roof with tie-beams, kingposts, and short arched braces. Perp N porch of two storeys with a tierceron-star vault. At the W end of the N aisle is a fireplace. – PLATE. Cover Paten, inscribed 1577; Spoon, inscribed 1637; Bread-holder, 1717/18; Flagon 1778/9; Cup, 1781. – MONUMENTS. Brasses to John de Walden, c.1350, bust only; to Thomas de Bushbury † 1409 (10 in. and, originally, 20 in. figures); and to William Skelton † 1448 (28 in. figure). All chancel floor.

MANOR HOUSE. Of the C15, which is rare in Berkshire. Chalk and stone. Buttressed. Many windows with cusped ogee-headed lights, and also one with depressed uncusped lights. On the ground floor the old windows have transoms. They light the hall. In addition the porch and the inner doorway with quatrefoils in the spandrels. The porch was in its upper part rebuilt in brick in 1697. Moulded beams inside the hall with carved bosses. (On the first floor a room with a moulded wooden cornice and a traceried frieze. Also between this room and the room above the porch a screen with trefoil-headed openings; VCH. Original roof with wind-braces; NBR.) The village lies on the slope of the downs and is largely built of chalk.

KINGSTONE FARMHOUSE, ⅜ m. NE. Dated 1730. Chalk front, sarsen sides. Five-bay façade of two storeys, quite plain. Door hood on brackets. Pitched roof.

WAYLAND'S SMITHY, 1 m. NE and just N of the Ridgeway. This monument has long been known as one of the few examples of a chambered tomb in the county, but excavation conducted in 1962–3 revealed an earlier monument on the site. This consisted of an earthen long barrow flanked by quarry ditches and covering a mortuary house of stone and timber which contained the remains of thirteen disarticulated and semi-articulated corpses. At a later date the mound was enlarged by the digging of a second ditch outside that of the long barrow to provide additional material to cover a chambered tomb which was added to the broader s end of the long barrow. A straight façade of upright sarsens flanked the entrance to the chamber, and further smaller sarsen slabs were set up as a kerb to support the material of the mound. After the recent series of excavations the monument was partially restored and it is now under the guardianship of the Ministry of Public Building and Works.

THREE BARROWS, *see* Idstone.

ALFRED'S CASTLE, ROUND BARROWS, and ROMANO-BRITISH SETTLEMENT, see Ashdown Park.

₂₀₈₀

ASHDOWN PARK

_{40b} Built for the first Earl of Craven, who also built Hamstead Marshall. For Ashdown we have no date, nor an architect. The style suggests about 1660. It is the perfect doll's house, proof of a longing for neatness and all-round order typical of the years after the Civil War and architecturally of the years following the Jacobean riot. The house itself is of five by five bays, very high, and has on the entrance side at some distance two detached office ranges. All this stood originally – *see* Kip's engraving – in a forest with long straight avenues in all four main directions. The source of the composition is Holland, and the style, wherever it appears in England about 1660, is also at least partly inspired by Holland. Chalk and brown stone dressings. Hipped roofs, the house itself with a balustrade on top and a belvedere cupola, just as had been done at Coleshill a little before, and earlier still (before 1638) at Chevening. The chimneys are so grouped in house and office ranges that they stand like pricked-up ears. The house has three storeys above a basement, the offices one. There is very little of adornment, just the stone balustrade to the garden entrance, and the balcony and pediment of the middle window on this and the entrance side. The windows have stone crosses, except on the ground floor, where they are given two transoms. Steep-gabled dormers. Entrance passage with a big open pediment to the doorway towards the main garden room. Between the scrolls of the pediment a bust. To the r. an arch leads to the staircase, which runs right up to the top. It has extremely strong dumb-bell balusters. Two rooms towards

the gardens have leaf coving, one of them also a wreath in the middle of the ceiling. The chimneypieces are Georgian and have been brought in recently.

ALFRED'S CASTLE, on Swinley Down. This is a small, roughly circular, univallate earthwork enclosing some 2½ acres. The rampart was originally faced with sarsen boulders, many of which were removed for use in the construction of the house. The earthwork is broken by gaps on the NE, NW, and SE – the latter at least appears to be original. This earthwork lies within a very much more extensive ditched enclosure which is only visible as a crop mark from the air. The site is unexcavated, but surface finds from the area include sherds of Iron Age A and B, Romano-British, and Saxon pottery, indicating a long and complex history.

ROUND BARROWS, S of Swinley Copse. Two good bowl barrows, one covered by trees. Both are approximately 3 ft high; one is 54 ft in diameter and the other 70 ft.

ROMANO-BRITISH SETTLEMENT, in the extreme SW of the parish of Ashbury, just W of Botley Copse. The settlement stands on a slight rise to the N of a dry valley and consists of a roughly rectangular enclosure of 1½ acres bounded by a broad shallow ditch with an inturned entrance in the middle of the S side. The site lies at the centre of a group of CELTIC FIELDS, and is directly linked to these on its E side. The site is unexcavated, but large quantities of Roman pottery are to be found in its ploughed interior.

ASHRIDGE FARM see WOKINGHAM

ASTON TIRROLD AND ASTON UPTHORPE 5080

The parish boundary runs along the middle of the main S–N road, with Tirrold to the E, Upthorpe to the W.

ST MICHAEL, Aston Tirrold. C11 S doorway, similar to the W doorway at South Moreton. Earlier still, it seems, though clearly *ex situ*, the doorway from the N aisle into the vestry. These large stones and their arrangement indicate Anglo-Saxon workmanship. E.E. S transept with lancets, but the S window Dec, with flowing tracery. Later E.E. the chancel, see the stiff-leaf capitals of the priest's doorway and the bar tracery of a S window. The E window has intersecting tracery instead. Perp W tower. The N aisle with its arcade is of 1863. – SCREENS. In the S porch two lengths of timber arcading coming probably from screens, the E one early, say early C14, the W one Perp. – PLATE. Chalice, Paten, and probably Cover Paten of 1754.

ALL SAINTS, Aston Upthorpe. Nave and chancel in one. In the nave a small Norman window and the remains of a S doorway. What is the date of the timber N porch? The VCH suggests the C17. Chancel of 1859–60 (BC), by *P. C. Hardwick*. His presumably also the pretty bell-turret with spirelet. – BENCHES. Perp ends, backs, and fronts re-used.

PRESBYTERIAN CHAPEL, Aston Tirrold. 1728. Two arched windows flanked by two (altered) doorways. Hipped roof. Blue and red brick. The end walls have two windows and show two roofs. Nothing special left inside.

At Aston Tirrold the MANOR HOUSE close to the church has a lovely E front of the early C18. Chequer brick. Seven bays, segmental shell-hood on carved brackets.

COPSTILE, on the main road S of the inn, is also of seven bays. It is of red brick with brick quoins and has a straight hood over the doorway, again on carved brackets. Pitched roof.

THE FILBERTS, facing the playing fields, is dated 1745. Plain three-bay front of red brick. Pitched roof.

FISHING LODGE. C18 Gothick. The ground-floor windows with ogee arches, above quatrefoil windows.

IRON AGE HILLFORT, on Blewburton Hill. Excavations in 1949 and 1953 revealed a number of phases in the settlement of the hilltop. The earliest occupation, dating to the C4, consisted of a group of circular huts enclosed within a palisade which provided the only defence. The second phase consisted of the construction of the bank and ditch. The rampart was revetted on the inner and outer faces with timber and was separated from a V-shaped ditch by a berm. These defences were broken on the W by an entrance 37 ft wide. This work may be dated to *c.* 300 B.C. The fortifications were then allowed to fall into disrepair, and at a date which cannot be precisely determined (? C1 B.C.) the ditch was recut and the material from it added to the existing rampart, which was now of dump construction. The W entrance was narrowed to 25 ft and the rampart flanking the gate revetted with dry-stone walling. This phase was the work of Iron Age B groups. The end of this period is equally difficult to date, but must have been some time in the first half of the C1 A.D. That its end was a sudden and violent one is attested by the bodies of animals crushed by the collapsing ramparts and the burning of the gateway. This destruction could be attributed to the westward-expanding Belgae or to Roman attack.

AVINGTON

3060

See p. 359

ST MARK AND ST LUKE. A memorable little church, sheltered under a gigantic cedar tree. The church is entirely Norman, with nearly all the windows original: three stepped E windows, two W windows, one above the other, and also a S doorway with divers zigzags. Inside more thrills to come, the broad, rather sagging chancel arch with scallop capitals, beakhead, zigzag at r. angles, and pellets in the arch, and capitals of open-mouthed beasts. In the S doorway beakhead was also planned, but not carried out. The chancel is of two bays, and it was once rib-vaulted (cf. Devizes). The responds have scalloped capitals, the ribs of the first bay had beakhead (a unique motif?), the E corners had the ribs on brackets with more open-mouthed beasts. The SEDILIA are a plain Norman arch. Of the C13 the doorway at the E end of the nave, the 'low-side' window, and the N doorway. – FONT. Even this is Norman, and it is moreover exceptionally interesting. Tub-shaped, eleven narrow arches with figures squeezed in, including a bishop, a man and a devil, two devils, an atlas of the Italian type carrying – what?

14b

BAGNOR MANOR FARMHOUSE *see* SPEEN

BANISTERS *see* FINCHAMPSTEAD

BARCOTE MANOR *see* LONGWORTH

BARKHAM

7060

ST JAMES. 1860–1 by *John B. Clacy & Son*; chancel and transepts 1887. S porch tower with high shingled spire on a wooden bell-stage. The older parts flint, the later stone. Pointed-trefoiled windows. The roof corbels like Japanese puzzles in which three-dimensional pieces have to be fitted in in ingenious ways. – FONT. Stone, late C18, in a Louis Seize mood. – PLATE. Paten given 1664; Flagon given 1729; Paten given 1775. – MONUMENT. Late C13 oak effigy of a lady (S porch).

BARKHAM MANOR. Red brick, Georgian, two ranges of differing date, and at the junction a handsome one-storeyed Tuscan portico with pediment. Niches l. and r.

LONGMOOR LAKE was made by John Walter of Bear Wood (*q.v.*).

BARLEY MOW INN *see*
LONG WITTENHAM

BARTLETT'S FARMHOUSE *see* ARBORFIELD

BARTON COURT *see* KINTBURY

BASILDON

ST BARTHOLOMEW. The W tower of blue and red brick was built in 1734. The rest of the church is over-restored (1875–6), but basically genuine. It dates from the late C13; see the cusped Y-tracery of the nave, the Geometrical tracery of the chancel side windows (circle with trefoiled cinquefoil), and the chancel E window of three pointed-trefoiled, steeply stepped lights under one arch. – FONT. Octagonal, Perp, simple. – MONUMENTS. Brass to John Clerk † 1497 and his wife. The figures, which are 12 in. long, are in the nave floor. – A C14 canopy, with cusped and subcusped arch, buttress shafts, and pinnacles, was re-used outside the church for a memorial to Sir Francis Sykes † 1804. – His monument proper in the church is very different. It is by *Flaxman* and has a standing, mourning widow, her face not visible. She stands by an urn on a high pedestal. The medallion portrait of Sir Francis is attached to the pedestal. – Sir Francis W. Sykes † 1843. Gothic tablet by *R. Brown*. – Mrs Benyon † 1822. By *Storey*. – Two Deverill boys drowned in 1886. Monument in the churchyard with portrait group, the boys in their swimming trunks.

ST STEPHEN, Upper Basildon. By *P. N. Perkins*, 1964–5. A square set diagonally with the altar across one corner and the seating on three sides around it. Seats for only 120, and very spacious for that number. Pyramid roof on eight steel ribs rising from the floor. Glazed lantern top and two odd oriels on two sides. High porch leaning forward as an aggressively steep gable. The church cost only £12,600.

Immediately to the E of St Bartholomew CHURCH FARM, C16, but with a picturesque late C18(?) front with battlements and a shaped gable.

BASILDON PARK. Built by *John Carr* for Sir Francis Sykes in 1776. The most splendid Georgian mansion of Berkshire. Bath stone. The house itself is seven by six bays, but the scale is large. There are in line with the entrance side three-bay one-storey links (behind which is an enclosed courtyard),

then three- by four-bay two-storeyed pedimented pavilions,
and then again three-bay one-storey walls. The composition
thus stretches out considerably, but the dominance of the
centre is guaranteed. This has a rusticated lowish ground
floor, then a *piano nobile* with, on the entrance side, a recessed
giant three-bay portico of unfluted Ionic columns and a pediment. The giant columns comprise the upper half-storey.
Towards the garden and the Thames the front has only five
bays, and three of them are, in the way Carr liked it, a broad
canted bay window. The entry into the house is a fascinating
adventure. One can go in through three arches in the rustication below the giant portico and through a door into a low
ENTRANCE HALL with four columns,* and then through an
intermediate room into a round GARDEN ROOM partly in the
bay window. This room has columns along the walls. But
from here only a small subsidiary staircase leads to the *piano
nobile*. Or one ascends one of the two relatively narrow staircases inside the space behind the three arches and thus comes
up to the portico and straight into the grand UPPER EN-
TRANCE HALL. Was perhaps an outer staircase planned?
The entrance hall has splendid paired pilasters and a coved
ceiling. On the walls, not in proper framed panels, medallions
and sphinxes. To the l. of the entrance hall is the LIBRARY.
The bookcase comes from Carr's Panton Hall in Lincolnshire.
To the r. of the entrance hall the SMALL DRAWING ROOM.
The chimneypiece seems Carr's, but the ceiling looks Early
Victorian, and it is indeed known that *J. B. Papworth* worked
at Basildon Park in 1839–44. Behind the entrance hall, in the
ample centre of the house, is the STAIRCASE HALL. The
staircase goes up in three flights with wide, open well. Iron
balustrade of discreet motifs between firm uprights. Above a
balcony and an arched gallery. The top windows are lunettes.
On the walls again no actual panels but spreading stucco with
griffins instead. At the NE corner of the house is the LONG
DRAWING ROOM with a two-column screen of pink scagliola
columns. The ceiling has a shallow segmental tunnel-vault
with rather more geometrical forms. The walls have panels.
Is this perhaps Papworth wanting to be in keeping with the
Georgian house? The chimneypiece again comes from
Panton Hall. The adjoining OCTAGON in the centre of the
front towards the river is evidently by Papworth, but the

* In this room are two seated figures of Egyptian women by *W. W. Story*,
the American sculptor; 1858.

DINING ROOM, in the SE corner, is once more original, with its chimneypiece. One BEDROOM on the upper floor has a groin-vaulted alcove, fine doorcases, and a fine plaster ceiling. – The EAST LODGES are octagonal with garlands just below the eaves. Gatepiers with vases. – The SOUTH-EAST LODGE is faced with alternating bands of flints and stucco and has pointed and quatrefoil windows.

THE GROTTO, ¾ m. WNW. White, informal house built by Lady Fane, who died in 1792. Inside one fine room with Adamish decoration. Lady Fane's grotto has completely disappeared and left no traces.

PEACOCK PAVILION, 1 m. SE. Built in 1956. The stonework came from Bowood in Wiltshire, i.e. a *Robert Adam* mansion. The pavilion was designed by its owner, Mr *G. Child Beale*. – The FOUNTAIN originally stood at Witley Park near Godalming and dates from the 1890s. The name of the sculptor is given as *O. Spalmach* (Studio *O. Andreoni,* Rome). – Much SCULPTURE, including a black Valkyria, cast by *Gladenbeck* in Berlin. – Also a statue of Shakespeare by *A. Salata.*

NOKE'S TOMB, Tomb Farm, 1½ m. SW, is in ruins. It was the mausoleum of a Quaker buried here in 1699.

(At LOWER BASILDON, according to the NBR, CHURCH HOUSE FARM has a sumptuous chimneypiece with demi-figure caryatids and a tympanum representing St George and the Dragon instead of a lintel. The photograph looks as if these pieces, obviously not belonging together, might be Flemish of about 1700.)

ROMAN BUILDING. In Church Field two mosaic pavements were found and destroyed by workmen in the C19. No other remains were located, but the pavements indicate the existence of a well-appointed Roman building in this area.

ROMAN VILLA, at Ealing, 1½ m. from Well House. The villa was of corridor type, 75 ft long and 45 ft wide. It included a hypocaust system and at least one mosaic floor with a guilloche pattern in red, blue, and white.

BAULKING

ST NICHOLAS. Long nave, chancel, and tiny bellcote. The chancel could be work of the Uffington masons. E.E. with lancets, a stepped group of three to the E, shafted inside. ANGLE PISCINA. E.E. also the very unusual stone chancel SCREEN, really just a doorway, but with openings l. and r. which may not be original. The nave doorway plain, of *c.*1200;

in the s wall two Dec windows. Nave roof Jacobean, with pendants from the tie-beams, but in fact dated 1708. – PULPIT. Jacobean (from Grittleton in Wiltshire). – PAINTING. Almost unrecognizable Nativity, N wall w, early C14. – PLATE. Cup of 1583; two Patens of 1715; two-handled covered Cup, inscribed 1723/4.

Baulking has an extremely large green.

BEAR PLACE see WARGRAVE

BEAR WOOD 7070

ST CATHERINE. 1846 by *Good* (BC; probably J. H. Good). The material good ashlar stone, the character still the thin one of the Commissioners' churches. Narrow w front, w tower with its w entrance the main entrance to the church. No aisles, high two-light Dec windows. The Dec details not all correct. High interior. – STAINED GLASS. In the chancel the original glass by *Wailes*; deeper colour than he used as a rule. – MONUMENT. John Balston Walter, John Walter's son, who was drowned while trying to rescue two others in the frozen lake. † 1870. The monument by *Matthew Noble*. Large angel in a sinuous stance. The relief below shows the frozen lake.

ESTATE HOUSING near the church, towards Sindlesham Green. Red brick with black diapers; gables. Even the pub conforms.

BEAR WOOD (Royal Merchant Navy School). Bear Wood was designed in 1864, i.e. a hundred years ago. As a piece of private architecture Blenheim or Hardwick could not be more remote. As far as scale is concerned, and the disregard for what we pygmies would call domestic comfort, Bear Wood is indeed nearer to Blenheim than to our poky villas. John Walter II, owner of *The Times*, bought the estate about 1830. His son John Walter III, reserved, handsome, conscientious, and of High-Church piety, got married in 1842, lost his wife, and married again in 1861. In January 1865 Mr Kerr and John Walter were working on the plans. *Robert Kerr*, then forty-two years old – Walter was forty-seven – had been a bit of a revolutionary when he was young, but had lately settled down, being appointed professor of architecture at King's College and publishing a book, *The English Gentleman's House*, which told readers all about the necessities and conventions of planning for wealthy gentlemen. The book came out in 1864. It was probably on the strength of the book that John Walter

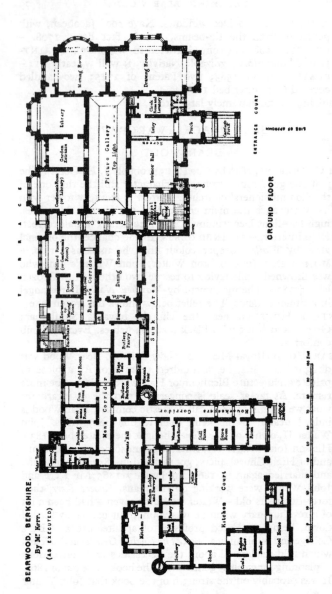

Bear Wood, by Robert Kerr, designed in 1864. Plans of ground and first and second floors (From Robert Kerr, *The English Gentleman's House*)

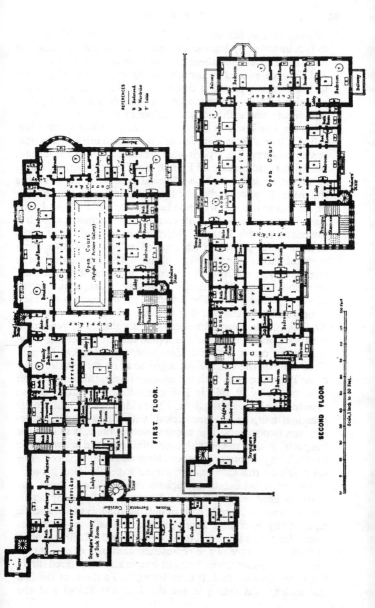

REFERENCES

B Bedstead
W Wardrobe
T Toilet

FIRST FLOOR.

SECOND FLOOR.

Scale, 1 Inch to 30 Feet.

selected him as his architect. The plans of Bear Wood were
in fact included by Kerr in the second edition of his book. He
must have considered them his crowning achievement to date,
and they are indeed so completely the epitome of High Victorian domestic planning that they are illustrated here. They
will also help an understanding of the following description.
The house was sufficiently complete in 1868 for a first staff
party for *The Times* to be held; but *The Architect* in 1870 still
called it 'aproaching completion'. It is of red brick with ample
stone dressings. The style is what we would now call Jacobean,
but with an admixture of French motifs. Kerr himself called
it 'of the irregular or Non-Classical type'. On the N side is
the main entrance, and at the l. end of the façade a long wing
projecting to the N. The s side has a terrace and overlooks the
59b   lake. The centre of the entrance side is symmetrical with a
tower and a gable l. and r. Projecting in front of the tower is
a deep porte-cochère with banded pillars. But this symmetrical part is only the r. end of the façade. The l. gable is in
fact ruthlessly cut into by a second, more massive and truly
enormous tower. The details of this are quite unauthorized
by any period style. The window arrangement expresses,
again ruthlessly, the fact that in this tower the staircase rises.
The top of the tower bristles with a palisade of pinnacles.
Further l., in the corner of the façade and the projecting wing,
is a round turret with a conical roof, unmistakably French.
This also has the window arranged so as to express the staircase. The wing ends with yet another tower, this one with an
ogee cap. The w side is less interesting, though it is also
asymmetrical. Straight gables. The s side has its l. half, i.e. its
principal half, again symmetrical, with three shaped gables
between two turrets. The continuation to the r. is once more
irregular, with a tower with a pavilion roof and a sw corner
tower. The prominent chimneys have alas been replaced. The
main exit on this side has two carved angels holding babies.

The plan behind these façades is as follows. From the
porte-cochère one reaches the Entrance Hall, 43 by 27 ft,
with a screen as in great halls of old. To the l. is the Staircase,
24 by 24 by 80 ft high. From the staircase hall straight s runs
a corridor to the s front. To the l. of this is the Dining Room,
to the r. the centre of the representational part of the house:
the Picture Gallery, which can of course also be entered direct
from the entrance hall. It is 70 by 24 ft. To the r. of the hall
and gallery and facing w are the Drawing Room and the

Morning Room, to the l. of the latter and due s of the gallery
the Library, the cross passage to the terrace exit mentioned
above, and a second Library or Gentleman's Room. To the l.
of this the cross corridor comes out, and then there is another
room also called Gentleman's Room. This clearly was the
Office; for it communicates with a Waiting Room for estate-
business callers with its own small exit.

What went on in the E half of the house and on the upper
floors is sociologically even more revealing. To the l. of the
dining room followed the Butler's Pantry, with access to a
corridor s of the dining room called the Butler's Corridor.
Then, to the l. of the Butler's Pantry, was the Butler's Bedroom with, attached to it, the Plate Safe. Here ended the
butler's territory. His corridor continued straight E as the
Men's Corridor with, off it to the s, Cleaning Room, Brushing
Room, Footman's Room, Gun Room, and a spacious room
called Odd Room. But to the N, in the wing, ran the Housekeeper's Corridor, and behind it were the Housekeeper's
Room, Store Room, Still Room, Women's Workroom. The
Kitchen etc. were yet further E on the other side of a courtyard.
The butler's and housekeeper's and the men's and women's
quarters met in the Servants' Hall.

On the first floor in the principal, i.e. w, half of the house
the area above the picture gallery formed an inner court, and
was surrounded by a corridor. Along this lay the principal
bedrooms, the s suite including the Boudoir. In the SE corner
were the Nurseries, though the School Room was above the
dining room. The ladies' maids slept to the E of this, the maids
in the Housekeeper's Wing.

On the second floor the Bachelors' Rooms were above dining
room and butler's quarters with direct access to the principal
back stair (on the N front), the Young Ladies' Rooms – separated, one is disturbed to see, from the bachelors only by a
corridor – above some of the principal s bedrooms. An internal
stair, connecting this floor with the first floor only, took the
young ladies to the Boudoir. At the SE corner was provision
for Strangers' Men Servants.

Those who study the plans might find more enlightenment;
e.g. the NE turret had the Luggage Entrance, the little French-
looking turret was the Women Servants' stair.

Now one or two details concerning the interior. The
Entrance Hall is in a ham Jacobean, but the normal hall exit,
i.e. the exit to the gallery, was a mirror. The Picture Gallery

of course is sky-lit. Drawing Room and Morning Room could be thrown into one by means of sliding doors with masterly marquetry. The woodwork was in fact made in private workshops on the estate. The brick was dug and made on the estate too. The stone is Mansfield carboniferous limestone. Gas was also produced in a private plant. The estate was 7,500 acres, including Finchampstead, Barkham, and Sindlesham. John Walter paid for the building of the schools at Finchampstead, Sandhurst, and Wokingham and for Woodyer's lavish St Paul at Wokingham. The lake to the S of the house is more than 40 acres in size. This is the lake in which, in the very year of the completion of the house, John Walter's eldest son was drowned. The house is now part of a boys' school, a fitting memorial.

HEADMASTER'S HOUSE. 1921 by *Prentice*.

CHAPEL. 1934–5 by *Sir Herbert Baker*. Red brick, with Perp windows and a flèche. The interior is an odd mixture of styles. Perp the windows and the open roof. But narrow aisle passages with arches of continuous mouldings, rather Early Christian in detail. Moreover, a rib-vaulted apse preceded by choir bays with shallow domes. A shallow dome over the lobby too.

GYMNASIUM. 1930. Opposite the chapel and forming with it and the N front of the house a *cour d'honneur*.

BEAUMONT COLLEGE *see* OLD WINDSOR

6060

BEECH HILL

ST MARY. 1867 by *Butterfield*, the N aisle 1873 (BC). Nave and chancel under one tiled roof. The walls flint with brick bands and chequers. Bell-turret, tile-hung below, weatherboarded above. The windows pointed-trefoiled and with plate tracery. Interior with exposed brick and stone dressings and patterns. The aisle arcade has square, only slightly chamfered piers and continuous arch mouldings – an early case of such simplification. High tripartite chancel SCREEN. – STAINED GLASS. Mostly by *Gibbs*, with his typical pronounced black lead lines. – N aisle NE window by *Kempe*, 1896.

See p. 359

BEECH HILL HOUSE. Messrs Betjeman and Piper give the date 1720. Brick. Seven bays and a full three storeys. Blunt top. Later porch. But inside the original staircase with carved tread-ends and a very handsome corner room with angle fire-

place, wooden surround and overmantel, panelling and door
surrounds with pilasters and friezes.

THE PRIORY. By the Loddon, with a canal or straight arm in
the garden. C16 or older parts are at the back. They are
timber-framed. The front range was added in 1648, see the
date on the porch. The façade is of brick and gabled. The
lower s range was also added. In the interior on the first floor
two splendid mid C17 chimneypieces with pilasters with
Ionic capitals, garlands, friezes with garlands, and overmantels with volutes down from halved Ionic pilasters.

BEEDON   4070

St NICHOLAS. Flint-built. Nave and chancel, timber bell-
turret with a shingled broach spire. Nave and chancel of
c.1200–30. In the nave lancet windows and a doorway, quite
simple, but the shafts with shaft-rings and a roll moulding
keeled. The chancel arch has broad flat leaves on the responds,
and this may be the earliest feature of the church. E.E.
priest's doorway, lancet windows with continuous roll
mouldings inside as well as outside. The E end three even
lancets and a round window in the gable. The interior of the
chancel has just that extra in the shaftings and leaf capitals of
the E window and the bit of dogtooth decoration which makes
one remember the church. If the lancets in the side walls
were all still there, it would make an uncommonly complete
piece. – PLATE. Cup and Cover, 1576.

MANOR HOUSE, N of the church. Early C18, with segment-
headed windows and pilaster-strips.

ROUND BARROW, on Barrow Hill, sw of Stanmore. This large
bowl barrow still stands over 7 ft in height, although it has
been considerably reduced by ploughing. It was excavated in
the C19, when a cremation accompanied by an incense cup
and a bronze dagger were found. The group can be dated to
the C16 B.C.

BEENHAM   5060

St MARY. 1859 by *Woodyer*, the chancel added in 1871 (BC).
Older only the brick tower, built after a fire of 1794. The
Victorian work is of flint, late C13 details. – The chancel
decoration was executed by *Miss Sharp* of Ufton Court, who
also painted the neo-Quattrocento Last Supper. – STAINED
GLASS. By *Hardman*, and typical of his style in imitation of
the early C14.

VICARAGE. Late Georgian, red brick, of three bays, the side
  bays on the ground floor Venetian, on the upper floor tripartite windows.

HILLFOOT, ⅝ m. E. Dated 1737, and characteristic of the date
  in the segment-headed windows and the bold brick cornice.

BENHAM PARK see SPEEN

BERE COURT see PANGBOURNE

4000
BESSELSLEIGH

ST LAWRENCE. In the grounds of the Manor, but by the main
  road. Nave and chancel in one, the roof with stone slates. The
  C13-looking twin bellcote is assigned to 1632 by the VCH.
  1632 is the date recorded in the chancel for the beautifying
  and repairing of the church by William Lenthall, Speaker of
  Parliament. Plain, unmoulded Norman s doorway. Late C13
  w and E windows (three stepped pointed-trefoiled lights under
  one arch), the E window with a cinquefoiled rere-arch. The
  other windows mostly Perp. Pleasantly unrestored interior. –
  Norman PILLAR PISCINA with decorated stem and top with
  decorated scallops. – FONT. C17, rather mid than late. Round
  stem with bands of rocky rustication. Small bowl with garlands. – PULPIT. C18. With tester. – COMMUNION RAIL.
  C18. – BOX PEWS. – TYMPANUM. With pendants. Probably
  of 1632. – TILES. A whole set. Are they C15? – PLATE. Cup
  and Cover, 1635. – (In the churchyard MONUMENT to the
  Rev. E. M. Walker by *Eric Gill*, 1932.)

SW of the church a lonely GATEPIER of the former house. It is
  typically mid C17 in style and remarkably similar to those of
  Sutton Courtenay Manor.

BILL HILL see ST NICHOLAS HURST

8070
BINFIELD

ALL SAINTS. w tower of dark brown conglomerate; Perp. The
  prominent stair-turret with its ornate ogee top is of course
  Victorian. The s aisle is of conglomerate too. The N aisle is of
  1848, the E end mostly of 1859, and what is pre-Reformation is
  Perp – except a s aisle s window which, with its cusped
  Y-tracery, must be of *c.*1300. The s doorway has fleurons in
  one moulding. Perp four-bay arcades of octagonal piers with
  moulded arches. The s chapel arcade looks somewhat earlier.
  An angel from a former house in the s chapel. – PULPIT. Dated

1628. Blank arches and arabesque. Back panel, its upper half with caryatids, and tester with strapwork cresting. – The HOURGLASS on an elaborate iron stand with the Arms of the 22b Farriers' Company in London, leaves and grapes, a lion, a pelican, and a wolf, is probably C17 (cf. Hurst). – Victorian iron SCREENS, W, N, and S of the chancel. – STAINED GLASS. In the SE window C15 glass, whole figures. – S aisle W by *O'Connor*, 1863. Violent colours and no stylization. – MONUMENTS. Brass to Walter de Anneforde, *c.*1360s, bust, 9 in. – Palimpsest brass. Inscriptions of the mid C16 and on the reverse part of a figure of a bishop or abbot. – Catherine Macaulay Graham † 1791, the historian and republican. Tablet with relief profile in a circular wreath. – George Hotham † 1806. By *Westmacott Jun.* Tablet with flag and sabre.

BINFIELD LODGE, ¾ m. NW. Late C18, brick, the distinguishing feature being the end bays, which are raised and carry a pediment. Curves down from this l. and r. and between them a lunette window.

BINFIELD PARK, ⅜ m. S. Built in 1775. Brick, of nine bays and two and a half storeys, with a three-bay pediment. A smooth front. Good GATEPIERS with pediments, and below them garlands.

MANOR HOUSE, ⅛ m. SE. C18, of five bays with hipped roof. Porch on Tuscan columns. Two later three-bay wings.

BINFIELD HOUSE, ¼ m. SW. Large, two-storeyed, late C18 brick house with delightful Gothick trim, including not only ogee-headed windows and a porch on slender shafts, but a Gothic Venetian window and a window in the form of a reticulation unit.

BINFIELD PLACE, ⅞ m. SW. The remains of a Jacobean manor house. Two gabled projections (probably out of a former three), one with original bricks.

Binfield Place faces the Windsor road (B road). The village of Binfield is S of this. It has its own church.

ST MARK. By *Sir Arthur Blomfield*, 1866. The damage done by a recent fire was sympathetically repaired by *Frederick Etchells*. Red brick with black-brick trim. Nave, chancel, and transepts. Lancet windows. The interior even more patterned: red and black brick and stone. Blomfield in his early years was much influenced by Butterfield. The effect is however not strident, as in Butterfield's churches, but curiously neat.

Opposite the church MOOR CLOSE, a Missionary College. The

original building is of 1881: red brick, with a tower and mullioned and transomed windows.

¼ m. SW of St Mark POPE'S HOUSE, Early Georgian, of red brick. Five bays, three storeys, with segment-headed windows. Doorway with flat pilasters but a fine open scrolly pediment with a big shell in the open top. The side elevation has a pedimented doorway too.

8080

BISHAM

Wooded hills form the backcloth to Bisham's two principal buildings – the church and the abbey – which are not visually connected, even when seen from the river which they both border.

ALL SAINTS. The Norman W tower is immediately by the Thames. Twin single-chamfered bell-openings. The tower arch is round and has one respond with a multi-scalloped capital, the other with waterleaf – which dates the tower to c.1170–80. The rest of the church is alas inside and outside all of the restorations, especially that of 1849 by B. Ferrey. The only exception is the Hoby Chapel with its windowless chalk wall. This is of the late C16. – REREDOS, N chapel. Four Late Gothic painted saints, probably East Anglian; very bad. – ROYAL ARMS. Of George III, painted, with a guilloche frame. – STAINED GLASS. The E window of the Hoby Chapel has interesting heraldic glass of 1609. – PLATE. Small Cup and Paten, the latter of 1765. – MONUMENTS. Interest is concentrated in the Hoby monuments in the S chapel. The earliest is that of Sir Philip † 1558 and Sir Thomas † 1566. It is of alabaster, a tomb-chest with the two bearded half-brothers, both in relaxed, semi-recumbent attitudes. Shallow arch behind. Long poem, worth reading in full. – Sir Thomas's widow Elizabeth married Lord Russell who died in 1583. She died in 1609. She kneels in widow's weeds under a canopy with columns. Behind her children, and others outside the columns. Also alabaster. Iron railings. – Margaret, wife of Sir Edward, † 1605. The finest of the Hoby monuments and indeed one of the most original monuments of the age. Again alabaster. On the high plinth a slender obelisk crowned by a heart. At the corners of the plinth four swans, the supporters of the Hobys. At the foot were originally four more obelisks (see the Buckler drawing). – The other monuments in the church are as follows. In the N chapel Purbeck tomb with short tomb-chest and canopy of three hanging arches on colonnettes with lozenge patterns. Pretty vault inside. Probably early C16. – Thomas Crekett † 1517. Brass, nave w wall, 16 in. figure. – George Kenneth Vansittart † 1904 aged 14. Kneeling Eton boy by *Morris Harding* under a Gothic canopy.

On the way from the church to the Abbey on the s side TOWN FARM HOUSE, timber-framed with brick infilling and a hipped roof. Then nice terraces of cottages, some timber-framed, but mostly Georgian.

BISHAM ABBEY. The house was an abbey only for three years. It was first a preceptory of the Templars, then in 1337 became an Augustinian priory, then in 1537 a Benedictine abbey. As such it was dissolved in 1540, and the estate was granted to Sir Philip Hoby in 1553. He began to build almost at once, and, after he died in 1558, his half-brother († 1566) continued. The appearance of the remaining buildings is accordingly complex and their evidence not easily understood. The s front is the most telling. Here one sees a C13 porch with a fine outer and an equally fine inner doorway and a quadripartite rib-vault. The doorways have colonnettes and extremely delicately moulded arches. On the door itself C13 ironwork. On the l. of the porch and lying a little back is the front of a range extending N at r. angles. To the s it has a good tall two-light upper window with bar tracery. The part of the front E of the porch is Hoby work, chalk below, stepped brick gables above, and windows with mullion and transom crosses and their pediments. As one enters through the porch one is in the SCREENS PASSAGE. To one's l. are five blocked arches. They went in the C13 to the kitchen and offices. The screen and the gallery above the passage may be of the C15. To the r. is the GREAT HALL of the Hobys. This was the Templars' Hall already, and evidently this Templars' house was not at all laid out like a monastery. It seems to have had the appearance of a manor house. The s wall of the hall is C13, though the chimneypiece is Hoby. The lower, stone part is very good and 39a typical of *c.*1560, i.e. with coupled columns and very dainty decoration. The wooden overmantel must be Later Elizabethan or Jacobean. The windows in the end walls are not original. The Hobys placed s of the original outer wall of the hall a set of rooms of theirs, the façade of which we have seen.

When the Augustinians came in, they built to the E of the hall a CLOISTER, of which only one range survives, a curious cloister indeed, low and irregular, with six arches, one and six narrow, two to five wide. The Hobys placed in front of the northern ones a canted brick bay window. The upper parts here and round the corner to the N and a projecting part to the N with large pedimented windows are all Hoby (except for the hall window already mentioned). The gables are stepped again. Slightly recessed rises a brick TOWER of an oddly irregular shape. This was being built in 1560. To the NW more C13 walling, but no features. Inside altogether, apart from the hall, not many features have been preserved.

To the S of the Abbey BARNS, one converted into a large private house, and a circular DOVECOTE.

TEMPLE MILLS, ½ m. SW, close to the river. Part of the present paper mill is the mill building of c.1790, red brick with a cupola. It has been attributed to *Samuel Wyatt*.

(WAYSIDE CRUCIFIX by *Eric Gill*, 1917. At the same time war memorial to F. S. Kelly and others.)

BLEWBURTON HILL *see* ASTON TIRROLD

5080

BLEWBURY

Blewbury has a curious layout. The A-road called LONDON STREET runs along the S end of the village, and from it the other village houses develop along a loop filled in in the middle and having the church in its centre.

ST MICHAEL. The exterior tells this: one small Early Norman window in the nave on the N side, one larger Later Norman window in the chancel also on the N side. There is one lancet in the N transept (but the E window is Dec with flowing tracery). There is another lancet in the S transept. Dec the chancel windows (E reticulated tracery). Perp S doorway with leaf in the spandrels and the N doorway with initials in the spandrels, and Perp also the ashlar-faced W tower with a pierced quatrefoil parapet. The interior confirms and enormously enriches this first impression. First of all the Norman church, at least the Late Norman one, had a crossing with no doubt a crossing tower. The crossing piers are there, all four, solid, just with nook-shafts. These shafts have capitals with broad flat leaves or waterleaf. That allows for a date c.1170–90. The arches are single-stepped and already pointed. That is in favour of 1190 rather than 1170. Set in the crossing but on corbels a rib-vault. The corbels indicate that the vault was not at once planned. Yet here the capitals again have waterleaf. The ribs consist in section of one half-roll and two quarter-hollows. The chancel – see the large N window – belongs to the same build, and this also is rib-vaulted. The ribs are of the same section and stand consistently on corbels too. A little later this cruciform church was enlarged to the S, and it was, for no good reason, enlarged in such a way that pieces of wall were left standing between all the new aisle arcade arches. The capitals of the semicircular responds still have trumpet-scallops, but also stiff-leaf. So again, c.1190 seems the date. Also the first three arches from the E are lower than the other two, yet the higher W arches cannot mean an extension of the Norman nave; for the C11 window faces them. All arches pointed and with only slight chamfers. The N arcade is C14 and extends only opposite the E arches of the S arcade. Octagonal piers, arches with sunk convex curves. The S chancel chapel looks c.1300 in its details. – PISCINA. A piscina survives which served a rood-loft altar. It looks as if it were the re-used top part of a Norman pillar piscina. – FONT. Perp, octagonal, with quatrefoils. – STALLS. The fronts with tracery. – SCREEN. To the S schapel, an unusual design for Berkshire. Wide, ogee-headed single openings with panel tracery over. – DOORS. The door to the rood loft is Perp and very pretty. – S door with C13(?) ironwork overlaid by wooden blank pointed arches. – STAINED GLASS. E window by *Bentley*, but with one beautiful early C14 angel in the head and fragments of another. – TILES. Some medieval ones in various places. – PLATE. Chalice, 1663; Paten, undated; Cup and Paten and Paten, 1725. – MONUMENTS. Brasses to John Balam † 1496, priest, 20 in. figure; to a Knight and two wives, c.1500, 27 in.; to John Latton † 1548, 18 in.; to Sir John Daunce † 1545, his wife † 1523, and their children. The 18 in. figures lie on a low tomb-chest. – Two effigies, defaced, in the churchyard N of the W tower. – John Macdonald † 1841, aged thirteen, small brass plate with a very rustic figure of Faith looking like Britannia. Brass was a very unusual material at that time.

s of the church the WILLIAM MALTHUS CHANTRY SCHOOL, built in 1709. Red brick, five bays, with an apsidal hood. SW of the church a single ALMSHOUSE of 1738, for the oldest man in the village, and a second of 1838.

Blewbury is full of attractive timber-framed houses, but there is no reason here to single out any, except perhaps HALL BARN, SW of the church on the loop, with, at r. angles to the house, a brick wing of three bays with giant pilasters and wooden cross-windows. They have odd frilly lintels. It is probably work of *c.*1660.

(In SOUTH STREET is a cruck-framed cottage. NBR)

In LONDON STREET a good recent house by *Martin Sylvester*, 1963–4. The same architect is, at the time of writing, engaged on a group of sixteen smaller houses on the W outskirts.

ROUND BARROWS. These two magnificent barrows lie on Churn Down, W of the rifle range. The N barrow is 12 ft high and 108 ft in diameter; the second site, 200 ft to the SW, is 123 ft in diameter and 12 ft high. Both sites were excavated in the C19 and again in 1935. They appear to have been erected over existing pits containing Iron Age pottery and are probably of Roman date, although their purpose is obscure: neither revealed any interments.

ROUND BARROWS, on Churn Hill. The E barrow is a fine example of the bell type, 54 ft in diameter and 6 ft high, separated from its encircling ditch by a berm 20 ft wide. A small bowl barrow almost touches it on its W side.

IRON AGE HILLFORT, Blewburton Hill, *see* Aston Tirrold and Aston Upthorpe.

ROUND BARROW, Compton Down, *see* Compton.

BOARS HILL *see* WOOTTON

²⁰⁸⁰ ## BOURTON

ST JAMES. 1860 by *J. W. Hugall*. Nave and bellcote and chancel. Kentish plate-tracery, if you please.

BAPTIST CHAPEL. 1851 by *W. F. Ordish*. Also nave and bellcote and chancel. The details Dec.

Bourton is a mid C19 village.

PINEWOOD, formerly Bourton House, Tudor and gabled, is by *Ordish* as well, and the tender in 1845 was for £6,650 (GS).

The SCHOOL is dated 1842, and there is neo-Tudor estate housing.

BOWYER'S FARMHOUSE *see* SWALLOWFIELD

⁴⁰⁷ ## BOXFORD

ST ANDREW. The W tower is of *c.*1692. Handsome large flint panels in brick framing. The church is mostly Victorian. N aisle of 1841, but the arcade (lozenge-shaped piers, continuous mouldings) probably by *J. O. Scott & Sons*, 1908. – FONT. Small octagonal bowl, with very simple panels, probably of *c.*1662. – PULPIT. 1618, with its tester. – COMMUNION RAIL. Of *c.*1700, thin, twisted balusters. – PLATE. Cup and Cover, 1786; Paten on foot, 1836. – MONUMENT. Jacob Anderton, rector, † 1672. Tablet. The 'predella' and piers built up of book-spines.

The church and the near-by houses form a pretty group by the Lambourn.

On the w bank street with brick cottages, also thatched roofs, and WESTBROOK HOUSE, five bays with a three-bay pediment into which a round-arched window reaches up. Is it early C18?

BOYNE HILL *see* MAIDENHEAD

BRACKNELL 8060

HOLY TRINITY, Chance Road, Bracknell. 1851 and 1859 by *Coe & Goodwin*. Flint, with a NE tower with shingled broach spire. The windows E.E. to Dec. The s aisle is as wide as the nave, and the N and s arcades are made to differ.

ST MICHAEL AND ST MARY MAGDALENE, Easthampstead. Quite an imposing Victorian church, though coarse. By *J. W. Hugall*, 1866–7. Only the w tower, which rises to a considerable height and has a yet higher stair-turret, is halfway up older than Victorian. The brickwork makes a Jacobean date probable. So the tower is finished in brick too, although the rest of the church is ashlar-faced. E.E. details. – PULPIT. Inscribed and dated 1631 on a large arched panel. Much arabesque. – STALL BACKS. Late C17, fine pedimented panels.* – SCREEN. Made up from traceried panels of the former Perp rood screen. – STAINED GLASS. The E window and several other windows by *Morris & Co.*, i.e. *Burne-Jones*, 1876. The E window represents the Last Judgement. It is a noble, if somewhat languid composition. Most figures in white robes, the angels with wine-coloured wings, the sky dark blue. – N aisle one window by *Kempe*, 1893. Very feeble next to the Burne-Jones. – PLATE. Cup and Cover, 1569; Almsdish, 1659; Paten presented in 1670. – MONUMENTS. Brass to Thomas Berwyk † 1443, demi-figure, 8 in. (nave E). – William Trumbull † 1678, large tablet, exceptionally sober. – Elija Fenton, poet, † 1730. Absolutely plain, but the inscription by Pope.

ST ANDREW, Binfield Road, Priestwood. 1888. The architect

* They came from Oxford Cathedral.

is *H. G. W. Drinkwater* (BC). Small, brick, with an apse and a tiny bell-turret.

ST JOSEPH THE WORKER (R.C.), Stanley Road. By *Clifford Culpin & Partners*, 1961–2. The dominant feature is a steep roof, 100 ft long. It appears as a triangle in the façade, with the lower part open as a porch and behind it the actual block of the church. So the roof seems to be a canopy. Low flat-roofed aisles project l. and r. of the steep roof. A metal cross, 22 ft high, rises out of a pool.

COLLEGE OF FURTHER EDUCATION. By *J. T. Castle*, the County Architect; completed 1963.

EASTHAMPSTEAD PARK COLLEGE, 1¼ m. w of Easthampstead church. Built in 1860 for the Marquess of Downshire. Red brick, large, of three storeys, in a kind of Jacobean and on a kind of E-plan. Shaped gables, broad porch. To the r. of this what in an original Jacobean house would represent the great hall window (with transom), but is here the staircase window. The fronts of the projecting wings differ, l. semi-octagonal, r. square. To the SE also a symmetrical front: arcade of ten arches on stumpy, square, tapering pillars.

METEOROLOGICAL OFFICE. 1959–61 by *Eric Bedford*, Chief Architect to the *Ministry of Works*, a good group.

PERAMBULATION. Bracknell in the early C19 was called 'a small thoroughfare hamlet', but 'adorned with many genteel residences and delightful villas'. The thoroughfare is the HIGH STREET. Here, near the w end, is the RED LION, of brick with odd horizontal courses. The side elevation is timber-framed with brick infilling. At the e end is the OLD MANOR HOTEL, also C17, also brick, with gables, and all much altered. Today's character of the High Street is that of a small-town shopping street: two-storeyed buildings and no events. But on the N side one modern terrace breaks in, with shops and curtain walling. That is the herald of the New Town, whose shopping centre is the BROADWAY, parallel to, and N of, the High Street, and reached by a pedestrian shopping lane. At the time of writing the Broadway is very incomplete and holds out no hope of distinguished architecture.

The NEW TOWN was incorporated in 1948. It was to have no more than 25,000 inhabitants. By the end of 1959 17,500 was reached. Now there are 25,000, and the target has become 60,000. A plan for the town centre was made in 1963 by *G. Rhys* and the chief architect to the Corporation, *E. A. Ferriby*.

At present only the following requires notice. E of the centre, by the roundabout at the E end of Broadway and the S end of Warfield Road, the Meteorological Office, *see* above, and Messrs MAC FISHERIES, 1961–2 by *E. A. Ferriby*, a curtain wall job, and a little further S the College of Further Education, *see* above. Yet further E, i.e. at BULLBROOK, the CASTROL RESEARCH LABORATORIES, 1962–3 by *Lam, Biel & Partners*, good, with an odd glazed top with tapering sides.

W of the town centre another industrial area. Little of individual interest. Messrs FERRANTI, Western Road, is by *E. A. Ferriby*, 1961–2. N of this blocks of flats, e.g. CAMPION HOUSE and BRYONY HOUSE, six- and four-storeyed, and quite good (1961–3 by *E. A. Ferriby*). Otherwise much humdrum housing.

New flats also at Bullbrook, e.g. BAY HOUSE, Bay Road, six-storeyed with a group of shops (also by *E. A. Ferriby*).

The one outstanding job – outstanding in whatever New Town it might have been placed – is POINT ROYAL, Rectory Road,⁶⁴ Easthampstead, just E of the Easthampstead shopping terrace. It is by *Arup Associates*, 1960–4, a hexagonal seventeen-storey point-block of 102 flats for single people or couples without children. Two sides of the hexagon are slightly concave, and – as cannot be avoided in a hexagon – the rooms are oddly shaped. There are six on each floor, with staircase, lifts, etc., in the centre. The block is of reinforced concrete, and is placed in a shallow bowl with car parking below. The slightly up-curved rim of the bowl allows daylighting for the car area and also acts as a ha-ha for the block. The structure of the block is exposed, and in fact set outside of, and detached from, the glazing of the flats. The block thus looks transparent at the edges, and the rooms can have glazing right to the floor level. The finish is raw and the *ensemble* very powerful. But rising as it does in lonely splendour, it cudgels down the whole scale of Bracknell. As a single climax it is placed too eccentrically, and it is also too massive, not tower-like enough. It calls for four or five more of identical design. They could then create their own environment.

Opposite Point Royal is the one-storeyed COMMUNITY CENTRE of white brick; nice and clean.

Of the genteel residences mentioned in the early C19, few remain which can be mentioned here.

OLD BRACKNELL HOUSE, Old Bracknell Lane, S of the station,

is of five bays and two storeys and has a pretty, semicircular Adamish porch.

SOUTHILL PARK, ⅝ m. SE of Easthampstead church. Large, of brick. One five-bay range C18.* The rest said to have been rebuilt in 1853. But the tower and the door look rather too Baroque for so early a date.‡

EASTHAMPSTEAD PARK, *see* above.

CHURCH HILL HOUSE, opposite Easthampstead church. This started life as almshouses and was rebuilt as the WORKHOUSE in 1826. The older part still exists, a two-storeyed red-brick range with a cupola.

CAESAR'S CAMP. Small univallate Iron Age hillfort of irregular plan enclosing some 20 acres. A prominent counterscarp bank is visible at some points along the defences. The two opposed entrances on the N and S are probably original, those on the E and W modern. The N part of the fort is now a public recreation ground.

6070   BRADFIELD

ST ANDREW. Except for the W tower and the N aisle by *Sir George Gilbert Scott*, 1847–8. The tower is C16 work, oblong flint panels framed in red brick. Battlements and higher stair-turret. As for Scott, he did feats of picturesque variety outside and inside this church. From the entrance to the churchyard one reads: N aisle with pointed trefoiled single-light windows, higher N chapel with geometrical tracery, vestry cross-gabled with plate tracery, and chancel with shafted lancets. The S side is again entirely different, with lancets and a S transept. Inside the consistent variety is even more striking. The N arcade is original Dec work. Low octagonal piers and double-chamfered arches. So the S arcade is of completely different form and height. Or take the N aisle windows (the W one is original) and Scott's S aisle windows, or the rib-vaulted apse. Here the AUMBRY has a shouldered lintel, the PISCINA rounded trefoil arches, the SEDILIA pointed arches. Decoration runs from zigzag to stiff-leaf. – Iron SCREENS. – STAINED GLASS. Mostly by *Wailes*, the W window signed. – PLATE. Cup and Paten, 1674; Set of 1800. – MONUMENTS. Obelisk in the churchyard to Henry Stevens, Lord of the Manor, † 1773. – Mrs Stevens † 1840. Small tablet framed to one's

* Alterations by *Soane* recorded for 1801.

‡ Goodhart-Rendel, *D.N.B.*, mentions Southill Park among the works of *Temple Moore*.

surprise in three-dimensional strapwork, something quite unexpected in Early Victorian funerary monuments.

BRADFIELD COLLEGE. Bradfield College was founded in 1850 by the Rev. Thomas Stevens, squire and rector. He used the site of Bradfield Place, and of this a number of fragments survive. They are first the lowest courses of walling and buttresses of a barn, originally 191 ft long. The best preserved buttress is at the SE corner of the school area close to the gateway. The others follow along the road to the W. Then there is some brick walling of very large bricks between the quadrangle and the church and, standing against the churchyard wall, a curious small polygonal brick building with a tiny polygonal, rib-vaulted lobby. It looks as if it might have been part of a gatehouse.

The quadrangle just mentioned is the main feature of the school. The various parts and stages along its E, N, and S sides are architecturally insignificant, but the W side is open to the country, and that is Bradfield's great asset. When the school started, it had only the N part of the E range at its disposal. This was Bradfield Place. It now looks 1840s-Tudor (except for the later tile-hanging), but the building is older. Stevens then added classrooms and dormitories in 1853 and 1862, to the S of the house, and they are the brick range with half-timbering.

In 1856 the DINING HALL was built, some way E of the house. This is a Gothic room with late C13 external details and wooden posts to divide it into a nave and aisles, and has tiles and chimneypieces with leaf decoration. But the *clou* of the room, and indeed of the school altogether, is the STAINED GLASS in the W lancets, designed by *Burne-Jones* when he was only 24 years old and made by *Powell's* shortly before 1859, before Burne-Jones had joined forces for good with William Morris. They are as a matter of fact much stronger and bolder than anything from Morris's workshops, and can only be compared with Burne-Jones's work at Waltham Abbey, Essex, of 1861. The colours are forceful, and the compositions are uncompromising too. In the l. lancet an angel, Eve, Adam delving, in the middle lancet the Tower of Babel, in the r. lancet two pages, Solomon and the Queen of Sheba, and a court scene. In the sexfoil above the Cross of St Andrew (the college is the College of St Andrew) and fishes; for Andrew was a fisherman. The E window by *Wailes* opposite is an anticlimax.

The hall belongs more to the ENTRANCE COURT than to the

buildings so far mentioned. This irregular court dates from
c.1865 (but the lengthening of Army House on the E side was
done only in 1889). The architect of these early parts of the
college is not certain. The most probable name is *Sir G. G.
Scott*, though Stevens himself was no doubt not a passive
client. Scott refers once to his strong will. Stevens had met
Scott in 1835 or 1836, and they had become great friends. A
daughter of Stevens married Scott's son John Oldrid, a
daughter of Scott Stevens's son. Another daughter of Stevens
married a Powell of the glassmakers' firm. The main buildings
ending the N and S wings of the quadrangle are Big School and
the chapel. BIG SCHOOL is of the 1860s and was completed,
with the library over, in 1872. The architect here was *John
Oldrid Scott*, but the style is the same as before. Flint and red
brick; gabled E end with lancets. Big School also is aisled. The
part between Big School and the manor house is later.

The CHAPEL is by *Oldrid Scott* as well and is architecturally
the best that the school has to offer. The W part is of 1890–1.
The building is of red brick with stone dressings in the Dec
style and has a lively short tower with recessed pyramid roof.
The narrow aisles are separated from the nave by polished
black columns. Tower, chancel, and sanctuary were added in
1901. Round the altar C17 PANELLING taken from the
Headmaster's House. The STAINED GLASS of the E window and the panels of opaque glass to its l. and r. are by
Powell's.

In the angle E of the church the WAR MEMORIAL. The panels
of slate with inscribed names added after the Second World
War are by *Will Carter*. N of the N range of the quadrangle,
between it and the church, is GRAY SCHOOLS by *W. G.
Newton*, c.1935–6, and rather anaemic.

Of other buildings of the college the best-known is the Greek
Theatre. The stage building dates from 1890 but received
its present façade in 1955.

Near the church and in the village are a number of Georgian
five-bay houses. One stands immediately NW of the churchyard, is of chequer brick, has a pedimented doorway, and,
with its timber-framed neighbour and the weir, forms a pretty
group. A second is in the village street, E of the church, by
the bridge. This is of red brick with vertical blue-brick strips.
Two more further N. One of these, HOME FARM HOUSE,
has its door-hood on brackets.

¾ m. SW is the OLD RECTORY, by *Ould*, 1882, and in his way

with timber-framing patterns of the West Country rather than of Berkshire.

⅝ m. s the WAYLAND HOSPITAL, former WORKHOUSE. This was built in 1835 and is still classical. It is on the usual workhouse pattern.

1½ m. sw is BRADFIELD HALL, dated 1763. It is a complex building, but the centre is in order. Façade of three bays, the middle one being a canted bay window. Entrance side curiously informal: two bays, the Tuscan porch instead of one, and a pediment over the middle of the rather high elevation. Between the arched main windows of ground floor and first floor oval windows. Inside, a groin-vaulted entrance hall leads to the saloon. (This is two storeys in height and has a gallery on four Doric columns. MHLG) STABLES to the E with cupola.

BRADLEY FARMHOUSE see CUMNOR

BRAY 9080

The centre of Bray is still a village centre, which is a relief in this commuters' country. But, where the Café de Paris used to be, there is now a river estate of flats.

ST MICHAEL. A remarkably large church. Big and broad Perp s tower with porch and higher stair-turret. In the porch tierceron-vault of an unusual pattern. The inner doorway with continuous Perp mouldings. But inside the church the arcades of six bays are early C14, judging by their arches.* Low octagonal piers. The two-bay arcades to the chancel chapels early C14 too.‡ Externally the s doorway is of the same period, and so must be the (re-done) windows. Perp N and s chapels; but everything externally hopelessly over-restored. Victorian in a more positive way the chancel arch with its naturalistic decoration and the chancel roof (architect *T. H. Wyatt*, date 1859, according to BC). – FONT. According to the churchwardens' accounts of 1647, yet entirely Perp of the standard type. – STAINED GLASS. E window by *Wailes* to *Street*'s design (BC). – Chancel s by *Henry Holiday*, made by Powell, 1868. – MONUMENTS. Brass to Sir John de Foxley † 1378 and two wives. The typical ambiguity of vertical and horizontal representation is here especially telling. The three are seen on a bracket, and, although that implies that they are

* The E bay of the N arcade was rebuilt in 1860.
‡ Also rebuilt in 1860.

standing, he in fact has his helmet behind his head and a dog at his feet. The canopies are missing. It must have been a very fine piece when it was complete. The figures are 2 ft 6 in. long. – Brass to William Laken †1474 (s aisle), a 13 in. figure. – Brass to William Norreys † 1591. Tablet in architectural surround with an egg-and-dart frame (N aisle). – William Goddard † 1609, founder of Jesus Hospital. Large tablet with two frontal three-quarter figures. Black columns, wide open pediment. The inscription reads

'If what I was thou seekest to know,
These lynes my character shall show,
Those benefits that God me lent,
With thankes I tooke, and freely spent:
I scorned what plainess could not gett,
And, next to treason, hated debt;
Loved not those that stirr'd up strife:
True to my friend and to my wife.
The latter here by me I have,
We had one bed, and have one grave.
My honesty was such that I
When death came, feared not to dye.'

– Brass of c.1610. Architectural surround with guilloche and a steep pediment. No name, no date. The inscription as worth while as the previous one:

'When Oxford gave thee two degrees in art,
And love possest thee master of my heart,
Thy colledge fellowshipp thow lefs't for mine
And nought but death could seprate me from thine.
Thirty-five yeares we livd'e in wedlocke bands
Conioyned in our hearts as well as handes
But death the bodies of best friendes devides
And in the earths close wombe their relyckes hides
Yet here they are not lost but sowen, that they
May rise more glorious at the Judgment day.'

– William Paule † 1685. Tablet with segmental pediment on columns. A wreath round the inscription. – Mrs Hanger † 1739. By *Peter Scheemakers*. No effigy; minor.
In the churchyard the CHANTRY CHAPEL OF ST MARY. It became a school in the early C17, and it was then that the wooden cross-windows were inserted. – Outside the s wall a RELIEF of a horse. Is it Norman? – The main access to the churchyard is by a timber-framed C15 GATEHOUSE. Brick

infilling, low passageway, and above it to the outside an oriel. Pretty lane from here to the main street. In the main street, at the N end, and overlooking the churchyard, CHANTRY HOUSE, C18, three-storeyed, the front later than the rest. The front has two canted bay windows and a doorway with Ionic columns and a pediment. Staircase with turned balusters and carved tread-ends. Further S in the main street some C15 cottages on the l., the CROWN HOTEL, a C15 hall-house, on the r.

At the S end of the village JESUS HOSPITAL, founded in 1627, a large brick quadrangle with twenty-eight dwellings, with their windows l. and r. of the doorway and their large dormer windows exceptionally generously dimensioned. The centre of the entrance side is higher and has to the outside a statue of the founder and l. and r. stone cross-windows. In the centre of the end wall the chapel with an original SCREEN. Four arches l., four r. of the entrance. Tapering pillars, no top decoration.

BRAY WICK HOUSE, ½ m. SW. The main front is dated 1675 and has a three-bay centre and two-bay moderately projecting wings. But there are no features, except the broad brick string course above the ground floor which projects slightly above every window. Behind, one corner of three by three bays is later and a little higher. (A staircase inside with balusters looking rather earlier than 1675. In one room nice thin Rococo stucco. Is it genuine C18 work?* NBR)

HOLYPORT HOUSE, Holyport Green, ¾ m. SW. A Queen Anne house of five bays with hipped roof and segment-headed windows. Earlier timber-framed rooms behind. The house overlooks HOLYPORT GREEN with several attractive houses, especially one picturesquely wonky-looking timber-framed house on the W side of the Green.

Behind Holyport House is GAY'S HOUSE, also C18. Brick, of seven irregular bays, with a porch on Tuscan columns. The windows on the r. of the porch are arched on ground floor and upper floor.

BRAYWOOD

8070

ALL SAINTS. 1866 by *Talbot Bury*. The church has been demolished.

BRIGHTWALTON

4070

ALL SAINTS. 1862–3 by *Street*. Rock-faced, in the late C13

* I was not allowed to see the interior.

style, with Geometrical tracery. SW tower with big shingled broach spire. The S arcade has short quatrefoiled blackish (blue lias: BC) piers, the clerestory quatrefoil and trefoil openings. – REREDOS. By *Earp*. – STAINED GLASS. By the font glass of *c*.1863, by an unfamiliar-looking hand. Mr A. C. Sewter, the foremost expert, attributes it to *Burne-Jones*. Children presented to Christ. Strong colours, but not strident. The faces with quite some tension. – PLATE. Small, ornate Cup, German, inscribed 1610; Paten, 1729; silver-gilt Paten, 1722. – BRASS to John Newman(?) † 1517. A 14 in. figure.

SCHOOL. By *Street*, 1863. Brick and stone dressings. Half-hipped roofs. Only the main window Gothic.

RECTORY. By *Street*, 1877. Brick and tile-hanging. Dormers. Good big chimneystacks.

WOOLLEY PARK, 1¼ m. NW. A late C17 house, remodelled by *Sir Jeffry Wyatville* in 1799. Cement-faced. The main façade with a big bow with attached giant Tuscan columns. Only two bays l., two r. of it. But Victorian additions l. as well as r. At the back a Tuscan one-storeyed veranda between projecting wings. (Inside, the staircase divides into two and is lit by a dome.)

5090   BRIGHTWELL

ST AGATHA. The S doorway of *c*.1200. Capitals with leaf. Round arch with a filleted roll. Of the same time the S arcade. Three bays, round piers, octagonal abaci, single-step pointed arches. The tower arch belongs too. Two slight chamfers. But the tower itself dates from 1797. Blue headers and red brick dressings. Arched bell-openings. Parapet. The N arcade is of about 1300, and the windows are in agreement with such a date. Late Geometrical tracery. Standard elements. Early C14 chancel. Windows with Geometrical tracery, but also ogees. Similarly the PISCINA and SEDILIA still look C13 but have ogees. The hood-mould of the group has head-stops. The S aisle fenestration is Dec too. Perp clerestory. – CHANDELIER. Brass; C18. – STAINED GLASS. Fragments, including a head, N aisle. – PLATE. Cup of 1599; small Paten of 1752; large Paten of 1771/2. – BRASSES. John Scoffyld † 1507, priest, 18 in. figure (S aisle). – Robert Court † 1509 and wife, 20 in. figures (nave). – Richard Hampden † 1512 and wife, 15 in. figures (nave).

BRIGHTWELL MANOR, S of the church. Georgian; blue headers and red dressings. Three storeys, five bays, plain arched doorway.

N of the church a HOUSE with a C17 part with mullioned windows.

BRIMPTON

5060

ST PETER. 1869–72 by *John Johnson*. All flint and quite big. The tower is in fact a brick tower of 1748, faced with flint and provided with a broach spire. The style chosen for the church is Dec. Inside, piers of polished granite. Nave and aisles, transepts, and symmetrical vestry and organ chamber, the latter opened by a two-light window to the chancel. – STAINED GLASS. N transept N by *Willement*, *c.*1856 (Betjeman and Piper). – Chancel S 1859 by *Lavers & Barraud*. – PLATE. Cup and Paten, Late Elizabethan; Paten, 1800.

MANOR FARM. Next to the house the former CHAPEL OF ST LEONARD, a plain oblong flint building with a Norman N doorway (tympanum with a big cross), a N lancet, and a Dec E window of three stepped lights, nicely done.

BRIMPTON MILL. Dated 1731. Brick, of five bays, with a weatherboarded gable.

ROUND BARROW CEMETERY, in the S of the parish, close to the Hampshire border. The group consists of two bell barrows and three bowl barrows. They vary in diameter from 60 to 100 ft and in height from 4 to 8 ft.

BROADLANDS see SUNNINGHILL

BROADMOOR see CROWTHORNE

BROCKHAMPTON FARM see LAMBOURN

BUCKHOLD

6070

HOLY TRINITY. 1836 by *Sampson Kempthorne*. Nave and chancel and bellcote. Lancet windows. Cemented walls.

BUCKHOLD HOUSE (St Andrew's School). By *Alfred Waterhouse*, 1884–5. Large and quite freely grouped. Red brick and yellow terracotta. Gothic and Elizabethan forms mixed. In the entrance hall ceramic pictures by *Doulton's*, including a view of their own Gothic works at Lambeth, and also a view of Boston, Mass. – Octagonal COWSHED.

BUCKHURST PARK see SUNNINGHILL

BUCKLAND

3090

ST MARY. The church possesses an exceptionally wide early C12 nave, the dimensions of which are given by the N and S

windows fairly high up and the N and S doorways. The very
tall S doorway has two orders of shafts with one-scallop
capitals and strong roll mouldings. Hood-mould with saltire
crosses. The N doorway is lower but otherwise similar. The
nave battlements of course are later, probably Perp. The
church is cruciform with a crossing tower with E.E. lancet
bell-openings. The piers on which the tower stands are unfortunately restored beyond redemption. E.E. also the N
transept – see the remains of lancets in the W and N walls.
The chancel must be Dec, judging by the N recess with ogee
gable and ballflower decoration and the S recess minus the
leaf and fleur-de-lis friezes which must be a later cutting. The
SEDILIA and PISCINA with pointed-trefoiled heads also Dec.
But all that evidence is externally obscured by the fact that
the chancel and N and S transept windows and the nave W
window of three to five lights have mullions running dead into
the arches. The same motif with even the arches straightened
out occurs at Uffington. The VCH in both cases calls it E.E.
But can that be? On the S transept here a date 1787 is inscribed. But if the C13 is too early, 1787 is too late. It looks a
C17 repair. However, nothing is recorded, and why would such
consistent repairs have been needed? Good chancel roof with
tie-beams, kingposts, and many carved bosses. Extremely rich,
glittering S transept DECORATION with mosaics. Made in the
1890s by *Powell's* (BC). – FONT. Perp, octagonal, with
quatrefoils and tracery motifs. – PULPIT. Jacobean, similar
to that in Shrivenham church. Angle pilasters tapering. Blank
arches with fake perspectives. – BOX PEWS and PEWS,
including open balustraded fronts. – TOWER GALLERY high
up. Balustraded; Jacobean. – CHANDELIERS. In the transepts. One was given in 1733 (VCH). – SOUTH DOOR. The
ironwork is of the C12. – STAINED GLASS in the S transept,
probably part of the general decoration. It looks *Powell's*,
and the date of death recorded is 1888. – SCULPTURE. In the
piscina small Italian C17 alabaster relief of the Adoration of
the Shepherds. – Three funeral HELMETS in the N transept;
C17. – PLATE. Cup of 1565, an early post-Reformation date;
Paten of 1638; Plate of 1697; large Flagon of 1721. – MONU-
MENTS. William Holcot † 1570. Triangular niche in the
chancel N wall. He was a lay-preacher after the Reformation.
Under Mary he recanted. He made a will for his heart to be
kept in a casket in this niche. The shape may allude to the
Trinity. – Sir Edward Yate and his daughter who died in 1648.

Black and white marble altar with 'frontal' of strapwork and
garlands. 'Reredos' with the same elements. The garlands
are a progressive motif. Good quality. – Sir John Yate † 1658.
Tablet with black columns, garlands in the 'predella'. The
top already an open scrolly pediment. – Elizabeth Perfect.
Coade stone, i.e. by *Coade & Seely*, 1802. Weeping putto by
an urn.

St George (R.C.). 1846–8 by *Hansom* (Mr D. Evinson) or
W. W. Wardell (BC). Whichever it was, the church looks as if
it was remodelled in the later C19. Nave and chancel, bellcote on a mid-buttress. High N chapel with Kentish tracery.
The rest of the tracery Geometrical.

Buckland House. Built in 1757 etc. by the younger *Wood*
of Bath for Sir Robert Throckmorton. Buckland House as
built was not as large as it is now, but it was the most splendid
of smaller Georgian houses in the county. *Romaine Walker*
about 1910 added the wings to the house itself, not the low
outer wings, and thereby doubled the accommodation. These
wings as seen from the grounds project beyond the centre and
look perfectly convincing. From the entrance, on the other
hand, they stay in line with the centre, and the result is an
unhappy crowding of link windows. Wood's design was a
square and low links to outer pavilions. The square is of five
bays and two and a half storeys and has an exceptionally high
ground floor, exceptionally, considering that it is rusticated
and that giant columns start only above it. Yet the main rooms
are on the rusticated, not on the upper level. The giant
columns are Corinthian and carry a pediment, and the frieze
is enriched throughout by leaf garlands. The main upper
windows are framed by aedicules. The pavilions cruciform
but with diagonals in front of what would be the re-entrant
angle. Romaine Walker, needless to say, added the unfortunate porch. It is not known whether he also altered the low
ENTRANCE HALL with its coupled pilasters. He certainly
re-did the STAIRCASE, though in its original place. The
two fully preserved rooms in the centre block are the saloon
and the adjacent room behind the stairs. The SALOON is
higher than the other rooms and has a coved ceiling with
medallions and swags and in the flat centre a much baro-
quized stucco version of Reni's 'Aurora'. Big chimneypiece.
Door-hood on brackets. The adjacent room has a Rococo
plaster ceiling and a very fine late C18 chimneypiece. The
centre towards the garden is oddly of six, not five bays.

Paired doors lead therefore out of the two main rooms to the
open stairs and the terraces. Original also the interiors of the
end pavilions. In the E pavilion the LIBRARY with a ceiling
painted all in one (i.e. not in compartments) by *Cipriani* and
Rebecca to Cipriani's design, and with decoration gone
Adamish. The W pavilion on the other hand is grand in the
sense of the façade. It is called the CHAPEL, but if it was that,
it must have had the altar at the W end, which is unlikely.
The interior is all left in stone. Corinthian angle pilasters in
groups. Columns only in the W arm of the cross. The frieze
again with garlands. The windows flanked by colonnettes.
The chimneypiece still has a head with rays as its centre – still,
as this is a William Kent motif. The room is not really vaulted.
There is only a broad coving with penetrations.

In the grounds are an ICE HOUSE, N of the N end of the
house and the NW corner of the Manor House, in the trees.
It is largely above ground and thatched. The front is a portico
of three arches, W, N, S, and has ample grotto rustication on
the portico openings. By the lake is a rustic BOATHOUSE built
of upright logs. Further W a pedimented EXEDRA, derelict,
and a good deal further W, i.e. NW of the house, a ROTUNDA
of unfluted Ionic columns with a dome. The urn inside is by
Romaine Walker and commemorates the Knight of Kerry.

MANOR HOUSE. A late C16 or C17 house with mullioned and
transomed windows was converted in the late C18 into
Gothick STABLES to Buckland House. Of the old house the
E side still has a canted bay window and a window immediately l. and a window immediately r. of it, making a total of
fourteen lights. To the l. and r. of this part the Gothick
architecture, i.e. windows with Y-tracery. The front towards
Buckland House has polygonal angle towers and nine bays in
between, the centre an archway. The façade is crenellated and
the battlements rise as a shallow gable above the archway.
There are of course also quatrefoil windows.

Much ESTATE HOUSING.

BUCKLEBURY

ST MARY. The churchyard is entered by cast-iron gates of
1827 (signed by the firm: *N. Hedges*). The church is of flint
and possesses a very ornate Late Norman S doorway. The
inner order has rosettes, faces, four-petalled flowers, etc. The
next order has shafts with decorated capitals. In the arch
pellets and zigzag. In the centre of the hood-mould a fearsome

face crowned by an orb and a cross. C13 N arcade of three separate openings cut into the former wall. Double-chamfered arches. Perp W tower* with W doorway and W window. C18 pinnacles and spire. – FONT. Octagonal, strongly moulded, probably C14. – PULPIT. Later C17? Just panels framed by guilloche. – BOX PEWS. – COMMUNION RAIL. With twisted balusters, c.1700. – WEST GALLERY. The date 1824 might well apply to it. – STAINED GLASS. The chancel E, N, and S windows by *Brangwyn*, 1912, N aisle window by the same (date of death commemorated 1917). Strong colours, clearly and dramatically told stories, in a kind of realist Expressionism. – PLATE. Cup, 1576: Cover, 1577; Paten on foot and Flagon, 1811; Almsdish, 1824. – MONUMENTS. Sir Henry Winchcombe † 1703. Two putti and a coat of arms under a looped curtain framed by pilasters and a pedimental top. – Also three HELMS, two SWORDS, and a pair of GAUNTLETS.

RECTORY. A handsome early C18 brick façade of three bays with giant pilasters. One-bay pediment. – In the garden two large bronze figures: Reclining Figure by *Henry Moore*, 1961–2, but done in plaster c.1956. – Draped Reclining Woman, 1957–8 by the same. The setting is ideal.

BUCKRIDGES see SUTTON COURTENAY

BULLBROOK see BRACKNELL

BURGHFIELD

ST MARY. 1843 by *J. B. Clacy*, a rather terrible neo-Norman effort. Brick, with a W tower. Its top stage is polygonal. A stumpy spire on top. Two unhappy porches in the angles between tower and nave. Wide nave and wide transepts. The chancel built by *Bodley & Garner* in 1892 (BC), in the Dec style, and carefully, as one would expect. The E window is above the reredos. – FONT. Cut in the C14, with blank panelling, out of a circular tub-shaped Norman font. – STAINED GLASS. The E window by *Burlison & Grylls* (BC); not at all bad. – PLATE. Cup, 1632; Paten on foot, 1714. – MONUMENTS. Early C14 effigy of a Knight, damaged, but must once have been very fine. Angels by his pillow, crossed legs. – Richard Neville, Earl of Salisbury, † 1460. Two recumbent stone effigies; defaced.

* On the SE buttress relief of a man with a wheel. It looks C18. It has been suggested that it might be a rebus referring to the Winchcombe family who were Lords of the Manor, and in this case might well be earlier.

OLD RECTORY, ¼ m. NW. Brick, Georgian, five bays with three-bay pediment. Door surround with pilasters, triglyph frieze, and pediment.

BUSCOT

ST MARY. By the Isis, i.e. the Thames, outside the village. Perp W tower with W doorway and W window. Nave and chancel separated by a chancel arch of c.1200. Two orders of simple stiff-leaf; zigzag arch. In the chancel one N lancet and one low-side lancet. Unrestored N side of the church. Inside, cinquefoiled rere-arches indicate that what seem wide early C19 lancets were originally two-light windows. – PULPIT. Three panels are a re-used Flemish triptych, early C16. Two other panels English Early Renaissance, probably domestic. – LECTERN. Splendid, Spanish, C17; of wood. – STAINED GLASS. The E window by *Burne-Jones*, i.e. *Morris & Co.*, 1891: the Good Shepherd. By the same a window in the chancel on the S side; c.1895. – PLATE. Silver-gilt Cup and Bread Holder, 1711; Cover Paten and Flagon, 1779. – MONUMENTS. Brasses to Husband and Wife, c.1500, 2 ft figures. – Monument to Margaret Loveden Loveden † 1786. Two putti by a grey obelisk. At the foot relief of Charity. She is giving money to a poor man and bread to a girl. – Elizabeth Loveden Loveden † 1788. In front of an obelisk, reclining on a couch. A baldacchino above her on the r. An angel appearing from the l. and holding her hand. Both by *Robert Cooke*.

OLD RECTORY. Fine house of c.1700. Five by three bays, two storeys, hipped roof. Stone, and roofed with stone slates.

The VILLAGE HALL with cupola at the end of the short village street and the village WELL of four square pillars and a four-gabled roof, as well as a number of houses, were done for the Hendersons, i.e. the first Lord Faringdon, by *Sir Ernest George* in the 1890s. In the village street MANOR FARM-HOUSE, dated 1691, five bays, two storeys, hipped roof, like the Old Rectory. But wooden cross-windows and doorway on carved brackets.

BUSCOT PARK. The house may have been built about 1770. It is of nine bays and two storeys with a pedimented three-bay centre. To the N two generous symmetrical bows. In 1889 *Sir Ernest George & Peto* added a big wing and altered the house itself. The wing was pulled down and the house brought back to its original appearance by *Geddes Hyslop* just before the Second World War. The work was done for Lord Faringdon.

Hyslop also added two detached classical ranges at a distance and in axis with the house. They end on either short side in a Tuscan portico. One has a cupola, and a tunnel-vaulted passage through its centre. In this wall PAINTINGS of Labour Party and generally Socialist subject matter; and also of the family having tea. They are by *Lord Hastings* (then Lord Huntingdon), who studied under Diego Rivera, and were done in the thirties.

The entrance hall has at its back a screen of two red scagliola columns with Ionic capitals. The overdoors with recent Grecian paintings by *Elroy Haldall*. The ceilings of the rooms to the l. and r. are distinctly Adamish. In the centre room on the garden side another, more elaborate, such ceiling. Round the walls in thick gilded neo-Renaissance frames the 61 series of *Burne-Jones's* Sleeping Beauty (Briar Rose), painted in 1890. The frames were designed by Burne-Jones too. Fine chimneypiece with detached termini-caryatid maidens. Vaulted passage along the centre of the house between the front and back rooms. In one of the two bow-fronted back rooms is yet another excellent plaster ceiling. The overmantel is in the Chippendale–Chinese fashion. The *chinoiserie* paintings, however, are recent. The staircase hall has an Adamish ceiling too. But the composition of Roman Doric columns in the window wall is Hyslop's.

BUSSOCK WOOD *see* WINTERBOURNE

BUTTERSTEEP HOUSE *see* ASCOT

CAESAR'S CAMP *see* BRACKNELL

CALCOT   6070
2 m. w of Reading

CALCOT HOUSE. 1755 for John Blagrave. A splendid seven-bay house, unfortunately provided with a later roof. Red brick, all headers. Basement and two storeys. Three-bay portico with brick pilasters carrying finely carved Ionic capitals. Pediment with a Venetian window squeezed into it. Doorway with attached Tuscan columns and a triglyph frieze. The back just as impressive. The house here forms the end of an oblong stable court with three ranges and four corner pavilions with hipped roofs. The staircase has an iron railing with scrolls, quite modest. Walls with good stucco panels. The extension to the second floor is recent. The principal

room has a modest plaster ceiling. – LODGE on the Bath Road
three by three bays with giant blank arches.

ALMSHOUSES. 1852. Quite pretty. Red brick and blue diapers.
One-storeyed.

CARSWELL MANOR *see* LONGWORTH

4080

CATMORE

ST MARGARET. Two Norman doorways, the s one with a head
at the top of the hood-mould. The rest of the Norman features
overwhelmingly Early Victorian, an effort to make a modest
Norman church showy Norman. The work is of before 1850,
as in that year the church was called 'lately carefully restored'
(BC). The nave roof with collar-beams on arched braces and
wind-braces is of 1607. The pendants betray the date. –
FONT. Tub-shaped, Norman, with a top band of defaced
decoration. – PLATE. Paten on foot of 1723(?); Almsdish of
1834.

7070

CAVERSHAM

ST PETER. Norman s doorway. One order of shafts, zigzag up
the jambs and in the arch, partly at r. angles to the wall. The
abaci have saltire crosses. Re-set Norman window in the w
wall of the N vestry. Perp N wall. The s aisle is an addition of
1878. The tower was rebuilt in 1878 (BC). Low arcades inside,
with round piers. Good Perp N chapel. Panelled arches on a
pier the capital of which has carved angel-busts, a Windsor
motif. The chapel has a N window, now inside, a little later
yet than the other N windows. The chancel was lengthened
in 1924–5 by *Sir N. Comper* (BC). – FONT. Norman, of Purbeck
marble, a round basin, but at the angles raised spurs with
concave outlines. – CHANDELIER. Of brass, dated 1743. –
Former WIND VANE. Dated 1663. Now on a staff. – PLATE.
Silver-gilt Flagon and two Patens, inscribed 1753. The flagon
is a piece of Elizabethan Revival.

The church lies above the site of CAVERSHAM COURT, now a
public garden by the Thames. Of the buildings a GARDEN
HOUSE remains, brick, C17, and the STABLES, also brick and
C17.

The centre of Caversham is now all Reading. At the main
crossing, at the angle of GOSBROOK ROAD and South Street,
the BAPTIST FREE CHURCH, 1875–7 by *Waterhouse*, red
brick, Gothic, and in Gosbrook Road *Waterhouse*s' WEST

MEMORIAL INSTITUTE, of 1865-6, also brick and also Gothic. It was the Free Church before the present one was built. At the corner of HENLEY ROAD and PEPPARD ROAD is QUEEN ANNE'S SCHOOL, 1894 and later. It includes Amersham Hall, built as a Nonconformist boys' school by *Waterhouse*, probably *c*.1865. The chapel is by *Sir Reginald Blomfield*. At the top of Peppard Road is the entrance to CAVERSHAM PARK, a stuccoed mansion of 1850-2, in the Palladian tradition. This is, however, across the Oxfordshire border.

Finally, at the far w end of SURLEY ROW, a somewhat Italian lane, OLD GROVE HOUSE, Elizabethan, of flint set in square panels, framed by brick bands. Gables, unusual chimney-stack.

In 1964 a beginning was made on a large HOUSING ESTATE taken out of Caversham Park. It is an area of 156 acres and will in the end have 1,500 houses. The plan is entirely on the Radburn principle of strict separation of pedestrian and vehicle circulation. The designers are *Diamond, Redfern & Partners*, with *Paul Ritter* as the planner. The site runs from Peppard Road to Hurley Road.

CHADDLEWORTH

4070

ST ANDREW. The s doorway is Norman. It has zigzags up the jambs, meeting at the angle. Arch with two zigzags. Hood-mould on heads, with a nice simple trail. In the original chancel a Norman N window. In the nave an early C13 N lancet. Early C13 also the short, unbuttressed w tower. The hood-mould over the w window is re-used Norman work. To this modest church *Street* in 1851 added a chancel, deliberately unconcerned, it seems, with the scale and character of the church. His chancel is of blue and red brick, is higher, has a slate roof, and displays bigger and heavier windows. On the N side of the church two family chapels, the eastern one of 1706, the western of 1765. – The PULPIT is not Georgian, but imitation-Georgian. – RAILS to the family chapels. – Creed and Our Father. Nicely bordered WOODEN BOARDS, dated 1757. – PLATE. Cup and Cover, 1585; Cup, 1717; Paten, 1788; Salver, 1790. – MONUMENTS. Exceptionally many tablets, but no major monuments. In the chancel Thomas Nelson † 1748 with two standing putti. – In the nave on the N side two Mrs Nelsons † 1618 and 1619. Above the inscription ogee arches. – Bartholomew Tipping † 1757, big. – Chardin Musgrove † 1768, with a standing mourning female by an urn. By *King* of Bath. – On the S side two more Bartholomew Tippings † 1718 and † 1737. – In the western family chapel yet another Bartholomew Tipping † 1798. Signed Westmacott Junior, i.e. the future *Sir Richard Westmacott*. Competently and restrainedly Grecian.

CHADDLEWORTH HOUSE. Of *c*.1830. Blue and red brick. Five bays. Tuscan porch. Pedimental gable.

POUGHLEY FARMHOUSE, 1½ m. S. Now inside an Air Force establishment. This was the site of a priory of Augustinian Canons founded *c*.1160. (A part of the W range of the priory buildings is now incorporated in the E façade of the farmhouse. Blocked late C13 two-light window with pointed trefoiled lights. Small figure of a seated monk, re-set. VCH) To the ENE of the façade excavations have shown an aisleless chapel, probably with a W tower.*

ROUND BARROWS *see* Great Fawley.

₃₀₉₀

CHARNEY BASSETT

ST PETER. Small, next to the larger Manor House. Embattled nave. Curious Jacobean bellcote. Perp two-bay N arcade (octagonal pier, depressed double-chamfered arches). But the interesting thing of the church is the Norman work: i.e. the outer moulding of the S doorway with radially set faces, their tongues out and forking like beards, and the tympanum set up inside. This shows a standing man holding two gryphons and bitten by them. He is called in the literature Alexander, but the representation does not fit the Alexander story. – PULPIT. Perp, of wood. – STAINED GLASS. C15 fragments.

MANOR HOUSE. Centre and two projecting wings, the S wing being the late C13 solar wing of a hall-house. The centre, where the hall was, and the N wing are a C19-Tudor rebuilding. The C13 wing has a rectangular projection to the E. The ground floor has windows which are small slits, except for one two-light window under a round arch. The head is re-set. In the N wall is a doorway to the former house, and also a large fireplace with a shouldered lintel. On the upper floor was the solar, and to its E the chapel. Two-light windows in both. The chapel E window has bar tracery. In the S wall a pointed-trefoil-headed lancet. Roof with tie-beams, crownposts,

* Mr S. E. Rigold adds to this 'a good piece of C14 arched-braced roof with a well-preserved louvre'.

and four-way struts. In the w wall of the N wing is a re-set quatrefoil opening also of the C13.

CHERBURY CAMP. The low-lying situation of this fort would appear to render it indefensible under modern conditions. It has been shown, however, that during the life of the fort access to the low knoll on which it is constructed would have been barred by a stream on the N and W and by an extensive area of swamp on the E and SE. Access was by means of a narrow neck of higher ground on the NE. The defences consist of three concentric banks and ditches, best preserved on the NW. These fortifications are broken by gaps on the N, S, and E sides; only the last is an original entrance. This E entrance had a metalled surface in which cart ruts had been worn and gave way in the interior of the fort to a finely cobbled street. Finds from the ditches suggest that the fort was the work of Iron Age B groups, probably at the beginning of the C1 A.D.

CHAVEY DOWN
2 m. E of Bracknell

8060

HEATHFIELD SCHOOL. The school chapel is by *Street*, 1850, i.e. very early.* Nave and chancel in one, tiled roof, small bell-turret. Straight-headed three-light windows with ogee-headed lights. The interior was entirely remodelled *c*.1960. The school buildings, near the chapel, include a re-erected Georgian shopfront of doorway and two bow windows.

CHERBURY CAMP *see* CHARNEY BASSETT

CHIEVELEY

4070

ST MARY. Unbuttressed C13 w tower with Perp bell-stage, and a very fine C13 chancel. The E wall has three lancets, with continuous roll mouldings outside, continuous roll mouldings and shafts with stiff-leaf capitals inside. The roof has one tie-beam on arched braces with traceried spandrels.‡ The side walls have lancets. The nave is of 1873, by *J. W. Hugall.* – FONT. Octagonal, Perp, with quatrefoils. – PULPIT. Jacobean, with blank arches and arabesques. – MONUMENT. Mrs Fincher † 1688. Small. Square brass plate in a stone surround of leathery or doughy forms, more like 1650 than 1688.

* Or is this even the church by Street mentioned in the *D.N.B.* as designed for Bracknell before 1849?
‡ It probably also served the purpose of supporting the lenten veil.

CHIEVELEY HOUSE, SE of the church. Red brick, five bays, hipped roof, the doorway with a straight hood on three brackets, one of them an angel-head.

VICARAGE, N of the former. Five bays with a one-bay pediment and a hipped roof.

(PIG FARM COTTAGE. Of cruck construction. NBR)

PRIOR'S COURT, 1 m. E. Late C18. Seven bays, the first and last two raised by one storey and pedimented. In the raised part a lunette window. The centre has a porch with four (re-used?) Corinthian stone columns. (In the house some C14 STAINED GLASS, e.g. monkeys playing musical instruments – see *Newbury District Field Club*, II, 1872.)

IRON AGE HILLFORT, in the middle of Bussock Wood. This small 10-acre fort is of univallate construction on the N and W and has two banks on the E and S, where the gentler slope would favour attack. There are a number of gaps on the E side, but without excavation it is impossible to say which are contemporary with the ramparts.

CHILDREY

3080

ST MARY. Quite a big church. The nave basically early C13 – see the two doorways, that on the S side with a hood-mould of dogtooth. But the windows are Perp and the upper windows – a heightening – Late Perp. Then the chancel, higher than the nave. This is late C13 – see the windows with pointed-trefoiled lights and a circle over. Also cusped Y-tracery and SEDILIA and PISCINA with pointed trefoiled heads. The Easter Sepulchre on the other hand must be later – late C14 at the earliest, see the Perp panelling behind the ogee gable. The foliage, however, is still near the Dec. Much oak leaf. After that the transepts – see the Dec E window and the low tomb recess in the N wall (cf. below). But the big window over this is Perp again. Broad Perp w tower with w doorway with decorated spandrels and a typical broadly moulded arch to the nave. The date of the transepts is internally confirmed by the arch into them. No chancel arch at all. – FONT. Of lead, *c.*1200, with small upright figures of bishops taken from the same few moulds. A very interesting piece. – SCREEN. One-light divisions; not much of it old. – BENCHES. A few old, with simple poppy-heads. – STAINED GLASS. In the N transept, much of it C15, but in small parts. – PLATE. Paten, hall-marked 1496, with the Vernicle; Cup, C17. – MONUMENTS. The low tomb recess in the N transept

is Dec. It has an ogee arch, ballflower, ogee cusping, and a
fine, slender cross-legged effigy, hand at his sword, shield
held high up. – Purbeck marble tomb with short tomb-chest
and canopy on a straight under-edge. Brasses of William Fete-
place † 1516 and wife, kneeling, in shrouds against the back
wall. – Many brasses: William Fynderne † 1444 and wife
(chancel floor). 52 in. figures, but little of them left. High ogee
canopies. Interesting inscription in distichs. – Headless priest,
12 in. figure, c.1450. – John Kyngeston † 1514 and wife,
Trinity above, 30 in. figures (chancel floor). – Joan Walrond,
Mrs Strongbow, † 1507(?). Small figure in a shroud, beautiful
Trinity above (s transept floor).

BOWL BARROW, 50 yds NE of the Ridgeway and w of Hackpen
Hill. This fine barrow is 90 ft in diameter and 4 ft high. The
site was excavated in the C19, when an unaccompanied
primary cremation was found.

CHILTON

4080

ALL SAINTS. The blocked N doorway Norman, the s doorway
probably too. The chancel arch is of c.1200 (unmoulded,
pointed). So is the priest's doorway. The s arcade (in an odd
position) must be early C13. Big round pier, round abacus,
single-chamfered arches. The chancel of c.1300, see the E
window of the same type as those of the s chapel of Brightwell,
i.e. arches upon arches. Two N lancets with ogee-trefoiled
heads. w tower 1847. – STAINED GLASS. E window designed
by *J. F. Bentley* and made by *Westlake* (BC), 1873. – PLATE.
Chalice and Paten, late C17.

CHILTON FOLIAT

3070

CHILTON LODGE, w of Leverton. 1800 by *W. Pilkington*.
Monumental five-bay façade of ashlar, only one and a half
storeys high but generously spaced, with a giant Composite
portico to which a wide staircase leads up. Pediment over the
portico. The ground-floor windows l. and r. of the portico
are set under blank arches. On the E side a porte-cochère, on
the w side an attached wing, both said to be by *Sir Arthur
Blomfield*. STABLES of brick behind.

The rest of Chilton Foliat is in Wiltshire; *see The Buildings of
England: Wiltshire*, p. 151.

CHOLSEY

5080

ST MARY. Quite a major church. Cruciform, of flint and stone
and essentially Norman, with a chancel lengthened in the C13.

There must have been a similar church here already in the
C11; for the crossing tower has long-and-short quoins. They
may be Saxo-Norman overlap of course, and the crossing
piers are too much remodelled to make sure whether a Saxon
core is possible. Of the crossing arches, however, the capitals
of the W and E responds seem trustworthy up to a point, and
they are rather after than before the mid C12. Two have
decorated scallops, one of them with two little heads inserted.
Norman moreover two S transept windows and one N transept
window, one larger nave S window, and the S doorway with
one order of shafts and zigzag in the arch. The transepts
originally had apses to the E. The arch to one remains, the
outline of the other has been excavated. So it is likely that the
Norman chancel also ended in an apse, in which case the plan
would have been that of e.g. Norman Melbourne (Derby-
shire). That the chancel is a lengthening can be seen on the N
side, where the sill frieze breaks off at a certain point. On the
S side it runs all along. The S side has five lancets and the
priest's doorway with a continuous roll moulding. The E
window is of three lights, the middle one sharper and taller
than the others and with three uncusped, unfoiled circles
above – a typical motif of c.1275. Inside the lancets are shafted,
and they stand so close together that one shaft serves two of
them. The shafts have fillets. The E window shafts are
excessively long and have shaft-rings and leaf capitals. The
SEDILIA are simply stepped seats below the lancets. Of later
contributions it is enough to list the S transept S window of
the type with arches upon arches as its tracery, i.e. a type of c.1300,
and the N transept N window, which seems of about the same
date, but is of 1877–8. The top parts of the tower are Dec; the
pretty little doorway to the tower staircase is Perp. – BENCH
END. One, with poppy-head, in the chancel. – (DRESSER.
From Trautmannsdorf Castle near Merano in the Tyrol,
c.1700. In the vestry. – SCULPTURE. A Norman piece, probably from a scallop capital, in the N wall of the intermediate
chamber of the tower.) – TILES. A few under the E crossing
arch, more in the S transept. – PAINTING. Taking the Sacrament to a Sick Person at Traù. By *A. W. Rimington*. –
STAINED GLASS. By *Kempe* chancel S 1891, N 1900. – PLATE.
Cover Paten, 1577; Chalice and Cover Paten, 1646. – MONU-
MENTS. Defaced effigy of a Lady, early C14. – Brass to John
Mere, vicar, † 1471. A 14½ in. figure.
MANOR FARM. It is here that the materials were re-used of the

BARN which had been the largest anywhere and was de-36a
molished in 1815. Its length was 303 ft, and its height 51 ft.*
The roof was supported by square stone piers, about 35 ft
high, with chamfered angles. The outer walls were only 8 ft
high, i.e. the expanse of roof was tremendous. The date of
the barn is not certain, but the early C13 or even the late C12
seems likely – cf. e.g. the chamfered angles of piers of the late
C12 at Byland Abbey or the rounded angles of the piers of the
late C12 Canons' Barn at Wells.

(BREACH HOUSE. By *E. P. Warren*, 1905. In the William-and-
Mary style. Recessed centre with two-column veranda.
Hipped roof. *C.L.*, 1909)

FAIRMILE HOSPITAL (Psychiatric), ¾ m. W of Moulsford.
Built in 1867–70, designed by *C. H. Howell*. Red brick with
gables and a tower. Additions by *G. T. Hind*, 1898. The
George Schuster Hospital is by *Powell & Moya*, 1955–6: one-
storeyed and roughly cruciform; a good, clearly articulated
design.

CHURN DOWN *and* CHURN HILL *see*
BLEWBURY

CLEWER *see* WINDSOR, pp. 300, 304

COCK MARSH *see* COOKHAM

COLD ASH   5060

ST MARK. 1864–5 by *C. N. Beazley*. Nave with bellcote, chancel
with polygonal apse. Brick, with bands of stone and vitrified
brick. Lancets and late C13 tracery. – PULPIT. Of stone,
circular, with a broad band of severely geometricized flowers,
entirely in the style propagated by Henry Cole and his circle.
– Low metal SCREEN. – STAINED GLASS. E by *Clayton & Bell*
(BC). – Apse N and S by *Kempe* 1891.

CONVENT (Franciscan Missionaries of Mary). Red brick, with
a tower. The chapel by *W. C. Mangan* of Preston, 1934–6.

(THIRTEOVER HOUSE. By *Leonard Stokes*, 1898. A large,
handsome house, in Stokes's free neo-Tudor.)

COLESHILL   2090

ALL SAINTS. The church makes an odd group from outside,

---

* According to Professor Horn, the second largest is at Vaulerand in
France (*c.*233 ft), the second largest in England at Beaulieu in Hampshire
(224 ft).

and is odder and more confusing inside. There is what looks
like a Late Norman respond facing not E or W but N, and
what looks like half a respond facing as improbably. They
belong to the S arcade and represent a normal round pier and
a semicircular respond cut down (when?). Capitals with flat
leaves, and also some trumpet scallops. The arch is double-
chamfered and later. To the W of this bay is another completely muddled one. To this leads the E.E. S doorway, which
has a rounded trefoiled head. The N arcade on the other
hand is perfectly normal: three bays, round piers, round
abaci, double-chamfered arches – i.e. late C13. A half-bay has
been added on the W, showing that the W tower is a later
addition. It is indeed Perp; with W doorway (hood-mould on
angel busts), W window, bell-openings with Somerset tracery,
battlements, and eight pinnacles. A vault was planned inside.
Dec the S porch, higher than nave and chancel, and Dec
the S transept – see the two ogee-headed recesses in the S wall.
The N aisle has a pierced quatrefoil parapet. But what is one
to make of the large quatrefoil E window of the chancel? Is it
C17 or C18? – The STAINED GLASS in it was brought from
Angers. It is early C16. – BOX PEWS in the S transept. –
PLATE. Two silver-gilt Cups and Patens, inscribed 1776. –
MONUMENTS. Effigy of a Lady, early C16, holding a scroll?
(S transept). – Sir Henry Pratt † 1647 and wife. White and
black marble. Two effigies, she recumbent and below, he
semi-reclining, but also dead, a little above. – Viscountess
Folkestone † 1751, by *Rysbrack*. Two putti hold an oval
medallion with two profile portraits. The whole against the
usual obelisk. – Mark Stuart Pleydell, 1802 by *Coade & Seely*.
Tall, elaborate Gothic canopy.

COLESHILL HOUSE was gutted by fire in 1952 and subsequently
entirely pulled down. What remains is only four pairs of gatepiers eminently characteristic of the mid C17. The house was
in fact built *c.*1650–62. It was designed for Sir George Pratt
by his cousin *Roger Pratt* in consultation with *Inigo Jones*.
There are also drawings for Coleshill by *John Webb*. The consultation with Jones included the architecture as well as the
plaster ceilings. The house was the best Jonesian mid C17
house in England. It had nine bays and two storeys, and a
big hipped roof, a top balustrade, and a belvedere cupola.
High, square chimneystacks with far-projecting cornices stood
prominently and symmetrically on the roof. In the roof were
pedimented dormer windows, their pediments alternatingly

triangular and segmental. The staircase of Coleshill, completed in 1662, was one of the most beautiful in England. Two
arms rising in a spacious hall, first away from one another,
then parallel up to the landing. Balusters already with leaves
up the bulb at the foot. The string with thick fruit garlands.
Oval niches with busts in the walls. Typically Jonesian plaster
ceiling with strong beams with guilloche. In the panels
wreaths. More opulent were the plaster ceilings of the saloon
and the library.

The STABLES have projecting wings. Mullioned windows.
The cupola looks late C18. The DOVECOTE probably dates
from the time of the house and is circular.

STRATTENBOROUGH CASTLE FARM. An eye-catcher from
Coleshill, 1 m. distant to the s. Dated prominently 1792. It is
really a farm with barns, but the house was given a back
towards Coleshill with two sham tower fronts castellated and 51a
various big arrow-slits and large, unmoulded cross-windows.
It is of stone, but towards the top of brick, as though it were
a repair of a stone ruin, and the windows are blocked. One of
the barns has a stepped gable, the other an elaborately
bricked-up enormous sham window of five lights, partly
ruinous. Below this window is a genuine C11 tympanum. 13
What church does it come from? It has the lamb in a circle
in the middle and l. and r. wild tendrils in an unmistakable
Ringerike style, i.e. an C11 Danish-Viking style.

COLEY see READING, p. 207

COMBE   3060

A very isolated hamlet s of Walbury Hill, the highest elevation
of Berkshire.

ST SWITHIN. Nave and chancel. Timber bell-turret with N
and s aisles, almost as in Essex. The s doorway arch may be
of c.1200, the chancel of the early C13 – see the pointed
chancel arch with one slight chamfer and the N lancet windows.

COMBE MANOR FARM. C18. Irregular five-bay façade with the
intrusion of an older big chimneybreast. (Entrance hall with
a screen with semi-elliptical openings and pilasters. NBR) On
the garden wall a pretty C17 GAZEBO of brick, square, with
Ionic pilasters near the angles and a pyramid roof. Raised
window surrounds. The gazebo is dated 1667.

COMBE GIBBET, on the LONG BARROW on the ridge between 2
Walbury Hill and Inkpen Hill. Very high, and with a cross-

bar for two. The long barrow itself is Neolithic, nearly 200 ft long and 75 ft wide at its broader E end, where it stands 6½ ft high. The flanking quarry ditches are clearly visible and are 15 ft wide and 3 ft deep.

WALBURY CAMP, on Walbury Hill, at a height of 974 ft. This is the largest hillfort in the county, enclosing an area of 82 acres. The univallate defences enclose a roughly trapezoid area. The principal entrance, with inturned ramparts, is at the NW corner. The fort has not been excavated, although circular depressions in its interior suggest the former presence of huts.

COMPTON

ST MARY AND ST NICHOLAS. The W tower C13, see the S window with plate tracery and the flat, broad staircase projection. The other details Perp. The body of the church mostly of 1850. N aisle 1905 by *J. O. Scott* (BC). – REREDOS. Designed by *E. P. Warren*, 1893 (BC). Gothic, with Crucifixion in the centre and much better side panels with foliage, a chalice, and the Instruments of the Passion. – PULPIT. Of *c.*1700. With garlands at the angles – an attractive piece. – LITANY DESK. With three Netherlandish C16 panels, Crucifixion and two saints. – PLATE. Salver of 1754; Paten on foot of 1798; Jug of the late C18; Cup probably of 1804. – BRASS to Richard Pygott and wife, *c.*1500; 20 in. figures.

Much HOUSING for the Agricultural Research Station.

A cruck COTTAGE in the Wallingford Road.

PERBOROUGH CASTLE. An Iron Age hillfort on Cow Down. The site is roughly circular in plan, the defences enclosing an area of 15 acres. It has been considerably damaged by cultivation, which has almost completely obliterated the rampart on the S and SW. The best preserved section is on the N, where the bank, ditch, and counterscarp bank are clearly visible. The only contemporary entrance appears to be that on the N. The five large hollows in the fort's interior are probably marl pits.

The banks of CELTIC FIELDS are faintly visible in the interior and can be more easily seen NW of the fort, especially in the wood to the W of Cow Down Barn.

ROUND BARROW, on Compton Down, adjacent to Grim's Ditch, on the Blewbury–Compton boundary. The barrow is of bowl type, 90 ft in diameter and 7 ft high, surrounded by a clearly visible ditch 12 ft wide. A hollow in the centre suggests that it has been opened, although no record of this work survives.

COMPTON BEAUCHAMP

2080

St Swithun. Small, by the moat of the house. Built of chalk. Nave and chancel, transepts, and thin unbuttressed w tower with pyramid roof. The tower seems C13, see the low and narrow arch to the nave. C13 also the chancel, see the N lancet and the SEDILIA, just a stone bench with low arms. The E window is Dec with reticulated tracery. – FONT. Perp, plain, with quatrefoils. – PAINTING. The gay chancel painting with vine trails and, in the window jambs, palm fronds is not rustic Regency, but by *Lydia Lawrence*, c.1900. – STAINED GLASS. In the N transept E window fine early C14 Crucifixus. In the chancel E window equally fine Annunciation and a third figure. – PLATE. Cup of 1668/9; Paten of 1737. – MONUMENTS. Several major tablets, especially Rachel Richards † 1737 and Ann Richards † 1771. The inscription of Rachel's and the putto heads in the roundel of Ann's are admirable.*

RECTORY. 1849 by *H. E. Kendall*. Chalk and limestone with steep gables.

COMPTON HOUSE. The house dates from the early C16, about 1600, the later C17, and about 1710. It is the latter date which faces one as one approaches. A tall, three-bay, two-and-a-half-storey centre with giant Doric pilasters on a ground floor with banded rustication. Top balustrade, and lower, recessed two-bay wings. All this is stone-faced. Through the centre one enters an oblong courtyard and faces a late C17 stone front of four bays and two storeys with cross-windows and a pedimented doorway. The l. and r. sides of the courtyard are lower and older and have small mullioned windows. Outside, the E, W, and S sides of the house are all brick. In the E wall is just one early C16 window of two lights with uncusped arched lights. Fine S view towards the distant gates. N of the N range, at r. angles, are separate wings of the later C17 with wooden cross-windows.

---

* In addition to the above, Mr Samuel Gurney mentions to me in a letter the REREDOS, ROOD, COMMUNION RAIL, etc., all by *Martin Travers*, and a piece of SCULPTURE, a head of Christ in the S transept, said to come from the C6 church of St Sergius and St Bacchus at Constantinople.

COOKHAM

HOLY TRINITY. Flint, partly mixed with stone. Low, broad w
tower. Nave and aisles and chancel chapels. The nave is
Norman, as one N window shows. In the early C13 the short
N aisle and the N chapel were built – see their lancet windows
and the wide, low arch with nailhead to the chancel.* Also a
late C13 N doorway, blocked. Late in the C13 the s aisle and
s arcade were built, and also, it seems, the N arcade was remodelled. Octagonal piers, moulded capitals. The arches on
the s side double-chamfered, on the N side double-hollow-
chamfered. The s aisle windows with Y-tracery. C14 s chapel
with two tomb recesses. The oddly placed second doorway
in the s aisle should be noted. Late Perp the w tower with
higher stair-turret. C18 repairs to the N chapel in brick. The
roofs with tie-beams and kingposts. – STAINED GLASS. The
E window of c.1840. – TILES. Plenty of medieval tiles in the
chancel. – PLATE. Two Chalices and Patens of 1818. –
MONUMENTS. Brasses in the N chapel to John Babham † 1458
(14 in.), floor, to William Andrew † 1503, his wife, and her
second husband (16 in.), floor, to Richard Babham † 1527
and wife, kneeling (10 in.), N wall. – In the chancel on the N
side monument to Robert Peake † 1517 and wife. This is a
Purbeck marble monument with a canopy of three hanging
arches on twisted columns (cf. Bisham). Brasses 18 in. long
on the short tomb-chest. Pretty vault inside the canopy. – In
the s chapel Arthur Babham † 1561. Tablet with small
kneeling figures. – Sir Isaac Pocock, drowned in the Thames
1810. By *Flaxman*. White relief. His reclining body in a boat
held by his niece. The oarsman in shallow relief behind.
Beautifully executed, and with genuine feeling. – C. Ashwell
Boteler Pocock † 1887. Bronze tablet; Arts and Crafts. –
Fred Walker A.R.A., tablet with head by *H. H. Armstead*,
1877 (w wall).

The church lies close to the Thames. By the entrance to the
graveyard CHURCH GATE HOUSE, timber-framed. The river
is crossed by an iron BRIDGE of 1867. Shallow arch on iron
columns. Low parapet with pierced quatrefoils. s of the
church a good group of late C17 to early C18 houses, notably
WISTARIA COTTAGE with handsome carved modillions, its
neighbour EAST GATE with a door pediment on carved

* The VCH says that the Norman-looking jambs, as if of a former two-
bay arcade, are 'modern'.

brackets, and the finest, TARRY STONE HOUSE. This is chequer brick, of five bays with parapet. Doorway with seg-mental pediment. The window above flanked by pilasters and with a cut-brick pattern in the lintel. Opposite the house the TARRY STONE, a large sarsen stone. At the start of the HIGH STREET the STANLEY SPENCER GALLERY. *Stanley Spencer* was born and lived at Cookham. The High Street has kept its villagey scale well, even if shops have been made in most of the house fronts.

(FORMOSA PLACE. C18. Three storeys, five bays, the middle ones forming a broad, shallow, canted bay. Pointed windows with intersecting glazing-bars. NBR)

ROUND BARROWS, to the N, on Cock Marsh. A group of four bowl barrows, the largest of which is 90 ft in diameter and 7 ft high. Three of the barrows were excavated in the C19. Two yielded Early Bronze Age cremation burials and the third a Saxon inhumation accompanied by a shield and an urn.

ROBIN HOOD'S ARBOUR, see Maidenhead, p. 176.

COOKHAM DEAN   8080

ST JOHN BAPTIST. 1844 by *R. C. Carpenter*. Flint, humble. Nave, chancel, low s aisle, and bellcote. Early C14 style. The interior a pure white. – STAINED GLASS. In the chancel good glass of *c*.1860, i.e. consciously primitive but with odd ten-sions in the faces, almost like Toorop, i.e. perhaps influenced by Moxon's Tennyson. The date of death recorded is 1860. – In the N wall a *Kempe* window of 1893, still with much dark brown and dark red.

(THE COPPICE. By *T. H. Lyon*, 1904.)

COX GREEN see MAIDENHEAD

CRANBOURNE   9070

ST PETER. 1849 by *Benjamin Ferrey*. Flint, nave with bellcote and chancel. Dec style. The s chapel with red brick bands *c*.1866. This has plate tracery. Ferrey's chancel is remarkably ornate inside. – STAINED GLASS. A wide variety of designers and of quality. At the top of course the w window which is by *Morris* (Cana), *Ford Madox Brown* (Christ and a child), and *Webb* (ornament), and of 1862. Beautifully tender scenes. Also by *Morris*, probably himself, a one-light s chapel window of about 1861.* In a s aisle window *Kempe* glass as early as 1878. – The two-light window with St Peter and Cornelius is of 1896 and by *Selwyn Image*, executed by *Powell*. The Rev. B. Clarke adds to this two s nave windows by *Hardman*, the s chapel E window by *Clayton & Bell*, and the chapel w window by *O'Connor* (of 1865).

FERNHILL PARK, ⅜ m. E. Partly of c.1740, partly of c.1900.

CROWTHORNE

8060

ST JOHN BAPTIST. 1873 by *Blomfield*, the chancel added in 1888–9. Red brick and black brick bands. Steep bellcote over the nave E gable. Cross-gabled aisles. Geometrical tracery. Low, apsed w baptistery. Wide interior, also red and black brick. Unmoulded brick arches. – STAINED GLASS. E and SE windows 1894 and 1889.

BROADMOOR INSTITUTION. The original plan by Major-Gen. *Joshua Jebb*. The opening was in 1863. Brick, with small arched windows. The high walls go without saying.

ROAD RESEARCH LABORATORY, 1 m. N. Big and good new buildings by the *Ministry of Public Building and Works (J. Moss)*.

WELLINGTON COLLEGE, *see* p. 260.

CRUCHFIELD HOUSE *see* WINKFIELD

7080

CULHAM COURT
1¼ m. E of Remenham church

Built in 1770–1 for Robert Mitchell. The architect is unknown. Red brick, of five spaciously placed bays. Elegant proportions altogether. To the N and s the three centre bays project slightly and are pedimented. To the N a Venetian doorway, to the s a single doorway with pediment. Some pretty plaster-work inside, especially the ceiling of the drawing room to the N. Stone staircase with elegant, simple wrought-iron railing. (On the first floor a vaulted cross corridor.)

CUMNOR

4000

ST MICHAEL. The story starts on the s side of the nave, where there is part of a Norman corbel-frieze. At the same time or a little later the w tower was begun. It has a w doorway with one order of shafts and a round arch and an arch towards the nave with three orders of shafts, scallop capitals, and a pointed

* I owe these details to the ever helpful Mr A. C. Sewter.

arch with roll mouldings. That would take one to *c.*1200. The
bell-openings are indeed lancets with continuous thin roll
mouldings, two to each side. Inside the tower a splendid spiral
staircase, dated 1685, instead of the usual ladder. The chancel
belongs to the same time as the nave, see the one small
Norman N window (with a pointed rere-arch). On the s side
a later C13 window, on the E side a Dec one (reticulated
tracery). Dec N aisle, especially the doorway, Dec s transept.
Here again reticulated tracery, and also a window with a triangle top and lozenge shapes for the tracery (cf. North
Hinksey and Theale). One window of *c.*1300 in the s side of
the nave. Perp clerestory with a fleuron frieze. Wide nave.
The N arcade Early E.E. (circular piers, octagonal abaci,
arches with one chamfer and one hollow chamfer, hood-
moulds with heads and leaf paterae). Dec arch to the s transept. The two big tomb recesses in the s wall are cusped and
subcusped, but have no ogees, whereas the PISCINA has. Two
head corbels l. and r. of the E window. The chancel arch goes
with the arcade arches, and the short shafts of the responds
have in fact flat stiff-leaf on one capital, two rows of knob-
like leaf on the other. In the chancel traces of the window of
*c.*1200 which was replaced by the later C13 one. – PULPIT.
A Jacobean two-decker, the clerk's part specially roomy. –
STALLS. Good poppy-heads with heads, IHS, etc. – COM-
MUNION RAIL. With alternating twisted and fluted balusters;
Early Georgian. – Another(?) which is heavily Jacobean serves
as the chancel screen. – SCULPTURE. Statue of Queen Elizabeth I, said to have been erected by the Earl of Leicester in
the garden of Dean Court Cumnor, now rather unhappy in
the vestry part of the N aisle. – STAINED GLASS. Odd bits in
the N aisle. – W window by *Kempe*, 1889; E window by the
same, 1901. – PLATE. Silver-gilt Cup with chased ornament,
1571; Cover Paten, 1723; two Cups, 1808. – MONUMENT.
Anthony Forster, *c.*1572. Forster was supposed to have
murdered Amy Robsart who fell down the stairs of Cumnor
Place to her death. A Purbeck marble monument of the
familiar early C16 type, i.e. tomb-chest with much-cusped
quatrefoils, big canopy with a quatrefoiled frieze, and quatrefoil panelling inside the canopy. The brasses against the back
wall. But instead of buttresses, columns. Are they the contribution of 1572 to an older monument or Easter Sepulchre, or
is this a case of extreme traditionalism?

THE BEAR AND RAGGED STAFF, w of the church. The front

with symmetrically projecting gabled wings looks C17, but at the back a mullioned window with arched lights, i.e. a C16 form.

BRADLEY FARMHOUSE, $\frac{5}{8}$ m. SSE. Seven bays, two storeys, brick.

CURRIDGE
1¾ m. SE of Chieveley

SCHOOL, MASTER'S HOUSE, AND CHAPEL. One little brick group by *S. S. Teulon*, 1854–5.

CUSCOTE MANOR *see* EAST HAGBOURNE

DAVIS STREET *see* ST NICHOLAS HURST

DEDWORTH

ALL SAINTS. By *Bodley*, 1863. Plain, small brick church with a remarkably square and solid bellcote. Tracery of *c.*1300–30. Conventional s arcade. – STAINED GLASS. This is what makes a visit imperative for anyone walking around Windsor. The glass is by *Morris & Co.*, of 1863–87. The E window with Nativity by *Burne-Jones*, Crucifixion by *Rossetti* (made in 1861), and Resurrection by *Morris* himself. The s aisle middle window of 1873, St Anne by *F. M. Brown*, St Catherine by *Morris*. The first window from the E in the s aisle is of 1877, the N aisle middle window of 1881, and N aisle first from W and s aisle W of 1887. They are all by *Burne-Jones*. The Annunciation is specially lovely.

ST LEONARD'S HILL, 1 m. SW. The St Leonard's Hill estate has been broken up. It is now a gradually growing estate of prosperous houses in their gardens. One of the original mansions still stands: ST LEONARD'S of *c.* 1771 but almost entirely rebuilt in 1872 for Sir Francis Tress Barry. It looks rather 1840s, however, cemented and castellated. The other major mansion, of 1876 by *C. H. Howell*, is in ruins. It was extensive, Frenchy, with steep pavilion roofs and a square tower.

ST LEONARD'S DALE. A stuccoed Georgian house of only three bays and one and a half storeys. The side windows tripartite with a blank arch decorated fan-wise. The top centre window of lunette shape. Doorway with demi-columns.

DENCHWORTH

ST JAMES. Of dark rubble. With a NW tower, a N aisle further

E separated from the tower, and a S transept. Mostly Perp windows, one of them (chancel S) with tracery a little nicer than usual. Plain Late Norman S doorway. The interior reveals that the N aisle was originally C13 (see one respond) and the S transept Dec (see the arch with its continuous sunk-quadrant mouldings).* – PULPIT. Not Perp, but 1889. – PLATE. Chalice and Paten of 1587/8. – MONUMENTS. Brass to Oliver Hyde † 1516 and wife; 25 in. figures. – Brass to William Hyde † 1557 and wife and many children. They all kneel. – Five tablets to Geerings in the S transept, 1690 to C18.

MANOR HOUSE. Four-bay later C17 front (cross-windows), but one ground-floor window C15. Where does it come from? Early C18 shell-hood over the doorway. Near the house an oblong building known as the WOOL STORE. This is dated 1708, but still has mullioned and transomed windows. However, they are placed symmetrically l. and r. of the doorway. But, on the other hand, the doorway still has a Tudor head. The building has a hipped roof.

DENFORD   3060

HOLY TRINITY. By *J. B. Papworth*, 1830–4. Gothick. Demolished.

DENFORD HOUSE. Stone house of three bays, spaciously planned. On the entrance side the centre is recessed, and a semicircular porch is set in front of it, with paired Tuscan columns. On the S side there is a big central bow instead. Three-bay wings are added. They are dated 1839. The MHLG calls the house 1832 and by *Sir Jeffry Wyatville*. But Colvin mentions several items at Denford House as by *Papworth* and of 1827–8.

DIDCOT   5090

ALL SAINTS. In a W part of Didcot which has managed to remain villagey. The church is Dec, but much pulled about. Three-bay S arcade, Dec at least in the W respond and the second pier, though this looks as if it had been wrenched out of true into a diagonal position. One Dec S window with

* Mr Ferriday drew my attention to a 'gross attack' on *Street*, who restored the church in 1852. It came from the Rev. C. H. Tomlinson and was published in the *Building News* on 15 September 1876 and answered by Street on 20 October. Mr Tomlinson calls Street 'a certain young man from Oxford called Street'.

segmental head. The chancel is higher than the nave. Timber bell-turret with shingled spire. – STAINED GLASS. Some fragments in the w window. – MONUMENT. Excellent effigy of a mitred Abbot, probably Ralph de Dudecot † 1293/4. Purbeck marble.

ST PETER, in the New Town. 1890–8. No architect known, except for the tower, which is by *Waterhouse* (GS). The church itself with its broad lancets looks 1830 rather than 1890. – PULPIT. From Long Wittenham and originally perhaps from Exeter College, Oxford. Dated 1634 and unusual in design. No arabesques, just strapwork.

(A COTTAGE of cruck construction is near the church. Information from the Rev. J. W. Gann.)

DONNINGTON

CASTLE. Sir Richard de Abbesbury was granted licence to crenellate in 1386. The castle he built was oblong, with four round corner towers, two square towers intermediate on two sides, a mighty gatehouse on a third sticking far out, and the fourth projected beyond the two towers with canted sides as a half-hexagon. It seems as if, apart from the gatehouse, there have been only timber buildings. The gatehouse is of three storeys and has its own round towers, an archway with a broadly moulded four-centred arch, and inside a lierne-vault in two bays, the centre of each in the shape of four kites, cusped.

CASTLE HOUSE. The house is of brick and has an C18 front, but is older. The front in fact has two gables above the Georgian fenestration. Seven bays, two storeys. High, narrow doorway with pediment.

HOSPITAL. Built in 1602, restored and re-opened in 1822. Red brick, one-storeyed, round a courtyard with a covered way on wooden posts. Central porch to the street. Big, diamond-shaped chimneys.

DONNINGTON GROVE. The house, a little Gothic gem, was built before 1772 for James Pettit Andrews, F.S.A., author of a history of England, many archaeological papers, and An Appeal to the Humane on behalf of Climbing Boys. His architect was *John Chute* of the Vyne, friend of Horace Walpole. The house is of blue brick, only three by three bays, of three storeys, and castellated. The s front has a porch projection in the middle, rising the whole height and provided with a charming porch of bamboo-thin clusters of Gothic shafts, a

Chippendale–Gothic doorway, and an oriel window above of a complex shape. The windows have mullions, arched lights, and hood-moulds. To the E the centre is a broad canted bay window. The small entrance hall has a simple Gothic plaster vault, in full contrast to the surprisingly spacious staircase hall with an arcaded gallery right round the upper floor and a central lantern. The stair balustrade is of cast iron. (On the upper floor the principal s room has Gothic plasterwork round the tops of the chandeliers.) As a N attachment about 1785 a large drawing room was added, very chastely classical. In the grounds a three-arched BRIDGE across the stream which is dammed into a lake, and a Gothick FISHING LODGE. Brick STABLES with stepped gables.

Donnington village has become part of Newbury. DONNING-TON SQUARE for instance has consistently town houses. It is not a square, but a crescent, and it must initially date from about 1840. Semi-detached houses, some under one gable, one with two gables, also one with two towers of the Italian villa style and another with two towers and Jacobean trim. Interrupting this chronological, if not visual, unity is OLNEY LODGE by *W. Hunt*, the design for it shown at the Royal Academy in 1901. Red brick and tile-hanging, Tudor, but with a low, rather Baroque angle tower and Art Nouveau lettering, quite resourceful.

DOUAI ABBEY *see* WOOLHAMPTON

DOWN PLACE
1¾ m. SE of Bray

9070

The house has an L-shaped river front, both parts Georgian. The later is of nine bays and has as its feature a wide shallow bow with Greek Doric columns, i.e. early C19; the earlier, at r. angles, has two smaller bows, a doorway between, and a pretty staircase with carved tread-ends. To the l. of the later façade a quite incongruously added Gothic one-bay bit, with a tall pointed window and a fancy Dec canopy over it.

OAKLEY COURT, immediately SE, is an eerie experience at the time of writing. It is a Victorian Gothic mansion of 1859 in full decay, with ivy half-covering the porte-cochère and green-houses with broken panes.

At OAKLEY GREEN, 1 m. SE, the OLD MALTHOUSE, E of the Red Lion, is timber-framed with two gables whose barge-boards may be original (MHLG). The suggested date is C16.

4090

DRAYTON

St Peter. Perp w tower, unbuttressed. The chancel was re-built in 1872, but the windows are old. In the nave the masonry is old, but the windows are all renewed. S porch of 1879 by *E. Dolby* of Abingdon, a very nice job. In the chancel a simple doorway of about 1200 and at the E end a group of three stepped lancet lights with continuous roll mouldings. The S transept has lancet windows. Most windows of the church Perp. Perp also the N arcade. The piers of the four-shafts-and-four-hollows section. The arches four-centred. In the nave a PISCINA with dogtooth, i.e. C13 again. – PULPIT. Jacobean, with arabesque. – (BENCH ENDS. Those on the S side of the nave are mostly original.) – SCULPTURE. Six panels of an alabaster altar of the familiar type and all of the familiar iconography; C15. – STAINED GLASS. The E and W windows designed by *J. F. Bentley* and made by *Westlake* in 1872. – In the N aisle Ascension designed by *Bell* and made by *Powell*. – PLATE. Salver of 1727.

In the HIGH STREET quite a number of enjoyable houses, ending with the MANOR HOUSE. This consists of two parts, both Georgian, the higher r. one of three bays, blue and red brick, with a doorway with Corinthian pilasters and a seg-mental pediment, the l. one of red brick with pilaster strips and stone lintels to the windows. Good iron GATE and GATE-PIERS.

By the GREEN, at the junction of the Abingdon and Sutton Courtenay roads, the BAPTIST CHAPEL of 1834, with pointed doorway and pointed window, and GOTHIC HOUSE, with pointed windows and a lattice porch.

4000

DRY SANDFORD

St Helen. 1855 by *J. B. Clacy*. Nave and chancel and apse. Bellcote over the E end of the nave. Lancet windows. The interior quite dignified, with a rib-vault in the apse. – Stone PULPIT, accessible by an outer stair, and READER'S DESK.

Church Farmhouse, s of the church. Stone, five bays, two storeys, hipped roof.

Between this and the church a symmetrical imitation-Georgian house, well done, but the date 1959 is a surprise. (By *E. H. Vaux*.)

Plenty of Oxford housing.

EALING *see* BASILDON

EARLEY *see* READING

EASTBURY

3070

ST JAMES. 1851–3 by *Street*. Nave and N aisle under one big roof. Bellcote at the E end of the nave. N arcade with plain polygonal piers into which the arches die. The W window of the aisle is round and has three spherical triangles as tracery.

To the E former SCHOOL, by *Street*. Flint with brick quoins and bands and brick tympanum between the windows and their pointed arches. Half-hipped roof. Much Butterfield influence.

N of the church the brook with a little bridge, and on the other side a little square. On it the CROSS: patterned base and long shaft. To its W a house of blue headers and red dressings, and NW of that a similar one dated 1791.

At the SE end of the village PIGEONHOUSE FARMHOUSE. This has a date 1620, and to this may well belong the flint part of the house with the mullioned windows and also the large octagonal DOVECOTE (flint with brick quoins and pyramid roof) with 999 nesting holes.

At the NW end of the village MANOR FARMHOUSE, brick, early C17, with mullioned and transomed windows and a good chimneypiece inside, with caryatids.

EAST CHALLOW

3080

ST NICOLAS. The W front is of 1858, with the funny stunted tower of 1884. But behind this is a medieval church, with a C13 N arcade of three bays (low piers, square with four demi-columns, good moulded capitals, double-chamfered arches), a chancel arch of the same date, and an arch to a S chapel with a typical early C14 continuous moulding. – LECTERN. Dramatic eagle with a snake. Is it *c.*1850, and is it Continental? – STAINED GLASS. In N windows some C15 parts of figures.

EAST GARSTON

3070

ALL SAINTS. Outside the village. Basically Late Norman, see the crossing tower (cf. Lambourn) with its E and W windows, the S doorway with shafts with trumpet scallops or stiff-leaf and a deeply moulded arch including a keeled roll, and the blocked N doorway with a slight chamfer. The transepts have

Norman masonry too. The N chapel is Dec, as the continuous mouldings to the chancel show, and also the eminently curious E window of three steeply stepped lights and huge over-cusped pointed trefoils above the lower ones. The arch to the S transept is Dec also. The chancel is of 1875 (*J. W. Hugall* according to BC). The S arcade looks *c.*1900 but is in fact of 1882 (by *Ewan Christian*; BC). Not one of the crossing arches is original. – PILLAR PISCINA. Norman, *ex situ.* – PULPIT. Jacobean. A part of the back board in the vestry. – REREDOS. In the N chapel, with paintings probably by *Westlake* (*see* below). – PAINTING. On the nave E wall Tree of Jesse, by *Westlake*, said to be copied from a church at Florence. Reredos and wall painting both very creditable. – PLATE. Cup and Cover, 1576; Cup, 1675.

MANOR FARMHOUSE. Close to, and parallel with, the church. Seven bays, two storeys, brick, with a hipped roof.

EAST GINGE *see* WEST HENDRED

EAST HAGBOURNE

ST ANDREW. Early C13 S arcade of three bays. Round piers, octagonal abaci, one-step pointed arches. Bases with spurs. The S chapel is of two bays and probably just a little later. Pier with coarse and heavy stiff-leaf, double-chamfered arches. C13 chancel windows, though the five-light E window and the clerestory are Perp. Chancel arch on big head corbels, one a *triciput*. Then the N arcade and N chapel arcade. The N chapel can be dated, as there are brass inscriptions to the woman 'qui fieri fecit istam capellam' and to her husband as 'fundator istius Ile', and they died in 1403 and 1414. That is eminently interesting, as the chapel is entirely Dec – see e.g. the reticulated tracery of the E window. The tower arch also is Dec, though the ashlar-faced tower appears all Perp from outside. Charming bell-canopy on top. Perp also the walls of S chapel and S aisle. Nice gargoyles, etc. Low-pitched nave and chancel roofs with tie-beams. C17 S chapel roof with pendants. – FONT. Octagonal, Perp, nothing special. – PULPIT. A little of Perp woodwork. – STAINED GLASS. Excellent, small early C14 Nativity and Virgin in a N window; much red and blue. Also fragments in the N chapel E window. – PLATE. Cup and Paten, 1664; Flagon, 1736; Cup, 1738.

Delightful group of timber-framed houses NE of the church round the village CROSS. The shaft has on one side two niches.

Much timber-framing in the main street as well, and also No. 7, partly timber-framed, partly Georgian blue and red brick. At the end of the main street, where it meets the B-road, another CROSS, mostly C19, and close to it GRANGE COTTAGE of five bays, brick, with wooden cross windows.*

CUSCOTE MANOR, ¾ m. w. Timber-framed, C17, with fretwork bargeboards and one tripartite, typical later C17 window. The wider middle-light is arched below the straight top of the window, i.e. the so-called Ipswich motif.

EASTHAMPSTEAD see BRACKNELL

EAST HANNEY   4090

ST JAMES. 1856 by *Street*. Nave and chancel under one tile roof, though with a chancel arch inside. s porch at the w end. No visible bellcote. Goodhart-Rendel commented: 'Entirely different from the Puginist type of nave and chancel chapel.'

EAST HENDRED   4080

ST AUGUSTINE OF CANTERBURY. Perp w tower of ashlar with w doorway and four-light window. N aisle and N transept Dec. s aisle and s porch very Victorian, especially the porch entrance (1860–1 by *Woodyer*). But inside, the arcades of four bays are E.E. with piers carrying very thick, lush, and somewhat brobdingnagian stiff-leaf capitals. C14 chancel PISCINA with shelf and gable. The two-light opening into the organ chamber is of course Victorian. Perp s (Eyston) chapel. Two bays, thin piers with the four-shafts-four-hollows moulding. The chancel roof is boarded above the altar and has moulded rafters, purlins, and carved bosses.‡ – PULPIT. Jacobean, with strapwork, arabesques, and a knob-like head in the centre of each main panel. – SCREEN. To the s chapel, tall, of one-light divisions; good. – STALLS. With tracery from a screen dado. – CHEST. Now the N transept altar. Rich later C16 work with heads in roundels and caryatids. Is it Flemish? – LECTERN. What date can this be? The stem rises from a foot with a shoe stepping on three crocodiles. – STAINED GLASS. Bits in the s chapel. – PLATE. Large silver-gilt Cup, 1632; Paten, inscribed 1632; Flagon and Almsdish, 1783; all

* According to Mr D. R. Sherburn there is a cruck cottage at East Hagbourne.

‡ The Rev. F. G. Addenbrooke draws my attention to a *ceilure* or canopy of honour above the former rood.

London. – BRASS to Roger Eldysley † 1439, a 25 in. figure (N transept, floor).

ST MARY (R.C.). 1865 by *C. A. Buckler*. Nave, N aisle, and chancel. Turret in the corner of the nave and a S sacristy. Spirelet. Early C14 style with Kentish tracery. – STAINED GLASS. By *Hardman*. – Also one window in the English wood-engraving–Expressionism. – Next to the church a large brick PRESBYTERY and in it light-oak furniture and crockery said to come from *Pugin*'s house at Ramsgate.

JESUS CHAPEL, at the E end of the village. Oblong, of ashlar, Perp, with a Perp E window and a W doorway with segmental arch. The Priest's House, attached to the chapel, is timber-framed and assigned to the late C15.

On the way from the Jesus Chapel to the church a number of good timber-framed houses, in particular KING'S MANOR, with brick infilling and stone slate roof. Gateway and barns. Also THE STORES, with two symmetrical gables and brick-nogging.

HENDRED HOUSE, E of the church, has a C13 chapel. The date is determined by two lancet windows. The E window is Dec. Some foreign STAINED GLASS in the windows. The house itself must be late medieval, as the chimneypiece with a quatrefoil frieze in the hall is *in situ*. The façade does not give away a date. It is regular with two short projecting gabled wings, but the consistent hood-moulds look *c.*1840. The back regularized probably early in the C19.

ROUND BARROW, in Scutchamer Knob plantation, just S of the Ridgeway. This fine barrow still stands 11 ft high and is 120 ft in diameter. It is surrounded by a ditch 5–8 ft wide and 5 ft deep. In the lowest levels of this ditch were found sherds of Iron Age pottery. No trace of a burial was found during the excavations.

ROUND BARROW, on East Hendred Down, N of the Ridgeway. The barrow is 75 ft in diameter and $2\frac{1}{2}$ ft high. The site was excavated in 1934, when the bones of two horses were found overlying numerous sherds of Romano-British pottery. The barrow has no ditch, and was formed by scraping up the surrounding topsoil.

EAST ILSLEY

ST MARY. Dec W tower, N aisle of 1845, the rest C13. In the chancel dogtooth hood-mould of one lancet window and pointed trefoiled windows and a pointed cinquefoiled window with a circular one over (E). In the s aisle the w window of the same type, the E window with plate tracery, the arcade of three bays with round piers. Their abaci are odd and seem to have originally been square. Also the arches have only a slight chamfer. So while the rest is all later C13, this arcade is probably as early as c.1200. The N arcade is of 1845. In the chancel an AUMBRY with dogtooth. – FONT. Said to be Norman, but very doubtful. – PULPIT. Jacobean. With the usual blank arches and arabesques. – SETTLE. With Early Renaissance medallions containing heads and with caryatids. Probably assembled from odd dismembered parts. The piece reached the church only in 1963. – COMMUNION RAIL. Of c.1700, with alternating turned and twisted balusters. – PLATE. Cup of 1733; Almsdish and probably Flagon 1846. – BRASS to Katherine Hildeslea † 1606. Latinists should read the inscription.

EAST ILSLEY HALL. Quite a swagger Early Georgian house. Five bays, two storeys, blue and red brick. Segment-headed windows with aprons, panelled parapet, the centre part oval.

KENNET HOUSE, opposite. Probably a little earlier, say c.1700. Six bays, straight-headed windows. Shell-hood on carved brackets. Staircase with twisted balusters.

EAST LOCKINGE see LOCKINGE

EAST SHEFFORD see LITTLE SHEFFORD

EATON HASTINGS

2090

ST MICHAEL. There is no village to go with the church, which lies close to the Thames. Brown stone. Nave with bellcote and chancel. In the nave N wall an Early Norman window and the remains of the doorway, with a plain tympanum. The priest's doorway in the chancel looks c.1200. So does the chancel arch, with an abacus with saltire crosses still Norman, but a pointed arch with a slight chamfer. The s doorway to the nave has a rounded-trefoiled head, i.e. is C13. So are the chancel lancets and the SEDILIA, a recess with two shafts on heads and with big stiff-leaf capitals. The E window (three stepped pointed-trefoiled lights under a round arch) looks yet a little later. The s aisle has disappeared, but its arcade is preserved, late C13 too. Circular piers, double-chamfered arches dying into the imposts. – PULPIT. Jacobean. – STAINED GLASS. Small St Matthew and small Risen Christ by *Burne-Jones*, i.e. *Morris & Co.*, 1872–4. – PLATE. Elizabethan Cup; Bread Holder of 1717–18.

EDDINGTON
¾ m. NE of Hungerford

ST SAVIOUR. 1868 by *Sir Arthur Blomfield*. Nave and chancel; bellcote. Brick. Bar tracery.

EMMBROOK *see* WOKINGHAM

ENBORNE

ST MICHAEL. Nave and chancel, two cross-gabled N aisle bays, and a small timber bell-turret. The interior reveals that the church was originally Early Norman or Saxon and that aisles were provided as early as the mid C12. They are of two bays plus a W bay and were evidently (which is unusual) built N and S at the same time. Also the W bay, which follows beyond where the original W wall had been, must have been decided upon at once. Evidence is the identity of style throughout. Short round piers, square abaci, capitals with many scallops, many flutings, or stylized leaves. Bases with spurs. Arches with two slight chamfers. The chancel arch responds are contemporary too, though the arch is C19. E.E. chancel with lancet windows, shafted inside, and a DOUBLE PISCINA whose position shows that the Perp W wall runs further W than the E.E. E wall. Terrible S side, probably of 1893 (when the N transept was added), but re-set in it a single-chamfered Norman doorway and the head of a small Norman window. – FONT. Norman, tub-shaped. Narrow blank arches, and under them mysterious vertical objects of divers kinds. – One old plain BENCH (N aisle W). – PAINTING. In the chancel on the N side a beautiful Annunciation. Large figures. Early C14. – PLATE. Cup, 1663; Paten, 1679; Paten, 1801.

Nice farm buildings by the church.

ROUND BARROW CEMETERY, *see* Newbury, p. 185.

ENGLEFIELD

ST MARK. The church lies in the grounds of the house, surrounded by trees, the typical High Victorian estate church. It is by *Sir George Gilbert Scott* and was built in 1857. Scott used a good deal of the C13 church on the spot, dating from the time when the village was around it. E.E. the spacious S

aisle and s arcade. The E window is three stepped lancets
with continuous rolls, the w wall has a small doorway (re-set ?)
and an over-restored foiled window above. In the s wall the
main doorway with one order of shafts with moulded capitals
and a whole order of what can only be described as uncarved
beakheads, a surprisingly late occurrence of this motif. Inside,
the E windows have Purbeck marble shafts with rings and
leaf capitals. To the l. a beautiful image bracket with three
bands of E.E. decoration. The s lancets, two pairs of them,
are also shafted (not Purbeck) and have leaf capitals. The w
pair is largely C19, and it is altogether uncertain whether the
s aisle really went as far w as is supposed. The s arcade anyway stopped short of the present w bay, which is Victorian.
The rest is E.E., with circular piers with stiff-leaf capitals,
circular abaci, and well moulded arches. In the nave N wall a
re-set length of an E.E. arch. Scott's church has a N tower
with a stone broach spire and two tiers of lucarnes. It makes
the church stately, not regional, and eminently Victorian. –
PILLAR PISCINA (N chapel). Norman, with decorated base,
shaft, and top. – SCREEN (between N chapel and chancel). Of
one-light divisions. – PLATE. Cup and Cover, 1577; Paten
and Paten on foot, 1821. – MONUMENTS. In the s aisle in
recesses Knight with crossed legs, early C14, and Lady,
wholly re-cut, C14. – Also in the s aisle Mrs Benyon † 1777. 31a
By *Thomas Carter.** An excellent, surprisingly Berninesque
scene with the lady on the ground collapsing and women
attending to her. Big drapery behind. – Also two completely
unenriched yet perfect tablets: † 1789 and † 1805. – In the
chancel N wall Purbeck marble monument to Sir Thomas
Englefield, c.1500. Large tomb-chest with enriched quatrefoils. Canopy with pendants, cresting, and vaulting inside.
The brasses were on the E wall, not the tomb-chest lid. So
the monument probably served as an Easter Sepulchre. – On
the nave N wall Marquess of Winchester † 1675, a large tablet
of black and white marble, very simple, without any curly
decoration, and – strangely enough – without name or date.
Instead a poem and then in beautiful italics a passage from
Dryden. – Richard Benyon † 1854. Relief of the three Maries
at the Sepulchre in a Gothic surround. – In the N chapel:
Small alabaster tablet of 1605 to John Englefield, his wife and
son. One recumbent effigy, two kneeling ones below. Several

* Mr Gunnis, with his customary kindness, allowed me to publish this
attribution, which is based on a bill he has found in the Benyon papers.

obelisks. – Milburg Alpress † 1803. Small tablet with a very small kneeling woman and her sturdy little boy by an urn.

RECTORY. Near the church, also in the grounds, wholly on its own. Stone, Tudor, gabled. By *P. C. Hardwick*.

ENGLEFIELD HOUSE. 'Englefield House is a handsome Elizabethan structure, completely modernized inside and out', says the VCH. The paragraph on the house ends: 'The whole exterior now presents a not unpleasing example of the mid-Victorian Elizabethan style.' That clearly will not do. There is no mention of the date – 1886 – when a fire made rebuilding necessary, nor a mention of the architect responsible – *Richard Armstrong* of London. Nor is there a reference to the fact that when Dance painted the house in the late C18 and Constable in 1832, its front did not look materially different from what it looks like now, except that the front door is now closed and Victorian pinnacles stand against the sky. The s and w fronts look Elizabethan, but they cannot according to their style be of before 1559, and between 1559 and 1589 the owner, Sir Francis Englefield, was away from England as a Catholic, and the temporary occupants were hardly likely to rebuild. Then, in 1589, it went to the Earl of Essex, and after his execution in 1601 it remained with the Queen and then the King until 1611. Between 1611 and 1622 it was the Earl of Kelly's. From 1635 onwards it belonged to the Marquess of Winchester. When was it built, then? It does look Elizabethan rather than Jacobean, and so 1590–1600 is perhaps the most probable date. Three-storeyed stone façade with flint patternings. Central porch and two bay windows. The windows of ground floor and first floor with pediments. Round the corner on the w side another bay window, a slender four-storeyed porch tower, and another narrower bay window. The E front has the massive Victorian entrance tower with porte-cochère. This is ashlar-faced and replaces a tower apparently in brick like the w tower. To its r. C18 brickwork is exposed, and a big blocked archway. This represents the place where up to the Victorian time the main road passed the house.* In the corresponding part of the w front there is also C18 work, i.e. a ceiling and a chimneypiece.‡

* Mr W. J. Smith, the County Archivist, to whom I owe the information on the fire and the rebuilding, has few Bunyan papers for the mid century. But the new road was built in 1854, and Murray's *Handbook* in 1860 calls the mansion 'recently built' and briefly mentions the tower.

‡ *The Beauties of England and Wales* say that the house was modernized by Paulet Wright. He died in 1779.

Of the same time the ceiling of the large dining room in the E corner of the front. The principal rooms of the house are large and Victorian, notably the hall under the tower, running up through two storeys and open to a wide gallery or corridor on the ground as well as the first floor. Their decoration was not included in Armstrong's bill of 1886, which amounted to £2,556 17s. The LODGES in the road have the date 1862.

FAIRMILE HOSPITAL see CHOLSEY

FARINGDON

2090

ALL SAINTS. One of the richest churches of Berkshire. It is set across the top of the Market Place and against the trees of the grounds of Faringdon House. Nave and aisles, transepts with appendages, chancel and N chapel, and low crossing tower. The odd details of the tower are of 1645. The nave is Norman, as is at once shown by the clerestory windows, the corbel frieze of the N aisle, and the flat buttresses at the W end. The W doorway and the five-light W window of course Perp. Long early C13 chancel with lancet windows, in the E wall three, separated and slightly stepped. Also priest's doorway, still round-arched with one slight chamfer. The evidence of the transepts is complicated outside as well as in. The S transept with its W chapel is a Victorian job anyway (1853 by *Hugall*). The N transept is C13, but its W chapel is C14 (reticulated tracery of the N window), and the baptistery and vestry attachments W and E are again Victorian, though the baptistery doorway is a re-set Norman piece with a big crenellation frieze in the arch. The jambs with two odd flat lobed bands, each lobe hollowed in the middle. Very good Perp N aisle windows, just two, but each of six lights with a transom. Perp N chapel. Inside, the arcades which correspond to the clerestory windows turn out to be a little later than these would have made one expect. Round piers with elementary stiff-leaf capitals and octagonal abaci. Round arches with mouldings. The responds differ, the W responds being stiff-leaf corbels, the E responds one semicircular, the other flat. That looks c.1200. So the W buttresses probably belonged to the nave before it had aisles. Richly shafted crossing arches also of c.1200. The capitals mostly big upright stiff-leaf, but also still trumpet-scallops. Pointed arches. In the chancel SEDILIA with cinquefoiled pointed arches, buttress shafts, and pinnacles, dogtooth and coarse crocket leaves. The

PISCINA has a moulded-trefoiled arch, i.e. belongs to the date of the chancel, whereas the sedilia must be of the later C13. The arch from the N transept to the former N aisle with its billet frieze belongs to the time of the arcades, the arch to the N chapel is C15 (as is the arcade of the chapel towards the chancel: octagonal pier, double-chamfered arches), but the arch is set within a larger C13 arch. The details between transepts and W aisle of course Victorian. – FONT. Octagonal, with Perp tracery motifs of different patterns. – SOUTH DOOR. C13. Splendid, with agitated scroll-work, several parts ending in dragons' heads. – STAINED GLASS. In the S transept W chapel by *Wailes* (TK). – S transept E by *Kempe*, 1888. – PLATE. Salver, 1721; large Flagon, 1733; large Cup and Paten. – MONUMENTS. In the chancel: Brasses on the N wall to Thomas Faryndun † 1396 (13 in.), his wife Margaret † 1402 (13 in.), John Parker † 1485 and wife (25 in.), Katherine Pynchepole † 1443 (13 in.), John Sadler † 1505 (13 in.). – In the N chapel three standing monuments, described by Lord Torrington as 'lumbering marbles'. Jane Pye † 1706. By *Edward Stanton*. White marble and black columns, no effigy, putti on the open curly pediment. Top urn. – Anna Pye † 1729. Grey marble; no figures. – Henry Pye † 1749, their husband. Obelisk with portrait of his son in oval medallion. Vase below. – N transept: Sir Thomas Unton † 1533. Alabaster. Two effigies on a tomb-chest. Shields in wreaths in fields of colonnettes and shell arches, i.e. Early Renaissance. – Purbeck marble monument with the usual flat-bottomed canopy, with a trellis vault inside. Against the back wall kneeling brasses of Sir Alexander Unton † 1547 and wives. – Sir Edward Unton † 1583. Large tablet of alabaster and touch. Twin arches, no effigies, but small allegorical figures. – Sir Henry Unton † 1596. Alabaster and touch tablet. The life-size kneeling lady now detached from any monument belonged to this one. – Henry Purefoy † 1686. Standing monument with two weeping, naked putti. Cherubs' heads in flat relief above. Vase at the top. In the style of Gibbons.

FARINGDON HOUSE, N of the church, with a direct and perfect view towards it. Begun *c.*1780 and called by Lord Torrington in 1785 not yet finished. Five bays, two storeys, top balustrade, and hipped roof. Stone, stuccoed. The centre bay raised to two and a half storeys and framed by a giant arch. Broken pediment. Tuscan porch with niches l. and r. L. and r. of this front, pedimented doorways start quadrant walls. The garden side is different. Here a two-armed open staircase rises to a terrace which rests on five elliptical arches. Otherwise, except for three pediments – two windows and the doorway – there is no decoration. Fine entrance hall with a two-armed staircase which rises to a landing on three arches. Broad frieze at half-height. Elegant stucco work, especially the overmantel with an urn in the dining room. – ORANGERY of three glazed bays with a pediment. The arrangement in front with four splendid urns of *c.*1700 is recent.

Next to the church good GATEPIERS, apparently of the mid C17 (cf. Coleshill), and a three-bay Early Georgian house with segment-headed windows.

PERAMBULATION. On leaving the church one should first have a look at two houses along the churchyard in CHURCH STREET, one Early Georgian, of brown stone, two bays, with a raised pedimented centre and an arched window sticking up into the pediment, the other, called CHURCH FARM HOUSE, also Early Georgian, of five bays, with segment-headed windows and an ample shell-hood over the door. Then straight into the MARKET PLACE. It is L-shaped and has along its sides no houses of special interest, except the CROWN HOTEL, which, behind its Georgian front, hides a very pretty courtyard with an early C14 range and an open Jacobean staircase. This leads to the front rooms, one of which has a decorated plaster ceiling. In the BELL HOTEL opposite also minor plasterwork. On the w side of the hotel a mullioned window. But what makes the Market Place is the TOWN HALL in the middle, late C17, on Tuscan columns, with a hipped roof. From the Market Place E, through London Street to LONDON ROAD, and at its end SUDBURY HOUSE, handsome, colour-washed, with two symmetrical bows. From the Market Place w to a road fork at which the CORN EXCHANGE, 1863, in a funny debased Gothic with a totally unmonumental, asymmetrical front. The r. fork is GLOUCESTER STREET, with several C18 houses including OAKLEA, *c.*1700, of four bays with a hipped roof. Then along a l. turn, GRAVEL WALK, lies WESTBROOK HOUSE, Early Georgian. The doorway has alternating rustication, the first-floor windows are segment-headed except for the middle one, which is straight but has a moulded surround. (The house is said to have a date 1705 inside. MHLG) Just beyond the turn into Gravel Walk, in LECHLADE ROAD, i.e. the immediate continuation of Gloucester Street, the FRIENDS' MEETING HOUSE, early C18, small, with a big hipped roof.

WORKHOUSE (former), Ferndale Street. 1846 by *Foder* of London.

LORD BERNERS' FOLLY. 1935 by the *Duke of Wellington*. Brick tower, 140 ft high, with an arcaded look-out room and an octagonal top with battlements and pinnacles. It must be the last of the follies.

FARLEY HILL

ST JOHN EVANGELIST. 1890–2 by *G. Truefitt*. The tender was for £1,535 (GS). Red brick, roof reaching low down. Turret with spirelet at the SE corner of the nave. Wide nave, brick, with a wagon roof. It is a well-enclosing interior. Tripartite chancel arch.

FARLEY HALL. Built about 1730. Brick, still in the tradition of Queen Anne. A fine, spread-out composition culminating in the circular lantern with its diagonally set coupled columns. The centre of the house is of seven bays with a slight three-bay projection to the entrance, a very deep one to the garden. Straight-headed windows, panelled parapet. This centre is connected by three-bay links with lower four-bay pavilions The doorway to the entrance has fluted composite columns and an ornamental bolection frieze. To the garden there are Ionic columns instead. The entrance hall is the climax of the house. It is about square, and reaches up the whole height of the house. The cupola moreover is open. One looks up into its pilasters and windows. The ceiling round the cupola is painted with mythological scenes in the Veronese tradition by *Lanscroon*. They represent the Triumph of Cybele, Venus and Vulcan, Neptune and Amphitrite, and Jupiter and Juno. On the back wall at first-floor level five painted rural scenes put in much later. They are by *J. F. Nollekens*. On the other walls at the same level a wooden communication balcony. The doorways, two l., two r., are excellent on ground and first floors. On the ground floor they have Doric pilasters and pediments, on the first floor Ionic pilasters and no pediments. Good chimneypiece with a large central head. In the middle room towards the garden handsome doorways too. They are balanced in the opposite wall by two shell niches. Behind that blank wall lies the staircase, accessible from the entrance hall. It has column balusters and carved tread-ends. In the dining room garland decoration along the top of the walls and on the chimneypiece, again with a head. Splendid overmantel with a large urn in relief. The doorways have open scrolly

48b

pediments with shells in the middles. Stucco ceiling with a central painting of deities.

FARLEY CASTLE. Built in 1809–10 by *W. Fellows*. A brick castle with Gothick windows, brick hood-moulds, turrets, and battlements. Quite sizeable and asymmetrical in composition. To the NE a MONUMENT. Column with a sundial and the lead figure of Father Time. Dated 1723.

HALL'S FARMHOUSE, ¾ m. E. Brick, and originally of five bays. Between each ground-floor window and that above it a sunk panel. In addition brick quoins not only to the angles but l. and r. of every window – a motif which Sir John Summerson would no doubt list as Artisan Mannerism. When was the house built ? About 1675 ? Hipped roof. Later doorway.

FARNBOROUGH
4080

ALL SAINTS. Ashlar-faced Late Perp w tower. The church of flint. The nave is Norman, see the one N window and the simple N doorway. – C13 PILLAR PISCINA. – On the E wall two identical MONUMENTS, tablets of † 1668–83.

RECTORY. Grey vitrified bricks and red-brick dressings. Five bays, panelled parapet. Segment-headed windows. The house was built in 1749. The porch with set-in columns; the upper storey with a round-arched window and the top lantern are later, say *c.*1800.

FAWLEY *see* GREAT FAWLEY

FERNHAM
2090

ST JOHN. By *J. W. Hugall*, 1861 (GR). Nave with bellcote and chancel. Brown stone and stone-slated roof. E.E. details. – STAINED GLASS. E window († 1867) by *Wailes* (BC).

FINCHAMPSTEAD
7060

ST JAMES. The church has a wide view to the s over Hampshire. 1b Brick tower, built in 1720, yet still with the bricks laid in English bond. Arched bell-openings, square pinnacles. The body of the church is Norman. Two N windows are exposed inside, and the E end is an apse. Also there is a nicely decorated PILLAR PISCINA. Perp chancel arch and N windows. The small N doorway is Perp too, but dated 1590. The room into which it leads has a wide arch to the chancel, and that also could well be of 1590. – FONT. Norman, tub-shaped, with beaded diagonal bands. – PLATE. Silver-gilt Cup and Paten,

1591. – MONUMENTS. Elizabeth Blighe † 1635 and her little daughter. Small brass plate. Mrs Blighe is standing, holding the child by her hand and placing her other hand on a skull which lies on a column. – Richard Palmer † 1670. Tomb-chest with black marble lid.

EARTHWORK. The church stands on a rectangular platform enclosed by a bank in which the s and E walls of the churchyard stand. The site is unexcavated and cannot be precisely dated.

Near the church a gabled and enormous red brick house, looking like a rectory.

WEST COURT, 1¼ m. w. Late C17 brick house of seven bays with a hipped roof. Inside, the staircase with twisted balusters is preserved but re-used. Re-used also a Jacobean overmantel and Jacobean panelling with pilasters.

BANISTERS, 1¼ m. SW. 1683. Long, even brick façade with tiled roof. Two-storeyed porch. Horizontal (later) windows. Brick frieze below the eaves. The porch has brick pilasters below and an oriel above.

NEW HALL, 2 m. WSW. White, picturesque group of buildings by a ford.

1 m. E of Finchampstead is a ¾ m. long AVENUE of high red-woods.

4090
FRILFORD
1 m. NW of Marcham

Two big mid C19 stone villas, one with a pair of chalet gables, the other with a pair of Jacobean shaped gables. Why should they have been built here?

IRON AGE AND ROMAN SHRINES, see Garford.

PAGAN SAXON CEMETERY, on Frilford Heath, N of the river Ock. From the mid C19 large numbers of graves have been discovered in the area. Both urned cremations and inhumations are represented. The cemetery is a poor one, however, and grave goods few. They include small saucer and cruci-form brooches and iron knives.

5070
FRILSHAM

ST FRIDESWIDE. Mean brick w tower and less mean brick s porch, both said to be 1834. Genuine Norman N doorway with one order of shafts, scallop capitals, and a lintel with seg-mental underside. The s doorway plainest Norman. Two renewed Norman N windows, one belonging to the then nave, the other to the then chancel. Nave roof with tie-beams, collar-beams on arched braces, and wind-braces. – PULPIT. Simple, Jacobean. – READER'S DESK. Also simple, also Jacobean. – SOUTH DOOR. With minor early ironwork overlaid by minor battening. – PLATE. Chalice, flat semi-globular Bowl, and Cover Paten, only the latter inscribed 1712.

S of the church a pleasant, utilitarian MILL house.

FRILSHAM HOUSE, 1¼ m. ENE. By *S. Gambier Parry*, 1896. Neo-William-and-Mary, brick with brick quoins and a symmetrically gabled façade. The building is L-shaped, and the other arm of the L has a long irregular front.

FURZE HILL *see* LITTLE COXWELL

FYFIELD

4090

ST NICOLAS. Of about 1200 the N and W doorways. They have deeply moulded round arches, and the capitals of the shafts go from trumpet-scallop (N) to upright stiff-leaf (W). Dec chancel, the E window of four lights with reticulated tracery. The priest's doorway has a hood-mould on unrestored heads. Much was done to the church after a fire in 1893. That explains the S side and the octagonal part of the tower. But the comical S porch with its outsize pinnacles seems to be of 1867–8, by *J. C. Buckler* (BC). Perp N arcade with octagonal piers and an arch moulding not of a usual section. In the chancel an ornate Perp PISCINA and an ornate Perp pedestal, a CREDENCE TABLE, it is assumed. – MONUMENTS. Sir John Golafre † 1442. Effigy above, corpse below. A terrifying[26b] representation. – Lady Katherine Gordon, the White Rose of Scotland and widow of Perkin Warbeck, † 1527. Tomb-chest with elaborate decoration set in a high recess with straight canopy. But how much of this is original? Nearly all of it is of a composition material harder than stone, and probably dates from after the fire of 1893. Even the openwork spandrels and the scale are not convincing. – George Dale † 1625. With an incised bust. He points to a skull. – In the S transept parts of rescued late C17 to C18 tablets.

FYFIELD MANOR. A remarkable survival. A stone house of *c.*1320 complete with its hall, porch, and service wing. Only the solar wing is missing. The porch doorways have mouldings and decoration (ballflower) typical of the date. At the former high-table end of the hall, doorways of the same mouldings to the former chamber and the former staircase to the solar. In the opposite wall of the hall, i.e. in what was the screens passage, three doorways formerly to buttery, kitchen, and pantry. Above these, visible by its timber work from outside, a solar. Mighty tie-beams, queen-posts, cusped arched braces, and cusped wind-braces. Three bays. Above the porch a small wooden two-light window with one reticulation unit. Externally the evidence of the great hall is concealed by an Elizabethan front with three-light windows and three (or four) gables.

MANOR FARMHOUSE, by church and manor. Of *c*.1700. Five bays, two storeys, hipped roof. Doorway with straight hood on brackets.

WHITE HART. The chantry founded by Sir John Golafre († 1442; see above), with the priest's house attached. C15. The hall is the full height of the house and has a roof with collar-beams on arched braces and wind-braces. The priest's house has always been two-storeyed. It has its staircase at the back. The present dining room was the priest's study, the present public bar the kitchen.

1090

GARFORD

ST LUKE. Nave and chancel in one, plus a N aisle, and a timber bell-turret. There was apparently previously a C13 W tower. Some old windows are also re-used (e.g. lancets in the chancel), and the nice C13 S doorway with continuous roll mouldings. But mostly the church is by *Edwin Dolby* of Abingdon, 1880. – (SCREEN. C15 parts are incorporated. – HOURGLASS STAND. Wrought iron. VCH)

IRON AGE AND ROMAN SHRINES, in the field W of Noah's Ark Inn. The earliest structures revealed by excavation were a number of timber-built round huts, associated with Iron Age A pottery, and grain storage pits. Towards the end of the prehistoric period a small shrine or sacred enclosure was constructed. It consisted of a horseshoe-shaped ditch enclosing a double row of timber uprights beside one of which an iron ploughshare had been deliberately buried. In front of these posts was a square-cut pit containing the votive offerings of a miniature bronze sword and shield.

At the end of the C1 A.D. a Romano-Celtic temple was built on the village site, overlying one of the earlier Iron Age huts. The temple consisted of the usual square cella with sides 25 ft long enclosed within a portico 55 ft square. The site appears to have been venerated well into the C5.

Also in the C1 a second religious building was erected on

the site of the earlier Iron Age shrine 80 ft to the s. This was a stone-built, circular structure 36 ft in diameter. The precise nature of this building is uncertain, but in view of its position overlying the earlier shrine it may be regarded as religious in function and reflecting the continuity of worship on the site.

GOOSEY

3090

ALL SAINTS. At the sw end of a wide green with houses on both sides which are almost too small. Nave and chancel in one, roofed with stone slates. C19 bell-turret. The roof inside with tie-beams and kingposts with two-way struts. – STAINED GLASS. Some C15 work in a s window.

GRAZELEY

6060

HOLY TRINITY. 1850 by *Benjamin Ferrey*. Flint. Nave, chancel, bellcote, late C13 details. – (STAINED GLASS. E window by *O'Connor*.)

GREAT COXWELL

2090

ST GILES. At the end of the village. Nave of *c.*1200. The N wall has two small lancets. In the s wall a jolly lot of odd windows, the earliest early C14 (with cinquefoiled rere-arch). The chancel N side of the same date as the nave, though the chancel arch must be mid C13, the s window with bar tracery (a spherical triangle) later C13, and the E window (three stepped pointed-trefoiled lights under a round arch) late C13. Inside the E window two plain lancet niches. Do they go with the N side? A window like the E window also in the tower W wall, but the top of the tower is Perp; battlements and gargoyles. – PULPIT. Jacobean. – COMMUNION RAIL. Later C17, with flat balusters of dumb-bell outline. – NORTH DOOR with impressive, large-scale tracery. It might well be of *c.*1300. – STAINED GLASS. In the E window clear glass panes with engraved shields. 1792 by *Eginton*. – PLATE. Chalice inscribed 1680; Paten probably of the same date. – BRASS to William Morys, *c.*1500; 18 in. figures.

COURT FARMHOUSE. Late C17 stone farmhouse. Front of five bays, the ground-floor windows with stone crosses. Pitched roof. To the farmhouse belongs the magnificent BARN which *See* p. 359 William Morris (whose country-house was only a few miles away at Kelmscott) called 'as noble as a cathedral'. It is of stone and roofed with stone slates, and is 152½ ft long and 51 ft high. The date is C13. The buttresses are still shallow, also in their set-offs. Entrances by a transept and an archway opposite the transept. The archways are segment-headed and have two continuous chamfers. Posts divide the barn into nave and aisles. The collars and straight braces, transverse as well as longitudinal, are strong and serviceable and entirely utilitarian.

GREAT FAWLEY

3080

ST MARY. 1866 by *Street*. A serious, almost forbidding church with a beautiful view to the N over the Downs. Small, rock-faced stones. Nave and aisles, higher chancel. S tower with pyramid roof, apse. Later C13 window details, but in no way an imitation-late-C13 church. Three-bay arcades, low circular piers of dark marble. Vaulted chancel, the ribs on marble shafts, the windows also marble-shafted. Stone PULPIT and low stone SCREEN, both with the use of marble. – REREDOS with Crucifixion, by *Earp*, the mosaic work by *Salviati*. – STAINED GLASS. One excellent two-light window by *Morris*, especially fine the round Nativity in the tracery circle. Probably of c.1866.

SOUTH FAWLEY MANOR HOUSE. An imposing Jacobean house, built in 1614 by Sir Francis More. Front with two gables and a third a little recessed. Porch under one half of the second big gable. Two orders of pilasters, the upper exceedingly elongated. Round the l. corner one more gable, and then an embattled tower containing the staircase. Good, solid woodwork with heavy vertically symmetrical balusters. The staircase leads up through two storeys.

ROUND BARROWS, in a N–S line on the S spur of Woolley Down. All three sites were excavated some years ago, with inconclusive results. The N barrow produced an unaccompanied inhumation, but in the others no trace of interments was found. On the evidence of the pottery the excavators inferred that the barrows were constructed in the Iron Age.

GREAT SHEFFORD

3070

ST MARY. The only church in Berkshire with an original round tower. It is probably Norman.* In the chancel E wall remains of a former Norman triplet. The S doorway is Norman too, though it is pointed. Shafts with beast's-head capitals. Arch with zigzag at r. angles to the wall. So the arch was probably made pointed from being originally round. Perhaps it was done early in the C13, at the time of the nave N lancet

* The top stage of the tower is octagonal.

and the N doorway with its two slight chamfers, the tower
arch of three chamfers (the inner on small heads),* and the
lancet windows in the chancel. In the chancel also one window
of *c.*1300 (cusped intersected). – FONT. Norman, tub-shaped,
with four bands of foliage, one and two complementing each
other, three a running pattern, four individual symmetrical
figures. – REREDOS. 1912. Painted by *Byam Shaw*. – PLATE.
Paten of 1728; Cup of 1730; Flagon of 1815. – In the churchyard CROSS with, at the angles of its base, heads.
(MANOR FARMHOUSE. Probably C16. Angle buttress at the
NE corner. MHLG)

GREENHAM

4060

ST MARY. By *Woodyer*, 1875–6. Flint, lancet windows, an
arrow of a bellcote. Fine unified interior, especially the
chancel. This has at the E end five closely set lancets shafted,
a prettily painted roof, and painted and stencilled decoration
round the arch and on the walls. Stencilling also on the nave
and aisle walls. All this painting is of after 1888, the year
when a N aisle was added. The baptistery is of 1895 (BC). The
aisle and the baptistery piers are of marble. The work up to
1895 is all Woodyer's. – STAINED GLASS. The Tree of Jesse
is Netherlandish of 1618, but made to look C20 by setting the
figures in clear glass.

GREENHAM LODGE. By *Norman Shaw*, 1875. A fine view to
the N. Red brick, inspired evidently by Shaw House, but only
in making the façade symmetrical on the E-pattern. Norman
Shaw the motif of the twin enormous windows at the ends of
the short wings. Twice at each end four lights with four
transoms. The porch doorway moreover a typical Shaw piece,
white in a Baroque variety. Inside, the hall-screen, the
panelled staircase to its l., and the Great Hall to its r. deserve
attention. The hall is panelled high up, but there is still space
on the long wall for three oriels to look into it. The chimneypiece is something tremendous. The overmantel stretches
right up to the closely beamed ceiling with panels of gilt
leather. The whole of this overmantel stands on two columns.

GRIM'S BANK *see* ALDERMASTON

GRIMSBURY TOWER *see* HERMITAGE

---

* The transition from the square W end of the nave to the roundness of
the tower is by squinches.

GROVE

4090
ST JAMES. 1901 by *P. A. Robson* (GR). With an odd bellcote in an odd place. Derelict at the time of writing. – FONT. Of wood, said to have been used by Dr Pusey.

GROVE FARMHOUSE, ⅜ m. ESE. Dated 1684. Chequer brick, three bays, wooden cross-windows, doorway with bolection moulding.

(ORCHARD VIEW is a cruck cottage. NBR)

HAINES HILL *see* ST NICHOLAS HURST

HALFWAY HOUSE *see* KINTBURY

HALL PLACE
1½ m. SSE of Hurley

8080
Built *c.*1730–5 for William East, a wealthy London man. The architect is not known. The estate is entered from the E by a castellated LODGE with arrow slits of shapes typical of the Gothick of 1760 or so. A straight avenue takes one to the house, others go S and N, and one used to go E. At the end of the N avenue a lead STATUE of Diana on a high base. The house is of red brick and has its façade on the entrance side. Seven bays, basement and two and a half storeys, parapet. At the angles giant pilasters. One-storeyed three-bay links lead to five-bay wings projecting at r. angles. The drawing room is very splendid. Stucco ceiling and stucco wall panels, some with big intertwined dolphins, two with profile portraits in cartouches. They are no doubt the work of the Italian *stuccatori* who worked in such places as Ditchley and Sutton Scarsdale. There they are *Artari*, *Vassali*, and *Serena*. Door frames with Corinthian pilasters and pediment. Sumptuous chimneypiece. On the mantelshelf two big volutes. At the top, below a baldacchino with looped-up curtains, two putti holding a portrait medallion. In the anteroom to this room a more classical chimneypiece with two eagles on the top. In another room a chimneypiece the overmantel of which has a relief in an elaborate frame on which perch two eagles.

HALL'S FARMHOUSE *see* FARLEY HILL

HAMPSTEAD NORRIS

5070
ST MARY. Quite large. Short broad W tower with flatly projecting staircase. In spite of the Perp doorway, window, arch to the nave, and battlements surely an early tower. The nave

sw quoin even looks Saxon. s doorway of *c.*1200, simple,
with a billet hood-mould. The N doorway of the same time,
still simpler. E.E. chancel with lancets and in the E wall three
widely spaced lancets with continuous roll mouldings inside.
Nave roof of 1635 with collar-beams, arched braces, and
pendants. Chancel arch of 1879–80 (by *Arthur Baker*; BC). –
FONT. 1768. Of semi-globular shape. The stem and foot
meant to be Gothic. – SCULPTURE. Knight on horseback, the[15]
figure over 2 ft high. C13. He is charging; prancing horse. It is
an excellent piece of sculpture, but what can it have belonged
to? – PAINTING. Beautiful, if faded, large seated C13 figure
of the Virgin against an arch. – MONUMENTS. John James
† 1818. By *Westmacott*. Grecian and quite plain, but with an
inscription worth recording

> Could stone articulate, could earth declare,
> What noble virtues are recorded here
> The widowed voice might now be spared to raise
> Its feeble numbers, to an husband's praise.
> Yet how instructive is it to relate,
> The painful history of that husband's fate.
> A fate – that in its mournful progress told
> A lesson, equally, for young and old,
> So young, so gifted, and alas! so blest
> By fortune, nature; By the world carest.
> Struck in the opening of his brightest day
> To fatal malady, became a prey.
> Ah loved and more than my existence prized
> Heaven mark'd thee for its sweetest sacrifice
> Two lingering years, brought on the fatal hour
> And all the misery, fate had in its power.
> When to the world, and to his weeping wife
> A long farewell, announced departing life.
> Still with the tears the joyful accents fell
> From lips where truth was ever wont to dwell
> Dying he said 'See what devotion gives!
> I know, I feel, that my redeemer lives.'

– Lowlsey Family. In the churchyard. Square monument of
cast iron. Seven steps with inscription and an iron spire. Mid
C19. – CROSS in the churchyard. Base only, but with Perp
panelling.
MANOR HOUSE, to the E. Irregular, with one stepped gable.
Doorway with pilasters and pediment. Long, aisled, weather-
boarded BARN.
ROMAN VILLA, *see* Hermitage.

4060

HAMSTEAD MARSHALL

ST MARY. C18 W tower of brick. Plain Late Norman S doorway, C14 N aisle, the E and W windows round-arched, with Late Dec tracery. Perp N arcade of two bays. Wide depressed arches, the responds with broad shafts and broad hollows. Good restoration by *Sir Charles Nicholson*, 1929. – FONT COVER. Jacobean; openwork. – Two-decker PULPIT. Early C17. With tester. – BOX PEWS. – WEST GALLERY on columns of bottle-like entasis. – COMMUNION RAIL. Of *c.*1700. – PLATE. Cup and Paten given in 1622.

MANOR HOUSE. Built for the Earl of Craven by *Sir Balthasar Gerbier c.*1660, on the pattern, it is said, of Heidelberg Castle to please Elizabeth of Bohemia (and the Palatinate). Continued by *Winde*. Burnt in 1718. Kip's engraving of a solid block, eleven by eleven bays, three storeys high, with dormers, a hipped roof, and three belvedere cupolas, looks emphatically English of *c.*1660 and not a bit like Heidelberg. All that remains is a number of pathetic GATEPIERS, some on their own, some still attached to garden walls. Three pairs are of stone, one with balls on top, the other two with urns and pineapples. Gibbonsish garlands in small panels. The other pairs of brick and decidedly early C18. As for the earlier, it is interesting to note that, according to Mr Gunnis, *Thomas Strong*, one of Wren's masons, worked at the house in 1675.

42d
& e

42f

MOUNDS, in the park. These three large mounds are probably castle mounds rather than barrows.

MILL. Early C19. The house has a raised centre with chamfered corners, i.e. it is an elongated octagon.

HARE HATCH *see* WARGRAVE

HARTLEY COURT *see* SHINFIELD

4080

HARWELL

ST MATTHEW. *The Times* in 1962 reported that to the W of the present tower remains of a nave had been found. The walling showed herringbone laying, so that an C11 date is likely. At the same time a pewter CHALICE was found which dates from *c.*1200. It has a cambered lid with a raised cross whose arms are chalices and whose foot is stepped. It may have come from the tomb of the man to whom the plain N and S doorways are due, and the three-bay arcades with round piers, early, i.e. upright, stiff-leaf capitals, octagonal abaci, and single-chamfered arches and the transepts with lancet windows (N smaller than S) and arches corresponding to the arcade responds – elements all of *c.*1200. The W tower may have been begun at the same time, but the bell-openings have plate tracery of elementary motifs, and that is mid-century. There is an excellent Dec chancel, less so outside, as the five-light E window is over-restored, than inside. Here the chancel arch has two lively horizontal figures instead of capitals, and by the side of the priest's doorway sits a yet jollier little man with a bottle. Dec SEDILIA and PISCINA too.* – SCREEN. The shafts with shaft-rings probably early C14 like the chancel, but the top parts Perp. – COMMUNION RAIL. Of *c.*1700; twisted balusters. – CHANDELIER. Brass. Dated 1766. The centrepiece moulded, not a ball. – PLATE. Pewter Chalice, *see* above; two Chalices and Patens given in 1724.

GEERING ALMSHOUSES, on the main S–N road (the A-road). 1715. One-storeyed, brick, with a recessed centre with an arcade of three widely spaced arches and small segment-headed windows in the wings. The tops of the wings still have shaped gables. The centre of the recessed part is raised, with the parapet curving up to it.

The best house of Harwell is MIDDLE FARM. It has its C14 hall with embattled central truss, kingpost, and fourway struts, and a little pargetting of 1589, when a floor was put into the hall. The front and back doorways with the former screens passage also survive, and two of the doorways from this to the kitchen and offices. The service wing may represent a hall of the late C13. Also tie-beams, crownposts, and fourway struts. One barn has crucks. Several other good timber-framed farmhouses.‡

ATOMIC ENERGY RESEARCH ESTABLISHMENT, 1½ m. SW. It started in 1946 and now covers 441 acres, plus 93 of housing, playing fields, etc., plus 100 of research laboratories of other bodies. Two reactors, Dido and Pluto, and the improbable-looking Tandem Generator are the most prominent objects. Among the other buildings none is outstanding.

* Messrs J. M. Fletcher and P. S. Spokes draw attention to the original ROOFS, scissor-braced in the S transept, with crownposts and two collars in the nave, with octagonal crownposts in the chancel. Their dating is *c.*1220–40 for transept and nave, *c.*1305 for the chancel.

‡ Mr J. M. Fletcher of Harwell has listed the following CRUCK COTTAGES at Harwell and obtained provisional radiocarbon datings for them: in CHURCH LANE LE CARILLON, *c.*1425, and DELL COTTAGE, *c.*1445, in SENNINGS LANE SCHOOL HOUSE, *c.*1600.

HATFORD

3090

ST GEORGE. Norman N window, S doorway, chancel arch, and
   priest's doorway. The doorway has scallop capitals, one with
   a small head, and zigzag in the arch. The window has an
   inner roll moulding. The chancel arch has scallop capitals
   too, and a one-step arch. All this points to *c.*1130–50. The
   priest's doorway is late C12 (one slight continuous chamfer).
   Late C13 several other windows (chancel S, nave S, and
   especially chancel E: three stepped pointed-trefoiled lights
   under one arch). Also late C13 a tomb recess in the chancel N
   wall. The church is ruinous, and the W end has been converted
   into a MAUSOLEUM for the Rev. Samuel Paynter † 1893. Red
   granite sarcophagus, four grey granite columns carrying a W
   gallery. – PANELLING. Jacobean. On the E wall. – MONU-
   MENT. Defaced effigy of the late C13(?). His hands hold his
   heart.
HOLY TRINITY. 1873–4 by *W. Wigginton* at the expense of the
   rector. Small, with a SW porch tower. Walls of grey crazy
   paving. Nave and short chancel. Details late C13. – PLATE.
   Cup and Cover, 1581; Paten, inscribed 1640.
S of Holy Trinity a terrace of six cottages. Brown stone. Big slate
   roof with two tiers of irregularly arranged dormers. Said to
   be by *Street* (D. Cole).

HEATHLAND

8060

2 m. SSE of Wokingham

ST SEBASTIAN. 1864 by *Butterfield.* Nave and chancel in one.
   Red brick and blue brick diapering. Small bell-turret with
   Jacobean balusters. Timber S porch. N aisle on two plain
   wooden posts. – STAINED GLASS. W window by *Gibbs.*
The NINE MILE RIDE runs E–W from S of Easthampstead to
   S of Arborfield Garrison. It is a ride originally cut through
   Windsor Forest, and it does not seem to represent a prehistoric or Roman road. Still in 1928 the *Little Guide* called
   it 'remarkably lonely, as it hardly possesses a single house'.
   Now it is for long stretches lined with bungalows. Who
   allowed them in? The result is ribbon development at its
   most fatal and fatuous. The tourists' pleasure is spoiled by
   the bungalows, and the bungalow dwellers' by the tourists' cars.

HERMITAGE

5070

HOLY TRINITY. 1835, in the Norman style, i.e. long, round-headed windows and a Norman w porch. The chancel by *Maurice Hulbert* (BC) is enterprising for 1887, with brick dressings exposed inside. – FONT. Neo-Norman.

GRIMSBURY TOWER, ½ m. SE. Inside an earthwork stands an octagonal brick tower with battlements and a pyramid roof behind. The ground-floor windows are pointed, the upper ones have an odd shape of ogee curves leading to a moulded top.

ROMAN VILLA, in a field on Well House Farm, below the high ground of Cold Ash. The site was discovered during ploughing operations in the C19. No plans were made of the structures found, but they included a substantial building, 108 ft long, containing at least one mosaic pavement. The villa appears to have been destroyed by fire at the end of the C3.

HILLFOOT see BEENHAM

HINTON HOUSE see ST NICHOLAS HURST

HINTON WALDRIST 3090

ST MARGARET. Essentially later C13, though much re-done. The s transept s window (three stepped pointed-trefoiled lights under one arch) is typical of the late C13. In the rere-arch two little fluted corbels. The w tower is Dec. – PLATE. Cup of 1725; large Paten of 1809. – MONUMENT. John Loder † 1701. Good cartouche.

HINTON MANOR. Early C18 front of five bays and two storeys. Door-canopy on elegant brackets. The E side of the house has early C17 details, including two cross-windows. The house stands in a moat, and this and a MOTTE to the SW are supposed to belong to a motte-and-bailey castle.

EARTHWORK, in an oak copse on Windmill Hill. The site is rectangular in plan and is enclosed by a single bank and ditch with traces of a counterscarp bank in places. The area enclosed measures 270 ft by 60 ft. The site is unexcavated, but on the analogy of similar structures in the area may date to the C1.

HOLME GREEN see WOKINGHAM

HOLYPORT HOUSE see BRAY

HOP CASTLE see WINTERBOURNE

HUNGERFORD 3060

ST LAWRENCE. 1816 by *Pinch* of Bath. Large and uninspired.

Bath stone exterior with aisles and an apsed chancel. Many
9b clumsy pinnacles, especially big on the w tower. The windows
have intersecting tracery. The piers with their carved capitals
and the arches are of 1880–1. – FONT. Octagonal, Perp, with
quatrefoils. – STAINED GLASS. In the s aisle w window glass
of c.1816, typical, with its deep yellows.* – The E window by
Lavers & Westlake, 1887 (BC), and not an ornament. – MONU-
MENT. Defaced and footless Knight of c.1350 (N aisle E).

The VICARAGE is a C17 cottage with wooden mullioned and
transomed windows and later additions.

Visiting Hungerford from the Bath Road, one starts at the
corner of the BEAR HOTEL, low, white, with a Tuscan porch,
and RIVERSIDE, brick of c.1800, a cube of three storeys and
three bays with parapet and tripartite windows. Only the
WESLEYAN CHAPEL opposite the two on the N of the Bath
Road is somewhat painful: 1868–9 by *Willson & Wilcox* of
Bath. Pale blue and red brick, with a (ritually) sw turret and
heavy E.E. tracery. Then s across the Kennet, Nos 12–13
BRIDGE STREET, five bays and a pair of identical doorways,
with broken pediments. Across the canal and into the HIGH
STREET. The house on the l. is a delight, with an iron bridge
as access to the first floor and other decorative iron work. Bow
window to the canal. Opposite a timber-framed cottage. The
High Street is wide and nearly straight. The scale and
character are undisturbed, though shops of course have
invaded many of the ground floors. Specially pleasant No. 11
of four bays with alternating blocks of rustication for the
window surrounds, No. 16 of six bays with a hipped roof, and
the house opposite with a nice doorcase. Then the railway
bridge and to the r. to the Green, at the end of which stands
the church. Back, and then alas the TOWN HALL. This is of
1870, not detached, only three bays wide plus a tower bay, fussy
and with an undefinable cap on top of the tower. The ground
floor of the three bays is a loggia. Red brick and yellow terracotta.‡ To the l. down PARK STREET, to the HOSPITAL,
former WORKHOUSE, of 1840, still in a utilitarian sub-
classical style, with pedimental gable (no longer a real pediment), brick, fifteen bays long. Back to the High Street and
on the r. No. 27 with four gables, three large, one small

* The Rev. K. Tagg tells me that the glass until recently had the signature
of *W. Collins*, Wilkie Collins's father.
‡ Mr Angus Marshall, the Town Clerk, tells me that the architect was
Ernest Prestwick of Leigh in Lancashire.

(c 17 ?), No. 28 of five bays, blue and red brick, No. 107 opposite, also blue and red, but three widely spaced bays. The
windows have blank segmental arches with free motifs. The
CONGREGATIONAL CHURCH is of 1840, stuccoed, with
giant pilasters and no pediment. No. 33 is the most ambitious
house: five bays, blue headers and red dressings, and four
(not original) gables. No. 34 has two minimum Venetian
windows on the ground floor – and that is the end.

THE YEWS, New Town. Early c 18, blue brick and red dressings.
Segment-headed windows.

STANDEN MANOR, 1¾ m. SSW. Early c 18. Blue headers and
red dressings. Six-bay front with the end pairs of bays somewhat projecting. Parapet, hipped roof, segment-headed
windows, widely spaced. On the side a big bow has later been
inserted.

NORTH STANDEN FARM. The c 13 chapel has been demolished.

HURLEY

8080

HURLEY PRIORY was founded before 1087 as a Benedictine
house. What remains of it is the nave of the church, now the
parish church (see below), and the refectory range to its N.
The latter is part of an inhabited house now and has to its S,
i.e. towards the cloister, two Norman-looking doorways not
regarded as medieval by the VCH, and small pointed-trefoil-
headed windows over, and to the N the remains of three large
early c 14 windows. Excavations have shown that the church
initially had a long aisleless chancel and an apse, was lengthened in the c 13 and given a straight E end and a straight-
ended N aisle, and lengthened again in the c 14, when it got
new chapels. Beneath the crossing interesting evidence of the
Saxon predecessor of the church was found. It seems to
represent a crossing and two turrets or towers to its immediate
E. The E range of the cloister was found in a c 13 state, with
the chapter house oblong, its doorway enriched by colonnettes.
The dormitory above it stretched as usual a good deal further
N than the N wall of the refectory. E and SE of the chancel
remains of Ladye Place, a Tudor mansion, were found,
including a crypt of two naves and four bays below a wing
projecting W from near the S end. This has been regarded as
the infirmary undercroft. To the W of the church are a round
DOVECOTE and a BARN, both assigned to the c 14.

ST MARY is no more than the oddly long and narrow nave of
the priory church. The proportions are decidedly Anglo-Saxon.

The windows of the church are Norman (except for one large Dec s window), and so are the doorways, except that that to the w is partly and that to the e entirely of *Hakewill*'s restoration of 1852. Hakewill also did the neo-Norman stone SCREEN separating the altar space from an e vestry. – FONT. C15, with coarse blank panelling. – BENCH. Just one old one with poppy-heads. – PAINTINGS. Moses and Aaron from the reredos; C18 (by the w door). – PLATE. Cup of 1655 with Cover of 1635; Paten on foot of 1693; and Flagon of 1695. – MONUMENTS. John Lovelace of Ladye Place † 1558 and his wife † 1579. A typical Early Elizabethan monument, i.e. with columns and no figures. Superstructure with arms and two eagles as finials. – Richard Lovelace † 1602 and his son Sir Richard. Upper parts of the figures only. From a lost monument (vestry). – Viscountess Ashbrook † 1810. By *Flaxman*. Tablet with two kneeling putti. – Lt-Commander Hipolyto J. Da Costa † 1823. By *Theophilus Clifford* of Marlow. White and black marble tablet; large.

HOUSE, 250 yds s. By *Hartry, Grover & Halter*, 1963–4. Small and architecturally convincing.

HURST *see* ST NICHOLAS HURST

2080

IDSTONE
¾ m. sw of Ashbury

A hamlet of chalk, Sarsen, and brick. Specially rewarding the Rectory Farmhouse and the Parsonage Farmhouse. At the entry to the hamlet from the B-road a later C17 three-bay house, formerly the TRIP THE DAISEY INN, with a recent relief showing a hound doing just this. Symmetrically placed mullioned windows.

THE THREE BARROWS, s of Old Ditch, on Idstone Down. These three bowl barrows all measure approximately 50 ft in diameter and 5 ft in height. The central and western examples have depressions in their centres, although there is no surviving record of their excavation.

INHOLMES *see* WOODLANDS ST MARY

3060

INKPEN

ST MICHAEL. Nave and chancel in one; tile-hung bell-turret. Plain C13 s doorway, the hood-mould on two defaced heads. Traces of a large s window. Interesting restoration and remodelling by *Clayton Crabbe Rolfe* of Oxford, 1896, i.e. the s porch, the charming Arts-and-Crafts Gothic s window with its partially flying rere-arch, and the N arcade with the lozenge-shaped piers and continuous mouldings. The nave must have been much widened, as the timber posts of the bell-turret now stand free. – PLATE. Set of 1758. – Silver-gilt Chalice and Paten, given in 1903; designed by *Bodley*. – MONUMENTS. Effigy of a Knight, the legs lost. Defaced, but it looks late C13. – Tablets of *c*.1738 and *c*.1763.

OLD RECTORY. Built about 1695. Seven bays, but in a typical *c*.1700-way the windows next the centre are much slimmer than the others. Hipped roof with dormers with triangular and segmental pediments. Sashed windows, but at the back still some of the original wooden mullion and transom crosses. Entrance hall with two arches on a Roman Doric column and the staircase behind.

WEST COURT HOUSE, ¼ m. NE. Red brick. The N part with the porch early C18, the s part later C18.

SCHOOL, 1 m. NE. By *Street*, discussed in *The Ecclesiologist*[58a] in 1850 and indeed most remarkable for that date. Brick, tile-hung gables and tile-hung blank pointed arches above windows. It is all so informal and domestic and un-High-Victorian that it seems an immediate preparation for Shaw.

KIRBY HOUSE, 1¼ m. ESE. Fine entrance side of 1733. Five bays, two storeys, segment-headed windows. Parapet and pedimental gable with an arched window. Brick. Blue headers and red dressings. Raised brick quoins. The doorway must be recent, but there is a splendid doorcase round the corner which was perhaps originally here. Columns and carved brackets for the hood. The house of 1733 here borders on a higher addition of 1761. This also has a five-bay façade, but all is more widely spaced. The staircase is of 1733 and has turned balusters and carved tread-ends.

LONG BARROW, Gallows Hill, *see* Combe.

KENNINGTON

ST SWITHUN. Cruciform, of yellow brick, free neo-Georgian. By *Lawrence Dale* and the Vicar, the Rev. *S. S. Davies*, 1956–8. Central altar inside.

The old church stands to the l. of the new. It is in the Norman style, of 1828, by *Daniel Robertson*, an early date for neo-Norman. It is a plain rectangle without separate chancel, but with a Norman bellcote. Plain long windows. The w doorway is startlingly well imitated, even to a capital with a little Sagittarius.* Two orders of columns. Roll mouldings.

(MANOR HOUSE. Dated 1629 on a beam. Stone ground floor with C 16 two- to four-light windows with round-arched lights. Timber-framed upper floor, also of 1629, with Late Georgian windows. In two back rooms fine plaster ceilings, vine, pomegranate, strapwork, and arabesque.)

KILN GREEN see WARGRAVE

4090
KINGSTON BAGPUIZE

ST JOHN BAPTIST. 1799–1800 by *John Fidel* of Faringdon, but apsed and internally altered by *E. Dolby* in 1882. W doorway with inset Tuscan columns and above atrocious little Dolby-Norman windows. Pediment. Pretty cupola with wooden columns. The side windows and E window set in large blank arches. – PLATE. Paten, 1724/5; Cup, Paten, and Flagon 1727/8. – MONUMENTS. Edmund Fettiplace † 1710. Inscription below canopy with two putto-heads and two urns. – John Blandy and wife, 1762. Obelisk with two oval portrait medallions.

KINGSTON HOUSE. The date must be about 1720. Tall brick house. Seven-bay centre with raised pedimented three-bay centre. Lower wings. Quoins. Vases on top. The ground-floor windows all arched, the upper ones segment-headed. Doorway with rusticated surround in which the flanking pilasters partly disappear (cf. Radley House). It is a Lutyens effect, two hundred years ahead of its time. Triglyph frieze. The window above with curves widening down towards the sill. The entrance side (former back) is identical, but has a simpler doorway. The side elevation is of four bays with a four-bay pediment. The original entrance hall has two discreetly decorated stone chimneypieces. Behind it the staircase (now entrance) hall. The wooden staircase rises in two arms (as it used to do at Coleshill) and reaches an upper balcony or gallery in the middle of which is a spacious shell niche. Pretty turned balusters with fluted bulbs near the foot (also as at Coleshill). In one room a beautiful Rococo chimneypiece. – In the garden a SUMMERHOUSE of chequer brickwork with a lower storey, which has a shallow brick dome. The back faces a terrace, and to that side the upper floor is ground floor. It

* I hear from the Rev. S. S. Davies that this is a rebus of the name of the builder: Bowyer.

has a few steps leading to a doorway and l. and r. not apses but halved apses – a very curious motif. – Very good iron GATES.

STONE HOUSE, in the Faringdon road. Of *c*.1700. L-shaped, the main part of five bays with stone mullion-and-transom-cross windows.

RECTORY, ½ m. s. Built in 1723. Five bays, two storeys. The middle bay stressed by alternating rusticated giant pilasters. Porch with rocky grotto rustication similar to that of *c*.1750 at Pusey House. Mr Colvin has recently found that the house was designed by *Dr Clarke* of Oxford.

BRIDGE, 2 m. N. Six semicircular approach arches and then six pointed medieval arches, the middle one widest, and with ribs and traces of ribs.

KINGSTON LISLE

ST JOHN BAPTIST. Small, with a timber bell-turret with spire-let. Norman chancel, see one N window. Nave of *c*.1200, see the N doorway and buttressing. The chancel E window is Dec (reticulated tracery) and has inside niches l. and r. C17 nave roof with tie-beams and pendants. – PULPIT. Later C17 with tester. – BENCHES. The ends straight-topped with tracery and arms, Instruments of the Passion, etc. – SCREEN. Jacobean; simple. – PANELLING. Chancel E wall, Jacobean. – NORTH DOOR. With splendid iron hinge-work of *c*.1200. – PAINTING. Large figures of St Peter and St Paul in the jambs of the E window. In the head of the Norman window roundel with head of Christ. On the N wall Herod's Feast and Be-heading of St John. All these are C14. – STAINED GLASS. Chancel s. A little with a head. – PLATE. Chalice and Cover, 1576; Paten, 1640.

KINGSTON LISLE HOUSE. The architectural history of the house, the interior of which is most ingenious and dramatic, is oddly obscure. The only fact known is that the house appears on a trade-card of *c*.1830. This is the card of a builder of Lechlade, *Richard Pace*. Mr Colvin reports that wings etc. were added in 1812. That is all. The centre of the house has seven bays with arched windows and attic windows over. Three-bay pediment, former doorway with Gibbs surround and stone bands and keystones. That is mid Georgian, and so is the modestly Rococo plasterwork of the former entrance hall. The garden side instead looks early C19, with three bays of widely spaced tripartite windows and a broad doorway with Greek Doric columns. Of the wings one has a big bow and contains the billiard room, the other has the present entrance at its end. This leads to a monumental passage with coffered tunnel-vault. At the far end of this are two windows, very high up, because the conservatory used to be here. One of the windows is in front, the other on the l. Facing the latter is the entrance to the centre of the house, and here a very large, functionally quite unnecessary procession of rooms has been created to continue at r. angles what the entrance hall had begun. The first part has a vault with fans in the corners, the second has sculpture placed boldly on the cornice, the third has an oblong groin-vault, and the last a half-vault with fans. In the latter two parts of the composition the staircase rises. Two flights of it are flying, and the balustrade is of wrought iron with s-scrolls. The staircase arrangement is such that it can connect the most unexpected levels. It is not known who designed this fascinating procession of spaces and could convince the client of such a waste of space. Messrs Betjeman and Piper suggest *Basevi* or *Cockerell*. The most likely date is c.1825–30.

ROUND BARROW, N of Kingston Lisle and E of Fawler. Large round barrow, 75 ft in diameter and 7 ft high. The mound is now covered by trees.

KINTBURY

ST MARY. Not a small church. Nave, transepts, chancel, w tower. The restoration of 1859 has made the church virtually Victorian. Norman s doorway with zigzag arch, what little is original of it. C13 w tower, broad, with clasping buttresses. One-light bell-openings. Tower arch to the nave with nook-shafts carrying stiff-leaf capitals. Later C13 N transept, though the arch looks early C13 (one slight chamfer). However, the N window has intersecting tracery. The s transept is of brick, was built in 1713, but is thoroughly victorianized. – PLATE. Flagon of 1683; Almsdish of 1688. – MONUMENTS. Jonathan Raymond † 1711. Not easily seen. Two busts and an urn on a pedestal between. – This motif was then taken up by *Peter Scheemakers* and *Thomas Scheemakers* who made the monuments to Sir Jemmet Raymond † 1754 and Jemmet Raymond † 1767 respectively. The former also has two busts and a raised urn between, the latter has on the pedestal the bust of the husband, and the busts below are of two wives. – Brass to John Gunter † 1624 and wife. She has her hat on.

WALLINGTONS, 1⅛ m. SW. Early C17, but far too drastically restored in 1892. Front with two gabled wings. Four gables on the side elevation. Mullioned and transomed windows.

BARTON COURT, ⅝ m. NNW. 1772. Chequer brick, of two and a half storeys. Five-bay front, the centre window Venetian.

LODGES of Kintbury House, 1 m. N, on the Bath Road. Gothic, one-storeyed, white and pretty, but not half as pretty as

HALFWAY HOUSE, the favourite of all travellers on the Bath 5ıb Road. It is a late C18 toll-house on the turnpike and looks exactly like a Staffordshire piece. A square with four corner towers, castellated, with round-arched and pointed-arched windows.

KIRBY HOUSE see INKPEN

KNOWL HILL 8o7o

ST PETER. 1840, with a flint chancel by *W. Scott Champion* of 1870. The old part is by *J. C. & G. Buckler*, of brick, with lancet windows and a hexagonal bell-turret with spirelet standing on a shallow projection. – STAINED GLASS. Three saints by *Hardman* from St Michael Oxford, as restored by *Street* in 1854.* – MONUMENT. Jane E. Smith † 1852. By *William Theed*, 1854. Small white standing figure.

LAMBOURN 3o7o

ST MICHAEL. A large and interesting church with a prominent crossing tower. Late Norman from the W end to the crossing, i.e.: W wall with doorway, two orders of shafts, one with shaft-rings, arch with two zigzags meeting to form three-dimensional lozenges, hood-mould on beasts' heads. Remains of the window above with a continuous roll moulding. Circular window in the gable. Then the aisle W windows and the lower parts of the crossing tower. The plain N and S doorways look a little later. C13 N transept, see the E lancet. The N window is Perp. Dec S transept, see the S window. Perp chancel E window, Perp tower top with three-light bell-openings, polygonal angle buttresses, and pinnacles, and Perp the only ornate part of the church, the outer S chapel with battlements and pinnacles. The inner S chapel E window looks *c.*1800. Now the interior. All four crossing arches are in a good Late Norman state. Keeled shafts, Late Norman capitals, pointed arches with three slight chamfers. The four-bay arcades can

* Information received from the Rev. Basil Clarke.

hardly be earlier, yet still have square abaci for their piers, i.e. this early feature was kept long. Round piers, bases with spurs, capitals with scallops, also Norman foliage. Round arches with two slight chamfers. The arches from the aisles to the transepts pointed with one slight chamfer. The N arch disturbed by a Perp inner flying buttress for the crossing tower (when the top was put on). Typically Dec arches (sunk quadrant mouldings, continuous) from the W to the N chapel and from the chancel to the S chapel. Perp arches from the chancel to the N chapel (four shafts and four wide hollows, four-centred arches), from the outer to the inner S chapel (shafts and deep wave), and from the S chapel to the W. This arch has a hunt in small figures in the hollow of the arch and heads and flowers in the hollow of the jambs.

FURNISHINGS. FONT. Later C17, with swags (N chapel). – PILLAR PISCINA. Norman, with leaf capital, later used as a stoup (N aisle). – SCULPTURE. Small Mannerist profile relief of Charles I with two angels l. and r. Alabaster, from Lambourn Place ('King and Martyr'). – STAINED GLASS. In the N chapel C16 figure and bits. – Outer S chapel, c.1855, by *Willement*. – S and N aisles by *Kempe*, 1890 and 1894. – PLATE. Silver-gilt Chalice-Cup, 1587; Paten, inscribed 1631; Flagon, secular, inscribed 1701; Almsdish, early C18; Bread Holder, 1746–7. – MONUMENTS. John of Estbury † 1372, and his son. Brasses, demi-figures, 14½ in., S chapel. – Sir Thomas Grandison and wife. Brasses, demi-figures, 14 in. long; also S chapel. – John Estbury † 1508. Good brass figure, 33 in. long, on a tomb-chest with shields in round panels. – Sir Thomas Essex † 1558 and wife. Alabaster. Effigies on a tomb-chest with shields and very elementary balusters. At his feet a dolphin (N chapel). – Thomas Garrard † 1583 and wife. Tablet with kneelers (chancel N). – Thomas Garrard † 1619 and wife. Brasses, she wearing a hat (chancel S). – Charles Garrard † 1710. Tablet with two putto heads at the foot (S transept). – CURIOSUM. The village STOCKS in the N chapel.

Round the church much to see. The former VICARAGE to the SW, a Jacobean composition, brick, with two big side and a smaller middle gable, but the fenestration all Later Georgian, round-headed windows with Y-glazing bars, and in the centre two Venetian windows. To the N the wall with many sarsen stones. In it a small C17 doorway from Lambourn Place, with strapwork at the top. Then the very picturesque ALMS-

HOUSES of 1852, by *T. Talbot Bury*, castellated façade with a higher turret. This display leads not to a bishop's palace, but to the sweet cloister of the almshouses, small, low, and of timber. Behind the almshouses down a lane to the WESLEYAN CHAPEL of 1835, brick, three bays, round-arched windows.

To the E of the church the MARKET PLACE. In it the VILLAGE CROSS, steps and tall shaft genuine. At the principal corner the RED LION. Façade of light grey sarsen stones in brick frames. Round the corner in NEWBURY STREET different: blue and red brick and giant brick pilasters. In the street two specially good houses: IVY HOUSE of three bays, blue headers and red dressings, broad doorway with Tuscan columns, triglyph frieze and pediment, and No. 21, six bays, with narrower windows l. and r. of the pretty Adamish doorcase. Columns and pediment with fan-motif in.

In the HIGH STREET, running S from the Market Hall, also two attractive houses: No. 3 with pargetting in simple patterns and a doorway with a fan-motif in the pediment, and COLLEGE HOUSE, Early Georgian, of light grey sarsen stone with brick dressings, seven bays, segment-headed windows, l. and r. of the door narrower windows, three-bay pediment. Also in the High Street, like any other house, *Street*'s SCHOOL, Gothic, blue and red brick, of 1850, nothing particular.*

BROCKHAMPTON FARM, ¾ m. SE. The l. part flint with mullioned and transomed windows, the r. part five bays, not regular, with segment-headed ground-floor windows. Blue headers and red dressings. The windows are sashed, but originally had wooden crosses, see the side and the back.

THE SEVEN BARROWS, on the downs to the N. This fine cemetery of twenty-four round barrows includes examples of bell, bowl, and disc barrows and two twin barrows – two mounds surrounded by a common ditch. Excavations conducted on a number of these sites in the C19 recovered several crouched inhumation burials accompanied by beakers and urn cremations.

LONG BARROW, just N of Seven Barrows Farm, at the S end of a wood, on the boundary of Lambourn, Sparsholt, and Kingston Lisle parishes. The mound is orientated E–W and is 220 ft long. It expands to a width of 70 ft at its E end, where it still stands 4½ ft high. There are flanking quarry ditches, 15 ft wide, round the S end of the barrow. At the E end numerous

---

* The NBR notes one cruck cottage on the authority of Addy, and *C.L.* has illustrated one (29 October 1927). It may be the same.

sarsens project from the mound and suggest the presence of a chamber at this point.

MEMBURY CAMP. Only the NW corner of this fort is in Berkshire, the remainder lying across the county boundary in Wiltshire. The fort is of univallate construction, enclosing an area of 32 acres. The defences are broken by an entrance on the NW. The site has been damaged by cultivation and is now much overgrown.

4070

LECKHAMPSTEAD

ST JAMES. By *S. S. Teulon*, 1858–60. A 'hard' church and a wilful one in some features. The church has a crossing tower, but it is no more than a timber bell-turret. Also it has transepts, but they are no more than glorified dormers in so far as their end walls are flush with the nave wall and the aisle roofs go on below them. The church is of flint, with red-brick dressings including broad bands. The chancel is surprisingly short for 1860. The inside is all brick, red, yellow, black, and with diapers. The chancel arch stands beyond the crossing, and the crossing is no more than two pairs of cusped braces. – FONT. Norman, of cup shape, with leaf friezes at top and bottom. – PULPIT. Jacobean, with two tiers of the familiar blank arches. – COMMUNION RAIL. The balusters partly turned, partly twisted. Early C18. – STAINED GLASS. E window by *Lavers & Barraud* (BC). – PLATE. Elizabethan Cup; Paten on foot, 1723.

3080

LETCOMBE BASSETT

ST MICHAEL. Norman chancel, see one N and one S window. The N doorway, though it is probably re-set, would prove a Norman nave. One order of shafts, capitals with the four Signs of the Evangelists in the four big scallops of the two capitals. Tympanum with a pattern of incised squares, perhaps not original. The chancel arch narrow and the abaci of the responds decorated with crisp, close leaf trails. Chancel E and S windows *See* p. 359 later C13 with elementary bar tracery. Nave and S aisle, including S arcade, 1861 by *Butterfield*. Thin W tower, also later C13?

HILLFORT, on Segsbury Down, just N of the Ridgeway. This Iron Age fort is of univallate construction with a slight counterscarp bank which can be traced for some 200 yds on the NW. The area enclosed is about 26 acres. The rampart was probably faced with sarsen, and sarsen blocks are still visible projecting out of the turf. Probably only one of the gaps in the defences is original. It is marked by the out-turning of the rampart. Sherds of Iron Age A and B pottery have been found on the surface in the interior of the site, and a Saxon burial was discovered in the s stretch of rampart in the C19.

BOWL BARROW, at the junction of Letcombe Bassett and Lambourn parishes, just E of Stancombe Farm. The barrow is 45 ft in diameter and 4 ft high and is surrounded by a ditch 12 ft wide. The site is now covered by trees. Excavations in the C19 produced no evidence of a burial beneath the mound. To the NE is a second ditched bowl barrow, 41 ft in diameter and 4 ft high. The depression in the centre of the mound marks the position of the C19 excavation.

LETCOMBE REGIS 3080

ST ANDREW. Nave and chancel and W tower. The tower, except for the top, is C13 work. Lancets and two-light bell-openings with a polygonal shaft and a leaf capital. Tower arch with one slight chamfer. The s windows Victorian, on the N side Perp windows and smaller ones over them, as though the s side had had a Perp aisle with clerestory. – FONT. Tub-shaped, Norman, with a scalloped top band. – STAINED GLASS. Some original fragments, including one small Christ in Majesty. – PLATE. Elizabethan Cup and Paten; Flagon of 1720.

ROMAN VILLA, see Wantage.

LEVERTON 3070

A sweet model village of c.1800, or at least a sequence of five pairs of thatched cottages in a row.

CHILTON LODGE, see Chilton Foliat.

LINDEN HILL see WARGRAVE

LITTLE COXWELL 2090

ST MARY. Nave with bellcote on the E gable, and chancel. The bellcote is really the most interesting thing here. It is a genuine later C13 double bellcote with plate tracery. Norman nave, see the plain s doorway. Norman chancel, see the plain priest's doorway. The responds of the chancel arch are Norman too. One nave s window of c.1300. The others Perp, as is the transomed four-light window in the chancel. The chancel E window is Victorian, but the niches to its l. and r. inside are in order. – WEST GALLERY. With remains of the former rood screen. – CHANDELIER. Brass. Moulded centre. Dated 1729. – PLATE. Cup and Cover, 1584.

CHURCH HOUSE, E of the church. Brick, Early Georgian. A remarkable house of five bays. The end bays low, with an arched window and a rising parapet. The next bays with canted bay windows and the centre with a Tuscan porch. The parapet rises above the middle pedimentally, and there are three oval windows in it above the three middle bays. All this is very typical of *c.*1720.

IRON AGE HILLFORT. This badly damaged site lies on Furze Hill, with commanding views over the Vale of White Horse. The site was described in the C19 as being rectangular, but now only a length of double ditch on the W side is well preserved.

₃₀₇₀

LITTLE SHEFFORD

HOLY INNOCENTS has recently been demolished.

OLD CHURCH. This also looks disused. It is small, of nave and chancel with a small timber bell-turret. One Norman N window. Otherwise Perp windows. – STAINED GLASS. In the E window two figures of the early C16. – PLATE. Set of *c.*1630–40. – MONUMENTS. Sir Thomas Fettiplace † *c.*1442. Alabaster. Two recumbent effigies on a tomb-chest with angels holding shields. Wide-spread wings. – John Fettiplace † 1524. Purbeck tomb recess with tomb-chest and canopy. The canopy is straight and stands on quadrants. Vaulted inside. Brasses against the back wall, kneeling.

₈₀₇₀

LITTLEWICK GREEN
3 m. SSW of Maidenhead

ST JOHN EVANGELIST. 1893 by *E. J. Shrewsbury*. Nave and chancel and bellcote; also transepts. – REREDOS. A most surprising and interesting early Quattrocento PAINTING of the Adoration of the Magi, North Italian, with many contacts with Germany. Could it be from Verona? The panel would seem a *cassone* in a photograph, but is 10 ft long. Also many attractive and unusual iconographic features.

2ob

VILLAGE WELL. C17. The posts with the roller and its handles are all complete. Tiled roof.

LITTLE WITTENHAM
₅₀₉₀

The village lies under the Wittenham Clumps, indeed two clumps on the hill, and the church is close to the river Thames.

St Peter. The w tower is Dec below, Perp above, and has a higher stair-turret. The body of the church is of 1863, by *C. Buckeridge*. Nave and chancel, E.E. style. – Typical round stone PULPIT. – STAINED GLASS. e window by *Clayton & Bell* (BC). – PLATE. Chalice and Paten Cover, 1577–8; Flagon, 1696–7; silver-gilt Cover Paten, 1714–15. – MONUMENTS. Brass to David Kidwelly † 1454, a 14½ in. figure. – Brass to Cicely Kidwelly † 1472, good. The figure is 35 in. long. Both chancel floor. – In the chancel a tomb recess. The tomb-chest has quatrefoils. Depressed arch and buttress-shafts. On the tomb-chest brass to Geoffrey Kidwelly † 1483, a 2 ft 6 in. figure. – Sir William Dunche † 1611. Only parts remain, especially the two effigies of alabaster, she recumbent, he on his side with his head supported by his arm. Also two obelisks. – William Dunche and his wife. Jacobean brass plate. The date of death is left open.

Sinodun Camp, on Castle Hill, commanding a fine view of the Thames valley. The hill has been defended by the construction of a roughly heart-shaped enclosure consisting of a deep ditch and high outer bank. There is a single entrance on the w. Little is known of this fort, which is unexcavated, although Iron Age and Roman pottery have been found in the ploughed interior and a ROMANO-BRITISH SETTLEMENT lies 200 yds w of the entrance to the camp. Pottery from this site suggests occupation from the c1 to the c5.

LITTLEWORTH 309b

The Ascension. Built in 1839. Architect: *H. J. Underwood*. Nave and bellcote, w porch. The chancel rebuilt in 1876. Inside PAINTED INSCRIPTIONS in a nice mid c19 Book of Hours style.

Radcot Bridge, 2¼ m. n of Faringdon. Three ribbed arches, the first and third pointed and quite possibly c14. The middle arch later. This is the best medieval bridge in Berkshire.

LOCKINGE 408b

All Saints. Norman n doorway, with a big crenellation frieze in the arch. In the s chapel a re-done and re-set Norman window. The chancel of the early c14. The e window has Y-tracery, and l. and r. of the coarse chancel arch are ogee-headed niches. Plain SEDILIA without ogees. Some original paint left. The arch to the s chapel looks earlier than the

6*

rest of the chancel. The W tower dates from 1564, the S aisle from 1886. – PULPIT. Jacobean, with blank arches and arabesque. A ledge on corbels for putting books or notes on. – WEST SCREEN. Made up of Jacobean panelling. – NORTH DOOR. Good, heavy ironwork; C14? – SCULPTURE. Relief of the Annunciation; Italian, C17. – CHANDELIERS. Three, of brass, from Corfu, C17 or C18. – STAINED GLASS. E window designed by *Lady Jane Lindsay* (BC). – PLATE. Cup, 1576; Paten, 1677. – MONUMENTS. Mrs Grace † 1633. With kneeling effigy. – Many tablets.

The mansion was pulled down after the Second World War. The ORANGERY remains, close to the church, among barns. Blue and red brick, Early Georgian, with seven segment-headed glazed openings.

The village of East Lockinge is a village of estate housing of the 1860s.

WEST LOCKINGE FARM, ½ m. NW. Georgian. Blue and red brick, five bays, hipped roof, and later enlargements.

LONGCOT

2090

ST MARY. W tower of 1722, a rare date for Berkshire. Arched windows. Nave and chancel are C13 work. Evidence is the fine N doorway with stiff-leaf captals and a moulded trefoiled arch, one chancel N lancet, and perhaps also the chancel arch. The N windows of the church a nice mixed lot, including one two-light Dec and one four-light Perp. – PULPIT. Jacobean. Many motifs, also knob-like heads as pendants of paired blank arches.

LONG WITTENHAM

5090

ST MARY. Basically a Norman church. One chancel N window survives, and the chancel arch. Wide single-step arch on decorated capitals, one with two monsters. E.E. the chancel, as shown by one lancet, the S arcade of four bays with round piers, stiff-leaf capitals, and double-chamfered arches. It makes no allowance for the S chapel or transept, which is indeed a little later – say of *c.*1275 as against *c.*1250. Good S window of three pointed-trefoiled lights with two trefoils and a big sexfoiled circle. Dec S and N aisle walls, the N wall with one window with cusped intersecting tracery and a doorway with a characteristic moulding. The N arcade has standard components. The capitals are likely to be C14. Perp clerestory and perhaps S porch. The porch is of timber and may go back to the C14. – FONT. Of lead, circular, Late Norman. A broad band of rosettes and wheels, just two moulds repeated all the time. Below, a narrower band of small figures of a bishop under an arch. – The font was later encased and the Jacobean FONT CASE now serves as a table. – Jacobean also the FONT COVER. – PULPIT. Simple, Jacobean too. – What is more surprising is that the STALLS with their poppy-heads are Jacobean. – Jacobean SCREEN to the S transept. This and the stalls come from Exeter College Chapel, Oxford. – TILES. Some C15 tiles round the font, some S aisle E. – PLATE. Cup and Cover of 1576. – MONUMENTS. In the S transept an amazing monument. It is a PISCINA of pointed-trefoiled 17b form, but the top of the arch cannot be seen, because it is hidden by two small angels with wings standing up. And the piscina itself has in front of the basin a miniature effigy of a Knight. It must be of about the same time as the S window. – At the E end of the S aisle a plain Dec tomb recess.

CRUCKFIELD COTTAGE (No. 18), S of the village cross, is of cruck construction. It is L-shaped, with three pairs of crucks in the longer arm of the L.

CHURCH FARM contains one blade of a cruck truss and its BARN two complete bays. Mr J. M. Fletcher bases the dating of the cruck truss of the farm to c. 1440 and of the barn to c.1550 on a provisional radiocarbon investigation.

BARLEY MOW INN, $\frac{7}{8}$ m. N. Three bays of cruck construction. Crucks are here visible externally.

ROMANO-BRITISH SETTLEMENT. In the fields immediately adjacent to Northfield Farm are numerous crop marks indicating the presence of ditched enclosures and a variety of circular and rectangular buildings of an extensive settlement. Some of these features were excavated in the C19 and produced Romano-British material.

LONGWORTH

3090

ST MARY. Nave with clerestory, embattled S aisle. Several late C13 windows. The rest, including chancel and W tower, all Perp. However, inside a much earlier story. The original nave was enlarged to the N, by one and then another C13 aisle arch. The arches stand on corbels and have two slight chamfers. Then, in the late C13, a complete four-bay S aisle was built (round piers, round abaci, double-chamfered arches), and the N aisle was lengthened by two bays. Finally both aisles were cut off when the W tower was built. Perp N chapel of one bay. – REREDOS. Arts and Crafts, the paintings by *Kate Bunce*, the much more attractive beaten metal frames by her sister (BC). – SCREEN. Jacobean, with extremely elongated columns and strapwork top. – STAINED GLASS. The large Crucifixus in a cyclamen-coloured robe with vines rising l. and r. is by *Heywood Sumner* and as early as 1900 – again very much Arts and Crafts. – PLATE. Tall Cup, no marks; small Paten on foot, inscribed 1629 (by *W. Fawdrey*); tall Flagon (by *W. Fawdrey*); Chalice, 1721; silver-gilt Almsplate. – MONUMENTS. Brass to John Hinde, rector † 1422, demi-figure, 12 in. – Brass to Richard Yate † 1498 and wife, in their shrouds, 27 in. figures. – William Bowles † 1801. By *Westmacott*. Seated young man and two standing women, one comforting the other. – In the churchyard s wall a simple Perp doorway.

OLD RECTORY. Three parts, one gabled, c16, with a mullioned window with arched lights, the second Early Georgian, four bays, brown stone and raised brick window frames, the third late c18. The doorway of this part, however, seems to belong to the second part.

BARCOTE MANOR, ½ m. NE. Brick mansion in the Tudor style, built in 1875. A very irregular composition with many gables. The staircase window makes one think of *Kerr*.

CARSWELL MANOR, 1 m. ENE. The W range contains genuine early c17 work (e.g. mullioned and mullioned and transomed windows), the rest is partly of 1840 but mostly of 1898. Parts of the staircase are early c17, and so is the handsome DOVE-COTE with its four gables.

LOWER BASILDON see BASILDON

LUCAS HOSPITAL see WOKINGHAM

LUCKLEY see WOKINGHAM

LYFORD

ST MARY. Rubble-built. Nave and chancel and timber bell-turret set on strong braced and scissor-braced posts visible inside. In the chancel N and S lancets and one low-side window with pointed-trefoiled head. Lancets also in the nave on the S side. With them goes the N doorway (one continuous chamfer). The upper windows are Perp and indicate a heightening. – PULPIT. Jacobean, with the usual blank arches. In them large stylized tulips. – SCREEN. By the turret-posts. Perp, with single-light divisions; modest. – BENCHES. A few, the ends undecorated.

LYFORD MANOR. Dates 1617 and 1621. Of dark rubble. Gabled, irregular.

HOUSE, NE of the church. Chequer brick, five bays, dated 1717. (LYFORD GRANGE. Edmund Campion was arrested here.)

LYFORD MANOR FARM. Timber-framed. The core a later C16 range of two rooms divided by a wall with two back-to-back fireplaces (cf. Priory, Marcham). S and NW additions of the early C17, staircase addition later C17. (See Spokes and Jope: *B.A.J.*, 1959)

ALMSHOUSES. Brick, three sides of a courtyard. The oldest parts look no older than Georgian.

MACKNEY *see* SOTWELL

MAIDENHEAD   8080

The centre of Maidenhead lies less than a mile W of the bridge across the Thames which connects Berkshire with Buckinghamshire. The Bath Road traffic used it and then, until the Maidenhead by-pass was built, ended in a hopeless jam in the High Street. So the axis of Maidenhead runs E–W. It is not a town of architectural events and what minor events there are lie between the centre and the bridge.

ST ANDREW AND ST MARY MAGDALENE. The church of 1822–5 by *Busby* (of Brighton) has recently been pulled down* and a new church was built in 1964–5. It is by *Lord Mottistone & Paul Paget*, and according to the design‡ in a rather thin and spiky modern style, basically Gothic in outline. – PLATE. Two Flagons, 1629; Chalice and Paten, 1657; Paten, 1725.

ALL SAINTS, All Saints Avenue, Boyne Hill. 1854–7 by *G. E. Street*. The two W bays by *A. E. Street*, 1907–11. Before that time the steeple stood clear and the group was even more remarkable than it is now. It is a group of varied outline and frontages consisting of steeple, church, and gate to a courtyard with parsonage, parsonage stables, schoolmaster's house, and school house. The whole is of brick, the church with stone stripes, the other buildings with vitrified blue brick stripes etc. The style is *c.*1300 or, as *The Ecclesiologist* wrote in 1854, 'an ornate Geometrical Middle Pointed'. The interior of the

* The old building had been condemned as unsafe by the Diocesan Surveyor.
‡ Seen at the time of writing.

church red and blue brick. The coupled trefoil clerestory windows do not stand above the arches below, but they are symmetrically placed all the same. The E window is set high up. Stone PULPIT and low stone SCREEN. *The Ecclesiologist* summed up: 'We have seldom been more pleased with a design than with the one before us'.

ST JOSEPH (R.C.), Cookham Road. 1884 by *Leonard Stokes*. Brick, flint, and stone. Gothic. Aisleless with transept. Over the S transept a tower with a spike.

ST LUKE, St Luke's Road. 1866–70 by *G. R. Clarke*. Large, rock-faced. Plate tracery. The prominent spire 1894 by *J. O. Scott*. – STAINED GLASS. E window by *O'Connor*, 1871.

ST MARK, St Mark's Road. 1873 by *Charles Cooper*.

ST PAUL, High Town Road. 1887–9 by *E. J. Shrewsbury*. Red brick.

ST PETER, St Peter's Road, off Furze Platt. 1897 by *E. J. Shrewsbury*. Red brick, with a short, embattled SE tower, added only in 1961.

METHODIST CHAPEL, Castle Hill and King Street. 1859. Yellow brick, and rather like a Commissioners' church.

TOWN HALL, St Ives Road. 1960–2, pale red brick and stone. Remarkably large, and in a weak, retardataire neo-Georgian, i.e. what would have been conservative already in 1936. By *North & Partners* with *Sir Hubert Worthington*. – REGALIA. Small silver-gilt Mace, London, 1604; large silver-gilt Mace, London, 1776; Cup, Dublin, *c*.1775; Cruet, London 1801; silver-gilt Cup, *c*.1810.

POLICE STATION, Broadway. 1906 by *J. Morris*, the County Surveyor. Very red, i.e. brick and terracotta with typical battered buttresses. Asymmetrical tower (cf. Wokingham). Quite fun.

FREE LIBRARY, opposite the town hall. Small, pretty, in a free Baroque with a cupola. By *Arthur E. McKewan* and *G. H. V. Cole*, 1904.

CLOCK TOWER, King Street. 1897 by *E. J. Shrewsbury*. Brick and stone, fancy Tudor, with a wooden lantern. No architectural merit.

ST MARK'S HOSPITAL, the former WORKHOUSE, I m. W. 1836 by *Cooper & Son*.

The only sensible PERAMBULATION is from the corner of King Street and High Street first for a few minutes W to see the villas of *c*.1840 and then on the way out towards Reading (i.e. in CASTLE HILL and the BATH ROAD) and then E along the

HIGH STREET, where the small-town shopping has suddenly been given a jerk by a group on a large-town scale. Two rows of two-storeyed shopping terraces leading to an eight-storey office block on very high stilts (by *Ian Fraser & Associates*).* The best houses of Maidenhead are further E in BRIDGE ROAD. First SMYTHS ALMHOUSES of 1659, a row in dark brick, one storey and gabled dormers. Nice coat of arms. To the r. additional ALMSHOUSES, 1895, redder brick and a number of pavilions. Further E a few pretty Georgian brick houses, the best OLDFIELD LODGE, lying back behind a wall with gatepiers decorated by nice paterae. Lodge with pointed windows. Yellow brick house with handsome Venetian doorway and windows. These houses are on the S side. On the N side lying back some 50 yards behind other houses RAY LODGE. Tall and stately, red brick. To the S one-storeyed portico of four wooden Roman-Doric columns with pediment. To the N tall thin Tuscan columns as a colonnade coming forward above the outer stairs to the main entrance. Two-bay pavilions l. and r. Back to the S side, and hideous between these Georgian houses the former SHOWBOAT roadhouse, white and modernistic, of 1932–3 and already a complete period piece. By *E. Norman Bailey* and *D. C. Wadhwa*. Just before the bridge a road leads S to the REITLINGER MUSEUM, formerly OLDFIELD, a typical rich Maidenhead house of *c*.1895. Black and white, extensive and irregular. Further S on the FISHERY ESTATE of the 1880s more such houses. Back and to the BRIDGE, a beautiful piece of 1772–7 designed by *Sir Robert Taylor*. Seven main water-arches with rocky rustication on the voussoirs. Fine balustrade. The bridge cost £19,000. To its S the RAILWAY VIADUCT by *Brunel*, 1837–8. Brick, with two long semi-elliptical arches said to have been the largest brick span ever (128 ft each). It is the bridge which appears in Turner's *Rain, Steam and Speed*.‡

* Since writing this a second high block, eleven storeys, glass and brick infilling, has gone up in the High Street a little further E, on the site of the old town hall. This is by *Hildebrand & Glicker*.

‡ As the inverted triangle of streets of which the High Street is the base remain intolerably congested by local traffic even after the completion of M4 a plan for central redevelopment was commissioned from Lord Esher of *Brett & Pollen* in 1961. This plan proposes a loop road cutting N from the station across back land W of King Street, and then E along the S edge of Kidwells Park to join the old A4 a little W of Smyth's Almshouses. This will enable the High Street (where pavements are only 4 ft wide) to be cleared of traffic and paved from wall to wall. Pending this improvement, an extension of the shopping centre S on to the back land inside the triangle has already begun,

NORDEN FARM, Altwood Road, s of the Bath Road. The survival of a farm. Behind a screen of black weatherboarded barns a plain Late Georgian brick house of three bays with a Tuscan porch. New housing around.

ROBIN HOOD'S ARBOUR, in Maidenhead Thicket, just s of the road to Stubbings House. The site is a sub-rectangular, ditched enclosure covering ¾ acre. The area is defended by a single bank and ditch with a counterscarp on the w and s. A section cut through the N line of the defences proved the ditch to be 16 ft wide and 2 ft 9 in. deep. The gap in the w defences is original, and from it a track led to a sunken paved stockyard in the interior. The scanty finds included sherds of Belgic pottery dating from the early c1.

ROMAN VILLA, at Cox Green, between Northumbria Road and the Maidenhead by-pass. The site was discovered from the air, and nothing is now visible on the ground, for much of the area is covered by a housing estate. The villa was excavated in 1959 and shown to have a fairly complex building history. The earliest structure, built in the early c2, consisted of a simple rectangular building, 63 ft long and 26 ft wide, divided into a small living room and a large hall which probably served both as kitchen and cattle shed. In the mid c2 a corridor was added to the NE, the original building provided with further partition walls, and a bath suite built on its SE end, the whole forming a villa of winged corridor type. The main feature of the third building phase, which cannot be precisely dated, was the provision of a greatly elaborated bath wing. In the final phase, in the late c4, this bath building was once again simplified. The villa lay within a ditched enclosure which was probably dug at the same time as the third building phase of the villa and had silted up during phase four.

4090 MARCHAM

ALL SAINTS. 1837 by *William Fisher* of Oxford. He used the c13 w tower (unbuttressed, one-light bell-openings), the N chapel E wall with its three widely spaced, stepped lancets, the arch from the N chapel to the chancel with stiff-leaf

with two-storey shops and the two blocks of offices referred to on p. 175. s of the latter a new central square is to be formed, with a Central Library and more shops, all served by a large three-decker car park projected into the centre from the loop road over the top of King Street.

responds, and the Perp s doorway with a continuous frieze of large, individual leaves in one jamb and arch moulding. The vault inside the tower with hollow-chamfered ribs on four face corbels is a Perp addition to the tower too. Otherwise symmetrical arrangement of tall, transomed, straight-headed Perp windows of 1830 proportions. Equally characteristic of 1830 is the interior, one large, wide space. What distinguishes it is the E end, where the chancel and N chapel now appear like twin chancels, their W arches treated identically. – BENCH ENDS. Plain, straight-headed, with linenfold panelling. – PLATE. Elizabethan Cup. – BRASSES to Edmund Fettiplace † 1540 and wife. Kneeling 15 in. figures.

The HOUSE s of the churchyard has some mullioned windows.

MARCHAM PARK (Denman College). Of the early C19. A seven-bay, two-storeyed stone house. The side is of six bays with symmetrically arranged tripartite windows. Stone staircase with wrought-iron balustrade of simple S-shapes.

PRIORY, ½ m. SE. An oblong range with mullioned and mullioned and transomed windows with arched – lights C16 no doubt, and according to external appearance first half, though Messrs Spokes and Jope prefer c.1570. The doorway mould-ing, however, is of a Dec type. Inside, the wall through which lead the two doorways to the former offices. The hall is divided into two rooms by a fireplace opening into both. Next to this in the far room is a spiral staircase.

MARLSTON 5070

CHURCH. Mostly by *Butterfield*, 1855. Nave and chancel, bell-turret with shingled spire. Lancets and Dec windows. Of the medieval church the N doorway of c.1200. One order of shafts with scallop capitals. Arch with a slight chamfer and a roll moulding. The s doorway, heavily pointed-trefoiled, is Butterfield's. – PILLAR PISCINA. Norman, with decorated scallops. – STAINED GLASS. E window by *Kempe*, 1901.

MARLSTON HOUSE (Brockhurst School). By *Edward Burgess*, 1895–9, for the Palmers of Reading. Large, of brick with stone dressings. Rib-vaulted octagonal porch, big Elizabethan hall window to its l. The garden side with four gables and three canted bay windows in a very odd, very deliberate, syncopated rhythm. In the hall very high overmantel, with elongated pilasters and caryatids yet higher up.

MEMBURY CAMP *see* LAMBOURN

MIDGHAM

ST MATTHEW. From the Bath road it seems to lie on the hill entirely on its own. 1869 by *John Johnson*. Flint; nave, chancel, N chapel, and a SW spire. The interior sumptuous with polished granite piers, one exceeding fat to help support the tower. Roof on brackets with faces, chancel arch with angels. And so on. A two-light window opens into the organ chamber. The carving was done by *Farmer & Brindley* (BC). – STAINED GLASS. E window *Ward & Hughes* (BC); nothing to commend it. – PLATE. Paten hallmarked 1531, with the Vernicle.

MILTON

ST BLAISE. Unbuttressed W tower with an unmoulded round arch to the nave, called C18 by the VCH. Nave, N aisle, and chancel almost entirely by *Woodyer*, 1849–51. The chancel higher than the nave and more ornate. Strange coal-hole composition. – STAINED GLASS. Fragments of old glass in several windows. – E window by *O'Connor*, 1851. – PLATE. Plate, London, 1679; Cup, London, 1765.

MILTON HOUSE. The C17 centre is most interesting. What is its date? 1660? 1670? Can it be much later? It is called newly built in 1696. Five bays, a high three storeys, brick of not specially careful quality. Giant pilasters above ground-floor pilaster strips. The giant pilasters have Ionic capitals and waistbands; which turn out to be raised panels with fleurs-de-lis. Odd flat raised upper quoins. The garden side identical with the entrance side. Short wings of 1776 by *Stephen Wright*, with oblong projections in the middle on the entrance side, canted on the garden side. Nice one-storey offices. Inside, one room has a plaster ceiling of the time of the house. Panels with wreaths, round and oval, in a very satisfying pattern, of Inigo Jones derivation. Oak and laurel. Original and equally characteristic one chimneypiece with two rustic maidens with cornucopias in the overmantel and thick, compact garlands l. and r. of the fireplace. It may be by *William Bird* (cf. Pusey). The chimneypiece in the room with the plaster ceiling is late C18 with a splendid Kentian overmantel of *c*.1740. Also original the staircase through all floors with sturdy turned balusters. In the l. wing the library and the chapel, both Gothick, and the library quite delicious – absolutely complete with fireplace, bookcases, and window decoration, including odd pendants. The chapel is plainer.

Thin-ribbed ceiling with pendants. In the windows STAINED GLASS, the side windows Netherlandish C16, the altar windows English late C14 bits and pieces from Steventon village. The glass was put in in 1772. – VESTMENTS. Bishop Challoner's vestments of 1760 are preserved in the house.

MONKEY ISLAND
⅞ m. SE of Bray

9070

Access by way of a suspension footbridge. On the island a hotel and a house. They were the third Duke of Marlborough's fishing lodge and pavilion and were built *c.*1744. He owned the estate of Whiteknights outside Reading. The fishing lodge has rusticated walls (of wood?). In the centre is a raised octagon with lunette windows and a room in front of it with a canted bay window. In this room paintings of monkeys fishing, shooting, etc., by the monkey specialist *Clermont*. The house, known as the Temple, has a r. part of three bays with rusticated ground floor with giant columns above with a large Venetian window. The ground floor was originally open where there are now arches. (Inside lively stucco decoration of Neptune, sea deities, etc.) Added on the l. a plain lower five-bay house.

MORTIMER COMMON *see* STRATFIELD MORTIMER

MOULSFORD

5080

ST JOHN BAPTIST. By *Sir G. G. Scott*, 1846.* Small, by the Thames. With a bell-turret with shingled broach spire. The N arcade, low, with arches dying into the octagonal piers, looks late C19, but no work at that time is recorded. – PLATE. Chalice of 1774.

OLD VICARAGE. At the time of writing in the course of conversion into an Old People's Home. The architect is *H. A. J. Darlow*.

FAIRMILE HOSPITAL, *see* Cholsey.

NEWBURY

4060

Leland calls Newbury one of the three most important cloth towns in Berkshire, the others being Reading and Abingdon. The climax of the trade is marked by the life and the riches of John Smallwood, alias John of Winchcombe, alias Jack of Newbury.

* According to the VCH. His fee was £64.

He lived around the year 1520, and a fanciful C17 chronicle of his life tells us of his two hundred looms and the two hundred men, the two hundred pretty boys, the two hundred maidens and hundred women who worked for him. Nor was he the only wealthy clothier. We hear of others including the Dolmans, and under Queen Elizabeth Thomas Dolman was the – apparently much envied – leader of the trade (*see* Shaw House, p. 213). In the C17 and C18 the national importance of Newbury may have decreased, but local prosperity does not seem to have suffered much. Newbury in any case had the additional advantages of a situation on the Bath Road. The plan of the town clearly expresses this dual situation. The town itself has as its spine the S–N streets S and N of the river Kennet, but at the very N end the Bath Road crosses from E to W.

6 ST NICHOLAS. The church is the great monument of the wealth of Newbury in the Late Middle Ages. It is a Perp church throughout, large, ashlar-faced, and the work of one generation. It was built *c.*1500–32, the nave at the expense of John Smallwood. The church is embattled throughout. The W tower has massive polygonal buttresses and big pinnacles with their own battlements and pinnacles. On it a date 1532. The windows are of four to six lights and of three lights in the clerestory. The arcades have five bays, and the piers are of a variety of the standard section of four shafts and four hollows in which the shafts towards nave and aisle are trebled. Only one pier, the second from the E on the N side, is different. It has a wave moulding instead of the plain hollow and a capital band all round instead of capitals only for the shafts. The chancel arch and the pretty chancel roof are of 1858 (*Woodyer*). The nave roof is Perp and has the initials of John Smallwood. – PULPIT. Unusual and quite splendid. Above the familiar blank arches square panels with thick leaf frames. The pulpit was presented in 1607. – GATES to the chancel. Low, of iron, 1704. – STAINED GLASS. All by *Hardman*, designed by *Powell* and *Maycock* (BC). Not good. – MONUMENTS. Brasses to John Smallwood † 1519 and wife, 27 in. figures. – Griffith Curteys † 1587. With kneeling figures under arches (chancel S, outside). – Many tablets in the church. – CURIOSUM. Charity Boy, painted on board and cut out. He comes from a school founded before 1713.

From the street the churchyard is entered by two very pretty Gothick archways. It is likely that they are connected with a payment to *Fuller White* in 1770.

St George, Wash Common, Andover Road. The old church humble red brick, the new Italian in taste, white, pantile-roofed. Tunnel-vault with penetrations. By *F. C. Eden*, 1933 etc. The w end is not yet built.

St John, Newtown Road. 1955–7. By *S. E. Dykes-Bower*. Red brick, large, in a kind of neo-Romanesque, neither period nor modern.

St Joseph and the Sacred Heart (R.C.), London Road. The old, small, featureless red brick church of 1864 stands by the side of the new, large, inappropriately Early Christian or Byzantine or Italian Romanesque, equally red church with its separate high campanile. Only the top of the campanile goes a kind of free Renaissance. The church has a semicircular porch with green marble columns and inside the area round the altar space developed in the Byzantine way of the inscribed cross, i.e. a groin-vaulted crossing, high, short chancel and transept bays, and lower corner features with balconies. Central altar; canopy on marble columns. The church is of 1923–8 by *W. C. Mangan*.

St Mary, Speenhamland, London Road. In 1876–9 *Street* added the present chancel to a church of 1830. In 1911 etc. *A. E. Street*, the son, replaced the church by a new and larger one. No tower. Ashlar facing. Geometrical tracery. Imitation Perp piers inside. The best thing about the church is the chancel decoration. This was done by *Burlison & Grylls* in memory of someone who died in 1884 (BC).

Methodist Church, Northbrook Street. 1837–8. Stone-built, in the lancet style.

Town Hall, Market Place. 1876–81 by *James H. Money* (BC). He imitates Waterhouse. Blue and red brick, a tower on the l., a much higher one on the r., differing in a characteristically Victorian way. The peculiar hardness of it all is very similar to Waterhouse's.* The building cost was estimated at a mere £4,345 (GS).

Museum, Wharf Road. The most interesting house in Newbury. Built in 1626–7. Commonly called the Cloth Hall, but it was built (with money left by John Kendrick of Reading) as a municipal cloth-weaving workshop to give employment to the poor. Three wings were intended, but only one was built. Timber-framed, the ground floor with six columns carrying segmental arches, each with a pendant. One would

---

* plate. Two silver-gilt Maces, one c17, the other 'somewhat later' (vch).

assume that they were originally open, but the doorway to the w is original with its straight hood on brackets. Massive overhang. Top gables. The building is continued to the E by the so-called CORN STORE, a long timber-framed building with an outer upper gallery. Originally the Kennet wharf was close to it. This extremely interesting structure has been ruined by the town, which put a snack-bar and other shops and offices in, all in connexion with the messy bus-station-cum-car-park in front of it. What is the date of the Corn Store? Mr R. Neville Hadcock suggests c.1660–80.

GRAMMAR SCHOOL, Enmore Road. 1885 by *Power & Hughes*. Red brick, nearly symmetrical. Tudor.

58b ST NICHOLAS SCHOOL, Enmore Road. 1859 by *Butterfield*, and as original and aggressive a job as any of his. The school stands at a corner and has a tower there. This tower is set back from the two ranges between which it stands and has moreover canted sides. On top of that the upper windows towards Enmore Road are dormers under four shark-teeth-sharp gables.

CORN EXCHANGE, Market Place. 1861–2 by *J. S. Dodd* (BC). Stone, restrainedly Italianate. Three bays, with pairs of giant pilasters, only the angle ones differing from the others. Pediment all across. Arched windows.

FALKLAND MONUMENT, Andover Road. 1878. Granite obelisk on a high base, with minor Gothic details below.

PERAMBULATION. We start in the Market Place, which is of Victorian interest chiefly and of minor interest at that. Apart from the Town Hall and the Corn Exchange the principal building is the WESTMINSTER BANK. Broad and stone-faced along the N side. It is of 1864, by *J. Chancellor*, and was to cost £3,653 (GS). The style is that at the time called Italian Gothic. To the E of this, in WHARF ROAD, No. 5 is the first of many Early Georgian houses to come: red brick, five bays, three storeys, segment-headed windows, parapet with one blank lunette in the middle. Later doorcase.

First s, along CHEAP STREET, with little to see. Nos 33–4 keep the bargeboards to the gables, dated 1679. The ST MARY'S ALMSHOUSES of 1864 are poor-man's Gothic. No. 8 has a straight hood on carved brackets above its side entrance.

From the s end of Cheap Street w by Station Road and then a little s or by St John's Road and then a little N to an interesting corner. On the E side of NEWTOWN ROAD, facing a green, RAYMONDS BUILDINGS, or Lower Raymonds Buildings, dated 1796, a long range of plain, classical almshouses. Twenty-five bays, two storeys, pedimental gable in the centre. Across the street, just s of the new Christian Science church, UPPER RAYMONDS BUILDINGS, 1826 and Gothic. Straight-headed two-light windows, and in the raised middle a giant arch. To the immediate E of this range of almshouses, in ARGYLE ROAD, is a remarkable group of buildings. At the N end of the short street on the E side is a high Early Victorian house attached to which, with its E end on Newtown Road, is the LITTEN CHAPEL, a small Perp chapel with two small genuine Perp windows and an original roof. The E end is cut off by the road. The chapel is said to have been connected with the Hospital of St Bartholomew and later served as the Grammar School. It has a handsome roof with collar-beams, queen-posts, and wind-braces. In Argyle Road itself ST BARTHOLOMEW'S HOSPITAL, a U-shaped brick building of two storeys with a hipped roof. It dates from 1618, but the windows have mullion and transom crosses, and this looks later C17 and could go with the date 1698 on the cupola. Opposite BARTHOLOMEW MANOR HOUSE (with a front of 1927–8, but the building behind medieval, Tudor, and Queen Anne, including e.g. an Early Tudor chimneypiece opposite the porch. The building may have been farm buildings originally, was made into a house in the C16, and became Raymond's Almshouses in 1676). The similar-looking house next to it is all restoration.

N of Argyle Road runs BARTHOLOMEW STREET towards the N, the Kennet, the town hall, and, in its N continuation, ultimately to the Bath Road. In Bartholomew Street the EIGHT BELLS, C16, one-storeyed, with three gables. Gothick window details. No. 28, much renewed, is of six bays, Early Georgian, with a pretty doorway (a staircase with twisted balusters and a room with nice late C18 stucco and chimneypiece; NBR). By the bridge, a good finish, a house with a broad, shallow canted bay window and the main windows with semi-elliptical heads. Opposite opens WEST MILLS, running along the side of the parish church. Here ST NICHOLAS HOUSE, Early Georgian, five bays, with semi-elliptical window heads, aprons below the windows, a parapet with arched panels, and a doorway with a pediment on carved brackets. Staircase with one twisted, one fluted, one plain baluster to each step. To its w a house with a porch on Tuscan columns and a frieze with decorated metopes. The HUNT ALMSHOUSES of 1729, rebuilt in 1817, are quite plain, but have a blank oval on the front. Then on the other side the good group of the MILL and after that No. 22, early C18, low, brick, with a big moulded brick frieze above the ground floor, and Nos 23–29, C17 cottages, called The Old Weavers' House.

Back and across the BRIDGE (one arch, balustrade) and into Northbrook Street, but first into NORTHCROFT LANE for the humbly Gothic three-bay CHILDS ALMSHOUSES of 1821. In NORTHBROOK STREET the best C18 houses of Newbury. It must have been a swagger street before shops invaded it and traffic killed it stone-dead. Nos 91–92, on the W side, is the most ambitious house, brick, seven bays, three storeys, giant pilasters, parapet – i.e. Early Georgian. Then on the other side No. 8, dated 1669, also brick, and very typical of its date in the articulation by pilasters for each floor. Two top gables. Staircase balusters a transition from the Jacobean to the dumb-bell shape. Nos 13–14 (Woolworth) is again Early Georgian, but quite plain. Nos 23–24 is timber-framed with brick nogging, as is visible along the N side. It is called Jack of Newbury's house, and it may indeed have been his. Inside an original roof with tie-beams, queen-posts, and wind-braces. No. 26 is of four bays, later C18, with pilasters framing the two middle bays. No. 61, on the other side, has a particularly pretty Adamish doorcase. Then, opposite, the former LITERARY INSTITUTION, dated 1834, stone, with Soanian incised ornament above, but details on the ground floor which tend to get a little looser. No. 24 is dated 1724. It is quite small but uncommonly ornate. Three bays, Composite pilasters on the upper floor and a Venetian window. Cypher and date. The parapet rises in the centre to a segmental shape. Northbrook Street continues as BROADWAY, and here no more needs attention than the Georgian shop front of No. 19. At the top of Broadway is the CLOCK TOWER, with a colonnaded base like a market cross. It dates from 1929.

The clock tower marks the place where Newbury meets the Bath Road. Along this wealthy houses also spread already early in the C18. First E, that is in LONDON ROAD. No. 40 has a flat Gothic three-bay front with battlements. The doorway has an ogee arch and thin tripartite shafts, the windows are straight-headed. Then, at r. angles to the road, a three-bay house with blue brick headers and red brick dressings and an arched middle window, and, forming an L with this,

DOWER HOUSE, early C18, very massive, of seven bays and three storeys, with the angle pairs of bays raised to a fourth floor and given pediments. These parts are red brick, the centre three bays blue and red with segment-headed windows. Plain doorway. The house was an inn originally. It is abandoned at the time of writing but ought to be preserved. Nothing after that.

Back to the clock tower and now E. In OXFORD STREET on the N side, hidden behind houses, the former THEATRE of 1802. On the S side No. 27, once more Early Georgian, five bays, segment-headed windows, but round-arched ground-floor windows and mid-window, and, a little further on, THE HIGH HOUSE, Late Georgian, of three storeys. Opposite is No. 2 BATH ROAD, a very fine house of five bays, blue and red, with strong angle pilasters, a three-bay pediment, and again segment-headed windows. The house has a date 1720 on the roof. The porch with Roman Doric columns and a pediment is later. SPEEN COURT, mid C18, blue headers and red dressings and with angle pilasters, was quite grand too, but has been spoiled by additions. GOLDWELL also mid C18, and also altered. It has its brick quoins, however, and the banded brick rustication of the ground floor. CASTLE HOUSES, Early Georgian, is not attractive to look at now. SPEEN HILL HOUSE is early C19, of three bays, with a porch, rendered. A fine cedar tree in the garden. After that the road passes on into Speen (see p. 224).

One outer item. In TYDEHAMS, off the Andover Road, two Early Modern houses, THE HAVEN, by *Thomas Tait*, 1929, a very early date for England, and SHEPHERDS, by *Pakington & Enthoven*, of 1934. It is typical that The Haven is still symmetrical, Shepherds is not. The source of the first is blatantly Peter Behrens's house of 1926 at Northampton, of the second Le Corbusier as broadcast in England by Connell, Ward & Lucas.

ROUND BARROW CEMETERY, on Wash Common. Three mounds here have the appearance of being Bronze Age bowl barrows, though since the mid C18 they have been thought to cover the remains of those killed in the battle of Newbury in 1643. The largest mound, in the side of the copse, is 120 ft in diameter and 9 ft high. The two smaller ones are surmounted by memorial stones to the victims of the battle.

NEW HALL see FINCHAMPSTEAD

NINE MILE RIDE see HEATHLAND

NOKE'S TOMB *see* BASILDON

NORTH HINKSEY

4000

The part by the church is still villagey, in spite of all the Oxford development around.

ST LAWRENCE. A Norman church, Norman the S doorway with one order of columns, scallop capitals and many zigzags in the arch, Norman the blocked N doorway and two N windows, Norman a re-set chancel S window. The chancel arch also seems Norman, but it is in fact by *John Macduff Derick* (BC). The W tower, short and unbuttressed, looks Norman too, but is in fact E.E., as shown by the W lancet. In the nave S wall a Dec window with a triangular head and lozenge tracery (cf. Cumnor and Theale). – FONT. Octagonal, of the pattern-book type, i.e. with eight different tracery designs, including reticulation. They are all Dec except for one, which is on the way to Perp. – PLATE. Cup and Cover, 1582; Paten, inscribed 1681. – MONUMENT. William Fynmere † 1677. Tablet with oval centre, garlands, etc., and two putti at the top. Probably by *William Bird* (cf. Pusey). – In the churchyard CROSS with the shaft still complete.

In the village Cottage No. 9 is symmetrical with one mullioned window l. and r. of the doorway, probably late C17.

One field SW of the Southern By-pass opposite the SW exit of the village street is the CONDUIT, dated 1634 on a buttress, but built in 1616–17 to supply water to the conduit house at Carfax (now in Nuneham Park). The conduit was given by Otho Nicholson, and the water passes below the river. Square, *c.*18 ft long, ashlar-faced with a pitched roof.

WESTMINSTER COLLEGE. By *Seely & Paget*, 1957–9. A large composition in grey brick and buff stone, in a mildly blocky neo-Georgian. The centre is the chapel with a white weatherboarded gable and bell-turret looking as if it had come straight from Connecticut. Below the chapel the library. If one considers the date of the design, it is surprising that the architects should have been happy in the tradition of C19 historicism, but it is more surprising that the client, an educational body, should not have insisted on something of this century. The large STATUE looking towards Oxford is by *John Matthews*.

5080

NORTH MORETON

ALL SAINTS. A voussoir stone (?) with beakhead decoration on a window ledge and the round S arcade piers are all that remains of the Norman church. The present church is mostly mid C13 to earliest C14. There are first the S arcade arches, double-chamfered, the chancel arch which corresponds, and the S chapel arcade of two bays, where the arches are hollow-chamfered. The W respond of this arcade is a three-quarter column and has a rich stiff-leaf capital. The S respond of the arch into the chapel also has stiff-leaf, and it looks as if some re-using had here taken place. This S chapel was then re-modelled and perhaps lengthened and widened. This may be connected with the foundation of a chantry in the church in 1299. To this date clearly belongs the large E window of a rare but not unique type: five lights, with, as its tracery, arches upon arches, diminishing to four, three, two, and filled by trefoils or quatrefoils (cf. e.g. the Wells Lady Chapel). The W window of the chapel, which is higher than the nave, has the same type of window reduced to three lights. Pretty frieze at the top outside with beasties. Angle PISCINA with ogee arches which otherwise are missing. Ballflower as well, which also occurs on two image corbels l. and r. of the E window. The chancel windows are late C13 too, see the Y-tracery and the details of the E window of three stepped pointed-trefoiled lights; Dec windows in the S aisle and the nave wall. Perp W tower of enormous stones. Pierced quatrefoil parapet. The arch to the nave with concave-sided responds. – STAINED GLASS. In the S chapel E window about the best glass in [18a] Berkshire. It is contemporary with the window and the chapel to which it belongs. The dominant colours are yellow, green, and brown. There are fifteen scenes altogether, and elaborate canopies. The scenes are from the lives of Christ (centre light), the Virgin (S light), and St Nicholas, St Peter, and St Paul. – Fragments also in the nave N and S aisle S.

Several worthwhile timber-framed houses, the most attractive COBBS COTTAGE with two gables and an oriel under one of them.

OAKLEY GREEN see DOWN PLACE

OCKWELLS MANOR HOUSE
¾ m. WSW of Bray

Ockwells Manor, built by Sir John Norreys some time between 1446 and 1466, is the most refined and the most sophisticated timber-framed mansion in England. It is true that its

perfection is partly due to the C20 restoration by *Fairfax Wade*,
but the façade, i.e. the E side, is in fact largely original. The
near-symmetry, but not-quite-symmetry, is certainly as it was
devised in the C15. The façade has two main gables over the
wide end bays, the l. one a little larger than the r., two minor
gables, of about the same size, but the l. one, belonging to the
porch, coming a little further forward than the other, which
represents the hall bay window, and the even hall windows,
one band (five plus five) of them, between the minor gables.
So the plan of the house seems the standard manor-house
plan and perfectly clear in the façade, clearer in fact than it
will turn out to be when one studies the interior. The hall
windows with plain arched lights are intact, the more play-
fully detailed windows belonging to the gabled bays are mostly
of the restoration, but the lacy bargeboards are again in fairly
genuine condition. To return to the anomaly of the plan
already referred to, the standard arrangement would be that
chamber and solar are to the r. of the hall, pantry, buttery,
and kitchen to the l. The former is the case at Ockwells, but
the kitchen and the buttery and pantry are in a separate W
range separated from the front range by a small courtyard.
The house originally had a chapel which came forward from
the SE angle of the façade. All that remains of it is a brick
wall with some plain windows and two doorways. The W and
S sides of the house are also brick, not half-timber. The NE
range is C19 or C20.

From the porch the HALL is entered through a doorway
the spandrels of which are carved with a griffin and an antelope. In the hall the screen is plain. The hall has an open
timber roof with collar-beams, arched braces, and one tier of
wind-braces. The roof rests on moulded posts, and the braces
are moulded too. Big stone chimneypiece. In the windows a
famous set of armorial STAINED GLASS, eighteen shields in
all. Behind the hall is the courtyard. The exit from the screens
passage leads into a dog-leg CLOISTER which runs along the
S and W sides of the courtyard and has uncusped arched
lights. The function of the cloister is to connect the screens
passage with pantry, buttery, and kitchen. Of this arrangement the most telling witness is now a serving hatch as big as
those at Hampton Court and with iron hinges. No satisfactory
explanation has yet been given for the shifting of the offices
from their customary position, nor is it known where the two
doorways in the S wall of the hall led.

In the room with the hatch is a chimneypiece with the date 1673, but judging by its style clearly of *c.*1550. The WEST PARLOUR has an Elizabethan chimneypiece with caryatids and a Spanish gold and red leather wall covering. A simpler Elizabethan chimneypiece with pilasters to the overmantel in the chamber beyond the high-table end of the hall. Jacobean STAIRCASE and yet another, simpler, Elizabethan chimneypiece in the solar.

To the E of the former chapel is a GATEWAY with a room above whose wooden window has tracery, and beyond the gateway is a BARN, of the same time as the house and also timber-framed. Near by a circular brick DOVECOTE with buttresses.

OLD WINDSOR

9070

Excavations at Kingsbury carried out in the last ten years have revealed the site and many details of the Anglo-Saxon and Norman town.

ST PETER. A C13 flint church by the river Thames. W tower with lancets, doorway, and tower arch with slight chamfers. The same slight chamfers for the S doorway and the chancel doorway. One genuine lancet in the chancel too. Handsome C14 nave windows, straight-headed. *Scott* restored the church in 1863–4, and his are the fine big shingled broach spire and the substantial timber porch. – FONT. Octagonal, Perp, recent. – PAINTINGS. Some original C13 ornamental painting in the chancel, more in the same style, but of the Scott time. – STAINED GLASS. Medieval bits in several windows. – S aisle one by *Kempe*. – PLATE. Set of 1701; Chalice and Paten 1750. – MONUMENTS. Mrs Sheridan † 1817, *Coade* stone; in the churchyard, S of the church. – Charles A. Murray † 1895. Recess with tomb-chest and recumbent effigy. Two members of the family upright against the back wall.

BEAUMONT COLLEGE. The Society of Jesus bought the estate in 1854 for its novices. The school was established in 1861. It started with Beaumont Lodge as its building, a house designed by *Henry Emlyn* of Windsor and built in 1790. It is of nine bays with a recessed giant portico and would be a Georgian mansion like many others, if it had not been for Emlyn's ill-advised invention of, and plea for, an 'English order' incorporating the Star of the Garter. That alone, if for example confined to the capitals, might have been innocuous, but Emlyn's idea was to couple columns, let them grow out of one painful squashed common lower part, and hide the place of the splitting by the Garter Star. Alas right at the top the columns remember again that they are Siamese twins and share one pair of volutes in the capital. Good staircase round an apsed space with an iron handrail. The range to the r. of the mansion is of 1865 and may be by *Hansom*. The range was extended to the E in 1870, also probably by Hansom. The CHAPEL was designed by Hansom in 1870. But the mural decoration in a highly surprising Raphael style, i.e. with 'grottesche' of the Pompeian and the Vatican loggie kind, is by *Bentley*, 1873–6. In the same years he did the high altar, reredos, tabernacle, and throne. The HIGH ALTAR is a ciborium with two angels, the REREDOS is in the Venetian Renaissance style with five painted saints, but also little pediments and garlands.* The room is tunnel-vaulted and articulated by pilasters. Penetrations in the vault. In 1884 *Bentley* enlarged the chapel by a low N aisle. Piers and segmental arches dying into them and the segmental aisle vault glazed in the centre of each bay.

ST JOHN'S (Beaumont College Preparatory School). By *Bentley*, 1888. Brick and yellow stone. French Renaissance. A symmetrical front with, l. and r. of the entrance, two short polygonal turrets and, on top, a white lantern turret. Gabled angle pavilions. On the l. the chapel projects, with Perp windows and a small turret on the side away from the façade. On the r. at an obtuse angle the kitchens and infirmary. The back is rather more Georgian in style.

OLD WINDSOR HOSPITAL, the former WORKHOUSE. 1835 by *Scott & Moffatt*. Not classical; already Tudor. Red brick with diapers. Gables and dormers. A symmetrical composition with a raised three-bay centre, two canted bay windows, and a cupola.

(THE PRIORY contains a small octagonal room in which a date 1762 has recently been found. This belongs to the conversions carried out for Dicky Bateman, as Horace Walpole calls him, by *J. H. Muntz*.)

PADWORTH

Church and house close together.

ST JOHN BAPTIST. Nave and apsed chancel, timber bell-turret. Roughcast. Entirely Norman. N and S doorways with decorated colonnettes and arches and also capitals with leaves

* The wing to the l. of the house of 1790 is by *Adrian G. Scott*, 1937.

and with volutes. The chancel arch quite grand in its proportions, tall, and again with busy leaf capitals. – COMMUNION RAIL. C17. – (PAINTING. On the E wall of the nave traces of a large St Nicholas with the miracle of the three boys below. Also, on the r. of the saint a recumbent figure.) – STAINED GLASS. In the apse by *Kempe*, 1891. – PLATE. Cup and Cover, 1664; Cup, 1742. – MONUMENTS. Mrs Loftus Brightwell † 1711, standing monument with a big base and two putti l. and r. of a coat of arms on the top. – Christopher Griffith † 1776. Signed by *J. Wilton*. Large female figure bending over an urn with a portrait medallion.

PADWORTH HOUSE. Built *c.*1769 by *J. Hobcraft*. Cemented brick. To the S seven-bay centre with lower three-bay wings, to the N nine and five bays respectively. The centre of the centre is pedimented on both sides. Doorway with Tuscan columns on the S, Ionic columns on the N side. Triangular and segmental pediments respectively. Plasterwork by *Joseph Rose*, especially the principal saloon and the entrance hall. In this the staircase runs up in three flights, the second right above the doorway. Very elegant stucco panels. The top landing carried on Roman Doric columns and itself with Adamish columns. The space below the landing is groin-vaulted; so is the landing itself. Good fireplace in the saloon. A Gothick fireplace comes from the fishing lodge.

FISHING LODGE, ½ m. N. A charming Gothick façade with an ogee-headed doorway between two niches and an embattled gable.

HOUSE, Padworth Common. By *Raymond Lockyer*, 1961. Well planned; modest appearance. The house cost just over £4,0 00.

GRIM'S BANK, *see* Aldermaston.

PANGBOURNE

ST JAMES. Brick tower with brick quoins. That fits the year when it was built: 1718. The battlements have stone angles. The church is of 1866, by *J. Woodman*. It is a spacious building with Late Geometrical to Dec tracery, and the strictly naturalistic capitals and the two-bay arcade to the organ chamber the Victorians liked so much. – PULPIT. Jacobean, with large blank arches and much arabesque work. – PLATE. Cup, 1677; Flagon, 1692; Paten, 1698; Cup, 1737. – MONUMENTS. Sir John Davis † 1625. Large, of grey stone, three recumbent effigies, coupled Tuscan columns l. and r. and a pediment. – Three daughters of Sir John Suckling

† 1658–61. Remarkably reticent and classical. Black and white marble tablet with an open segmental pediment.

By the w end of the church stands CHURCH COTTAGE by *Stokes*, c.1900. A little to the E of the church is THE SQUARE. Here, and along the bit of Whitchurch Road to the railway arch, a group of houses and shops also by *Stokes*, c.1900, a nice quiet, yet varied composition. Grey headers and red brick the r. building, roughcast the l.

Again by *Stokes* at the start of SHOOTER'S HILL, i.e. the Oxford road, a big house of 1898, the symmetrical façade with a bold upper overhang carried on two bay windows. Gables above and small Venetian windows in them; this also a happy composition. Further along Shooter's Hill a sequence of more run-of-the-mill Late Victorian houses, locally known as the Seven Deadly Sins.

PANGBOURNE TOWER (Nautical College), 1¼ m. SW. By *Sir John Belcher*, 1897–8. A very ambitious mansion, in a very free William and Mary style. Red brick, but the top of the high, massive porch tower on the entrance side of stone. The garden side is symmetrical, with a slightly recessed centre and outside the wings two lower porch bays with ogee caps. Above the centre of this façade appears a piece of balustrading and a belvedere cupola. Behind the whole of the recessed centre is one long room and behind that, i.e. along the entrance side, runs a gallery with a middle bay window. The doors to the gallery in its ends are of onyx.

E of the college DAVOLI, a new house by *K. G. A. Feakes*, very good in the new architectural idiom of the 1960s: two mono-pitches rising and defeated in their rise by two steep square chimneys of differing height.

PORT JACKSON, Lower Bowden, 1¼ m. WSW. By *Arnold Mitchell*, 1901. Brick and tile-hanging, asymmetrical and gabled.

BERE COURT, 1½ m. SW. Early Georgian, brick, of seven bays. Doorway with Tuscan columns and a triglyph frieze. The window above it round-arched. Entrance hall with charming stucco decoration. Three arches at the far end. Staircase starting in one arm and returning in two. Rather heavy cast-iron balustrade.

PARK PLACE
1⅜ m. SSE of Remenham church

The present house is by *Thomas Cundy*, 1870, in a rather dreary French Renaissance with a tower over one corner of the façade. Pavilion roofs. This house takes the place of that of

(a) *Scenery:* Maidenhead, river Thames

(b) *Scenery:* Finchampstead Ridges

I

Scenery: Combe Gibbet

(a) *Prehistory:* Ashbury, Wayland's Smithy (long barrow and chambered tomb)

(b) *Prehistory:* Uffington, White Horse, first century B.C. (?)

(a) *Church Exteriors*: Warfield church, east window, Decorated

(b) *Church Exteriors*: Windsor Castle, porch into the cloister, c. 1350

4

Church Exteriors: Windsor Castle, St George's Chapel, begun 1475

5

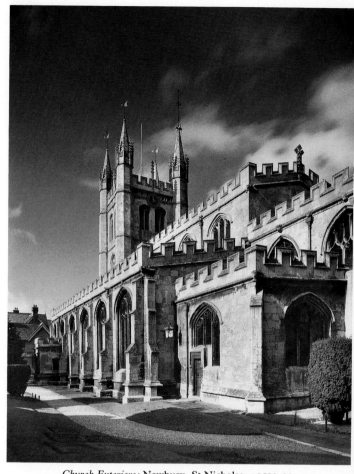

Church Exteriors: Newbury, St Nicholas, *c.*1500–32

Church Exteriors: Sunningwell, west porch, *c.*1560–70

(a) *Church Exteriors:* Ruscombe, south aisle, 1638–9

(b) *Church Exteriors:* Uffington, transept east windows, 1677–9(?)

8

(b) *Church Towers*: Hungerford,
by John Pinch, 1816

(a) *Church Towers*: Wallingford, St Peter,
spire by Sir Robert Taylor, 1777

9

Church Interiors: Windsor Castle, St George's Chapel, begun 1475

(a) *Church Interiors:* Abingdon, St Helen, fifteenth and sixteenth centuries

(b) *Church Interiors:* Shrivenham, 1638

Church Interiors: Windsor Castle, chapel (demolished), by Hugh May, 1684–6

12

Anglo-Saxon Doorway: Coleshill, Strattenborough Castle Farm, tympanum, eleventh century

(a) *Norman Doorway:* Charney Bassett, south doorway, tympanum, eleventh century

(b) *Church Furnishings:* Avington, font, twelfth century

14

Church Furnishings: Hampstead Norris, relief of a knight on horseback, late thirteenth century

(b) *Church Furnishings*: Windsor Castle,
St George's Chapel, door of Henry III's Chapel,

(a) *Church Furnishings*: Uffington,
south door, thirteenth century

(b) *Church Furnishings*: Long Wittenham, piscina-monument, late thirteenth century

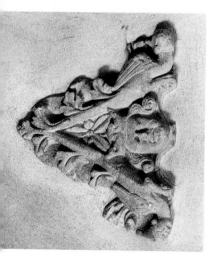

(a) *Church Furnishings*: Ardington, sculptural fragment, late thirteenth century

17

(a) *Church Furnishings*: North Moreton, stained glass, c.1300

(b) *Church Furnishings*: Warfield, screen and rood loft, fifteenth century

18

Church Furnishings: Windsor Castle, St George's Chapel, choir stalls, mainly by William Berkeley, 1478–85

19

(a) *Church Furnishings:* Abingdon, St Helen,
painted ceiling in north aisle, *c.*1390

(b) *Church Furnishings:* Littlewick Green, Adoration of the Magi,
North Italian, early fifteenth century

(a) and (b) *Church Furnishings:* Windsor Castle, St George's Chapel, west window, stained glass, early sixteenth century

(a) *Church Furnishings:* Stanford-in-the-Vale, wooden font and cover, early seventeenth century

(b) *Church Furnishings:* Binfield, hourglass stand, seventeenth century

Church Furnishings: Stratfield Mortimer, St John, Christ at Emmaus,
by N. H. J. Westlake

Church Furnishings: Longworth, stained glass by Heywood Sumner, 1900

(a) *Church Monuments:* Aldworth, members of the de la Beche family, early fourteenth century

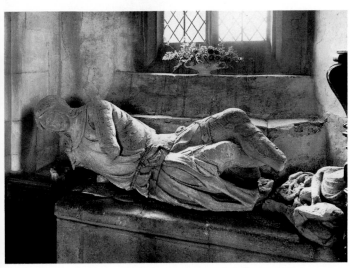

(b) *Church Monuments:* Aldworth, one of the de la Beche family, *c.*1290

(a) *Church Monuments:* Sparsholt,
oak effigy of a lady,
early fourteenth century

(b) *Church Monuments:* Fyfield,
Sir John Golafre †1442

Church Monuments: Aldermaston,
Sir George Forster and wife (detail), *c.*1530

(a) *Church Monuments:*
Shottesbrooke, William
Throkmorton †1535

(b) *Church Monuments:* Windsor Castle,
St George's Chapel, the Earl of Lincoln †1585
(*Copyright Country Life*)

Church Monuments: Bisham, Lady Margaret Hoby †1605

(a) *Church Monuments*: Bisham, Lady Elizabeth Hoby †1609

(b) *Church Monuments*: Reading, St Laurence, John Blagrave †1611

30

(a) *Church Monuments:* Englefield,
Mary Benyon †1777, by Thomas Carter

(b) *Church Monuments:* Speen,
Margrave of Anspach †1806, by Antonio Canova

31

Church Monuments: Windsor Castle, St George's Chapel,
Princess Charlotte †1817, by M. C. Wyatt

Church Monuments: Windsor Castle, Albert Memorial Chapel,
Duke of Clarence †1892, by Alfred Gilbert, detail

(a) *Abbeys:* Reading, twelfth century

(b) *Abbeys:* Abingdon, The Chequer, chimneystack,
late thirteenth century

(a) *Secular Buildings:* Windsor Castle, as in the sixteenth century. Engraving

(b) *Secular Buildings:* Windsor Castle, air view

(a) *Secular Buildings:* Cholsey, Manor Farm, barn, *c.*1200. Engraving

(b) *Secular Buildings:* Abingdon, Christ's Hospital,
1446 and seventeenth century

Secular Buildings: Donnington Castle, licensed 1386

Ockwells Manor House, 1446/66 (*Copyright Country Life*)

(b) Windsor Castle, Queen Elizabeth's Gallery, chimneypiece, 1583

(a) Bisham Abbey, great hall, chimneypiece c.1560, overmantel c.1600
(Copyright Country Life)

39

(a) Shaw House, completed 1581

(b) Ashdown Park, c.1660

Aldermaston Court, staircase, 1636 (*Copyright Country Life*)

Gatepiers (a, b, c, *Copyright Country Life*) (a) and (b) Coleshill House, by Roger Pratt, *c.*1650–62 (c) Sutton Courtenay, Manor House, mid seventeenth century (d) and (e) Hamstead Marshall, by Thomas Strong (?), 1675(?) (f) Hamstead Marshall, early eighteenth century

42

Swallowfield Park, doorway, by William Talman, 1689/91

Wokingham, Lucas Hospital, 1665 (*Copyright Country Life*)

(a) Windsor, town hall, by Sir Thomas Fitch, c.1687, completed by Wren, 1689–90

(b) Abingdon, town hall, built by Christopher Kempster, 1678–82

Windsor Castle, Queen's Presence Chamber, *temp.* Charles II,
carving by Grinling Gibbons

46

(a) Abingdon, Brick Alley Almshouses, built by Samuel Westbrooke, 1718

(b) West Hanney House, 1727 (*Copyright Country Life*)

(a) Hall Place, c.1730–5, chimneypiece
(Copyright Country Life)

(b) Farley Hill, Farley Hall, c.1730, entrance hall
(Copyright Country Life)

48

Hall Place, *c.*1730–5, drawing room, Italian stucco work (*Copyright Country Life*)

(a) Speen, Benham Park, by Capability Brown, 1772–5, portico

(b) Basildon Park, by John Carr, 1776, gates

(a) Coleshill, Strattenborough Castle Farm, 1792

(b) Kintbury, Halfway House, late eighteenth century

(a) Milton House, library, 1776 (*Copyright Country Life*)

(b) Windsor Castle, Great Park, Virginia Water, ruins from Lepcis Magna, erected 1826

Windsor Castle, Home Park, Frogmore House, 1792,
room decorated by Mary Moser

(a) Sandhurst, Royal Military Academy, by John Sanders, 1807–12

(b) Reading, Royal Berkshire Hospital, by Henry Briant, 1837–9

Windsor Castle, Crimson Drawing Room, door from Carlton House, *c.*1810

Windsor Castle, Grand Reception Room, by Sir Jeffry Wyatville, *c.*1820–30

Kingston Lisle House, staircase, *c.*1825–30

(a) Inkpen, school, by G. E. Street, 1850

(b) Newbury, St Nicholas School, by William Butterfield, 1859

(a) Wellington College, by John Shaw, 1856–9

(b) Bear Wood, by Robert Kerr, designed in 1864

59

Windsor Castle, Home Park, Dairy, by John Thomas, 1858

Buscot Park, *c.*1770, parlour, paintings by Sir Edward Burne-Jones, 1890

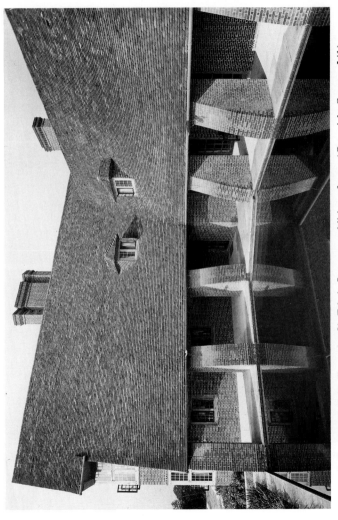

Sulhamstead, Folly Farm, by Sir Edwin Lutyens, addition of 1912 (*Copyright Country Life*)

Wokingham, Luckley, by Sir Ernest Newton, 1907

Bracknell, Point Royal, by Arup Associates, 1960–4

the Conway family, and the interest of Park Place is its grounds
as beautified by General Conway, who bought the estate in
1752. In his time the grounds were 900 acres in size. To his
period belong the handsome obelisk piers close to the entrance
to the house, and the OBELISK W of the house, but not the
seeming obelisk E of the house which turns out to be the little
top SPIRE of St Bride's in the City, erected by Mr Fuller Mait-
land in 1837. Conway work also the CYCLOPIC BRIDGE at
the foot of HAPPY VALLEY (now part of the grounds of
a house of that name). This was built in 1781–6. The stones
said to come from Reading Abbey are in fact much too
cyclopean for that. Every stone, Horace Walpole writes, was
placed by the general's own direction. The stones came from
fourteen different counties, and the bridge cost £2,000. On
the river side they are conglomerate and form voussoir stones.
At the top of Happy Valley the GROTTO, six tunnel-vaulted
entries into a cross-tunnel-vaulted long, low room with
niches. Here also, it is said, stones from Reading Abbey were
used. From here the Thames looks through the bridge as if
it were immediately beyond. In fact there is plenty of space
and e.g. a pretty early C19 COTTAGE with bargeboarded
gables which was built as a boathouse. Yet a little further s
an estate called TEMPLE COMBE and in this the DRUIDIC
TEMPLE, called by Horace Walpole 'little master Stonehenge',
a STONE CIRCLE found in Jersey in 1785 and brought over as
a gift to General Conway in 1787. The stones were all re-
erected accurately, and Walpole is right, as usual, when he
calls the monument 'very high-priestly'. The circle stood
originally on Mont de la Ville, St Helier, Jersey. In its original
form the tomb was covered by a mound of earth revetted with
drystone walling, but only the megalithic structure was erected
in the park. In its present form it consists of a stone-built
passage 15 ft long and 5 ft wide roofed with four capstones
leading to a circular area enclosed by a ring of thirty upright
slabs against which are built five cells roofed with capstones
but open to the centre. The diameter of this circle is now 27 ft,
although a contemporary plan made before its removal from
Jersey shows it to have been originally 21 ft in diameter. Some
slight additions appear to have been made to the monument
as a number of the stones are of a sandstone unknown in
Jersey but outcropping in Berkshire.*

* The house was rebuilt in 1963–4 to designs of *Hadley & Partners*.
Large, and all living quarters on one storey. A curvaceous design.

4070

PEASEMORE

St BARNABAS. The W tower is of red brick and carries an inscription: 1737 Will Coward Gent. built ye tower. The top of blue brick, however, and the recessed spire are of 1842, the date when the rest of the church was built, also of blue brick. In 1866 *Street* added the chancel (GS), and on that occasion probably also altered the windows and provided the N porch. – REREDOS. By *Earp* (BC). – FRONTAL. Five Netherlandish panels, C17 clearly by their ornament, but still entirely Mannerist in the figures. They are rustic but very forceful and deserve a careful look.

PERBOROUGH CASTLE see COMPTON

PORT JACKSON see PANGBOURNE

POUGHLEY FARMHOUSE see CHADDLEWORTH

PRIESTWOOD see BRACKNELL

PRIOR'S COURT see CHIEVELEY

6070

PURLEY

St MARY. Re-set inside the church is the Norman chancel arch. Single-scallop capitals, strong roll moulding, abacus with saltire crosses in chip carving – i.e. first half of the C12. Of the early C13 a re-set lancet and doorway in the vestry. In the chancel a partly original lancet on the N side. The W tower is of brick and dated 1626. But mostly the church is of 1870, by *Street*, and it is not a church that could contribute to his fame. – FONT. Norman, on short, stubby columns, decorated in different ways. – PLATE. Almsdish of 1683; Chalice and Paten of 1733. – MONUMENTS. Anne Hyde † 1632, tablet with small, stiff reclining figure on her side and a baby in the same position. Two obelisks. – Pretty tablet of coloured marbles, date of death 1772. – Good Grecian group of a family turning towards an urn on a high pedestal. On it the portrait of the deceased. A genius with an extinguished torch stands by the pedestal. This commemorates Anthony Storer, who died in 1818. No signature of a sculptor of this well-done monument.

The church is reached along a regrettable bungaloscape.

PURLEY PARK, ¼ m. SW. By *James Wyatt*, c.1800. Five-bay façade of Portland stone. Porte-cochère of pairs of Tuscan columns. The centre bay with the porte-cochère is framed by giant pilasters. Towards the Thames semicircular bow with detached wooden columns. On this side the house has only three bays. Entrance hall with two fluted Ionic columns. Staircase with a spare iron balustrade of an unusual design of interlocking ovals. Two delicate stucco ceilings.

PURLEY HALL, 1½ m. WSW. The front with two symmetrical canted bay windows and mullioned and transomed windows is of the early C17. The entrance side has a porch of 1869, the E front Early-Victorian-looking trim. Inside a fine if small entrance hall with grisaille wall-paintings in the *Thornhill* style: standing figures, trophies, etc. The staircase has slender twisted balusters and carved tread-ends. Its underside is part of the painting scheme. All this seems to be of *c.*1700, but on a rainwater head is a date 1719. Late Georgian SUMMER HOUSE by the lake; stone and flint rustication. 'Venetian' opening under a pediment. Inside a niche. Probably of the same time the LODGES. Whole flints and brick bands, circular windows, battlements.

PUSEY

ALL SAINTS. Built about 1745–50 for J. A. Pusey, who died in 1753. Oblong, with N and S transeptal chapels and a W porch. The top of the tower looks a remodelling of *c.*1840 – see the Italian villa type of roof, and the Grecian acroteria. It is in fact not on the Buckler drawing. The windows are arched, but the three principal windows Venetian. The chapels are separated from the nave by beautiful Venetian screens. Also a W doorway into the S chapel, internally pedimented. – SCULPTURE. Small German Entombment relief, *c.*1500. The background openwork traceried windows. – MONUMENTS. Incised slab to Henry Doggett and wife † 1480. – M. Dunch † 1679 by *William Bird*. Tablet with two awkward weeping putti. – The comparison with the neighbouring tablet of 1707 is telling. – Jane Pusey † 1742 and J. A. Pusey † 1753. By *P. Scheemakers*. Large monument with reredos background. In front of it young woman seated on the ground. Above bust of the husband in a medallion.

PUSEY HOUSE. Built in 1753. Stone, of five bays and two and a half storeys with two-storey wings and quadrant walls to entrance as well as garden. They have niches with busts and end in pedimented features. The niches have grotto-like vermiculated rustication. The doorway on the entrance side has Tuscan columns and a triglyph frieze. Entrance hall with a screen of columns to the l. Staircase with simple lyre-type wrought-iron railing. In the garden a Chinese BRIDGE across the lake and a square TEMPLE with a low dome. Quatrefoil frieze at the top of the square. In the temple a STATUE of Mrs Brotherton, née Pusey, dated 1759, and busts on tapering pillars in the four corners.

QUEEN ANNE'S MEAD see SWALLOWFIELD

RADCOT BRIDGE see LITTLEWORTH

RADLEY

ST JAMES. Mostly Perp, and curious in that the s arcade has sturdy and high wooden posts instead of piers and longitudinal arched braces instead of arches. Unbuttressed small w tower. Embattled s aisle. The diagonal chancel buttresses have pinnacles, and along the chancel N and s sides runs a fleuron frieze. – FONT. Norman, drum-shaped, with blank arches on colonnettes. – STALLS. C17, with C17 MISERICORDS, mostly with cherubs' heads. The surprising date may be connected with the damage suffered by Radley in the Civil War. – PULPIT. The Late Perp canopy is a rarity. It is said to have belonged originally to the Speaker's chair in the House of Commons. The broad back panel has partly Flamboyant and partly linenfold patterns. – STAINED GLASS. Much very interesting heraldic glass of the C16, supplemented very skilfully by *Willement*. In the E window also larger parts of an early C16 composition, French or Flemish. – In the w window a large portrait which also looks early C16. – PLATE. Paten, 1571; Cup, 1605; Almsdish, c.1700; Flagon, 1705; Brass Almsdish, probably Flemish C16, with the Virgin and Child and the Signs of the Evangelists. – MONUMENTS. Sir William Stonhouse † 1631 and his son † 1632. Large standing monument by *Nicholas Stone*. Recumbent alabaster effigies of husband and wife, he behind and a little above her. The son kneels large on the r. Other children in relief below. Shallow back arch and open top pediment. – Sir George Bowyer † 1800. By *Nollekens*. Tablet with circular inscription in a laurel medallion. Gun, flag, etc., below. – Davis family, c.1822. Dainty triptych with an urn. By *J. Lock* of Abingdon.

RADLEY COLLEGE. The nucleus is RADLEY HALL, built in 1721–7 by *William Townesend* of Oxford as mason and perhaps architect. Nine-bay house of red brick with stone dressings and especially quoins of even length at the angles and the angles of the centres. None of the centres have pediments. Three and a half storeys. Arched ground-floor windows. The entrance doorway has a rusticated surround in which the flanking pilasters partly disappear (cf. Kingston House). Volutes down the window above. To the garden good, simpler doorway with carved brackets. Radley College was started in 1847. Of that year is the very odd CAMPANILE (architect *Howard*), of brick, square in plan, but set diagonally and with far-projecting buttresses.* E of Radley Hall and connected with it by a covered walk is a forecourt with the CHAPEL l. (s) and the DINING HALL r. (N). This group is by *Sir T. G. Jackson*, the covered walk of 1891, the chapel of 1895, the dining hall of 1910. The boys' house opposite is of 1886. Older buildings to the N, i.e. round the campanile: SCHOOL, W of it, of 1848, UPPER DORMITORY W of this, of 1849, the OCTAGON attached to it on its W side of 1857, GALLERY DORMITORY, SW of the campanile, of 1859, and the GYMNASIUM, E of the campanile, also of 1859. Many later additions, those of between the two wars mostly by *H. I. Merriman & A. B. Knapp Fisher*. The NEW LABORATORY, E of the main older group, is by *W. G. Newton*, 1937, of concrete, with a radiating plan and horizontal windows, inspired by the same architect's laboratory at Marlborough. Eight CLASSROOMS were added in 1960–1. They are by *Gollins, Melvin, Ward & Partners*, a straight-forward curtain-walling job, uncommonly well detailed.

WICK HALL, 1 m. SW. Built *c*.1700. Five bays, the ones l. and r. of the doorway narrower. Two storeys, hipped roof. Wooden cross-windows. Fine shell-hood over the door. Staircase with twisted balusters. (Jacobean screen in the drawing room, and another in the library. NBR)

READING

7070

INTRODUCTION

Two basic facts must be considered to understand the history of Reading: its position characterized already by William of Malmesbury as a potential *diversorium ad populosiores urbes Angliae* for all travellers, and its Cluniac abbey founded by Henry I in 1121 and the king's favourite monastic establishment. A castle also existed but was destroyed already in 1151.

---

* They were added in 1855 to create ball-courts.

Later the cloth trade supported Reading, as it supported so many English towns. Leland states that the town 'standith by clothing', and Archbishop Laud's father was a Reading clothier. Defoe still called Reading 'very large, wealthy, handsomely built'. Of his time the evidence must now be sought out.

READING ABBEY

The abbey was founded as a Cluniac house by Henry I. It was colonized from Lewes and was for 100 monks. In 1305 there were 65, in 1445 only 35. The time of Henry I was probably the climax. Much survives, but all except the inner gatehouse in so fragmentary a state that is of little architectural even if of much picturesque value. The extent was considerable. It starts where the Perambulation on p. 204 is going to start, by the Market Place. The church of St Laurence (p. 199) was the parish church *ante portas* of the abbey, with the outer gate formerly attached to its s flank. N of the church, now entered from Valpy Street or a passage N of St Laurence's churchyard, is part of the HOSPITIUM of St John Baptist, a range of flint with a polygonal stair-turret of brick on the N side. The range dates from 1486, when it was converted into a school. A good deal further E than St Laurence, at the E end of Forbury, is the INNER GATEHOUSE (Abbey Gate). This is of the late C13, but was drastically restored by *Scott* in 1869. Flint and stone, with angle turrets. The outer N arch is pointed, the inner round. The s arch is round too. Remains of a rib-vault with fillets on the ribs. Large lancet windows. What survives of the church and the ranges round the cloister is E of the abbey gate, s of the Catholic church, and immediately w of the gaol. It is as follows. Nothing of the nave and aisles of the CHURCH except the SE respond of the nave, where it is attached to the N arch of the s transept, walling of the s transept quite high up, remains of the two E chapels of that transept, and, just s of the Catholic church, of the two E chapels of the N transept, nothing of the chancel with its ambulatory which would now be inside the gaol, then s of the s transept the tunnel-vaulted SLYPE and a room above, s of this the CHAPTER HOUSE, oblong and apsed, and, visible quite high up, the w wall of the DORMITORY s of the chapter house, the high s wall of the REFECTORY w of the dormitory wall, i.e. s of where the cloister lay, and the REREDORTER, at r. angles to the s end of the dormitory, i.e. across a drain split off the Kennet. Finally, back in the streets of the town, s of Abbey Square, something of the ABBEY MILL incorporated into the present Abbey Mills. C12 arches, one with zigzag, one with a single chamfer, and two smaller ones. The south gate to the abbey precinct lay at the w end of Abbey Square.

But by far the most interesting survival of the abbey is the CAPITALS and other fragments now mostly in the Reading Museum, but some also in the Victoria and Albert Museum. They are partly ornamented with beaded bands, rather wildly entwined, partly figured. One particularly strange capital has two bearded angels, another the earliest surviving representation of the Coronation of the Virgin. The size of the capitals makes it clear that they were originally in the cloister. Their style derived from that of the Canterbury crypt. Their date may be c.1130. Henry I was buried in the chancel of the church in 1136. The piers and the voussoirs of the arches were carved too. One fragment in the Victoria and Albert Museum shows beakhead, and probably represents the earliest occurrence of this motif in England. It can be regarded as the child of West French and Viking parents. Fragments from the abbey were used after the dilapidation and demolition all over the Reading region.

CHURCHES

ST LAURENCE. The church looks down the Market Place. Originally the outer abbey gate was immediately attached to its s flank. Early C12 the SE quoins of the nave, a small s window in the nave, and fragments of a doorway re-set in the N aisle. In 1196 the Hospitium of St John Baptist was founded (see above), and probably in connexion with this the church was enlarged, see the E wall of the chancel with three lancets, shafted inside, and the nave s doorway, still with waterleaf capitals. Round arch with a filleted roll. A little later the w respond of the N arcade with its arch springer (i.e. a N aisle was built) and the N chapel arcade of three bays with round piers and early stiff-leaf capitals still keeping close to the bell and close to the upper edge. Perp w tower with polygonal buttresses and a tall arch to the nave and a lower one to the N aisle which embraces the tower. The outer aisle wall has straight-headed windows. Of the same time the E respond of the N arcade. But the arcade itself was rebuilt in 1522. Perp also the nave roof with tie-beams and kingposts. – FONT. Octagonal, Perp, of 1522, nothing special. – PULPIT. A fine piece of the C18, with inlay work. – BENCH ENDS. With tracery panels and poppy-heads (chancel). – ORGAN CASE. By *Byfield*, 1741. Supported on big neo-Elizabethan posts. – PLATE. Flagon and Almsdish, 1631; two Cups and Patens, 1637; Flagon, 1638; Patens, 1701 and 1708; Almsdishes, 1735 and 1752; Wine Strainer, 1730/1; Head on a staff, 1790/1. – MONUMENTS. Brass to John Kent and wife, early C15. Demi-figures, 12 in. long (N chapel). – Brass to a man, early C16, 23 in. figure (ditto). – Brass to Walter Barton † 1538, 2 ft figure. Palimpsest (ditto). – Thomas Lydall † 1608. Low diptych with kneeling figures and three columns (N aisle). – John Blagrave † 1611, author of *The Mathematical Jewell*. Demi-figure, frontal, with sphere and quadrant. In the surround five small figures, l., r., and above. They represent the five regular geometrical solids. – Mrs Hamley † 1636. Kneeling figure (s wall). – Ann Haydon † 1747. Still with the figure kneeling. – Dr Valpy, 1838. Life-size standing figure high up under a giant arch. By *E. C. Hakewill*, executed by *Samuel Nixon* (BC). – Along the W half of the s wall Blagrave in 1619 built an arcade known as Blagrave's Piazza. It was six arches long and was pulled down in 1868.

ST AGNES, Northumberland Avenue. 1938 by *E. Ravenscroft*. Red brick, with an Italian low-pitch roof to the crossing tower.

ALL SAINTS, Downshire Square. 1865–74 by *St Aubyn*. E.E., with a bellcote over the E end of the nave. Ornate W doorway. Ornate mosaic W wall inside by the font. Very ornate chancel of 1889–90 with an apse. Fine tall proportions internally. – PULPIT. Of wrought iron.

ST BARTHOLOMEW, London Road. The church is by *Waterhouse*, 1879, the chancel by *Bodley*, 1881. Blue and red brick, lancet windows, bellcote. Low round polished granite piers. The finest thing is the chancel E wall with its Dec window high up.

CHRIST CHURCH, Christchurch Road. By *Woodyer*, 1861–2, enlarged 1874. An exceptionally rewarding High Victorian church and very typical of Woodyer. Big, with a NW porch steeple. E.E. style. The clerestory with bold blank tracery. The crockets of the gable over the porch entrance have remained uncarved and look like the New Brutalism. Inside, the arcade piers very personal, with closely set Purbeck shafts and big capitals with ever so many gablets and naturalistic flowers. Eastlake in 1872 called them 'difficult to accept as agreeable in an artistic sense'. The clerestory has openwork-cusped rere-arches. But the most astonishing and successful feature is the openwork tympanum in the chancel arch, an arched band of trefoils carrying reticulation. – The PULPIT is no doubt by Woodyer too. – Richly sculptured REREDOS by *Birnie Philip* (BC). – STAINED GLASS in the chancel and clerestory by *Hardman*, 1868 (BC).

ST GILES, Southampton Street. 1873 by *J. P. St Aubyn*, except for the C13 aisle walls and the Perp tower. The tower now carries a spire. Flint. Very rich E.E. chancel. – SCULPTURE. Fragments in the tower, including a large Norman capital. They probably come from the abbey. – STAINED GLASS. In the S chapel by *Powell's*, designed by *Wooldridge*, 1872. – PLATE. Silver-gilt Chalices and Covers of 1599 and 1618; Paten, 1632; three Flagons of 1636, 1637, and 1639. – MONUMENTS. Brass to John Bowyer † 1521 and wife; 19 in. figures. – Uncommonly many C18 tablets, including some of uncommon design (e.g. Thomas Paterson † 1746).

GREYFRIARS. The Franciscans arrived at Reading in 1233 and went to their present site in 1285. Money for the *opus fratrum minorum* was bequeathed in 1311. That fits the details of the church. It was in fact almost entirely reconstructed in 1863 (by *Woodman*), but on sufficient evidence. Nave and aisles, transepts, but no chancel. Everything E of the chancel arch remained destroyed. The N transept was built wholly afresh. Of the piers, which are square with semicircular projections, most are original. Moulded arches. In the transept windows intersecting tracery. The large W window with reticulated tracery. The big E bellcote is of course of 1863. – (TILES. In a showcase. With sporting themes.)

ST JAMES (R.C.), Forbury Road. 1837–40 by *Pugin*, in the Norman style which he would never have chosen even a few years later. His reason must have been proximity to the abbey ruins. The S aisle and the ambulatory round the apse are recent (*W. C. Mangan*, 1925). The N aisle was completed only in 1962 (*H. Bingham Towner*). – FONT. A C12 stone found on the abbey site. Block with interlacing.

ST JOHN EVANGELIST, Watlington Street. 1872–3 by *W. A. Dixon*. Big, with a SW spire. E.E. Coarse and rock-faced. The window dressings in buff and red stone.

ENGLISH MARTYRS (R.C.), Tilehurst Road. 1926 by *W. C. Mangan*. Brick. Demonstratively Italian. With a NW campanile and an octagonal crossing tower.

ST MARY (Episcopalian), Castle Street. 1798, but mostly
1840–2. The original architect was *R. Billing*. A fine Grecian
façade with six giant Corinthian columns and a pediment.
The cupola has been lost. The portico etc. is by *H. & N. Briant*
(BC).

ST MARY, St Mary's Butts. In the N wall a Norman doorway,
re-set. S arcade of *c*.1200. Four bays, round piers, capitals in
the transition from waterleaf to stiff-leaf, octagonal abaci,
round arches with one big chamfer. At the E end of the N
aisle an arch of *c*.1300 which must once have connected a N
transept with an E chapel. The chancel is of 1864, the N aisle
is of 1872. The W tower is as late as 1550–3: chequer flint and
stone, with polygonal buttresses. – FONT. Octagonal, with
quatrefoils, but not Perp. It was given in 1616. – SCREEN.
Under the tower arch. With a band of 1631. – PAINTING.
Christ and the Syro-Phoenician Woman. Attributed to
Lodovico Carracci. Given by (the later) Dean Milman. Large
(S aisle). – PLATE. Silver-gilt Cup and Cover, 1592; two silver-
gilt Patens, 1626; Flagon, 1628; large Flagon, 1652; Chalice
and Cover inscribed 1661; silver-gilt Spoon, 1668; large
Bowl, 1767; Almsdish inscribed 1776. – MONUMENTS.
William Kendrick † 1635. Two kneeling figures facing one
another. Top pediment, segmental and broken, already with
a thick garland between, i.e. on the way from Jacobean to
classical. – John Monk † 1809, by *Flaxman*. The expiring man
in a chair fortified by a standing figure of Faith.

ST PETER, Church Road, Earley. 1844 by *J. Turner*, the aisles
and chancel 1882–3. Grey vitrified brick. NW tower.

ST STEPHEN, Rupert Street. 1864–6 by *William White*.
Enlarged (S aisle and chapel) 1886. Brick, with bellcote and
plate tracery. E.E. Brick exposed inside. The capitals naturalistic or stylized.

CEMETERY. 1842–3 by *William Brown*. Classical entrance
gate and chapels with a Tuscan portico and pediment.

PUBLIC BUILDINGS

SHIRE HALL, Forbury. 1904–11 by *Hall & Warwick*. Stone.
Free Palladian and quite lively. Not big.

MUNICIPAL BUILDINGS, Blagrave Street. 1872–5 by *Waterhouse*. Addition by *Thomas Lainson*, 1879–82. Blue and red
brick. Large, Gothic, and asymmetrical, with a tower at the
S end. Inside an Italianate concert hall, in fact the plain brick
town hall of 1786 minus one bay.

TELEPHONE EXCHANGE, Minster Street. By *Stokes*, illustrated
in 1908. Five bays, symmetrical, not really in any period style.

UNIVERSITY, Whiteknights Estate. The Whiteknights Estate
belonged to the Englefields from 1606 to 1798 and then to the
Marquess of Blandford, later fifth Duke of Marlborough.
He had famous ornamental grounds with rare plants, described by Mrs Holland in 1819. His library was even more
famous. He overspent on it all, and in 1819 a twenty-three-
day sale of the library was held. The estate went to Sir Isaac
Lyon Goldsmid, bullion broker, in 1849. He was the first
Jewish baronet (1841). In 1867 the estate was divided into
six leaseholds.

Reading University started as a University Extension
College in 1892. It moved to London Road in 1904, the site
having been made available by the Palmer family (of Huntley
& Palmer). The same family gave an endowment of £150,000
in 1911. The college became the University of Reading in
1926 and acquired the new site in 1947. Of the six large
villas, or indeed country houses, on the estate four were by
Waterhouse: Erleigh Park 1859, Whiteknights 1868, Foxhill
(for himself) 1868, and The Wilderness 1873. The first of
these three is demolished and only the lodge remains. The
second and third exist, but the fourth also has gone, though
its stables survive. Foxhill is N of the lake, Whiteknights W
of Foxhill. Whiteknights Park, W of the narrow S part of the
lake, can only be attributed to Waterhouse. Mr Stuart Smith
has found no office evidence on the house. The new buildings
are disappointing, when compared with buildings of the same
years of other universities, old and new. There is really not
one that needs a detailed appreciation. Faculty of Letters by
Easton & Robertson, Cusdin, Preston & Smith,· completed
1957, Physics by the same, completed 1960, Sedimentology
by the same, 1962, Library by the same, 1963, Whiteknights
Hall by *Stanley Meirick*, University Grants Committee's
Architect, 1964.*

TECHNICAL COLLEGE, King's Road. By *Lanchester & Lodge*,
1950–5. Terrible, in the tamest squared-up neo-Georgian of
between the wars. – In front of the entrance every year a
different piece of sculpture is displayed.

---

* For the old buildings Mr Stuart Smith gave me all the information,
for the new, Mr J. F. Johnson. In a letter from Mr Johnson I was told that
in the meantime Windsor Hall and the Department of Chemistry have been
completed. They are also by *Easton & Robertson, Cusdin, Preston & Smith.*

READING SCHOOL, Erleigh Road. 1865–71 by *Waterhouse*. Red brick, long symmetrical front, Tudor. The centre is the hall and this – as we are *c*.1870 – has an asymmetrically placed turret. The chapel, also by Waterhouse, was added in 1873. Many later additions.

LEIGHTON PARK SCHOOL, Shinfield Road. The core is Pepper Manor, but much has been added. *Waterhouse* extended the main building on the SE in 1890 and built Grove House at the N end of the site in 1892–4. This has since also been extended. Townson House with the Libraries, etc., N of the main building, and Peckover Hall, to the NW of the former and E of Grove House, are by *Fred Rowntree*, 1910. Much more since, and especially after the Second World War.

ROYAL BERKSHIRE HOSPITAL, London Road. 1837–9. By *Henry Briant*. A splendid building. Bath stone. Monumental block with a giant portico of six attached Ionic columns and a pediment. The wings were added in 1861, and a further l. wing at r. angles with an end pavilion with Doric pilasters, perfectly in harmony with the original work, followed in 1881–2. This and also the Greek Doric colonnade with an upper floor are by *Morris & Stallwood*, a remarkable feat of keeping in keeping, at a time when this was very rarely done. The r. pavilion is of 1882 too, but the connecting link was only provided in 1912. Good, if not large, staircase under a lantern. The CHAPEL is in the state of 1882.

BATTLE HOSPITAL, Oxford Road. The former WORKHOUSE. 1866–7. Red brick, gabled, i.e. Elizabethan.

GAOL, Forbury Road. 1842–4. Red brick, castellated and symmetrical. By *Scott & Moffatt*.

STATION. 1840. A nice Italianate job of yellow brick with pedimented windows and a cupola.

PERAMBULATION

The town developed on the river Kennet, away from the water-meadows of the Thames. We start in the MARKET PLACE. It is a triangular space of no visual distinction. In the middle the SIMEON MONUMENT of 1804, a triangular pillar, designed by *Soane* and characteristic of him in all its details. On the W side the former CORN EXCHANGE, 1854 by *J. B. Clacy & F. Hawkes*, free, debased Renaissance, quite small, and then a timber-framed house with two oriel windows. On the S side No. 52 with giant pilasters, early C19. On the E side Messrs SUTTON'S, High Victorian Gothic, three generously spaced bays only, with a French pavilion roof. By *W. & J. T. Brown*, 1870–3. At the NW corner No. 25, also with giant pilasters, and also early C19. The house curves round and leads out of the Market Place. From this place to the N to Blagrave Street and the railway.

To the E to FORBURY GARDENS and the MEMORIAL to those fallen in the Afghan wars, an enormous lion by *George Simonds*, 1886. S of the gardens the new building of the PRUDENTIAL ASSURANCE, by *Fitzroy Robinson & Partners*, 1963–4, with an inner courtyard which will one day become a trunk road.

To the W from the N end of the Market Place along FRIAR STREET, with some early C18 houses with segment-headed windows on the N side. Then turn N into STATION ROAD to gaze at Nos 7–25, fantastic Latest Victorian, with a diversity of steep gables and very varied detail altogether. Yellow and red brick, by *Joseph Morris & Son*, 1901–3. At the station corner the GREAT WESTERN HOTEL, opened in 1844, a quiet, small palazzo.

At the W end of Friar Street turn l. and go down West Street to ST MARY'S BUTTS. N of the church the VICARAGE, five bays, 1727, with segment-headed windows,* and the house on its r., also Early Georgian, with a door canopy on sumptuously carved brackets. E of the church the DISPENSARY of 1840, a nice five-bay palazzo with short lower wings. The quoins are diamond-cut. Bath stone. Old houses also on the S side.

Now out to the W, first briefly along OXFORD ROAD, then along Castle Street. In Oxford Road minor early C19 expansion, e.g. MANNSON HOUSE with a Tuscan porch. Much more in CASTLE STREET. First still timber-framing and Early Georgian houses, especially No. 19, of five bays, with segment-headed windows and a doorcase with pilasters and a segmental pediment. The former CONGREGATIONAL CHAPEL with its Soanian ornament and its pedimental gable is of 1837, by *J. J. Cooper*. More Georgian houses, also of Bath stone. Then the VACHEL ALMSHOUSES, two rows of cottages at r. angles to the street. 1864–5 by *W. H. Woodman*. After that No. 63, HOLYBROOK HOUSE, mid C18, of five bays, with a very ambitious heavy doorcase. Columns mightily blocked. Laurel frieze. Carved spandrels. Keystone head. (Staircase with turned balusters, decorated Hall, Rococo ceiling in the Music Room, large garden down to the Holy Brook. MHLG) More Bath stone terraces. Then the street becomes CASTLE

* Pretty fireplaces and staircase (NBR).

HILL, and among further terraces, low Italianate villa gables begin to appear. The continuation of Castle Hill is BATH ROAD. At its beginning some brick houses of 1800, e.g. BRUNSWICK HOUSE (former Blue Coat School), five bays, three storeys, Tuscan porch.

Back to St Mary's Butts and s, down BRIDGE STREET. The only noteworthy house is SEVEN BRIDGES HOUSE, the original Simonds house by the brewery. Five bays, Roman Doric porch. By *Soane*, 1790. Off to the E, in CHURCH STREET, some minor Georgian houses. However, one of them, No. 8, has giant angle pilasters, though it is only two bays wide. It must be of *c*.1720. The continuation of Bridge Street is SOUTHAMPTON STREET, with more Late Georgian terraces. Note the doorways with set-in Doric columns. Parallel with Southampton Street, reached from the end of Church Street, is LONDON STREET, a wide Georgian street with many original houses left. Nos 73–79 are the best. No. 73 has odd door-hood brackets sideways as well as forward. The fine Grecian stone front with attached giant Ionic columns between angle pillars and a pediment was originally the SCIENTIFIC INSTITUTION, 1843 by *W. Brown*. At the N end of London Street to the E Queens Road with QUEEN'S CRESCENT, a long Bath stone crescent of 1832 etc., by *J. J. Cooper*. Then the HIGH BRIDGE of 1788, one arch with vermiculated rustication on the voussoirs, and so, by Duke Street, back to the Market Place.

Now E. First KING STREET with the GEORGE HOTEL, with its picturesque courtyard, and with BARCLAYS BANK opposite boasting a rich doorway in its palazzo front. The house is by *Henry and Nathaniel Briant*, 1838–9. Then follows KINGS ROAD. On the s side KENNET HOUSE, by *Cecil Elsom & Partners*, recent and decent. Then good groups of stone houses of *c*.1830, classical, also with pairs of tall bows as if they were copied from Brighton, and also with low Italianate gables. From the far end of Kings Road one returns along LONDON ROAD, seeing the development backward. The early C19 went out as far as No. 113, but there are plenty of High Victorian villas even further W, especially on the s side. On the N side good houses of *c*.1830–40 round ELDON SQUARE. Yet further W a white terrace with giant pilasters of only six bays, and then the best of all, Nos 45–65. This is, according to Mr Sherburn, of 1825–35, by *Richard Billing*. The doorways again have set-in Doric columns. Terraces also opposite, one of twelve bays with pediments over the end bays. A little before, off to the N in WATLINGTON STREET, is WATLINGTON HOUSE. The garden side is dated 1688 (rainwater-heads). Five bays, two storeys, hipped roof. The upper middle window is at a lower level than the others (staircase) and has a brick pediment. (Staircase with strong twisted balusters. Entrance hall with fluted pillars and two arches. NBR) The entrance side is C18. Back to the Market Place by Queens Road or Kings Road, and that finishes the perambulation of Inner Reading.

OUTER READING

CALCOT, see p. 109.

CAVERSHAM, see p. 110.

TILEHURST, see p. 242.

No proper perambulation can be suggested. The following individual items may be picked out.

s of London Road along REDLANDS ROAD, where No. 76 is said to have been designed by *May Morris*, William Morris's daughter. Also in Redlands Road ST ANDREW'S HALL (University Hostel), formerly EAST THORPE, by *Waterhouse* for Alfred Palmer, 1880. Additions, but the main rooms unaltered.* Again in Redlands Road SOUTH HILL, an attractive group of three pairs of houses, early C19, the side pairs a little canted forward. These side pairs have very clumsily detailed Greek Doric entrances. Then, just N of Christchurch Road, in HIGHGROVE STREET an old CONDUIT house of brick, 9 by 6½ ft in size.

SW and W, off WENSLEY ROAD at Coley is COLEY PARK FARM with a brick BARN (of six bays, dated 1619. Queen-post trusses. MHLG). To its W, just s of the Bath Road, a group of high-rise flats, by *C. H. A. Willett*, 1957–8. Of COLEY FARM itself only the massive gatepiers are left, at the N end of COLEY AVENUE, i.e. also in the Bath Road. N of the flats is Prospect Park and in it, placed on a hill, PROSPECT HOUSE, early C19. Stuccoed. Centre of five bays with a colonnade of unfluted Ionic columns and wings lying back a little. They have bow fronts and shallow domes. Nice staircase with simple iron balustrade.

Reading has much new housing other than what has been

---

* Mr Stuart Smith kindly told me of this.

mentioned. The town is growing rapidly, thanks to a position just far enough from, and just near enough to, London.

7080

REMENHAM

St Nicholas. Virtually of the time of the Victorian restoration (*Roland Plumbe*, 1870). But one large Dec two-light window on the N side is original, and the W tower with its polygonal buttresses (cf. Henley) is of 1838. Also, the apse represents a Norman apse of the past. – STAINED GLASS. In the apse by *Kempe*; 1909 (BC). – TILES. Ancient tiles by the pulpit. – IRON SCREEN. Presented by Sir John Noble of Park Place (*see* p. 192). The screen is a gate shown in 1873 'at the Siena exhibition'. (Does this not mean Vienna?) Elaborate, with vine trails. – Two BRASSES under the tower, † 1591 and † 1622.

TEMPLE, on Temple Island. 1771 by *James Wyatt*. An ornament belonging originally to Fawley Court across the river. It is extremely pretty and commands a full view of the mile to Henley. White, with a shallow bow front and an open cupola with columns. A perfectly harmless cottage behind.

REMENHAM COURT, ¼ m. s. White, with two symmetrical bows and a veranda on columns. Is is of *c*.1840?

CULHAM COURT, *see* p. 124.

ROBIN HOOD'S ARBOUR *see* MAIDENHEAD

ROOKS NEST *see* WOODLANDS ST MARY

7070

RUSCOMBE

St James. The chancel of flint is Norman. The small windows are pointed outside, but the rere-arches are round. Two windows in the E wall. The rest of the church, nave and tower, is of brick and was built in 1638–9. The two parts are not of the same build, see the difference in the brickwork and the way the W wall of the nave cuts through the buttresses of the tower. Interesting details of the three-light brick windows (cf. Winkfield, 1629) and bell-openings. The heavy wagon roof of the chancel is dated C14 by the VCH. – Between nave and chancel, inside, the C17 TYMPANUM with the Commandments. – Also of *c*.1639 the PULPIT with tester. – Two very simple C17 PEWS. – PAINTING. In the chancel, in the window jambs, traces of figures, assigned to the C13, but either very faint or restored into the likeness of Fra Angelico. – PLATE. Cup, 1630; Flagon, Paten, and two Almsdishes, 1821. –

MONUMENTS. Several C18 tablets, e.g. a purely architectural one, rather 1733 than 1774. – Richard Neville Neville † 1793 by *Flaxman*, simple, with two heraldic medallions with ox-heads. – Sir James Eyre † 1799, by *Sir Richard Westmacott*. A noble piece with a large asymmetrically placed standing female figure by an urn and a branch of weeping willow.

NORTHBURY FARM, formerly Ruscombe Manor. Timber-framed with brick infilling. Early C17. Front with three gables. It is only a part of the manor house.

ST LEONARD'S HILL *see* DEDWORTH

ST NICHOLAS HURST

7070

ST NICHOLAS. Flint with a brick tower. Mostly Victorian. The tower of 1612, Gothic, with C19 cupola. Norman N arcade, evidently tampered with and now inexplicable in more than one way. Norman W respond with multi-scallop capital and square abacus. Thin Norman circular pier with similar details, but the lower part of the pier fatter than the upper and ending in a collar as of a chipped-off capital. E respond as the others but with a capital too small, made for a tripartite respond and with what looks like chipped-off stiff-leaf. Unmoulded arches. Early C13 N doorway with two slight chamfers. The lancets of the N aisle would go with it. S arcade of 1875. In the C14 a W bay was added to the N arcade. Pretty head details. Also C14 heads on the vertical strips which must formerly have supported roof beams. – REREDOS. By *J. D. Sedding*, 1872. Alabaster, florid, with two biblical scenes: Expulsion and Nativity. – SCREENS. Perp, but much re-done. The top cresting openwork Jacobean and very enjoyable. – PULPIT. Simple, Elizabethan, with the usual blank arches. – HOURGLASS on a delightful wrought iron stand dated 1636. – PLATE. Silver-gilt Cup, Paten, and Flagon, 1611–12. – MONUMENTS. Purbeck marble wall tomb of the early C16 with canopy on a flat arch. Tomb-chest with quatrefoils. Later brasses († 1578) against the back wall (N chapel). – To its W brass plaque to Alse Harrison † *c.*1600, with the lady in a four-poster. She died in childbed. – Lady Savile † 1631. Long, tripartite, with three groups of kneeling figures. Each group under lifted curtains. Angels hold them l. and r. Alabaster and touch (N chapel). – Henry Barker † 1651. Recumbent effigy, very well done. A praying child on the l., a frightening skeleton on the r. Top with open curly pediment. Alabaster (N wall of

chancel). – Sir Richard Harrison † 1683 by *William Stanton*
(signed). Large tablet with kneeling figures facing one another.
She with a lively, if a little awkward turn. Behind them a
standing man, like an apparition. The group in a recess with
a trefoil arch. Segmental top pediment. White and grey
marble (chancel s).

s of the church BARKER'S ALMSHOUSES, founded in 1682.
Brick, flat, one-storeyed, with dormers. Entirely pre-classical.
E of the church the CASTLE INN, a pretty group, seen from
the churchyard.

HURST HOUSE, ¼ m. NW. Mostly of 1847, but with some
materials of a preceding house said to be of 1530. Only the
four heavy, straight-topped wooden doorways inside can be
of that date. The scanty remains of mullioned windows and
the brick chimneys must be Elizabethan. So is the fine
panelling with pilasters in one room.

HURST LODGE, ⅝ m. NE. C18 five-bay front with three-bay
pediment and a heavy recent door surround. Older bits behind.
One side has cross-windows and dormers, i.e. probably dates
from the later C17. The back is gabled.

HINTON HOUSE, 1⅜ m. NE. Built before 1589. Brick with blue
brick diapering. Entrance side with two gables and a polygonal
bay window with porch between. Mullioned and transomed
windows. Chimneystacks octagonal or lozenge. The house
was originally much larger. (Inside, a room with pilaster
panelling and an elaborate overmantel and another with
panelling and overmantel above the former. VCH)

STANLAKE PARK, 1⅝ m. NNE. Brick. Late C16. Three-gable
front, the centre a little recessed. Mullioned and transomed
windows. A canted C18 part later set into the similar back of
the house.

HAINES HILL, 1½ m. NE. A large house formerly of H-plan
with several courtyards. The oldest parts are late C16 or early
C17. Of that time is the long gallery, but the ends of this were
re-done in 1716. The front of the house is of 1760, and the
servants' wing of *c.*1825. The front has nine bays with a three-
bay pediment and a porch on Tuscan columns. The back has
gabled wings, but in the recessed centre is a large bow no
doubt also of 1760. One side of this back part has three shaped
gables (NBR). The interior decoration dates partly from *c.*1716,
partly from *c.*1760 (VCH).*

* I have not seen this house myself, as Mr A. Godsal refused my request
to see it.

HIGH CHIMNEYS, Davis Street, 1 m. SW. Brick, dated 1661 by scratching in on several bricks. Yet still the same type as Stanlake Park. Gabled, with recessed centre. Front and back almost identical, i.e. H-shaped. The windows, as against those of Stanlake Park, have wooden mullion and transom crosses. The doorways with canopies on scrolly, coarsely carved brackets.

BILL HILL, 1½ m. SE. Early Georgian. Blue bricks with red-brick dressings. Segment-headed windows, those of the first floor with stone keystones. Doorway with open pediment and the characteristic lines along the frieze leading up to a central point. Angle pilasters in three orders (giant pilasters would have been more typical). One-storey three-bay wings projecting at r. angles and connected by low links. Fine early C19 staircase with sparse, delicate iron balustrade. Gatepiers of brick with square urns and original wrought-iron gates. On the B road running S an oval STONE with a palmette at the top and an inscription commemorating the making of the road by subscription. The date is 1770. (The stone was moved here from Marchfield, Binfield. MHLG)

(HATCHGATE FARM. Barn of cruck construction. NBR)

SANDFORD see WOODLEY

SANDHURST

8060

ST MICHAEL. 1853 by *Street*, and enlarged in the sixties by *Woodman*. Coursed brown rubble. SW tower with wide open porch entrance and in it an imitation Norman doorway based on something real which had survived. Uninspired interior. – FONT. Furiously Norman, 'executed by one of the daughters of the late Rector'. – Much PAINTING on the walls. – MONUMENTS. Lady Farrer † 1892. Convincedly Athenian. She is seated in a chair, the family standing opposite. – A Jacobean brass († 1608).

ROYAL MILITARY ACADEMY, 2 m. ESE and really belonging to the Camberley area, i.e. the largest military area in England. The original building 1807–12 by *John Sanders*, after the academy, established in 1789 at High Wycombe, had moved to Sandhurst from Marlow. This original building is like a mansion, white, with a splendid portico and facing landscaped grounds and a lake – an appropriate place for young gentlemen to spend some formative years in. The portico is severely Greek Doric – a relatively early use of the order – and of six columns with a pediment. On either side twelve bays plus seven-bay wings plus three-bay pavilions, the outer blocks connected with one another and the centre by pillars. Large plain entrance hall and behind it, in axis, the former chapel, large as a ballroom, with segmental vault and an intruding Victorian Perp chancel window. The present CHAPEL is an independent brick building on an amazing scale and in an amazing style. It ought probably to be called Byzantine. As it now is, it consists of a nave of three bays, a chancel, and transepts, but at the start it was orientated differently, and the transepts were the whole building. Their front is Italian Romanesque rather than Byzantine, and it was consecrated in 1879. It was designed by *Captain Henry Cole*.* It had a short nave of two bays with weakly octagonal arcade piers, a crossing, a chancel like the nave, and an apse. Then, in 1922, Capt. *A. C. Martin* F.R.I.B.A. conceived the extension, and this was completed in 1937. Now one enters from the w through a feeble atrium and finds oneself in a church of three Byzantine inscribed-cross units, i.e. units of a square with a sail-vault plus a tunnel-vaulted nave continuation to the w and E plus four corner pieces. The new E end is an apse again, but the old chapel remained with its apse as transepts. The old apse with its MOSAICS and its marble revetments is the most sumptuous part of the building. Otherwise the interior is mostly white. One side apse at the E end has a good MOSAIC by *Boris Anrep*. – STAINED GLASS in the original apse E parts (four windows) by *Powell's*, in the w part (two windows) by *Laurence Lee*. – In the original apse two recent STANDS for books of remembrance by *Sir Hugh Casson*. – The very imaginative and lively ORGAN CASE is by *Sir Hugh Casson* too. It dates from 1950.

AMBERROW COURT, ½ m. N. 1885 by *W. Ravenscroft*. Light purple brick, C17 style, with gables, and an animated composition, with the porch set at an angle and a principal four-light window – a free version of the Ipswich type popularized by Norman Shaw. The arch here is segmental.

₄₀₆₀

SANDLEFORD PRIORY

The priory was founded for Augustinian Canons *c.*1200 and seems always to have remained small. Of the priory buildings one roof survives, but this is part of a large room of the house

---

* I owe the name to Mr Nicholas Taylor.

as rebuilt by *James Wyatt* in 1780–1. Wyatt appears Gothic here, not classical, as in the Pantheon in London, and Sandleford is supposed to be his earliest Gothic country house.* Symmetrical façade, cemented, seven bays, the outer pairs with embattled gables, the centre bay raised squarely and also embattled. Yet the ground-floor windows are round-arched. To the side a broad bow. At the back a wing extends with the two largest rooms, the first an oval preceded and followed by a small lobby with a screen of two columns to the oval, the second a large oblong with a final broad tripartite window with a segmental top. All this is classical and Adamish, though the exterior of the segment-headed end window has an ogee arch. It is above this large room that the C14 timber roof is preserved, a roof with closely set arched braces of Dec moulding, running up to a moulded longitudinal beam from which raking struts go up to the rafters. The entrance hall of the house is small, and it is followed by a larger room at the back which has thin shafts to the ceiling, a token of a former hall. What would then have been the screens passage is fan-vaulted in stucco.

SCHOOL GREEN *see* SHINFIELD

SEGSBURY DOWN *see* LETCOMBE BASSETT

SEVEN BARROWS *see* LAMBOURN

SHAW
4060

ST MARY. 1840–2 by *J. Hansom*, in the Norman style, i.e. long round-headed side windows of the lancet type, and a shocking W front with a very powerful W window, equally unauthorized long bell-openings, and a spire. The chancel is by *Butterfield*, of 1878. It is of flint and has late C13 windows. The interior of 1840 is characterized by the thin barn roof, that of 1878 by painted decoration. – MONUMENT. Sir Thomas Dolman † 1711. Enjoyable writing-master's writing.

SHAW HOUSE. The largest Elizabethan mansion in Berkshire, built for Thomas Dolman, clothier, and completed in 1581. Red brick, E-front, gabled. The projecting wings have four-4oa light single-transomed windows, but to the inner sides only large chimneybreasts. The recessed centre has three gables

* But Sheffield Park, Sussex, was in all probability begun well before 1779.

and a middle porch with two unfluted Ionic pilasters and a pediment. Greek inscription saying: 'Let no jealous enter'. The window above projects a little too and has a stone surround with the Latin inscription: 'The toothless envies the eater's teeth, and the mole despises the eye of the goat' – a highly unpleasant motto – and a pediment. The fenestration of the centre ought to be appreciated. It still stresses externally the place where the great hall lies. To the r. of the porch are three two-transomed windows, to the l. one and two one-transomed ones. The mullions incidentally are of an unusual and elegant H-section. The side has two symmetrical canted bay windows and a middle doorway with pediment on pilasters. The back has projecting wings too. Along the centre runs an c18 arcade, with a middle porch with a semi-elliptical head. There are no Elizabethan interiors. The internal features of the house are of the late c17 and the first half of the c18. The former date is that of the staircase with twisted balusters. The excellent stone fireplaces are of the latter, and the Rococo ceiling of the staircase is the latest part worth mentioning.

See p. 359

SHELLINGFORD

5090

ST FAITH. A very satisfying church. It has a Norman chancel arch with good decorated capitals and a single-step arch. Late Norman the s doorway with two orders of shafts, zigzag in the arch meeting at the angle. The hood-mould stands on beasts' heads but already has dogtooth decoration. Traces of a Norman N doorway too. The priest's doorway also of two orders, but the shafts have shaft-rings. Zigzag in the arch. Partially unbuttressed E.E. w tower with lancets, that to the s exceedingly long. The recessed spire was added in 1625 and rebuilt in 1852. The arch to the nave is broad and has a slight chamfer. Dec chancel, reticulated tracery in the E window. But to the N a three-light Perp window. This was originally probably the N window of a chapel; for inside the soffit of the arch and the jambs are decorated with quatrefoils. May be a tomb stood here. The nave s side has a three-light Dec and two four-light Perp windows, the latter with transoms. – FONT COVER. Jacobean. – PULPIT. Broad arched panels; not over-decorated. – BOX PEWS. By *Frederick Etchells*, c.1948. The Georgian Group has won, and things have come full circle. It is not so long ago that restorers almost automatically cast out box pews. – STAINED GLASS. In the E window two crowned female heads and more. Also old bits in the chancel and nave s windows. – PLATE. Silver-gilt Cup and Cover, 1597; Paten on foot, 1641. – MONUMENTS. In the chancel indent of the large brass to John of Bluebury, priest, who died in 1372. – Mrs Mary Packer † 1719. Large architectural composition. White and grey marble. At the lowest stage alternatingly blocked pilasters. Above a sarcophagus, a bust and two putti. – Sir Edward Hannes, physician of Queen Anne. Large tablet of reredos type with bust and putti. – Second Viscount Ashbrook † 1780. By *W. Tyler*. Brown, white, and grey marble. Obelisk behind a sarcophagus above which two putti by an urn in a diagonally rising composition. – Third Viscount, 1802 by *Flaxman*. Much smaller and plainer. Urn on a pedestal.

A long, low, even range sw of the church has several late medieval straight-headed windows. Two lights, arched tops. Probably early c16.

SHELLINGFORD HOUSE, NW of the church. A symmetrical two-gabled front of five bays. Mullioned windows with hoodmoulds. On the upper floor they run 2, 2, 4, 2, 2 lights. It all points to the mid c17. (The staircase with dumb-bell balusters and columns as newel posts and at the same time supports for the flights above confirms that date. NBR)

(The house formerly called THE GATEHOUSE, according to the Rev. D. G. Peck, has a good stucco ceiling of the early c17.)

SHINFIELD   7060

St MARY. The church has a Norman doorway with one order of colonnettes, thin scallop capitals, and a hood-mould on heads. The chancel is Dec, see the elementary flowing tracery of the two-light windows. The s chapel window has mullions and a transom, and the chapel is indeed dated 1596. The brick tower is yet later. It is dated 1664. It is broad, has polygonal clasping buttresses, several lively brick friezes, and a chamfered, round-arched doorway. Wide nave, wide aisle, Victorian arcade. The s chapel has a nice canted boarded ceiling with bosses. – FONT. High Victorian, with naturalistic leaves. The church was in fact restored in 1857. – PLATE. Almsdish of 1761. – MONUMENTS. Hugh Steward. Purbeck marble tablet with a coat of arms, an inscription on a scroll, and a sword below. On the hilt the date 1576. – Edward Martin † 1604 and wife. Tablet with small kneeling figures. – Henry Beke, wife and daughter. Dated 1627. Quite a swagger alabaster tablet. To the l. and r. of the three kneeling figures angels holding drapery open. The clothes also are amply draped.

SCHOOL GREEN, ½ m. SE. The SCHOOL founded in 1707 is still there, and it is effectively flanked by an extension of 1860 with a bellcote and another of 1889. The old building is of four bays plus the middle doorway and two storeys. Wooden cross-windows.

HARTLEY COURT, 1½ m. NW. The front Late Georgian, white, of five bays, with the first, third, and fifth tripartite. Hipped roof.

4090

SHIPPON
1 m. NW of Abingdon

ST MARY MAGDALENE. 1855 by *Sir G. G. Scott*. Nave and chancel. Bell-spirelet on the nave E gable. Geometrical tracery.

MANOR HOUSE, E of the church. Early C18. Five bays, two storeys, hipped roof. Doorway with pediment.

8070

SHOTTESBROOKE

ST JOHN BAPTIST. In 1337 Sir William Trussell established a college here, and the large and impressive church must be the immediate consequence of this. It is Dec throughout, a cruciform design with windows of flowing tracery, mostly just of two lights, but the E window of five with quite an exuberant pattern, and the N transept N window of three, decidedly wilful. The church is of flint, the chancel of knapped flint. The crossing tower carries a recessed spire with lucarnes right at the foot. Inside, the N and S crossing arches are triple-chamfered on the barest responds, just with a slight chamfer. But the E and W arches must be a later re-working. They are Perp in the responds, though Dec in the arch mouldings. In the chancel simple, ogee-headed SEDILIA and 'PISCINA. Opposite an ogee-trefoiled doorway. In the N transept below the N window are two tomb recesses, no doubt one William's. They have four pendant ogee arches each and a straight top and are separated by a steep-gabled niche with a bracket for an image and a pretty tipped-up vault inside. – FONT. C14 too. Ogee-headed panels, no separate foot or stem. – STAINED GLASS. Original bits in many windows. – E window by *Hardman* (BC). – PLATE. Paten, 1709; Paten, 1712; Chalice, 1714; Flagon, 1762. – MONUMENTS. Late C14 brass to a lady, 3 ft 6 in. – Brass to Richard Gyll † 1511, 25 in. Both N transept floor. – Also late C14 the excellent brass to a Priest and a Layman, 4 ft figures under canopies. – William Throkmorton, priest, † 1535. Moustached 28a stone figure carved into a stone block so that he appears to lie in his coffin. A band of stone is left standing across his waist, and on this are brass inscriptions. – Sarah Cherry † 1714. Small, bad bust under a baldacchino. – Also Cherry tablets of † 1699 and † 1703.

The COLLEGE has virtually disappeared. Thomas Hearne still saw 'the two spacious halls with their chimneys and the parlours and other remains' (*Gent. Mag.* 1840). The village which must have existed has also gone. So the church now looks the typical Victorian estate church, lying as close as it does to the house and in its grounds.

SHOTTESBROOKE PARK. Castellated brick mansion recently relieved of forty-one rooms including the fine staircase and drawing room. These were late C18, as the whole indeed appears to be. In fact the brickwork is partly Tudor. Polygonal angle-buttresses. The side where the rooms were demolished has been very handsomely tidied up by *Viscount Esher* (*Lionel Brett*). – By the side STABLES with a pretty cupola. Two long radiating avenues in front of the house.

SMEWINS, ¾ m. SE. Timber-framed house with two gables. Brick infilling. C16?

SHRIVENHAM 2080

ST ANDREW. This is an extremely interesting church, because it represents a personal solution to the building of a large church, when few were built. There was on the spot a church which was cruciform, and of this the central tower on its four arches (many continuous broad mouldings) remains and demonstrates a date about 1400. The roof line of the old continuation is also still visible, but that is all. All the rest was removed in 1638, when Lord Craven decided to build afresh. He built a large oblong outside the four arches, of nave and aisles and chancel and chapels, and added a W porch. This has entrances from N and S with four-centred heads and hood-moulds on big stops. The porch has a pediment too, the only classical feature. In the E wall of the church, set symmetrically at the ends of the chapel, are also two such entrances. Otherwise all is long, straight-headed Perp windows, with cusped arched lights and no tracery, of three, four (two plus two), and five lights. That is all. Inside, the arcade has double-chamfered 11b round arches on Tuscan columns with an excessive entasis, reminiscent of a certain bottle-shape. – FONT. Of Purbeck marble, C12, octagonal, with two shallow blank arches on each side – a familiar type. – PULPIT. Very good, and unusual. The usual blank arches made the pretext for false perspectives (cf. Buckland). Angle columns and balusters. Large tester. – BENCHES. Simple, straight-headed, and pleasant. – PANELLING. Nearly all the way round, plus a more decorated surround for the tower-stair doorway. – PLATE. Cup of 1577/8; Cup of the early C17; Flagon, 1624; two Patens, 1636; two Plates with allegorical figures, foreign. – MONUMENTS. Defaced effigy in the S aisle. Is it C13? – On the chancel E wall two nearly identical tablets: † 1713 and † 1734. – On the chancel W wall pretty tablet with garlands: † 1721. – Rothesia Ann Barrington † 1745. By *Thomas Paty* of Bristol. Coloured marbles. Obelisk and simple urn. It looks later. – Second Viscount Barrington † 1793. Designed by *James Wyatt* and carved by *Richard Westmacott*. A circular base and an urn on top. Now supported by a Victorian angel bust. – Admiral Barrington † 1800. With a big flag. By *Flaxman*. – Russell Barrington † 1840. By *T. Denman*. A roundel with a sweet ivy wreath.

In the main street ELM TREE HOUSE, a fine specimen of about 1700. Five bays, two storeys, hipped roof, later Tuscan porch. Wooden cross-windows. Staircase with twisted balusters. Next door the variedly grouped SCHOOL, Gothic of 1863.

STATION. 1840. Very small. Flint with Tudor windows and roofs far projecting like a canopy on the entrance as well as the platform side.

ROYAL MILITARY COLLEGE OF SCIENCE. The college was founded as the 'Advanced Class' at Woolwich in 1864, became the Artillery College in 1885, the Military College of Science in 1927, and moved to Shrivenham only in 1947. The main group of blocks is over 1200 ft long, of red brick, neo-Georgian, and entirely symmetrical. In addition garden-suburb-like housing. The officers' mess is BECKETT HALL, built in 1831–4 in a Tudor style for the sixth Viscount Barrington. The architect was *W. Atkinson*. The main rooms have plaster ceilings. In the centre the hall with a covered ceiling, the centre panels glazed. Close to the house by the lake is a SUMMER HOUSE, square, with a big (renewed) pyramid roof and stone cross-windows. Each side has two, close to a middle doorway. This does seem original work of c.1635.

SHURLOCK ROW   *8070*
1½ m. SW of Waltham St Lawrence

ALL SAINTS. 1870 by *J. Sharp*. Brick, with transepts, a low
apse, and lancet windows.

GREAT MARTINS. Brick, with two C17 gables and a considerable enlargement of *c.*1830 on the l.

SILWOOD PARK *see* SUNNINGHILL

SINDLESHAM   *7060*

SINDLESHAM HOUSE (Salvatorian Fathers). Plain Georgian
seven-bay front, stuccoed, with a three-bay pediment, a
Tuscan doorway, and two one-storeyed bows.

   Behind the house the new CHAPEL, 1963–4 by *R. J. Beswick*
of Swindon (and of the firm which won third prize in the
competition for Coventry Cathedral). Square, with one of the
fashionable folded roofs.

SINDLESHAM MILL, ⅝ m. NW. Pretty group. Three-storeyed
brick mill, long, with the ground-floor and first-floor windows
tied together by giant arches.

The GREEN is triangular, and along it runs Bear Wood estate
housing.

BEAR WOOD, *see* p. 79.

FOREST GRAMMAR SCHOOL, Winnersh, 1 m. N. Recent and
good.

SINODUN CAMP *see* LITTLE WITTENHAM

SMEWINS *see* SHOTTESBROOKE

SONNING   *7070*

ST ANDREW. Visually the church is Victorian (by *Woodyer*,
1853 and 1876 etc.). Really original parts are only the shaft of
the Norman PILLAR PISCINA inside, with spiral bands, the
bases of the N arcade piers, E.E., the lower part of the Perp
tower, and the arch N of the chancel. The VCH builds up a
whole architectural history, with C13 N aisle walling, early C14
S aisle walling, late C14 E parts of the N chapel, chancel E parts,
and aisle arcade piers on both sides. Pretty chancel decoration
by *Bodley*, 1903–6. – Very ornate REREDOS with figures in
tiers, Dec in style, as is the E window. By *Woodyer*, 1875 (BC)
and very characteristic of him. – SCREENS to N and S chapels.
Perp single-light divisions, much restored. – STAINED GLASS.

E window by *Hardman*, 1869 (BC). – One N window by *Kempe*, 1893. – CHANDELIER of brass, two tiers, dated 1675. – PLATE. Two silver-gilt Almsdishes of 1661 and an undated silver-gilt Spoon. – The church has a splendid set of MONUMENTS, starting with the brass on the chancel floor of Laurence Fyton † 1434, a 38 in. figure. – Several more brasses on the chancel floor, all Barkers, † 1546, † 1549, † 158 ?. – Also a child † 1627. – In the S aisle fragment of an Elizabethan monument: six small kneeling figures. – Lady Litcott † 1630 (S chapel), kneeling below curtains. Columns l. and r. Red and black marble. – Lady Anne Clarke † 1653 (N chapel). Demure bust in an oval recess with garlands. Segmental pediment at the top. – Charles and Elizabeth Rich † 1665 and 1656 (S chapel). Large, with twisted columns; no figures. – Sir Thomas and Thomas Rich † 1667 and 1663 (tower). A very remarkable monument, called by the *Ecclesiologist* in 1853 'the vilest paganism imaginable' (BC). Two large white identical urns on a black marble slab which is carried by four sad white putti. – Sir Anthony Barker † 1630 and his son † 1675 and grandson † 1694 (S chapel). Above the inscription two putti under a baldacchino. – William Barker by *Sir R. Westmacott*, c.1796 (Gunnis). A standing female figure drops a flower on an altar. Not an inspired piece. – Canon Hugh Pearson, 1883 by *Frederick Thrupp*. White recumbent effigy under an elaborate Gothic canopy linking chancel and N chapel.

The S wall of the churchyard is of Tudor (and later) bricks and reminds us of the fact that at Sonning was a PALACE of the Bishops of Salisbury. This was excavated in 1916, and evidence was found of the late C15 gatehouse, a large forecourt, the great hall, earlier C15, with porch and square bay window, the C13 solar range to its N stretching E, a small irregular court E of the hall and S of the solar, more chambers to the E of the court, and the kitchen some distance S of the hall.

N of the church is the Thames BRIDGE, probably later C18, of eleven brick arches increasing in size to the centre. From here THAMES STREET winds along and has on its N side FALCON HOUSE, Georgian, of brick, irregular, on its S side *Lutyens*'s DEANERY GARDENS, built for Edward Hudson, the owner of *Country Life*, in 1901. The theme which started Lutyens off was the ancient wall to the street, which he did not want to break. So one enters by very small arched doorways. The principal one of these leads into a low groin-vaulted passage which takes one to the front door of the house

proper. On the r. is an inner courtyard formed by the front
of the centre of the house and a wing projecting to the old
wall. In the courtyard a small pool with what Mr A. S. G.
Butler calls 'a chaste piece of sculpture'. The vaulted passage
belongs to a second wing, symmetrical with the other. The
main front of the house is to the s, and its principal feature is
a glorious bay window (of Norman Shaw inspiration). It
projects by three lights and has a six-light front. This bay lies
in axis with the hall fireplace and the pool in the courtyard.
But that axiality is broken by the entrance passage, which, as
we have seen, is asymmetrically placed in one wing. However,
the passage also is followed through to the s front, where it is
represented by a deeply moulded arched exit. To the r. of
this stands as a very dramatic accent a chimney with three
bold and high stacks set diagonally. The composition is as
splendid as that of similar elements at Tigbourne Court in
Surrey of 1899. The hall inside, behind the big bay window,
has wind-braces showing up in the walls.

At the top of Thames Street is PEARSON STREET. Here the
ROBERT PALMER COTTAGES, brick, of 1850, a set of almshouses. Then cottages and one five-bay house of c.1700, with
a doorway decorated by pilasters and a triglyph frieze. Then
the corner of the HIGH STREET with divers pretty timber-
framed cottages and Georgian houses, e.g. the WHITE HOUSE
with Soanian incised ornament. At the bottom the timber-
framed BULL HOTEL by the entrance to the churchyard. At
the top, i.e. in Pearson Street, across the view up the High
Street, THE GROVE, early C18, with three gables. The doorway has a canopy with pendants as fine as those of Queen
Anne's Gate, London.

At the s end of Pearson Street a C17 brick house on the r., and
en face the Victorian GATES and LODGE of Holme Park. This
is now the Reading Blue Coat School and has kept two figures
of Charity Children, a bluecoat and a greencoat boy.

SOTWELL   5090

ST JAMES. 1884 by *S. R. Stephenson*. Like a Surrey church.
Nave and chancel, timber bell-turret and shingled broach
spire. In the N wall inside a stone which looks like a Norman
capital.* – PLATE. Cup of 1780; Paten of 1836.

* The Rev. R. Gibbs writes that in addition the following remain from the
preceding church: C14 roof timbers, two C14 windows in the N wall, parts of
two C12 ones in the N and S walls, and part of a C13 doorway in the N wall.

SMALL'S HOUSE, Mackney, ½ m. SW. An extremely interesting Elizabethan or Jacobean stone house. The street front is of two symmetrical gables and three widely spaced bays, with a four-centred head to the doorway and three- and two-light mullioned windows. The back is slightly different, in so far as here was the entrance to the hall, i.e. there are four bays, with the doorway not in the middle and with a four-light window to its l. The sides have far-receding centres so that deep narrow courtyards are formed and only a small core remains in the middle of the house. Here the staircase is placed. It originally had no direct access from the street doorway. Strange also is the placing of the hall fireplace in the wall where one would expect in a large house the screens passage, a Yorkshire custom unexpected here.

SOUTH FAWLEY MANOR HOUSE *see* GREAT FAWLEY

5000

SOUTH HINKSEY

The part by the church is still villagey, in spite of all the Oxford housing around.

ST LAWRENCE. Nave and chancel and unbuttressed W tower. The present chancel is simple and pleasant Georgian work. The rest basically C13, see the chancel arch responds and some windows. – SCULPTURE. Miniature ivory pediment with St John and other figures. Is it continental of *c.*1850?* – PLATE. Chalice and Paten, *c.*1636.

SOUTHILL PARK *see* BRACKNELL

5080

SOUTH MORETON

ST JOHN BAPTIST. In the W wall a narrow C11 doorway. The s aisle has a S lancet and a S cusped lancet and other indications of the same style, i.e. one must assume that the aisle was added already in the early C13. Otherwise most windows Perp. Dec the nave W window (reticulation), Perp the S aisle buttresses with shields in panels. The church has a bellcote of 1849. Inside, the arcade is of two parts separated by a C19 arch said to replace a small round-arched doorway. The two W bays are of *c.*1200 (round pier, octagonal abacus, single-step arches),

* Canon A. G. Whye tells me that an identical pediment is at St Aldate's Rectory at Oxford.

the E bays of the C13 (round piers, double-chamfered arches). – PLATE. Paten, 1584; Chalice, 1786.

THE HALL, NE of the church, on the main road. Seven bays, blue and red brick. Windows with stone keystones. Panelled parapet.

SPARSHOLT   3080

HOLY CROSS. The N doorway is of the late C12, with its water-leaf as well as stiff-leaf capitals, its round arch, the odd, still Norman motif of the arch moulding, and the hood-mould still on beasts' heads. The S doorway seems a little later, though the arch is also still round. Stiff-leaf capitals. C13 W tower with later shingled broach spire. Typical late C13 bell-openings. Good early C14 chancel of chalk. Long Dec windows, parapet with cusped wavy fields. Dec also the S transept.* The S window is of four lights and has reticulated tracery. Nave S windows Dec and Perp. In the church the Dec contribution is confirmed. For instance the chancel arch and S transept arch both have continuous chamfers. More-over the chancel has its full equipment of EASTER SEPULCHRE, S tomb recess, SEDILIA, and PISCINA, all with ogee arches, with cusping and head cusps, and in the S wall of the S tran-sept are two tomb recesses of the same kind. With one goes a tomb-chest with small 'weepers'. Chancel roof on stone corbels with the four Signs of the Evangelists. – REREDOS. This is the lower part of a former E window. – SCREEN to the S transept. Shafts with shaft-rings instead of mullions, and cinquefoiled, not pointed, arches – i.e. C13, an exception-ally early date for a wooden screen. – BENCHES. In the chancel. The ends straight-topped and with tracery and emblems. – NORTH DOOR. With original iron scrollwork of the late C12. – STAINED GLASS. One head in a nave N window. – PLATE. Chalice and Paten of 1613(?). – MONU-MENTS. In the chancel tomb recess Knight, crossed legs, hood of mail, praying hands, two angels by his pillow. Clearly early C14, i.e. of the time of the chancel. – In the S transept, not *in situ*, three over-lifesize oak effigies, also early C14. Knight, the legs not crossed, and two Wives, one wearing a wimple. – Brass to William Herleston, priest, early C15. The figure is in the top of a cross and 25 in. long. – Lady, 12½ in., and upper half of Man, originally 21 in., both c.1510–20, and all three on the chancel floor. – Sir George Hyde

26a

* A N transept has disappeared.

† 1623. Tablet with strapwork (s transept). – John Pleydell
† 1591 and his wife † 1623. Of chalk. Wide tablet, oval, with
much carving around, strapwork, heads, etc. Strapwork top.

MANOR HOUSE, s of the church. Blue and red brick. Early
Georgian (VCH: c.1722). Five bays, segment-headed windows.
Three-bay pediment.

BOWL BARROWS, on the SW spur of Sparsholt Down. Two
well-preserved bowl barrows, 90 ft and 27 ft in diameter and
6 ft and 2 ft high respectively.

₄₀₆₀   SPEEN

ST MARY. 1860 and 1878. Flint and stone. W tower with pyramid roof. Medieval the N arcade piers, round, of Purbeck
marble. Double-chamfered arches. Also the Dec E window
with flowing tracery of a popular pattern. – PULPIT. Jacobean.
The sounding-board only. The rest is now at Aldbourne in
Wiltshire. – STAINED GLASS. Medieval bits in the N chapel. –
Uncommonly many MONUMENTS of interest. John Baptiste
Castillion, a Piedmontese, † 1597. Recumbent effigy with praying hands. Shields on the tomb-chest. Alabaster. – Lady Elizabeth Castillion † 1603. Stone effigy with farthingale and widow's
hood. – Jonathan Hicks and his wife who died in 1713. The
monument with extremely lively decoration of garlands, putti,
skull, hourglass, trumpets, etc., is no doubt by *Jonathan Hicks*
himself, who calls himself a 'freemason and carver'. –
William Craven and his mother who died in 1717. Big base
and rich coat of arms and drapery above. – Thomas Wyld and
his son. By *Bacon*, 1791. Kneeling female figure with a small
urn for the son. Profile medallion for the father at the foot of
_{31b} the large tablet. – Margrave of Anspach † 1806. By *Canova*.
His wife was a Baroness Craven. Enormously heavy tablet
with a kneeling, amply draped female figure by an amphora. –
William Brinton † 1823. By *Chantrey*. Altar with a profile
medallion.

MONUMENT at the corner of the A-road and the street to the
church. A truncated column and a metal ball. This is said to
have nothing to do with the Battle of Newbury and to have
been a lamp post.

The houses along the main road are the immediate continuation of those of Newbury. They start with the three-bay,
three-bay pediment, yellow brick SPEEN LODGE. Then,
after some desolation, SPEEN MANOR with a nice doorcase,
the HARE AND HOUNDS, dated 1756, with a five-bay NE

front with pedimental gables, LEIGHTON LODGE, blue brick with two canted bay windows, and so to SPEEN HOUSE, stuccoed, with a central bow window up the whole three storeys.

ELMORE HOUSE, SW of the church. Brick. Early C18, five bays, two storeys, hipped roof, with lower three-bay wings.

BENHAM PARK, 1 m. W. 1772–5 by *Lancelot (Capability) Brown*, who also laid out the gardens. Brown had gone into partnership with *Holland* in 1772. Built for the sixth Earl of Craven. Three storeys, stone, nine bays, with a portico of four un-50a fluted Ionic columns and no pediment. The central room has two grand chimneypieces with carved wooden overmantels and a delicate plaster ceiling. Several nice details in other rooms. The GATEPIERS and LODGES at the NE corner, i.e. on the A-road, are excellent too. The piers each have two pilasters with banded vermiculated rustication, a niche between, and a pediment. – At the NW corner the GATEPIERS have trophies on top and are said to come from Hamstead Marshall.

BAGNOR MANOR FARMHOUSE, 1⅛ m. NNW. C17; altered. Jacobean staircase (MHLG and NBR).

SPEENHAMLAND *see* NEWBURY, p. 181

SPENCERS WOOD 7060

ST MICHAEL. 1908 by *S. Slingsby Stallwood*. Red brick, also inside. Bellcote. Dec windows.

SCHOOL. 1890. Pretty. Grey vitrified brick and red brick patterns. Gables with bargeboards.

CONGREGATIONAL CHAPEL. 1902–3 by *W. Ravenscroft*. Red brick, with a tower, and cosy to look at.

STANDEN MANOR *see* HUNGERFORD

STANFORD DINGLEY 5070

ST DENYS. Flint, with a weatherboarded bell-turret. Brick chancel of *c.*1768 (Kelly). Inside, the church is both more interesting and more eloquent. To the original church a N arcade of two bays, one small and round-arched, the other wider, higher, and pointed, was added in the late C12. The piers are nook-shafted. Shortly after, in the early C13, the same was done on the S side. The capitals now had stiff-leaf. Soon also a W bay was added on the N side, allowing for a wider nave. The W lancet of the aisle is original. The chancel arch also is of the same type. The s doorway may be of the time of the s arcade. One order of shafts with stiff-leaf capitals. The arch very odd, trefoiled, but a rosette cuts into the top foil. – SOUTH DOOR. With the old hinges. – PAINTING. Remains of C13 wall painting. Masonry and scroll patterns. Also a King in the jamb of a N window. – BRICKS. Very interesting encaustic bricks, not tiles, now built into the N respond of the chancel arch. – PLATE. Paten, 1697; Chalice, 1718. – MONUMENTS. Brass to Margaret Dyneley † 1444, a 19½ in. figure. – In the churchyard elegant urn on a pedestal to Richard Carter † 1773.

GARDEN HOUSE, ¼ m. s. Five-bay Georgian house with a pedimented doorway.

RECTORY, SW of the former. Chequer brick, early C18, also of five bays. Three dormers in the roof with alternating pediments. Doorway with Ionic pilasters intermittently blocked. Big keystones and broken pediment.

STANFORD-IN-THE-VALE

3090

ST DENYS. Quite a large church, with quite a high w tower. The earliest evidence is the s doorway, still with trumpet-scallop capitals, i.e. late C12, and the N doorway with crocket capitals, probably of the same date. Then the w tower. The arch to the nave triple-chamfered, the bell-openings twins. These features indicate the late C13. The tower ended with a corbel-frieze, but was heightened later. Dec chancel with the E and one s window provided with tracery which includes the spiked trefoils usually called Kentish tracery. Perp N porch higher than the aisle. Crenellated s porch also Perp. Low nave with Perp crenellated clerestory. C14 aisles with straight-headed windows. The N aisle is continued as a vestry, unnoticeable outside. C14 also the arcades, with octagonal piers and double-chamfered arches which die into the piers. Traces of the C14 clerestory below the present one (above the spandrels, not the apexes of the arches). In the chancel an extremely interesting PISCINA with shelf and PYX CANOPY over. This also is probably Dec.* – FONT. Jacobean, the whole font encased in wood panels and provided with a wooden cover as well. – PULPIT. Jacobean, roomy, with close arabesque decoration. – STALLS. A few, plain. – STAINED GLASS. In the heads of chancel E and s windows original, i.e. early C14, figures. –

22a

* The pyx canopy is locally supposed to have been a RELIQUARY originally.

PLATE. Cup and Cover, London, 1585; Paten on foot, London, 1711; large Flagon, London, 1752.* – MONUMENT. Brass to Roger Campedene † 1398, rector. Oversized demi-figure, 28 in. long.

The village spreads out and has e.g. two greens. S of the church MANOR FARMHOUSE, early C18, four bays, brown stone and red brick dressings, two storeys, hipped roof. (Some nice interiors. The BARN is dated 1618 and has a tie-beam roof. NBR) N of the church RECTORY HOUSE, stone, C18, of three bays with a hipped roof. Further N, i.e. at Upper Green, STANFORD HOUSE, red brick, very high, three widely spaced bays of small windows. One-bay projection with pediment. Doorway with Tuscan columns and pediment. To the S, i.e. along the street towards the Wantage road, PENSTONE'S FARMHOUSE, a fragment, part C17, part early C18, i.e. with mullioned and with segment-headed windows. Then COXE'S HALL, dated 1733, and quite a dramatic Early Georgian front. Brick, roughcast. Five bays, segment-headed windows. One-bay projection carried up higher and provided with a pediment. The doorway and main window in the projection are round-arched. (Staircase with thin twisted and turned balusters. NBR)

MILL FARM, ½ m. S. Georgian, five bays, rubble, with raised brick window surrounds.

STANLAKE PARK *see* ST NICHOLAS HURST

STEVENTON   4090

ST MICHAEL. The earliest piece is one S arcade pier which is round and has a stiff-leaf capital. It seems to tell of a smaller church. The present dimensions belong to the early C14. S porch tower – see the bell-openings; S aisle – see the windows; N side – ditto; chancel – ditto. The Perp E window is over-restored. The W doorway, though round-arched, is Perp. Inside a curious muddle. The tower arches really have no capitals – just abaci slabs. One of them has ballflower (which suits the date), one fleurons. The S arcade between the tower and the E.E. pier is shapeless. The wide arch E of the E.E. pier has two hollow chamfers. – FONT. Octagonal, Perp, nothing

* The Flagon has an inscription: 'As an humble testimony of their Unfeigned thanks to Almighty God, For the Recovery of their three Children, Thomas, Sohpia and Charlotte from the Small-pox by Inoculation Anno 1752'. The interesting thing is, as the Rev. H. S. Fry points out to me, that this of course is many years before Jenner.

special. – PULPIT. Jacobean, the tester now a table. – BENCHES. With plain panels. Also a front with blank tracery. – ALMSBOX. 1633. On a hefty baluster. – STAINED GLASS. E and chancel N windows by *Warrington* (BC). – PLATE. Silvergilt Cup and Cover, London, 1571. – BRASS to Richard Do † 1476; 14 in. figures (chancel floor).

There was originally an alien Benedictine cell at Steventon. It lay S of the W end of the CAUSEWAY, the memorable feature of the village, a paved raised tree-lined way from church to green along which are all the houses of interest, starting with THE PRIORY, a timber-framed house with two differently projecting gables and behind it a hall which is supposed to have been the guest hall of the priory. It seems early C16 and has one central hammerbeam truss with tracery spandrels and a fireplace inserted later. Two tiers of windbraces. Contemporary service wing. The solar wing is late C14, with a kingpost roof. It is in good condition too. A N extension from the solar wing has been assigned to the late C15. Along the Causeway then, all on the S side, a number of worth-while houses, all timber-framed. Nos 103–107, part late C14 (W wing with kingpost roof) and part C17, with two equally projecting gable wings; Nos 77–81, also part medieval and part C17 with a stout chimneybreast to the street and a picturesque polygonal bay on its immediate l.; No. 67, early C17, though dated 1657, very pretty, with a little pargetting and under the l. gable an oriel, under the r. a canted bay. Fretwork bargeboards. Then come No. 57 with four steep gables and Nos 39–43 with crucks and cross-bracing in the gable, very well and completely preserved.* Further along, beyond the green, in MILTON LANE, an L-shaped house with wooden cross-windows, one of chequer brick with segment-headed windows, and a big thatched one with two gables on slightly projecting wings. The spacious GREEN has along its E and NW sides mostly council housing.

SCHOOL. By *Street*, 1864 and 1871. Addition of 1900.

(By the station COTTAGES in the Tudor style, of *c*.1840. They were built for the Great Western, and board meetings were held in them, as they were about halfway between London and Bristol. J. Betjeman and J. Piper)

STOCKCROSS

ST JOHN. 1839. Blue brick, with W tower, transepts, and lancet

* I am grateful to Mr S. E. Rigold for help on the dating of these houses.

windows. The chancel was lengthened in 1864 (BC). The church was almost entirely re-fitted by *Sir Ninian Comper* (BC). – STAINED GLASS. Comper's anaemic E window replaces that which is now blind and hard to see. – In two side windows assembled bits of former glass.

Some early C20 ESTATE HOUSING.

STRATFIELD MORTIMER

ST MARY. 1869 by *R. Armstrong*, the W end with two surprising flying buttresses. Vestry 1896 by *E. Swinfen Harris*. Quite a stately church, and certainly a busy exterior. Rock-faced, with a SE steeple. Broach spire with two tiers of lucarnes. Geometrical tracery. Five-bay arcades with round piers and naturalistic capitals. Small foiled clerestory windows. Much blank arcading in the chancel. – REREDOS. The paintings 1868 by *O'Connor*, better known for stained glass. – STAINED GLASS. Behind the organ a mixed lot, including small English C15 pieces. – Also a mixed lot of Victorian glass, most interesting the W window with large figures by *Clutterbuck*. – PLATE. Complete Set of 1869. – MONUMENTS. In the chancel a 6 ft 6 in. coffin-lid with an inscription referring to Aegelwardus, who is mentioned in the Anglo-Saxon Chronicle and died in 1017. An eminently important piece. – Brasses to Richard Trevet † 1441 and wife, 27 in. figures.

ST JOHN, Mortimer Common. 1882 by *William Rhind*, but this refers only to the present aisle. Nave and chancel and W tower by *Swinfen Harris*, 1896. Red brick. The W tower has four top gables. Lancet windows, nice boarded roof. – REREDOS. A painting by *Nathaniel H. J. Westlake*: Christ at Emmaus, in the Nazarene tradition. Christ strictly frontal. Behind him a cloth held by angels. Westlake was a pupil of Dyce and Herbert and later specialized in stained glass. – STAINED GLASS by *Kempe*, chancel and S aisle SE.

Just W of St Mary the SCHOOL of 1869, rock-faced, with a high tower crowned by a saddleback roof.

MORTIMER HILL, halfway between Stratfield and Mortimer Common. Georgian. Front with doorway between two canted bay windows. The doorway has pilasters, a triglyph frieze, and discs in the metopes.

MORTIMER HOUSE, ⅝ m. N. 1774. Blue brick headers and red brick dressings. Five bays, two storeys. The centre projects a little. Contemporary additions to the l. Terrible later porch.

Fine staircase with a wrought-iron railing with s-scrolls. On the walls decorative friezes. Glazed circular lantern.

ROUND BARROW CEMETERY, on Mortimer Common. This group of four Early Bronze Age barrows includes a very fine bell barrow with a mound 80 ft in diameter and 6 ft high surrounded by a ditch 9 ft broad and 1 ft deep.

WOKEFIELD PARK, ⅞ m. NNE. Large, but of at least two periods. The centre of seven bays with two-bay projecting wings is probably Early Georgian. The staircase with twisted and fluted balusters looks that date. It rises behind a screen of fluted Ionic columns. This centre and the articulated five-bay wings are all cemented. Are the additions and the remodelling of the centre c.1820 or later?

STRATTENBOROUGH CASTLE FARM
see COLESHILL

5080
STREATLEY

ST MARY. Short Perp w tower. The rest of 1865 by *Charles Buckeridge*. – REREDOS. 1893. Designed by *Pearson* (BC). – PAINTING. The Mourning of Christ. After *van Dyck*, the picture in the Berlin gallery. – PLATE. Paten, 1715; Cup, 1716. – BRASS to Elizabeth Prout † 1440, a 20 in. figure (chancel N wall).

In the HIGH STREET STREATLEY HOUSE, late C18, of five bays and three storeys, red brick, smooth, with a big doorcase of unfluted Ionic columns and pediment. Also some other Georgian houses higher up ending in ELM LODGE across the top, and some Georgian cottages below. But charming as they are, surely the most attractive architectural feature of Streatley is *W. Ravenscroft*'s conversion of old malthouses into a village hall, a tower and two private houses l. and r. This group of brick with tile-hanging and gables, built rather late for its style in 1898, lies between church and High Street and is varied and cosy.

8080
STUBBINGS
2½ m. w of Maidenhead

ST JAMES THE LESS. 1850–4 by *R. C. Carpenter*. Flint; nave, chancel, and N aisle; bellcote. Windows mostly of single lights with ogee tops. In the chancel encaustic PAINTING.

6070
SULHAM

ST NICHOLAS. 1838, with an E end of 1875. The church is

flint and stone, with a W tower, lancet windows, and the apse of 1875. Between nave and chancel a triple screen, i.e. three arches nearly the full height. – FONT. The bowl is of marble, semi-globular and of 1733. – PLATE. Paten, 1680; Paten on foot, 1691; Cup, 1729; Almsdish, 1732; Flagon, 1751; small Flagon, early C19. – MONUMENT. Small tablet to Jane Wilder † 1845. It comprises an incised panel showing her in prayer at a prayer desk, not strictly in profile. A very charming period piece. – John Wilder † 1892, rector for fifty-six years. The memorial is an enriched CROSS in the churchyard, Gothic of course, and of 1892.

SCHOOL. 1892. The windows a nice mixture of Gothic and Baroque. The architect may have been the incumbent, the Rev. J. *Wilder*, Provost of Eton College.

(At the W end of the village the STOCKS. VCH)

SULHAMSTEAD   6060

ST MICHAEL. 1914 by *E. J. Munt*; flint, Gothic, and really of no architectural interest at all. Moreover, redundant now.

RECTORY. Brick, Georgian, of five bays, with pedimented doorway.

FOLLY FARM. *Lutyens* made this house in two campaigns out of a timber-framed cottage existing on the site. The two campaigns took place in 1906 and 1912 and were undertaken for two different owners. Oddly enough, i.e. in contradiction to Lutyens's development, the first was classical, the second Tudor–Arts-and-Crafts. Lutyens had done Monkton House, Singleton, in Sussex in a classical style already in 1902, the courtyard of Papillon House in Leicestershire in 1903, and Nashdom at Taplow much more monumentally in 1905. Here, at Folly Farm, he built a complete William-and-Mary house from the S end of the cottage to the E, a front with a two-storeyed hall in the centre and two symmetrical projecting wings. The next owner wanted much more space, and Lutyens provided it by returning to his early Arts and Crafts style, handled in few other cases as brilliantly as in this belated one. The addition is to the W of the house of 1906, which was left entirely intact. The new wing runs W and then turns S–N, W of the cottage. This S–N part in the end became the largest of the house. Visually the climax is the pool with the roof extending low down over the cloister. From the S the house is thus frankly of two periods which the layman may well read as Tudor, with mullioned and transomed windows and a weatherboarded gable, and William and Mary, of grey and red brick. In the garden Lutyens, as so often, collaborated with *Gertrude Jekyll,* his earliest patron and promoter.

SULHAMSTEAD HOUSE. Early C19, white, of two storeys. Nine bays with a three-bay giant Ionic portico.

TYLE MILL. 1937–8 by Lutyens's disciple *A. S. G. Butler.*

BRAZENHEAD COTTAGES, ⅛ m. N of Folly Farm. Once one house. Timber-framing and brick infilling, C17, a nice composition with gabled projections l. and r.

6060   SULHAMSTEAD ABBOTS

ST MARY. Flint, a small village church with a timber bell-turret. The church may be of *c.*1200 altogether, though only the chancel windows and the N arcade remain as features. The windows are small, pointed outside, round inside, the arcade has an original W respond and two original arches with only a slight chamfer. The third arch is C14. – FONT. Norman, tub-shaped, with blank arcading. – MONUMENT. Brass to Ralph Eyer, 1524 (when he was still alive). It has the following inscription:

Extremum vitae finem, meditare, Viator
Tam cito cum videas omnia nata, mori,
In coelum converte oculos, amplectere laudem
Damnosasque Evae despice blanditias.

One wonders what the congregation thought of the accursed blandishments of Eve.

9060   SUNNINGDALE

HOLY TRINITY. The chancel 1860 by *Street,* the rest 1887–8 by *J. Oldrid Scott.* The coarser character of the work of 1860 is externally at once noticeable. Oldrid Scott is competent, but not attractive here. It is a big church with a steeple over the crossing and E.E. details. The GATES to the churchyard, of cast iron, are obviously older. They must belong to the previous church, which was built in 1839. – STAINED GLASS. One S window by *Kempe,* 1892. – MONUMENT. Prince Victor of Hohenlohe-Langenburg † 1891. Alabaster. By his daughter, *Countess Feodora Gleichen.* Recumbent effigy in relief. Italian Renaissance style.

COWORTH PARK FARM. Timber-framed and gabled. The MHLG calls it C15 and earlier.

SUNNINGDALE PARK, ½ m. N. Classical, of nine bays with attached portico, but a lush fancy-Gothic hall with gallery on columns round the upper floor. Large staircase. All this was done by *W. E. Lord* for Sir Hugo Cunliffe-Owen in 1930.

CHARTERS, ⅞ m. WSW. By *Adie, Button & Partners*. 1938. A typical case of the C20 style adopted willy-nilly, just in order to be up-to-date. The result is motifs only in an ensemble not conceived in the C20 spirit. White and cubic it is, and horizontal windows, even breaking round corners, it has, but the great hall in the centre has a front to the S with the giant pillars of the Fascist brand and the French windows to its l. and r. are of Georgian proportions. The interior was originally almost entirely period, and the model farm had pitched roofs with blue glazed tiles.

SUNNINGHILL

ST MICHAEL. 1808 and 1826–7. Yellow brick. W tower with a re-used Norman zigzag arch to the doorway. Wide S aisle, its W front flat-topped and crenellated, its windows with Y-tracery. The same in the N aisle. However, some of the windows were made Geometrical in 1888, when the chancel and S chapel were built in yellow brick with red-brick trim by *W. H. Crossland*, the architect of the Royal Holloway College. They are imitation-Perp and have complicated pinnacles. Interior of 1828 with thin cast-iron columns. Wide aisles, their stucco roofs original. The nave roof evidently of 1888. The chancel roof extremely busy, with cusping. – PLATE. Chalice of 1711; Patens of 1703, 1715, and 1834. – MONUMENTS. In the S aisle one by *King* of Bath († 1783). – In the churchyard columns to Sir H. R. and Lady Popham. She died in 1866. Relief with nautical instruments and names of battles: Copenhagen, Cape of Good Hope, North of Spain, Buenos Ayres.

CORDES HALL, in the middle of the village, ½ m. S. 1902 by *Joseph Morris & Son*. Brick and roughcast, with remarkably inventive brick windows crowned by curved hood-moulds and cross gables. Top lantern.

SILWOOD PARK, ½ m. E. Red brick and huge. Free Tudor with a freer tower. According to *The Builder* designed by *Waterhouse* in 1876. Executed with alterations by *S. Tugwell* of Bournemouth. It was meant to cost £22,800 (GS), but in fact cost £27,500.

TITTENHURST PARK, ¾ m. E. 1737, with additions. The

8*

exterior looks c.1830. White, two-storeyed, with a pretty Ionic porch. In the garden two weeping blue Atlas cedars, an extreme rarity.

BROADLANDS, 1 m. w of Sunningdale Station. By *Minoprio & Spencely*. Published in *Country Life* in 1934, and there shrewdly analysed as belonging to the 'middle' as against the 'left' of the modern style in its English form. The left is characterized as Corbusier–Mendelsohn–Connell–Chermayeff–McGrath, the middle as Stratford Theatre and Oliver Hill's Morecambe Hotel. *Country Life* praises Broadlands as 'not led away by the functionalist bogy'. It is brick, with a flat roof and a top frill of projecting brick ornament. Motifs of Spanish-Mission and Tudor can be noticed. The house replaces one by *Norman Shaw*, fortunately not one of his best.

(BUCKHURST PARK, 1 m. NE. Alterations and additions by *Edward Power* in 1873 etc. cost £6,000 (GS). In a mixture of styles. One part with neo-Tudor windows, another neo-Georgian with a veranda of columns. NBR)

4000

SUNNINGWELL

ST LEONARD. Mostly Perp, except for the jewel of a w porch. Ashlar-faced N transept tower and ashlar-faced s transept. Several straight-headed windows. The chancel is structurally earlier, see one blocked C13 s window. The w porch is supposed to have been given by Bishop Jewel of Salisbury, who died in 1571 and was rector of Sunningwell about 1551. It is seven-sided, with the entrance from the N, where it looks a regular octagon. At the angles are unacademic unfluted Ionic columns. The windows are small, Gothic, and cusped. Originally the porch carried a steep-pitched roof. – PULPIT. Very simple, Jacobean. – BENCH ENDS. With enormous, summary poppy-heads. Rather post- than pre-Reformation. – STAINED GLASS. The E window is most interesting. The design and the colouring are obviously inspired by the Pre-Raphaelites and Morris, but it is equally obviously not theirs. Adoration of the Shepherds and the Magi. The Virgin holds up the Child to them. Smaller figures below. Dark blue background of the main scene. Excellent leading pattern. The answer to the mystery of the attribution is that the window was designed by *J. P. Seddon*, who was a friend of Morris and the Pre-Raphaelites and restored the church in 1877. The glass, according to TK, was made by *S. Belham*. – PLATE. Cup of 1660.

BEAULIEU FARMHOUSE, SE of the church. What can the date
of the porch doorway be? The four-centred doorhead looks
late C16 or early C17. But can the open segmental pediment
be earlier than *c.*1660? The forms are all very thin.

SUTTON COURTENAY

ALL SAINTS. Late Norman W tower, broad, with clasping
buttresses. The doorway is imitation, but the window above
is genuine, with zigzag. Simpler windows N and S. Bell-
openings, twin, pointed, under a round arch, zigzag jambs.
Then a corbel-frieze, and above a Perp top storey. The arch
towards the nave is wide and single-stepped. Also Late
Norman the responds of the chancel arch, with decorated
scallop and intertwined-band capitals. The present arch is
later, but could not the S arcade E arch, evidently tampered
with, have been the chancel arch? It is now pointed but need
not have been originally. Big zigzag and crenellation motifs.
The rest of the S arcade and the whole N arcade of the notably
wide nave C14 with standard elements. C13 chancel with
lancet windows. A lancet, but cusped, also the N aisle W
window. Is it late C13? Late C13 anyway the N aisle E window
and also the identical S aisle E window (spherical triangle in
the top). The other N aisle and the S aisle windows wide and
Perp. The clerestory is puzzling. While the S side is Perp, the
N side has two decidedly Dec windows and three others which
could be early C14 too. Charming Perp S porch of brick, two-
storeyed. – FONT. Norman, tub-shaped, with narrow arcading
and odd tripartite leaf motifs at foot and top of each arch. –
FONT COVER. Jacobean. – PULPIT. Jacobean, with back post
instead of back panel, and tester. None of the usual arabesques.
– STALLS. Three in the chancel; plain. – SCREENS. The rood
screen with one-light divisions and the dado openwork with
the same simple tracery patterns. Was it always open? – Also
simple N and S parclose screens. – BOX PEWS. One is dated
1633. It is quite plain. – SOUTH DOOR. Perp, with tracery. –
CHANDELIER. Of brass. Dated 1821; still a Baroque pattern.
– PAINTING. A number of C17 inscriptions, one with the
naïve representation of six widows and their benefactor,
another, rather grander, with three Doric pilasters. – STAINED
GLASS. Fragments, huggermugger, in many windows. –
PLATE. Cup and Cover, 1584; Paten inscribed 1624; small
Cup, 1812; large Flagon, 1822. – MONUMENTS. Three Perp

tomb-chests with quatrefoil fronts: chancel N, used as an altar in the S aisle, and in the churchyard S of the chancel. – In the chancel N wall large tomb recess of the late C13. In it effigy of a priest, ruthlessly re-cut. It was probably early C14.

Sutton Courtenay is a large village and a rewarding one, both for the picturesque and the architectural traveller. Immediately W of the church is NORMAN HALL, a most remarkable example of a manor house of c.1190–1200. It is a plain stone rectangle, but has an excellent S doorway with one order of shafts, roll mouldings, and nailhead and dogtooth details. There is also, not quite in line, a N doorway with a continuous roll moulding and a small N doorway further E which is Perp and has charming little carvings up the jambs and the arch. Inside, on a beam, is the date 1626. This could apply to a renewal of the top part of the doorway. The hall was illuminated by lancet windows, of which some remain complete and some in traces. Roof with tie-beams, collar-beams on arched braces, and two tiers of wind-braces.

MANOR HOUSE, SW of the church, S of Norman Hall. The house as it is now, pink-washed, gabled, and bargeboarded, has great charm, in spite of its quite considerable size. It is U-shaped, open to the back garden and the river with two far-projecting wings framing a not too wide courtyard. This pretty picture hides the archaeological evidence (or conjecture), which is of the S wing being the C13 hall range (like Norman Hall) of the Courtenays and the E range being a C15 extension. In the S range the tie-beam roof with crown-posts and massive curved braces is hidden. Only the N range tells its story. It is the story of an enlargement of about 1670, and that date is made certain by the consistent use of Ipswich windows (for the term *see* Abingdon, p. 58). They belong to the first floor; for the ground floor is an open loggia with unfluted Ionic columns. On the first floor the windows are separated by pilasters. Garlands on their bases. On the outer side of the range the motif is repeated, but not original. Inside, a small Jacobean staircase with decorated string. In front of the E front a pair of GATEPIERS of the mid C17, almost identical with the one at Besselsleigh and similar to the piers at Coleshill. To the N a BARN with exposed timber on a stone base.

42c

THE ABBEY, S of the church. On the other side of the road, also in its own grounds. This never was an abbey, but it was a grange of Abingdon Abbey. It is a courtyard house with the W, N, and S sides of the C14. The W front is pretty and probably early C19 or Early Victorian from outside, with its castellated centre and its two gables. But in the l. gable is a genuine large window of the early or mid C14 with flowing tracery (the opposite number on the r. is not original), and round the corner to the N medieval windows continue. But inside, behind the battlements, is the original great hall, with its open roof with one mighty cruck truss carrying a kingpost and four-way struts. Specially massive purlins. The doorways to the front and the back have characteristic Dec mouldings too. The place where the solar staircase ran from the former high-table end can also be located by an upper doorway with a plain continuous chamfer. The room beneath the solar has moulded beams. – In the hall a screen made up of copious Jacobean panels.

Sutton Courtenay has plenty of enjoyable houses. Only the following can here be referred to. Going N from the church, first the ALMSHOUSES of 1820, one-storeyed, with the centre a little stressed. Then opposite COURTENAY LODGE, C18, chequer brick, of five bays with a hipped roof. Doorway with a hood carved inside with a basket held by two putti and foliage l., r., and top. Then gabled houses, one with two Ipswich windows, and opposite THE WHARF, an C18 core but mostly by *W. Cave*, c.1912. Neo-William-and-Mary with hipped roof and slightly projecting wings. One more good house round the corner, in Appleford Road, MILL HOUSE. This has to the W a whitewashed front with giant pilasters, probably early C19, to the street a porch.

s from the church in the MILTON ROAD a charming gabled house of 1631 with two oriels, their posts carved, and further s a fine group: No. 53 with two heavy ground-floor bay windows and a heavy doorway, Early Georgian alterations of an earlier house, No. 76 with a sweet symmetrical Gothick front and opposite a good bigger timber-framed house. In the DRAYTON ROAD GOSLINGS, timber-framed, with two low four-light windows probably original, and GILBOURN'S FARM, closer to Drayton than to Sutton Courtenay, also timber-framed, but with a doorway with segmental pediment on pilasters.

(BUCKRIDGES, $\frac{1}{2}$ m. SSE of the church. 1631. Gabled, irregular, with steeply gabled oriels and chimneystacks set diagonally. NBR)

SUTTON WICK FIELD *see* ABINGDON, p. 61

SWALLOWFIELD

ALL SAINTS. Flint. Nave and chancel in one; tiled roof. Bell-turret with brick-nogging. The nave is Norman, see the N and S doorways. The N doorway has two orders of colonnettes with scallop capitals and a round, moulded arch with zigzag. The chancel is Dec, see the elementary flowing tracery of the side windows. The E wall is Victorian. Two Perp nave windows. Late medieval also the sturdy timber supports of the bell-turret. They include scissor-bracing. – STAINED GLASS. A three-light nave window by *Hardman*. – In the N transept *Holiday*, 1884, not good. – PLATE. Flagon, 1639; Paten, 1651; Paten on foot, 1719. – MONUMENTS. Brass to Margery Letterford, mid C15 – a 15 in. figure. – Brass to Christopher Littcott † 1554, 28 in. figures (both chancel floor). – John Backhouse † 1649 and members of the Backhouse family (1669). Two large tablets with black columns, but not identical. – Funeral HELMS. – Sir Henry Russell † 1852. Tablet with ogee top. Profile in roundel. White marble.

SWALLOWFIELD PARK is not sufficiently known in its architectural history. What is known, is that the second Earl of Clarendon rebuilt it in 1689–91, that he employed *Talman*, and that in 1820 *William Atkinson* remodelled the house for Sir Henry Russell. What is Talman's? Certainly the monumental doorway re-erected in the garden. This ornateness is Talman's quite specially, and compares for instance with Drayton in Northants. Pilasters with garlands, corbels or brackets instead of capitals, broken segmental pediment with swags or drapes in it. The doorway once belonged to the house. The house is H-shaped with the wings projecting little to the entrance, much to the garden. Panelled parapet. This is essentially Talman's house, but internally the only feature characteristic of him is the surprising oval vestibule in the middle of the garden side with its stucco ceiling. The remains of one staircase (carved tread-ends, column posts) could also be his. The porte-cochère on the entrance side is of course Russell's. Two pairs of Tuscan columns. The entrance side is the S side. The E side is nine bays long and has a three-bay centre with giant pilasters. That also is something of which 1690 was well capable (see e.g. Talman at Chatsworth in 1687–96). To the W a complex and interesting development of the outbuildings. They are of exposed brick, the house is cemented. There is first an arcaded courtyard open to the w. It has nine by seven bays. Against the s side of the arcading stands a small house and the short side of the long flat stable block. Between the two the courtyard is entered by an archway with coupled giant brick pilasters. The stables have three archways, the middle one flanked by single pilasters, the outer ones each endowed with only one pilaster, as on the other side short wings project. The windows are segment-headed and have just one wooden mullion. The parapets are panelled. All this looks late C17.

Of the gardens of Swallowfield John Evelyn wrote that they were 'as elegant as 'tis possible to make a flat by art and industrie and no mean expense'.

BRIDGE in the grounds. Five plain arches.

LODGES. High Victorian. Brick with diapers.

BOWYER'S FARMHOUSE, ½ m. w. Dated 1749. Blue and red brick, five bays, wooden cross-windows. It certainly looks earlier.

QUEEN ANNE'S MEAD, 1¼ m. NW. A pretty three-bay front of chequer bricks and a front garden visible through an C18 wrought-iron gate.

SWINFORD BRIDGE   4000

Three approach arches either side and three larger mid-arches, the latter with rusticated voussoirs and balustrade. The bridge was built in 1777.

SWINLEY DOWN see ASHDOWN PARK

TEMPLE MILLS see BISHAM

THATCHAM   5060

ST MARY. Flint, quite big, with many gables, largely of the restoration of 1857 (by *Thomas Hellyer*). Original the Norman s doorway with zigzag, at least in a few parts. Original also the N arcade, clearly early C13. It is puzzling. The first bay is low, the others higher. The piers and arches have only a slight chamfer. There is a sign of a former w wall E of the first bay. Perp N aisle with its windows. – STAINED GLASS. s aisle w by *Powell's*, 1865, i.e. before they developed their characteristic Walter-Cranish style. – MONUMENTS. Tomb-chest with quatrefoils (s chapel) to Sir William Danvers † 1504. – Nicholas Fuller † 1620. Alabaster tablet with kneeling figures, the children below the parents.

CHAPEL, at the E end of the main street (A4). Founded in 1304, but the straight-sided arch to the S doorway Late Perp (cf. Theale, i.e. Oxford), the S and N windows probably C17, and the W porch Victorian. Two original, pretty niches l. and r. of it.

In the main street near the chapel on the N side a three-storeyed, three-bay house of brick and then a thatched timber-framed cottage.

Close to the church the VICARAGE, Early Georgian, of five bays, blue brick with red dressings. THATCHAM FARM, W of the Vicarage, is a handsome brick group with its outbuildings.

THATCHAM HOUSE. Victorian Gothic, brick and stone dressings, with an eccentrically placed turret.

MESOLITHIC SETTLEMENT, on a low terrace, just W of the Mow Brook and N of the railway embankment. The evidence from this site suggests temporary and intermittent occupation by groups of Maglemosean hunter-fishers. No traces of dwellings have been found, and the settlement is marked by hearths and a scatter of flint tools and flint-knapping debris. The flint equipment includes burins or gravers for antler and bone working, and a large series of small blades or microliths which served as arrowpoints or barbs in composite hunting weapons. Pollen samples and radiocarbon dates indicate settlement by Mesolithic groups from c.6000 to c.4000 B.C.

THEALE

6070

HOLY TRINITY. 1820–32 by *E. W. Garbett*, the tower by *John Buckler*. This is a church as remarkable for scale as for style. Regarding scale, it was all paid for by Mrs Sophia Sheppard, sister of Dr Routh, President of Magdalen College Oxford and Rector of Theale. Regarding style, the pattern is patently Salisbury Cathedral, and that was not a pattern likely to be chosen in 1820. 1820 looked to the Perp, 1840 to the late C13 and early C14. The early and mid C13 had no popularity. Lancet windows were used freely, but not to make up E.E. ensembles. Garbett's church is very tall, and seems more so by its pairs of very slender lancets in each bay and by the Salisbury buttresses. The tower is also E.E. It is open in a passage on the ground floor and is connected with the church by what seems to be a transept but houses a library. The façade of the church is also modelled on Salisbury, but the W porch gives the real date away. It is much too high and narrow in its proportions. Besides, such a W porch is not correct E.E. cathedral style. The porch is stone-vaulted. So is the handsome W gallery inside. The principal vaults however are of plaster. It is a great pity that *Oldrid Scott* added the apse. – STAINED GLASS. In the apse by *Kempe*, 1892. – MONUMENT. The 'chantry chapel' is that of Bishop Waynflete, removed from Magdalen College Oxford in 1830 by Dr Routh. Two doorways in the same style and probably also from Magdalen. Characteristic straight-sided diagonals in the tracery and straight-sided arches to the doorways (cf. Cumnor, North Hinksey). Inside, the cenotaph of Mrs Sheppard.

RECTORY, E of the church. Stone, classical, 1830, five bays with a three-bay pediment. Also built by Mrs Sheppard.

In the main street, near the E end, on the S side, some nice five-bay Georgian houses.

TIDMARSH   6070

ST LAURENCE. The church possesses a splendid Norman S doorway. The orders are all continuous and all ornamented: zigzag, chain, also trails and scrolls. The hood-mould has as its apex a fearsome head (of Christ ?) in a rounded trefoil, the top foil more than semicircular. C13 W lancets, C13 chancel lancets, and C13 polygonal apse, a great rarity in English parish churches. Madeley in Herefordshire is a parallel, but it is later. This one, from the apse arch and the supports of the (recent) plaster rib-vault (triple shafts with fillets, stiff-leaf capitals), is mid C13 at the latest. As impressive as the apse are the heavy timber supports of the bell-turret and its shingled pyramid roof. They have upper scissor bracing, and the posts as well as the tie-beam and arched braces are robustly decorated with motifs immediately derived from the Norman doorway. This is by a Victorian rector's wife. At first one would call it C17. – FONT. If C12, then entirely re-cut. – PULPIT. If C15, then only in very minor parts. – COMMUNION RAIL. C18. – PAINTING. In the jambs of one N and one S lancet faded C13 single standing figures. – PLATE. Cup of 1749; Paten on foot. – MONUMENTS. Brass to Margaret Woode † 1499, 19½ in. long. – Brass to Henry Leynham † 1517, 3 ft long. – Robert Hopkins † 1834. By *Whitelaw*. Big tablet with a small urn.

OLD RECTORY. 1856. Brick. Symmetrical three-bay front with steep gables. Gothic casement windows, but brick-filled tympana. Was *Street* the architect ?

TILEHURST

St Michael. s aisle of the early C14 (windows with Y- and intersecting tracery). Brick tower of 1737 with clasping buttresses, the rest 1856 by *Street*, including the rather wild spire with angle pinnacles, flying buttresses, and very large lucarnes. Flint church, not specially attractive outside or inside. – STAINED GLASS. Chancel E and s by *Wailes*, 1856, designed by *Street* (TK). – In the s aisle E window of 1869 by *Morris*, a Virgin and large angels on a patterned, deep blue ground. – PLATE. Silver-gilt Chalice and Cover, 1573; silver-gilt Flagon and Almsdish, 1737. – MONUMENTS. Brass to Gavin More † 1479 (13 in. figures). – Sir Peter Vanlore of Utrecht, a merchant, † 1627. Two recumbent effigies, praying. Children below and also, frontal, l. and r. Back arch with good strapwork and trophies. Alabaster.

St George, St George's Road. 1885–6 by *Sidney Gambier Parry*. Chancel 1893. Brick, with lancets and the bellcote over the nave E end. Polygonal apse. – (PULPIT. Jacobean; from Sonning.)

Church of Jesus Christ of Latter Day Saints, Readway. Modernistic, with thin tower carrying a spike.

At the s end of Church End Lane survives a timber-framed farmhouse. It ought to be kept. Down Kentwood Hill on the E side Kentwood Farmhouse, later C17, brick, with a hipped roof and wooden cross-windows.

TITTENHURST PARK *see* SUNNINGHILL

TOUCHEN END
1¾ m. SE of White Waltham

Holy Trinity. 1862 by *J. Turner*. Brick. Nave with bellcote and chancel. In the Dec style. The aisle windows all low, segment-headed, and of three lights, with reticulation units. Wooden posts between nave and s aisle, on the pattern of Winkfield. – STAINED GLASS. 1959, in an attractive, unexacting Expressionism. Designed by *Colin Shewring*.

TUBNEY

St Lawrence. 1844–7 by *Pugin*. It is in no way distinguished and might be by anybody. But the fact remains noteworthy that about 1845 so close to Oxford a Catholic architect could be chosen for an Anglican church.* Nave with bellcote and chancel. The bellcote on a mid-buttress. Minimum ogee-headed one- and two-light windows. Thin trussed rafter roof, in the chancel with an embattled wall-plate. The stencilled PAINTING of the chancel roof could well be Pugin's. – FONT. Given to the church by Queen Adelaide. Octagonal. Carved bowl supports and four carved panels.

TUBNEY HOUSE. The entrance side is plain Late Georgian but with two embattled pedimental gables over the ends. The side has all the windows with hood-moulds, probably Latish Georgian. But towards the garden is one C17 mullioned and transomed window and a canted bay window with steep Gothic openings. Also more battlements. Inside an ample staircase, apparently early C18.

TWYFORD 7070

ST MARY. 1846 by *Ferrey*, enlarged considerably in 1908–10 by *S. S. Stallwood* (BC). Flint, E.E., with a NW tower. Quite large. By Ferrey the S aisle and arcade. To the W of the church a ruinous tower said to belong to a former chapel of St Swithun.

In the HIGH STREET several nice houses, e.g. by the bridge the POLEHAMPTON SCHOOL house, plain, brick, of five bays. The school was founded in 1721.

In LONDON ROAD is APSLEY HOUSE, Early Georgian, rustic but very charming. Blue-brick headers and red-brick dressings. Five bays, segment-headed windows. The sill-zone with some elephant leg decoration. Pedimented doorway. A little further out the HARRISON ALMSHOUSES of 1640, a one-storeyed row with a porch. Projecting wings at the back.

UFFINGTON 3080

ST MARY. A church of *c.*1250 with a crossing tower. Its top storey turns octagonal, and a further storey was added after 1740. The windows of the church are mostly lancet pairs, and also triplets. Below these groups blank circles or roundels, for consecration crosses. Access to the church is by one grand and two unusual porches. The S porch is on a cathedral scale. Outer and inner doorways have mature stiff-leaf capitals. On

* The Rev. F. E. Rusby tells me that Pugin wanted a tower, but the cost of £645 was too much. In the end, the church cost £649, and Pugin received a fee of £30.

the buttresses niches with continuous mouldings. In the buttress gablets small figures. In the top gable also a figure composition. Large, unfinished panelled pinnacles l. and r. Rib-vault inside, the rib profile not one of the current ones. A second doorway with shallow porch leads from the E into the S transept. It is tunnel-vaulted. Is it explicable by the fact that the manor belonged to Abingdon Abbey? Was a house perhaps attached or close by in a monastery fashion? The third doorway is the priest's doorway, and that also has the uncommon feature of a gable. To its l. incidentally a three-light Dec window with reticulated tracery. Yet another curious fact is the very large sexfoiled circular window above the N doorway into the nave. Why was this made? The three lancet windows in the W wall of the nave have very odd tops, and these seem to belong to a restoration of 1677–9.* It is tempting to attribute to this date also the weirdest of all features of Uffington, the E chapels of the transept, two N, one S. They are of three lights with steep triangles, not arches, and the mullions simply running into them (cf. Buckland). It looks like Lethaby or E. S. Prior and certainly not like the C13. Would 1678 be an answer? Internally all is mid C13 again. Much shafting in the chancel. Original SEDILIA and PISCINA. Groups of triple wall shafts indicate the intention to vault. Springers indeed survive. The capitals of the shafts are polygonal, as though they were Perp. But they are not; for they recur in the impeccable transept E arcades. Each of the three chapels has a big PISCINA. The transept windows are shafted too. Finally the crossing arches, and they present something odd once more, the abaci with concave hollows as if they were Perp. It is all round a highly idiosyncratic style we find at Uffington, but surely not idiosyncratic enough for the transept E windows. – READING DESK. The ends are two bench ends. – SOUTH DOOR. C13, with very elaborate hinges. – PLATE. Cup of 1583. – MONUMENTS. Edward Archer † 1603. Stone, of reredos type. Two columns, straight top with strapwork. – John Saunders † 1638. Semi-reclining effigy, stiffly on his side. Coffered arch. Strapwork on the back wall.

(FRIENDS MEETING HOUSE, ¼ m. SE, i.e. E of Garrards Farm. 1711.)

S of the church UFFINGTON SCHOOL, a small oblong building

* The Rev. Basil Clarke quoted to me the churchwardens' accounts for 1677–9: 'Payd to *John Deane* for ye end wall of ye Church, pulling it downe & setting it up £25. 00. 00.'

of 1617* with mullioned windows. The building is of chalk, as is nearly the whole of Uffington.

VICARAGE. Asymmetrical, with gables and Gothic details. According to Messrs Betjeman and Piper by *Kendall*, 1849.

THE WHITE HORSE, ¼ m. NE. This great chalk-cut representa-3b tion of a horse is some 360 ft long and 130 ft high. It is the only undoubted prehistoric hill figure in England. The stylized treatment of the horse finds parallels in the horses on Belgic ceremonial buckets and on their coinage. The Uffington horse was probably cut in the C1 and may have served as a tribal emblem. It has never ceased to impress and puzzle people. Celia Fiennes praised its 'perfect proportions', Francis Wise in 1738 the 'skill in Opticks' of its makers and its durability, and Robert Dodsley in 1744 reported that it was supposed to have been made by Hengist. The horse had to be scoured every so often, and this, in the C17 at the latest, developed into a ceremony with all kinds of revels. In our less merry century the grooming of the horse is done by the Ministry of Public Building and Works.

BARROW. Just above the White Horse is an elongated pillow mound, 70 ft long and 40 ft wide, flanked by quarry ditches. The site was excavated in the C19, the central depression marking the position of this work. Forty-six Romano-British inhumation burials were recovered, and also an urned cremation, the latter perhaps a Bronze Age interment beneath a pre-existing round barrow.

UFFINGTON CASTLE, on White Horse Hill. The fort is of univallate construction with a single entrance on the NW. Little is known of the site, which has not been scientifically excavated, although some work on the ramparts in the C19 showed them to be faced with sarsens. The form of the ramparts suggests that the fort is the work of Iron Age A groups, although a silver coin of the Dobunni was found in the interior.

ROMANO-BRITISH SETTLEMENT, in the saddle joining Uffington and Woolstone Downs. The site consists of a small rectangular enclosure defined by a shallow ditch, 4 ft wide, with an inner and an outer bank visible at the SE corner. The site is unexcavated, but sherds of Roman pottery have been found in its ploughed interior.

MOUND, *see* Woolstone.

---

* Also dates 1634 and 1637.

UFTON GREEN *see* UFTON NERVET

6060

UFTON NERVET

ST PETER. 1861–2 by *R. Armstrong*. Early C14 style with shingled spire. – STAINED GLASS. E window 1862 by *Clutterbuck* (BC), still pictorial in the early C19 way. The nave windows by *Lavers & Barraud*, grisaille, i.e. brown outlines and some little yellow. – PLATE. Cup, Elizabethan. – MONUMENTS. Richard Perkyns † 1560. Early Elizabethan at its best. Unfortunately only the canopy is left: two fluted columns and a delicately decorated frieze. – Francis Perkyns † 1635. Two recumbent stone effigies on a tomb-chest with kneeling children, all badly preserved. – A very ancient yew-tree s of the church.

ST JOHN BAPTIST, Ufton Green, $\frac{7}{8}$ m. NW. All that remains is one flint wall with a marvellous huge hat of ivy.

UFTON COURT. Built *c.*1570–80. Large, timber-framed, with many gables. An E façade, with porch gable, each projecting wing with four side gables and one front gable and the connecting pieces between porch and wings with four gables each. That sounds perfectly symmetrical; in fact, it isn't, as of these latter gables those on the r. are in one plane, those on the l. not at all. The façade has two overhangs with moulded bressumers. The first-floor windows are slightly projected on brackets and have shallow pediments. The porch is deep and has ornamental front posts and also side balusters. It still leads into a screens passage and to an exit. The garden side was brick-faced in the early C18, but the doorway and the big chimneybreast tell of the still medieval arrangement of the Elizabethan hall. In the hall a thin-ribbed plaster ceiling with heavy pendants. Queen Anne panelling. In a room to the N also thin-ribbed plasterwork. It is divided by beams with carved decoration still entirely Early Renaissance, i.e. rather 1540– than 1580–looking. In the NE room modest mid C18 stucco and a mid C18 chimneypiece. (S of the screens passage the Elizabethan staircase, and S of this a small service room connected with the large kitchen by a hatch which is pre-Reformation in date and proves that at least this part of the house must structurally go back that far. The kitchen was originally open to the surviving trussed rafter roof. The SE wing must originally have held the chapel on the upper floor, and there are three ingenious priest holes. Francis Perkyns, who died in 1616, was indeed a recusant. VCH)

UPPER BASILDON *see* BASILDON

UPTON

5080

ST MARY. Flint-faced, nave and chancel and a timer bell-turret.
In the chancel two Norman windows, not identical. In the
nave one Norman window. Norman chancel arch with saltire-
cross frieze in the abaci.

WADLEY HOUSE
1¼ m. E of Faringdon

3090

Two parts, a plain seven-bay façade of 1768 with a doorway and
Tuscan columns and a pediment, and behind it an L-shaped
C16 part with mullioned windows with uncusped arched
lights, especially one in the gable facing E. A farm building has
three large Gothick quatrefoils.
To the N a three-bay red brick house with a one-bay pediment.

WALBURY CAMP *see* COMBE

WALLINGFORD

6080

The first charter was given to Wallingford in 1155 by Henry II,
who had here concluded the treaty with Stephen which ended
the civil war and secured him the succession. But Wallingford
had a guild merchant before then, and the castle also was in
existence and had indeed been in prominence, as the Empress
Maud had taken refuge in it in 1142. It is not known when the
town was laid out, but its plan shows clearly that it is a made
town. It is roughly square, with rounded corners, and its streets
are roughly parallel or crossing at r. angles. The main crossing
is that of Castle Street running N–S and continued in St Mary's
Street with the High Street running due W from the Thames
bridge. The castle fills the NE quarter, the NW quarter is still
mostly open (Bull Croft), the Market Place lies in the line of St
Mary's Street S of the main crossing. Ramparts are preserved
along the E and S sides and half the N side. Wallingford had ten
or eleven parish churches in the C12, but only four in the
C15. Now there are three. There was also a small Benedictine
priory.

ST MARY, immediately S of the Market Place. A flint church of
1854 (by *David Brandon*) except for the W tower. The tower
has polygonal angle buttresses.* – PULPIT. By *Onslow Ford*,

* It received pinnacles in 1660, and these (or copies) may be re-installed.

1888. Marble, with bronze reliefs of saints. Marble decoration also in the chancel, but of 1901. – STAINED GLASS. N aisle W by *Willement*, 1856. – PLATE. Paten, 1833. – MONUMENTS. Walter Bigg † 1659. Large tablet. The flat carving and the garlands and swags all typical of *c*.1660. Top segmental pediment with a skull. – (Thomas Renda † 1722. Signed by *E. Stanton & Horsnaile the Elder*. Gunnis) – In the chancel telling comparison between the tablets † 1746 and † 1826.

ST LEONARD. A Norman church, ill-treated by *Hakewill* in 1849, who added the totally uninspired W tower and the S arcade. But the church is genuinely Norman, see the herringbone masonry on the N side, the N doorway, and, after all, in spite of recarving, the splendid arches E of the nave and W of the apse. They are tall and wide and have decoration of small motifs such as saltire crosses, stars, etc. The capitals and abaci of the W arch are basket-weave, those of the E arch have two heads. – PAINTING in the apse. By *G. D. Leslie*, 1889 (BC). – PLATE. Two Chalices, Paten, and Flagon, 1812.

ST PETER. Nave and tower 1760–9. The delightful spire was
9a designed in 1777 by *Sir Robert Taylor*. It is not known if he also designed the rest. Flint tower, square, with an open Gothic octagonal bell-stage and the spire growing in a historically quite unauthorized curve out of it. The spire is openwork too, in four stages. It is rather cheeky for Sir Robert, but entirely convincing. The nave is of stone, with arched windows and a segmental vault. The apse was added in 1904 and is unfortunate. – STAINED GLASS. The E window is by *Morris & Co.*, of *c*.1918, and shows what the firm had come to twenty years after Morris's death. – PLATE. Silver-gilt Chalice and Paten 1769 and Almsdish 1777. – MONUMENT. Sir William Blackstone, the jurist, is buried here. Slab in the floor and Gothic monument of *c*.1841 outside on the S wall.

FRIENDS' MEETING HOUSE, Castle Street. 1724; a simple brick cottage.

CASTLE. The castle fills the NE quarter of the town. It has two ditches to N, W, and S, and one to the E, where the Thames was a further defence. On the N side the town ditch formed a third enforcement. The motte is at the S end of the inner bailey. On it mixed remains of masonry. More on the E side, with one early C14 window. More also to the SW. The masonry here belongs to the collegiate church of St Nicholas. It is of the early C16 and has one straight-headed three-light window. The whole is picturesque, but historically not very rewarding. The area is now the grounds of CASTLE HOUSE, a large gabled Tudor house of 1837.

TOWN HALL. 1670. To the Market Place the open ground floor has four sturdy columns, the upper floor just a Venetian window, and the roof appears pyramidal. To the sides five bays and a hipped roof. – REGALIA. Mayor's Badge, *temp.* Charles I; a silver-gilt Mace by *Thomas Maundy*, 1650; silver-gilt Cup and Cover by *Charles Shelley*, 1668; Shield, probably London, 1750–1.

CORN EXCHANGE, Market Place. Just one item in the terrace of the E side of the square. 1856, in a restrained Italianate. Stone, three bays, the windows arched pairs.

PERAMBULATION. This will have to fan out from the MARKET PLACE. On the E side LLOYDS BANK, of 1915 (by *F. W. Shann*), but looking entirely *c.*1830, of five bays. The middle window is arched and has a reeded surround. Pedimental gable. On the w side Nos 14 and 15, blue and red brick, with plain Venetian windows. Down S by ST MARY'S STREET. Not much to be seen, except the flat w terrace of ST LEONARD'S SQUARE, blue and red brick, *c.*1800, and Nos 28–29 of a similar character but with a minimum Venetian window on the second floor. The street then becomes READING ROAD and leaves the old town. Immediately on the E down a service road to the river and here ST LUCIANS, the most interesting house in Wallingford. It is of brick and pargetted and has a symmetrical w front with three gables and two castellated bay windows and looks Elizabethan. On the N a handsome range of outbuildings.

Continuing a little on the Reading Road on the E side AUGIER'S ALMSHOUSES. They are of 1681 and have three gables. The Gothic glazing bars are obviously early C19, but are the ogee head to the foundation tablet and the big Tudor roses on the other gables and the w porch really 1681?

Now N from the Market Place, again along ST MARY'S STREET. Here the WHITE HART, *c.*1500, with two gables and Gothic details at their foot. No. 1 is the corner to the High Street. Early Georgian, of five bays and three storeys, blue and red brick, with segment-headed windows and a parapet. This is the next point for fanning out from. To the N in CASTLE STREET a C16 timber-framed house with gables and overhang. To the w HIGH STREET in its less eventful part. At once on the N side Nos 62–63, blue and red brick, segment-headed windows, then No. 35, the Municipal Offices, low, widely spaced, red brick with angle pilasters and a parapet, early C19. Near the end, where the street stops being a town street, on the s side, FRANK H. JENKINS'S GARAGE, etc., a good modern job by *Hancock Associates,* 1961–2, black steel and glass, no fashionable gimmicks. After that a house with a Greek Doric porch on the same side and one on the N side preceded by FLINT COTTAGE, C17, with three even gables and mullioned and transomed windows.

Finally to the E from the junction of St Mary's Street and HIGH STREET. On the N side at once the former LAMB HOTEL, Early Georgian, blue and red brick, of two and a half storeys, quite plain, with a middle archway. Then the WESTMINSTER BANK, five bays, three storeys, plus one-bay additions l. and r. The five-bay part has angle pilasters. Later Georgian. After that the GEORGE INN, C16 or C17, with two gables and an oversailing upper floor. In the yard an C18 brick part with a re-set wooden C16 doorway and a Venetian window above. Off s for a moment into WOOD STREET for No. 12, blue headers and red brick, segment-headed windows, three storeys. On in the High Street, No. 74 with handsome C18 stabling with a cupola behind, and on the s side Nos 17–19, C16, picturesque, with an overhang. (Cellar beneath, vaulted in quadripartite bays, partly C14. MHLG) No. 75 again blue headers and red brick, three storeys, five bays. No. 76 lies back, is of stone, and has a Greek Doric porch, i.e. *c.*1820. Then the *clou* of Wallingford, CALLEVA HOUSE, Early Georgian. Five bays, three storeys, blue and red brick. Segment-headed windows. Upper giant brick pilasters on ground-floor pilaster strips. Parapet. Doorway with pilasters, triglyphs, and segmental pediment. (Staircase with slim twisted and fluted balusters and carved tread-ends.) Opposite the castellated GATES of Castle House (*see* above).

Here we are close to WALLINGFORD BRIDGE, a bridge of altogether seventeen arches, though only five of them span the river. Three of the arches are medieval and ribbed, perhaps C13, but the three middle ones with the handsome balustrade date from 1809. The arches to the l. and r. of these three are of 1751.

To finish with, a walk down THAMES STREET, opposite the Castle Lodges, is recommended, though the houses look their best rather from the Oxfordshire side of the river. First a stately three-bay one, with a stone E front and lunette windows on the second floor. Then CASTLE PRIORY, with a five-bay river front and good interior work. Then on the w side of the road a group of five houses and studio flats by *Morton & Lupton*.

WALLINGTONS *see* KINTBURY

WALTHAM ST LAWRENCE

St Lawrence. Approached under a majestic yew tree. w tower of flint and stone blocks, the doorway Perp, but the w window of *c.*1300 (finely detailed in cusped intersecting tracery). The very top early brick. The body of the church flint, with all details Victorian. The s transept front of 1847 with a rather bleak Victorian window. Internally, however, the church demonstrates a Norman origin. Two-bay arcades N and S with unmoulded arches separated by pieces of wall. Of the responds two have a very elementary row of flat leaves. These arcades of the short Norman church were continued E by two standard Dec bays. No chancel arch. – FONT. Perp. Octagonal. No separate foot or stem. Panelled sides. – PULPIT. 1619. Only the back panel with caryatids in its upper part is original. – SCREEN. The tracery heads are original and show that this was a Dec, not a Perp screen. – RAILING to the baptistery. Jacobean, and presumably not *in situ*. – CANDLE BRACKETS. C17, and very pretty with their decorative S-curve decoration. – PAINTING. On a N pier an early C14 figure and ornamental scrolls. – STAINED GLASS. E window by *Wailes*, probably of 1847, when the chancel was re-decorated. – w window by *Kempe*, 1877. – One N aisle window signed by *M. Schneider* of Regensburg, 1866. Why go to him? The glass is not even technically adequate. – PLATE. Chalice and Cover of 1661; Paten of 1783; Chalice of 1795. – MONUMENTS. Sir Henry Neville † 1593 and two wives and one daughter. Alabaster. Four kneeling figures. Flat top. – Katherine Thomas † 1658. A memorable monument. Urn of a curiously organic shape, somewhat like an inverted pear, on a short marble column, placed in a niche – no ornament whatever. – Dorothy Lewis † 1687. A pretty, scrolly cartouche. – Capt. Henry Neville † 1809. By *Sir R. Westmacott*. With a military still life.

From the church s the BELL INN, an impressive piece of C14 timber-framing. Attached to it a C15 timber-framed cottage with exposed brick infilling. Then IVY BANK FARMHOUSE, L-shaped and also timber-framed. Opposite a good recent brick house painted white. 1960–1 by *Paul Cornwall-Jones*.

After that COLTMANS, gabled Elizabethan or Jacobean brick, and KELLINGHAMS, again timber frame and brick infilling. At the s end of the main street by the war memorial PARADISE, brick, C18, with an irregular but attractive front and a side with tripartite windows. By the same green PARADISE FARM-HOUSE, C15 gable and C18 otherwise, and BORLASES, much altered but with a C15 core. The hall has its timber roof with wind-braces.*

₄₀₈₀

WANTAGE

ST PETER AND ST PAUL. The church can only narrowly be reached from the Market Place, and that is just as well. It is a large cruciform building with a crossing tower and dates essentially from the later C13. Externally this is visible as follows. The bell-openings of the tower are of two pointed-trefoiled lights with a circle over. Of the same date, it seems, the upper chancel windows, unless they are entirely of *Street*'s restoration of 1857. Street lived at Wantage from 1850 to 1852, when he moved to Oxford. He settled down in London in 1855. The chancel of the church was lengthened at the Perp time and the small s doorway then put in. The s chapel and transept E chapel are of course Perp too and can boast substantial gargoyles. This part and the corresponding N chapel alone are ashlar-faced. In the w wall of the s transept, to return to the C13, is a lancet. Otherwise more external Perp: nave windows and two-storeyed s porch. The w wall belongs to a lengthening of 1877 (by *Butterfield*); hence its prominent middle buttress. Inside the church, the arcades (except for the w bay) again C13. Round piers, round abaci, double-chamfered arches dying into the piers. The sw respond belongs to the same build, the NW respond is Perp. Roof supports of stone Perp too. Arch from the s aisle into the transept C13, but interfered with, from the N aisle Perp. But the s respond of the N transept E aisle (of two bays) has stiff-leaf and really seems the earliest feature of the church. The s transept E arcade is of the type of the nave arcades. The crossing arches are heavy and triple-chamfered, i.e. late C13 also. The arches from the chancel to the chapel are clearly Perp, but differ. Both sides have the familiar four-shafts-and-four-hollows section, but the N capitals are concave-sided. – PULPIT. Of 1857, i.e. probably designed by *Street*. – SCREENS. To the chancel chapels, of

* (FOUR ELMS. Above the door relief of four elms by *Eric Gill*, c.1926. Robert Gibbings then lived in the house.)

one-light divisions, Perp. – STALLS. The ends with tracery and big poppy-heads, the seats with MISERICORDS. On the misericords a pelican, a double eagle, shields, and mostly leaves. – CHANDELIER. A splendid piece with two tiers of arms; dated 1711. – STAINED GLASS. N transept E by *Willement*, 1848. – PLATE. Cup, London, 1571; large Cup, London, 1624; two Patens, London, 1722; large Almsdish, not English, inscribed 1725; two large Flagons, London, 1744. – MONUMENTS. Sir William Fitzwarin † 1361. Two alabaster effigies. Formerly with a canopy above the tomb. – Brass to Sir Ives Fitzwarin † 1414, a good 5 ft figure. – Brass to a Priest, *c.*1330 (2 ft). – Brass to a Man, early C16 (17½ in.). These are in the N transept. – Brass to Walter Talbot and two wives † 1522 (18 in.). This is in the S aisle. – William Wilmot † 1684. Wide tablet with columns and an open segmental pediment. Two frontal demi-figures, both at ease with one hand on the breast. A baby, pathetically upright, between them. The monument, which is signed by *William Bird* of Oxford, is supported on three angel busts. – John Stamp † 1728 and his wife 1741. The latter date must be valid, according to the Rococo detail. The two vases may even be an addition of *c.*1784. By *John Townsend Jun.*

METHODIST CHAPEL, Newbury Street. 1848 by *R. W. Ordish*. Modest Dec; stone.

CEMETERY. The CHAPEL is by *Butterfield*, 1850 (BC), a plain oblong building, of stone, with a circular E window. At the time of writing it seems doomed.

ST MARY'S CONVENT, Faringdon Road. Of the Anglican order of the Wantage Sisterhood, founded by Elizabeth Lockhart, inspired by W. J. Butler, later Dean of Lincoln. Stone buildings, the original ones by *Street*, 1855–6. They lie behind and to the l. of the present gatehouse, and the wing to the r. with which they form a courtyard was added in 1860. Street's designs are of course Gothic and of course unornamental. It is interesting, however, to see that his dormer windows are not at all Gothic and rather C17. Behind this is the original chapel, also by Street, and built in 1858–61. It is a plain oblong room with lancets on the N side and a large (altered) E window. The chancel side walls have arcading below and a circular window above. In 1866 and 1871–2 the refectory was built. It was altered in 1900. In 1878 the Noviciate was erected N of Street's buildings. This is by *Butterfield*, a long range with tall stone windows with segmental arches. In 1887 a new larger chapel was begun. It is by *Pearson*, with Geometrical tracery, high and rib-vaulted in stone. It originally went only as far as the screen and was lengthened in 1900. The curious, somewhat fussy re-arrangement of the E end, with stone piers acting as a canopy over the altar and three little vaults l., centre, and r., is by *Comper*, 1923.

RETREAT HOUSE, Priory Road, SW of the church. Also called ST MICHAEL'S. 1855, and initially by *William White*, probably changed in the process of building (BC). A very picturesque, though of course heavily picturesque, house of brown stone with thin brick motifs and pointed brick tympana above the windows. Porch set diagonally in an angle. The apsidal end of the upper chapel is an addition by *A. B. Allin*, 1888 (BC). Two larger, flat-fronted buildings were added yet later.

URBAN DISTRICT COUNCIL OFFICES, Portway. Inside the remains of the MARKET CROSS of 1580, with small defaced figures under arches.

ST MARY'S SCHOOL, Newbury Street. The main buildings lie right along the street, from l. to r.: new building of 1962 by *Lewis & Reedman*, brick, with the fashionable over-heavy concrete beams etc. and low bands of windows and an equally typical N view. Then *Butterfield*, 1874–5, but obviously heightened. This was done in 1900. Butterfield has small trefoil-headed windows. Then a five-bay Early Georgian house of blue and red brick with segment-headed windows and a pedimented one-bay centre projection. Doorway with brick pilasters and pediment. After that the CHAPEL, by *Ponting*, 1898–9. Red brick, fancy Gothic, with the motifs of several phases; asymmetrical turret with spire. The apse has a wooden tierceron-vault.

CHURCH SCHOOL, Church Street. 1850 by *Woodyer* (BC). Coursed stone with a hipped tower top.

KING ALFRED GRAMMAR SCHOOL. Stone, with two projecting wings. Gothic, and not symmetrical. By *J. B. Clacy*, 1849–50 with later additions. (The hall is attributed to *Butterfield*.) The Norman doorway of the former Latin School building in the churchyard was re-used. Little however is original. Arch with beakhead and lozenge decoration.

See p. 359

ST KATHERINE'S SCHOOL, Ormond Road. By *A. M. Mowbray*, 1897 (BC). Brick.

PERAMBULATION. We start in the MARKET PLACE. Its S side is excellent, and with its blue and red C18 brick houses a summing up of the regional Georgian style. The Market Place is nicely irregular in shape, particularly successfully to the w. The SE corner is No. 1, Early Georgian, three-storeyed, with segment-headed windows with aprons. Panelled parapet. No. 6 blue and red, this time the blue bricks all headers. Nos 7–8 also has blue headers and again a panelled parapet. No. 10 is a little lower, No. 11 stands forward a little and has a hipped roof. Segment-headed windows, aprons. Then, considerably back, the BEAR HOTEL of six bays with a pedimental gable in which, in a semicircle, the name in early C19 Egyptian letters. After that the Market Place narrows. Nos 29–30 stands across. To the Market Place it has a Victorian roof with Victorian dormers, but to the side a nice doorcase with scrolly open pediment on scrolly brackets and a (repainted) date 1708. No. 33 starts the N side. It has five bays to the s and once more segment-headed windows. At the back they still have the original mullion and transom crosses. Nothing after that, except that the E side makes quite a nice, uneventful *finale*. Off now to the E from the NE corner: WALLINGFORD STREET, with the best house in its garden derelict, and another, ROCKWELL HOUSE, of five bays, with wavy decoration of the bricks of the window lintels. Then s from the SE corner, down NEWBURY STREET. The best houses are both early C18, one now part of St Mary's School, the other opposite, also belonging to the school, which is of five bays and three storeys, yellow brick (an unusual choice) with red dressings, segment-headed windows, parapet. Then STILE'S ALMSHOUSES of 1680, brick, one-storeyed, with a hipped roof. Five very widely spaced bays.

From the Market Place W to the church and to its N the VICAR-AGE, 1850 by *Street*. Stone, asymmetrical, varied window shapes (and various periods of Gothic imitated). Gables.

From the NW corner of the Market Place straight N is GROVE STREET. At the corner of Mill Street yet another Early Georgian three-storeyed five-bay house of blue and red brick with segment-headed windows. Hipped roof. Another, humbler one of the same type further on, and then DALKEITH HOUSE, detached, of the early C18, but with two shallow late C18 bows. Now down MILL STREET with more blue and red, especially No. 20 of eight bays with brick aprons to the windows. Opposite, Nos 25–37 Victorian Gothic ALMSHOUSES, 1867 by *J. P. Spencer* (GS). One more blue and red five-bay house with segment-headed windows, and so to the convent. In DENCHWORTH ROAD, N of the convent, is WHITE

LODGE, one of the rare houses by *M. H. Baillie Scott*, Voyseyish in style and dating from 1899. Characteristic unmoulded mullioned window, and very characteristic gable pulled low on one side.

THE HAM, Ickleton Road, opposite the end of Ham Road which is the S continuation of Denchworth Road. Early Georgian, of three plus one bays. Venetian doorway and window. Hipped roof. At the back a wide canted bay window.

ROMAN VILLA. The site was discovered in a field on Chainhill Farm and excavated in the C19. The villa was of corridor type, 80 ft long and 36 ft broad, divided into five rooms of varying dimensions. A hypocaust system was found in the S room. Coins from the villa suggest an occupation from the early C2 to the beginning of the C4.

WARFIELD

8070

ST MICHAEL. One of the most rewarding churches around. Built of dark brown conglomerate. The N aisle E.E., as the N lancet and traces of more lancets establish. The rest mostly Dec, namely the N chapel and the chancel. The chapel windows have cusped Y- and cusped intersecting tracery. Y-tracery in the chancel too, but also one of the most ambitious designs of flowing tracery in Berkshire. Perp W tower of conglomerate and much stone. Short recessed spire. Perp N arcade of five bays (octagonal piers, double-hollow-chamfered arches), Perp arch to the S transept. The chancel arch on the other hand and the arches to the N chapel are Dec. They have consistent continuous mouldings of typical breadth and details. The chancel is most lavishly appointed, and, although much is over-restored (by *Street*, 1872–5), the effect is still of the most generous. SEDILIA and PISCINA with ogee arches, crocketed gables, and much foliage. The pattern continues into a screen behind the altar, creating a narrow vestry or relic chamber between altar and E wall (cf. e.g. Blakeney and Great Yarmouth in Norfolk). This screen is entirely of 1872–5, but is supposed to be based on original evidence. On the N side the EASTER SEPULCHRE has alas been mostly hacked off. In the N chapel were originally three tomb recesses with canopies, much as at Aldworth or Winchelsea. Excellent N aisle and nave roofs with tie-beams, collar-beams on arched braces, and wind-braces; heavy C14 timbers. – SCREEN to the N chapel. Four-light divisions, which is rare in Berkshire, and substantial parts of the rood-loft, which is rarer still. – BENCHES. Some ends have

4a

18b

tracery which was probably originally part of the rood-loft.
– STAINED GLASS. In the head of the E window some early
C14 censing angels. The rest of this window by *Burlison &
Grylls*, 1889 (BC). In the S transept S window some fragmentary
C15 figures. – In the N aisle W window one C15 figure.
– MONUMENTS. Thomas Williamson † 1611. Alabaster tablet
with kneeling figures. – Small kneeling figures also in two
fragmentary tablets in the N chapel. – John Walsh † 1797.
Lifesize female figure with an extinguished torch standing by
an urn in front of an obelisk. Unsigned. – Sir John B. Walsh
† 1825. By *Bacon Jun.* and *Samuel Manning*. Large tablet.
Half-naked male figure on a Greek couch with Faith(?)
standing by.

To the SE the VICARAGE, 1862 by *Poulton & Woodman*. Red
brick, gabled and varied.

To the S the PARISH ROOM, C17, timber-framed, and, at r.
angles to it, ST MICHAEL'S COTTAGE, C16 or C17, also
timber-framed.

WARGRAVE

7070

ST MARY. Burnt down in 1914 and rebuilt by *W. Fellowes
Prynne*. What remained of the old building was only the brick
W tower of *c.*1635 etc. Polygonal buttresses and (re-set) Norman
N doorway with one order of colonnettes with zigzag which
look as if they were *ex situ,* and with scalloped capitals
and a hood-mould with shallow lobes. In the fire a former
Norman N arcade was revealed: plain, slightly chamfered piers
and plain arches. – FONT. Octagonal, Perp, with cusped
quatrefoils. – STAINED GLASS. One S window, mildly Expressionist, by *John Hayward*, 1962. – PLATE. Cup and Cover
Paten, probably first half of the C17; Flagon, 1709; Paten
presented in 1763; Paten, 1837. – (In the SE corner of the
churchyard the HANNEN MAUSOLEUM, designed by *Lutyens.*)
In the village timber-framed cottages and Georgian brick houses,
the best of the latter WARGRAVE HOUSE at the corner of High
Street and School Lane and the former VICARAGE in High
Street. More striking the Norman-Shavian contributions,
especially WOODCLYFFE HALL, High Street, with a typical
Shaw oriel under the gable, and the WOODCLYFFE HOSTEL
in Church Street. The former is of 1901–2, the latter of 1905.
Both are by *Cole A. Adams.* Did he also do the LITTLE
HOUSE and the adjoining THAMES COTTAGE, both in the
HIGH STREET ? Also in the High Street, behind the White

Hart, the CONGREGATIONAL CHURCH of 1835, stucco, Gothic, with an embraced W tower. Further N the High Street becomes HURLEY ROAD, and here on the E side CHAPEL HOUSE of c.1800, white, with ogee-headed and quatrefoil windows, and FORD HOUSE, originally a tea-house of an adjoining mansion. Late C18, with a Gothic colonnade or veranda on the E side, returning on the N and S.

⅜ m. NE of the centre of Wargrave, in an elevated position overlooking the river, is WARGRAVE MANOR, early C19, white, with a broad bow in the centre, a long colonnade or veranda, and recessed two-bay wings. From here further NE, at Crazies Hill, CRAZIES, a house incorporating two two-storeyed pedimented porticoes of Tuscan columns, the cupola, and the entrance hall with Tuscan columns from the former Henley Town Hall, built in 1790.

½ m. E, at Holly Cross, FOX STEEP, a house by *Oliver Hill* of c.1923, all waney elm and roofs at odd levels, a Hansel and Gretel fantasy.

From Wargrave to the E, 1½ m. away, HARE HATCH, with the OLD HOUSE, E of the Horse and Groom, red brick, with a pediment to the N, and a little S of it THE HILL with a red three-bay front to which one-bay wings and a canted bay, used on the ground floor as a porch, have been added a little later. Further E, two houses on the N side of the main road. First HARE HATCH HOUSE, five bays, brick, the doorway and middle window in one giant blank arch, and on the side elevation two symmetrical canted bay windows. Then THE GRANGE, handsome, also red brick, of two and a half storeys. These four houses all appear to be late C18.

Yet further E, at KILN GREEN, on the S side of the road, CASTLEMANS, earlier Georgian and rather bleak. Tall, five bays, parapet. Then N of the road, from W to E, ¾ m. away the convent, ½ m. away Bear Place, ¼ m. away Linden Hill. The CONVENT OF THE GOOD SHEPHERD was Endelles Manor or Yieldhall and is by *John Belcher*, 1894, brick and half-timber. Gabled. Nice group of the porch and a brick tower. Very lively to the other side as well, with bay windows of different shapes and in different planes. BEAR PLACE is Georgian, red brick, with two symmetrical bow windows. The MHLG reports the existence of a contract of 1784 to build the house for £843. LINDEN HILL is stuccoed and less regular, but also has a front with two symmetrical bows. The tower is C19.

WASING

9060

ST NICHOLAS. Long nave and lower chancel, the timber bell-turret midway along the nave. These curious features find their explanation in the fact that the medieval church ended where the bell-turret is and the w part is an C18 enlargement. Another is the s transept. The dates of the enlargements are not quite clear. Dates 1761 (w porch), 1826 (w window), and 1839 (s transept) occur, yet these parts all look 1761 with their arched windows. The lancets in the chancel mark that part as C13, the nave windows are Perp. Coved C18 ceiling. But the very pretty plaster treatment round the windows inside seems impossible for the C18. It looks *c*.1875, the date of a restoration. The chancel arch certainly belongs to that time, but is not at all pretty. – PULPIT. Jacobean. – STAINED GLASS. The Moses probably early C19 or perhaps *c*.1835. – Many pieces of brought-in C16–17 glass, including some of 1649. – PLATE. Cup of 1671.

WASING PLACE was burnt out in the Seond World War. It was by *Hobcraft*, of 1770–3. A new house has since been built from the old materials, five bays with a five-bay pediment and a semicircular porch. The STABLES are charming, a symmetrical front with blank pointed arches and battlements.

WATCHFIELD

2090

ST THOMAS. 1858 by *Street*. Steep roof, down low over the narrow N aisle. Steeply gabled bellcote on a mid-buttress: the details late C13. Nothing of interest inside. – PLATE. Cup probably of 1636; Paten inscribed 1711.

WAYLAND HOSPITAL *see* BRADFIELD

WAYLAND'S SMITHY *see* ASHBURY

WELFORD

4070

ST GREGORY. 1852–5 by *T. Talbot Bury*, the round tower and the spire with eight dormers exact replicas of the medieval predecessor, Norman and E.E. Ornate vaulted porch. Elephantine tower arch, uncarved. Recesses in the aisles as if for tombs. Long vaulted chancel of three bays, lancets, wall arcading, black marble shafts. A piquant stone PULPIT comes out of the wall at the corner of N aisle and chancel arch. – FONT. Norman, tub-shaped, with intersecting arches. – PLATE. Set of 1737. – MONUMENTS. Brass to John Westlake, rector, † 1489, 17 in. figure. – Brass to John Younge c.1530, 16 in. figure. Both at the back of the sedilia. – Mrs Anne Parry † 1585. Kneeling figure; alabaster (s aisle w). – Francis Mundy † 1678. Oval, with coarse carving around. – Elizabeth Mundy † 1689. Bust in a round-arched recess, a little like Wilhelm Busch's Widow Bolte. – Thomas Shirley † 1780. Big standing monument without figures. Draped urn on a high base.

WELFORD PARK. The seven-bay w front of three storeys, brick, with giant pilasters stretched to the utmost of their capacity, is an early C18 refacing, or at least partly so; for some of it is brick in Flemish, some in English bond, and round the corner the house continues in English bond and is, with its hipped roof and its extremely curious brick details, something like 1660–70. The windows have raised frames and are vertically connected by a raised vertical band standing on the centre of each lower window. At the back this house has two projecting wings, but a big bow has later been set between them. The staircase with turned balusters, bulbous below.

8060

WELLINGTON COLLEGE

59a Wellington College was founded in 1853 as a national memorial to the Duke, who had died in 1852. It was to be a school for orphans of officers, and all the money was voluntarily subscribed. Fees should range from £10 to £20 per annum. The foundation stone was laid in 1856, the school was opened in 1859. The first headmaster, Edward White Benson, ended as Archbishop of Canterbury. The architect, *John Shaw*, is by and large unknown, though Wellington College alone ought to have secured a lasting reputation for him. He was over fifty when he was recommended for the job by *William Burn*, the architect, and commissioned. Burn knew Shaw's Royal Naval School at Deptford, now Goldsmiths' College, begun in 1843, which is in itself as remarkable a job as Wellington College: an extremely restrained, decidedly Italian design, with a giant middle portal as its only decoration. Commercial buildings by him are fussy and undistinguished. Wellington College is distinguished, it is not at all restrained, and some people may well call it fussy too. However that may be, for the history of Victorian architecture it is highly important; for it is in a style made up of Christopher Wren's Hampton Court and Louis XIII, and that mixture, purged of all fussiness, was going to be re-introduced by Nesfield at Kinmel Park some ten or twelve years later and to start the so-called Queen Anne fashion. Wren, according to *The Builder* (I, 1843, 218), had interested Shaw already in his early days.* It is remarkable that *The Builder* recognized Wren in Shaw; for *The Times* in 1859 called Wellington College 'a handsome edifice in the decorated Italian manner or mixed style'. *The Times* also liked its 'ruddy, cheerful glow'. Cheerful one may well call it, remembering the grim Gothic starkness of contemporary public schools. But the remarkable thing is that Wellington College, in spite of *The Times*, is just not Italianate in the sense of the 1850s nor the purer Cinquecento of Barry in 1850 (Cliveden).

Wellington College is built of red brick and Box stone. The estimates, excluding the chapel, were for sums ranging from £36,000 to £46,000.

In plan Wellington College has something of the axial flourish of Greenwich. For schools such axiality was by no means common, though the Woodard schools, in their unaccommodating Gothic way, also possessed it. But the tradition of the Victorian public school is one of less formal composition, collegiate in the Oxford and Cambridge way. The plan of Wellington College is of two square courtyards, one behind the other, with wings coming out at the N and S angles. The W and E ranges are higher than the N and S ranges and the cross range between the courtyards. In this cross wing is (or was) Large School, in the S range the Dining Hall with richly garlanded dormers and a lantern, in the N range in the middle the main entrance. It has giant columns and a pediment, and above it is a high clock-turret or lantern. The higher W and E wings have mansard roofs and in their middle, i.e. where the cross range meets them, each a high tower. The duality is reminiscent once more of Greenwich. In the upper storeys here are the dormitories. The two courtyards are arcaded.

We must now try to define the motifs which Shaw chose and connect them with the general picture of the style of the college. The mansard roofs of course are French, and the window surrounds on the main floor of the E and W ranges with their busy rhythm of brick trim are Louis XIII too. Also such things as the tower tops may have been intended to suggest France. On the other hand the hipped roofs of the other ranges, the segment-headed windows, the main portal (cf.

* 'The style of Wren of which Shaw has proved himself a master before.'

Trinity Library, Cambridge), and the dormers are William and Mary, and the arches of the cloisters are just Victorian and nothing else.

On the N front bronze STATUES of military heroes by *Theed*. The sculpture of the S front and the cloisters also by *Theed*.* The persons were selected by Prince Albert, who all the way along took a very close interest in the building.

Shaw had intended to have his chapel project from the S range S at the E angle and to match it by the infirmary projecting from the W angle. But this was not done. Whether Benson flinched from Shaw's style for a chapel or whether he flinched from a S orientation, in 1860 he went to *George Gilbert Scott*, a safe man and Gothic, and asked him to design the chapel. Shaw, very handsomely, agreed. Prince Albert, who had first thought of a reduced copy of Eton Chapel and then of a basilica (i.e. probably something Early Christian with round arches, as it was liked in Germany), in the end also agreed. The chapel was built in 1861–3 and faces E. It breaks the grand Baroque axiality of Shaw, and is of red brick, in the Geometrical style, with a main apse, a N chapel apse, and a very slender spire. However, the chapel apse and the aisles were added later, in 1886 and 1899 (by *Arthur Blomfield*). Arcading and rising amphitheatrical seating. Capitals with naturalistic foliage. The chapel is connected by a short Gothic arcaded passage to a big Gothic porch facing S, and this in its turn is connected to the main building by a longer colonnaded passage. – STAINED GLASS. W window by *Lusson*.‡ – In the apse by *Hugh Easton*, 1954, quite unbelievably behind the times, and moreover terribly genteel and thin-blooded. – (WAR MEMORIAL to the First World War. By *Lutyens*.)

The chapel is now part of a later E group of school buildings. N of the E end of the chapel dormitories of 1886 by *Arthur Blomfield*. At r. angles to these, i.e. opposite the N side of the chapel, Dining Hall, Common Room, etc., by *C. J. Blomfield*, 1906–7. Behind the range of 1886 further additions of 1927 and 1940.

WEST CHALLOW

ST LAURENCE. Nave and chancel in one, roofed with stone slates. Genuine early C14 double bellcote. Nice porch with

* Except for Count Alten by *F. W. Engelhard*, 1861.
‡ So Mr Nicholas Taylor tells me.

bargeboards of the C15. Simple N doorway of *c*.1200, with one order of shafts. – FONT. Tub-shaped. The decoration of the rim can hardly be Norman. – PULPIT. With some simple Jacobean panelling. – SCREEN. In good condition; one-light divisions. – STAINED GLASS. Old bits in the E window. – PLATE. Paten of *c*.1500 with the monogram of Christ; Chalice, 1605/6.

MANOR FARM. A dramatic early C18 front. Blue and red brick. Five bays, segment-headed windows. Stone keystones. Parapet. The centre bay is carried up one half-storey higher and crowned by its own parapet.

WEST COURT *see* FINCHAMPSTEAD

WEST HANNEY 4090

ST JAMES. Nave and lower chancel. Sturdy N transeptal tower. In the nave two Norman N windows. Also the Norman eaves line. N doorway Norman too, with various lobed decoration of the arch. Tower, end of the C12, with lancets, a doorway to the W, and, next to it, a lancet cut through a buttress. The arch to the church is triple-chamfered. The responds still have one trumpet-scalloped and one fluted capital. The E window, however, is Dec (reticulated tracery). Fine E.E. chancel arch. Rich stiff-leaf capitals on short shafts supported by heads. In the S transept late C13 windows with pointed-trefoiled heads. The S aisle follows after the S transept. Straight-headed Dec windows. Doorway with Dec moulding on – strangely enough – gablets. Blank-traceried parapet. Five-bay arcade. Square piers with demi-columns. Arches with the unmistakable sunk-quadrant mouldings. – FONT. Norman, tub-shaped, with neat vertical bands of rosettes. – PULPIT. Jacobean in style, but the (separate) back panel dated 1649. – SCREEN. Perp, one-light divisions. – COMMUNION RAIL. C17. – STAINED GLASS. Old bits in the S aisle. – BRASSES to a Priest, 4 ft figure, late C14; to John Cheynie † 1557, still with black-letter inscription; to John Ashcombe † 1592 and two wives, and to other post-Reformation people.

WEST HANNEY HOUSE (Old Rectory). Dated 1727 (MHLG).47b Blue and red brick. Six bays, two storeys, with a raised two-bay centre. The parapet curves up to it, and it has its own parapet. Segment-headed windows with stone keystones. The parapet is panelled. The four-bay side elevation has a raised two-bay centre too. Fine staircase with three turned balusters to the step.

WEST HENDRED

4080

HOLY TRINITY. By the brook, in a dip. Dec w tower, Dec N aisle doorway, Dec chancel with nice, steeply gabled buttresses. The arcades of three bays with octagonal piers and double-chamfered arches also possibly C14, though more probably later. – PULPIT. Jacobean. Spacious and panelled right to the ground, i.e. without foot or stem. – FONT COVER. Dated 1630. – Similar details in the re-used panels of the READER'S DESK and the PANELLING of the E wall. – BENCHES (N aisle). Straight-topped, with tracery. – COMMUNION RAIL. Later C17, with dumb-bell balusters. – TILES. Exceptionally many medieval slip-ware tiles in chancel and nave. – STAINED GLASS. Many small bits. – PLATE. Paten, 1662 or 1664; Flagon, 1674; Cup of C17 shape, 1787.

N of the bridge METHODIST CHAPEL, brick, 1830, with pyramid roof. SE of the bridge brick HOUSE of the early C18 with segment-headed windows still with wooden mullion and transom crosses.

(GINGE MANOR, East Ginge, 1¼ m. S. Partly C17, partly early C18. The S front of the latter date; five bays, doorway with straight hood on carved brackets. Also of that date the staircase with twisted and fluted balusters. MHLG and NBR)

WEST ILSLEY

4080

ALL SAINTS. Nave and chancel pre-Victorian, the chancel apparently C18. Victorian bellcote and N aisle and other alterations. The E window has a date 1878. The Victorian work is late C13 in style. C14 nave roof with tie-beams and collars, also wind-braces. – PULPIT. Jacobean; a fine, quiet piece. – BENCH ENDS. Two poppy-heads.

WEST WOODHAY

3060

ST LAURENCE. 1883 by *Sir Arthur Blomfield*. Nave and chancel in one, SE tower with pyramid roof. Plate tracery on lancets. – SCULPTURE. Three exceedingly pretty Rococo putti of wood. Bought in Scotland. – STAINED GLASS. The chancel windows by *Morris & Co.*, 1883 and 1890. – In the nave S side typical *Powell* glass.

WEST WOODHAY HOUSE. The house is a bit of a mystery.

There are three tablets recording the date 1635, and the stone doorway, now set in a porch, goes well with that date. But the appearance of the house otherwise, especially from a distance, would suggest 1675 rather than 1635. Two somewhat projecting wings recessed centre, hipped roof with dormers, no decoration, except raised brick quoins. The windows are sashed but probably originally had wooden mullion and transom crosses. Also, the brick bond is still English, and the windows have thin raised moulded brick surrounds. Can it after all be 1635 ? It would be yet earlier than the demolished Aldermaston Court (1636), Chevening in Kent (pre-1638), and Inigo Jones's house for Lord Maltravers (1639).* – Good GATES and GATEPIERS with vases.

WHITE WALTHAM ⁸⁰⁷⁰

St Mary. Flint, and dominated by the gross W tower of 1868 with its higher stair-turret turning circular at the top. Yet the building is old. Inside is a re-used unmoulded Norman arch (s of the tower), and the s doorway has two Norman capitals. Fine early C13 chancel with lancets N and S, and in the E wall three widely spaced stepped lancets with a round window in the gable. Inside, the E lancets have continuous rolls, and between them are odd high and very narrow niches also with rolls. The DOUBLE PISCINA has trefoiled arches on a detached column. Late C13 the N aisle W window (a quatrefoil done in plate tracery). Dec s transept s and one E window. The N transept is of 1889. The interior is even more High Victorian than the exterior. – STAINED GLASS. S transept s by *Mayer* of Munich, and so German! Big figures. – PLATE. Paten of 1694; Chalice of 1702; Flagon of 1709. – MONUMENTS. On the chancel floor two brasses to ladies: Margaret Hille † 1465 (14 in.) and Joan Decons † 1506 (18 in.). – In the tower standing monument to Constantine Phipps † 1723, by *W. Palmer*. No effigy, no figures; excellent workmanship. – Sir Benjamin Tebbs † 1796. Woman by an urn in front of an obelisk.

By the church a big aisled BARN. Another BARN with adjoining timber-framed cottages with brick infilling. Also W of the church the STOCKS and WHIPPING POST.

WICK HALL *see* RADLEY

* The whole substantial addition of 1880–1 has been pulled down. (Some original features inside.)

3070   WICKHAM

ST SWITHIN. Projecting Anglo-Saxon SW tower. Flint with
    ample mortar. Long and short quoins. Windows with outer
    splay. Bell-openings twin with mid-wall shafts. Victorian top,
    Victorian nave and chancel, Dec, by *Benjamin Ferrey*, 1845–9.
    Ferrey made the interior very sumptuous, again Dec, especi-
    ally the tower screen with much tracery and the canopies l. and
    r., all a background to his FONT. Also foliage capitals, a Dec
    REREDOS, Norfolk angels supporting the nave roof, and
    elephants (yes) supporting the aisle roof. They are of papier-
    maché and were shown at the Paris Exhibition of 1862.
    – PLATE. Set of 1804.
OLD RECTORY. An older house converted and much enlarged
    by *Ferrey* and provided with a spectacular Gothic bay window.
    The ARCHITECTURAL FRAGMENTS from Welford church
    which adorned the garden have all been destroyed.

        WINDMILL HILL *see* HINTON WALDRIST

9070   WINDSOR

                    WINDSOR CASTLE

                      INTRODUCTION

35a
& b Windsor Castle is the premier castle of England. It is also
England's largest castle. It covers about 13 acres. It has been a
castle since William the Conqueror, but the first stone buildings
were put up by Henry II between 1165 and 1179. Its position is
excellent from the point of view of commanding the Thames
Valley and of defence. The cliff on which the castle stands is
impressively steep to the valley. The climax of the defence
arrangements is the round keep. It stands on an artificial motte or
mound and is accompanied by three baileys, one to the W, a

smaller one in the middle, and the third to the E. The W bailey is called the Lower Ward, the middle one the Middle Ward, the E bailey the Upper Ward. This was no doubt already so at the time of William, and Henry II's walls followed the pattern. Since then the castle has grown steadily with, as a special impetus, the foundation of the Order of the Garter by Edward III in 1348 and with a large rebuilding programme by Charles II. But the architectural climax was the Romantic era from about 1800 to about 1830, and the social climax was, one is tempted to say, the age of Queen Victoria. The early C19 has given us the fairy picture of the castle from a distance, e.g. the M4 motorway. The castle contained a collegiate church with its college, and this college survives and occupies a third of the total area. The separate existence of the college and the castle must always be remembered.

By way of a preliminary exploration the castle ought to be circumambulated. Practically to most users of this book this will not be possible, as part of the circumference is not accessible to the public. What the tour will help to establish as firmly as ought to be done here from the start is that essentially all the features of the walls are C19–Romantic. Once this has been said, it can be pointed out that the three mighty rounded towers towards the town, i.e. Thames Street, and the walling between them are Henry III's, that Henry II's walling is most prominent in the Winchester Tower, NW of the round keep with stone blocks and narrow flint bands, in some walling to its W and its E, and especially the walling of the E side, and that the keep itself is in its lower parts Henry II too. Further towers of Henry III are on the s side, recognizable by their broad, big rounded projection (Henry III's Tower, Edward III's Tower – a perverse name). Charles II's work – he did much more than is preserved, as we shall see – is best visible in the square Victoria Tower at the SE corner and the NW part of the State Apartments, i.e. NE of the Round Tower. That range then recedes and has Henry II walling, but after that projects again and is pure George IV. The finer points of the outer walls cannot here be described.

We enter now by Henry VIII's Gateway, and shall look at the castle from there to the far E range.

HENRY VIII'S GATEWAY has to the outside broad polygonal towers. The archway has a four-centred head and continuous mouldings. Above it is the king's coat of arms and at the top are workable machicolations. The vault is simple: quadripartite with ridge-ribs. To the inside there is a large eight-light window, straight-headed and transomed, the lights still cusped. The turrets here are much thinner.

On leaving the gatehouse one has the first full view of the LOWER WARD, with the chapel facing full on, the one major building of fine buff ashlar limestone, Henry III's walling on the l. except for the tower in the sw corner all hidden by *Salvin's* building of 1862, the Horseshoe Cloister w of the chapel, and the quarters of the Military Knights, or at first the Poor Knights, the *milites pauperi* or *milites veterani*, a part of the Garter foundation. Their quarters continue the line of the gatehouse towards the Round Tower. Their first length is ashlar-faced and is an addition of Queen Mary Tudor to the further (ragstone) range of Edward III. The two ranges were over-restored by *Blore* in 1840–50. In the distance on the r. are the Round Tower and the Upper Ward.

It can be assumed that the chapel will be looked at first.

ST GEORGE'S CHAPEL

5The chapel was built to replace Henry III's chapel further E (on which more later) and its enlargement by Edward III, needed when the Order of the Garter was created in 1348. The new chapel was begun in 1475 and built from E to w. Progress was slow. By 1484 the chancel without its vault and the chancel aisles with their vaults were ready, the transepts and the nave minus the w bay begun. By 1503 the s transept was ready to receive the burial of Sir Reginald Bray. His munificence made it possible to complete the nave.* The w bay and w front were an afterthought, but all seems to have been ready by 1511. The contract for the chancel vault dates from 1506. The spasmodic building activity is due to the political vicissitudes of the decades in question. Eton and King's Chapels were willed and begun by Henry VI in 1449 and 1446, i.e. they were Lancaster jobs. Edward IV started St George's Chapel, and work had indeed all but stopped at Eton and King's about 1461. It was only resumed, *c.*1470 and 1477 respectively, when Edward felt safe and settled enough. In 1475, as we have seen, he started St George's Chapel. Henry VII had little interest in his Yorkist predecessor's initiative and probably changed his mind only

---

* The gradual completion is visible internally, by a change of stone descending from the N transept to floor level, which is reached one bay E of the w front. That the chancel aisles must have been in full operation in the 1480s is evident from the dates of the transfer of the bodies of John Schorne and Henry VI and the date of Edward IV's monument.

when he had decided to adapt the chapel of Henry III and Edward III as his tomb-house. That was in 1494. The master masons were *Henry Janyns*, documented from 1478 to 1484, but perhaps the original designer, and *William Vertue*, documented for the chancel vault. The chapel is 237 ft long as against Eton's *c.*190 and King's *c.*290. There has been so much restoration, chiefly in the last hundred years, that details can only rarely be accepted as the original carvers' work.* St George's Chapel differs from these two and the earliest major royal chapel, that of St Stephen in the palace of Westminster, in that it has a prominent transept. This transept – that is the most striking and a quite unexpected feature – is placed half-way down, not further E, as was the scarcely abandoned custom. The nave has seven bays, the chancel has seven bays. The transept has polygonal ends, which is again unexpected. A tower over the crossing was intended but never built. It would have been oblong, like that of Bath Abbey, begun in 1499. The balance between W and E with the transept in the middle is one of the signs of the impending Renaissance, or rather the readiness of England to receive the Italian Renaissance and its insistence on symmetry. The only feature which detracts from a full appreciation of symmetry is the difference between the polygonal chapels at the W and the E ends. The latter is an actual addition to the seven bays, the former corresponds to the first of the seven bays and caused this bay to be made wider than the others. The result, as we see it today with its three projecting polygonal bays, is curiously similar to Palladian or Baroque compositions. What obscures this prophetic harmony a little is the fact that the W chapel is one-storeyed and has an ogee roof, whereas the E chapel has two upper floors and a flat top.

The details are all very sumptuous, but the basic arrangements are uniform and repetitive. All the aisle windows are of four lights, with two embattled transoms and four-centred heads. All the clerestory windows are of four lights too, but in a two plus two arrangement, and have one embattled transom and

* Mr Maurice Bond, to whom I am extremely grateful for most generously given help, listed the major restorations for me as follows: *post* 1682, *Wren* removing the original King's Beasts and repairing roof and vault; 1782–92 *Emlyn* repairing stonework and adding screen, stalls, and staircase to the Royal Pew; 1841–5 *Blore*, including the reconstruction of the W window; 1863 *Scott* reconstruction of the E end of the chancel; 1866–72 *Scott* new W approach; 1878–86 *Pearson*, including new buttresses, parapets, gargoyles; 1920–30 *Brakspear*, complete restoration, new King's Beasts.

two-centred arches. The buttresses have niches, and there are flying buttresses above. Above the aisle windows is a frieze of beasts and then elaborate openwork battlements. Above the clerestory windows is a frieze as well, and then an openwork parapet. The upper buttresses end in plain pinnacles, or rather shafts, on which stand the royal beasts. The same system applies partially to the W chapel and completely to the transepts. In the re-entrant W angle of the transept is a porch provided in 1926, in the re-entrant E angle Bishop King's Chapel, a curious little excrescence of 1492–6.

The W front is grand enough, but was made yet grander by the wide staircase added in 1866–72. The façade is dominated by its fifteen-light window with four transoms and a four-centred head. The doorway is relatively small. Blank panelling l. and r., and a pretty frieze above. The three STATUES above the window are of *Coade* stone and were placed in 1799. Big angle-turrets with ogee caps. The N side of the chapel is fundamentally the same as the S side, but simpler in many details. The E side cannot be seen, owing to buildings to which we have to turn later. The E window is of fifteen lights too, but quite different in its design. Whereas the W window is even throughout, the E window is divided into four–seven–four with much larger panels and only two transoms plus a third at the level of the springing of the side arches. The chief tracery motif of these side arches incidentally is a square.*

10   The INTERIOR of St George's Chapel is wide rather than high. The effect is due partly to the consistent use of four-centred arches. In the case of the vault this is carried so far as to give the impression of a coved ceiling, flat all along the centre. The other dominant element of the chapel is the insistence on line rather than mass. In detail this ought to be observed. The arcades are high, much and thinly moulded, and, to the nave at least, entirely continuous in their mouldings, i.e. without any capitals. Above these follow blank panelling with pretty heads, a frieze, and then the clerestory windows whose two-centred arches can hardly be noticed, as the vault seems to cut into them. This vault is the marvel of the chapel, a complex design divided clearly into coving and ceiling. The ceiling part is emphasized by two straight longitudinal ribs running parallel to the ridge rib. The area of these three is

---

* Inside, the E window is surrounded by a moulding with angels making music.

arranged as stars with quatrefoiled circles as infillings and many bosses. The coving part has its ribbing of the palm frond, i.e. tierceron, type with liernes only in one small part. There are thirteen such ribs from each springer, three plus three into the penetrations for the clerestory windows, the next to the outer longitudinal ribs, the next the real diagonals establishing a basic normal quadripartite vault, the sixth just up the liernes, the seventh the transverse arch.

The aisles are treated quite differently. Here there are fan-vaults, and fan-vaults, at the time when the chapel was designed, were indeed still very exceptional for major vaults. The aisle walls are panelled and a frieze with battlements runs above them. The panelling is linked to the windows by vertical roll-mouldings, three to each bay, l., centre, and r.

The sw (Beaufort) and nw (Urswick) chapels have vaults starting with six little fans and leading up to a central star – a very handsome variation on the theme of the – it will be remembered: earlier – principal vaults.

The crossing has the one major fan-vault in the chapel. The crossing arches are broad and panelled, as is the inner surround of the w window as well. In the transepts the nave system continues, and it is delightful how the vaulting star fits in with the polygonal ending dictated by the polygonal end-walls of the transepts. The only difference in the elevation is that the E wall has in the inner bay a frieze of angel busts emphasizing the fact that here altars must have stood. In the s transept two niches with canopies of the reredos are indeed still *in situ*.

The chancel system is again the same, except that the aisle fan-vaults have octagonal instead of circular centres and the nave vault has a pendant as the centre of each star. There is only one anomaly in the chancel. The last two N bays are low, because above them the upper chantry of Edward IV was put in which later became the Royal Pew. It is accessible by a small newel staircase in the wall. It has an oriel to the w and a much wider one to the chancel. To the E of this yet another oriel was provided by Henry VIII some time probably in the 1520s. This is of wood, and extremely interesting in that it combines Gothic arches and panelling with Renaissance balusters. The fan-vaults of this low part of the aisle beneath the watching chamber have the central circles like the nave and not the octagons of the chancel, and Mr Harvey wonders whether this whole two-storeyed arrangement might not be an afterthought. The conversion to being the

Royal Pew belongs to George III and was done in 1785 by *Henry Emlyn*, a carpenter attached to Windsor Castle who developed into a gentleman and an architect.

The ambulatory behind the altar is a spot of great piquancy for the architectural historian. Henry III's chapel of *c*.1240 stood E of the present one, as will be seen later. This was its W entrance. The E wall of the ambulatory has three arches unmistakably E.E. The capitals have gone, but the bases and the moulded arches are eloquent enough. And, while this takes us for the first time to the beginnings of the Gothic in the castle, the other details of the ambulatory take us to the end. The cypher of George III will be noticed above the N doorway, and the panelled segmental vault also is his. The doorway leads into the VESTRY, and from here one can reach the STAIRCASE to the Royal Pew, early C19, with a nice cast-iron railing. It leads to a Gothick ante-room and then to the pew itself with the oriel. The niche in the N chancel aisle N wall by the start of the ambulatory is not explained.

In the S chancel aisle the corresponding niche has something to do with the SE chapel, which was originally the chapel of John Schorne, rector of North Marston in Buckinghamshire, who conjured the devil into a boot, died about 1290, and was transferred to St George's Chapel when Bishop Beauchamp of Salisbury became Dean in 1478. In the niche in question is a small squint to the E with a contemporary wooden grille. The chapel has a vault like those of the SW chapels, which were, as we have seen, in fact built later. Above the chapel is a room with a quatrefoil peep-hole down into the S chancel aisle. This is presumably connected with the years of the cult of Henry VI and control over pilgrims.

FURNISHINGS. St George's Chapel is as rich in furnishings as a cathedral, and in such cases the tradition of *The Buildings of England* is to discuss them topographically rather than chronologically or by types of objects. We start from the E end.

CHANCEL. REREDOS. Of alabaster, with carved scenes. 1863 by *John Birnie Philip*. – STAINED GLASS. The E window by *Clayton & Bell*; dull. – The two big CANDLESTICKS in the Italian Renaissance style are copies of two of the four made for Henry VIII and now in St Bavon at Ghent. They are of the 1530s. – MONUMENTS.* The exquisitely fine iron grille be-

---

* The monuments are treated fully and authoritatively in Shelagh M. Bond: *The Monuments of St George's Chapel*, one of the admirable *Historical Monographs relating to St George's Chapel*.

longed to the monument of Edward IV, † 1483, and is by *John Tresilian*. It is all a filigree of tracery. – Opposite, white marble recumbent effigies of Edward VII and Alexandra, 1919 by *Sir Bertram Mackennal*. To the N aisle, against the tomb-chest two small allegorical figures in the Alfred Gilbert tradition.

STALLS. The stalls were provided in 1478–85, the principal 19 carver being one *William Berkeley*. They consist of three tiers, the topmost for the Knights of the Garter and the dean and canons, the middle one for the Military Knights, the minor canons, and the choirmen, the lowest for the choir boys. Behind the top row are high, elaborate canopies with helmets and crests on them. In addition to the rows along the N and S walls, there are four return stalls each side to the W, against the screen. Between them and the N and S stalls is a short piece without seating. The N and S sides originally had twenty-one stalls each, but two each side were added in 1786–90 by *Henry Emlyn*, who made some other minor changes and did a great deal of repairing and extra carving – amazingly skilfully. In front of the stalls are desks, the lowest tier of them being of the C19. The desks are divided into blocks, and each block-end has a poppy-head with a scene to the W and a scene to the E and small figures of prophets. The desk fronts have blank tracery and scenes in tympana and spandrels carved in relief. Moreover, all the stalls have misericords, the elbows of the seats have carving, and an inscription – largely Psalm XX – runs along the front of the upper desks. It is impossible, within the scope of *The Buildings of England*, to list all the sculpture. Fortunately there is Montague R James's guide: *The Woodwork of the Choir*, 2nd ed., 1955. The following is no more than a summary. It is arranged in the order of Montague James's guide. First the link-pieces between return stalls and N and S stalls. They each have three figures and in addition vertical strips with small figures. The large ones are N: St George, St Katherine, the Virgin; S: St John Evangelist, St Edward, St Edmund(?). Of the small figures a number are by *Emlyn*, and it is not always easy to recognize them as such. – Then the other woodwork, N before S. The N return stalls have poppy-heads of the life of Edward III and of St George and the Dragon, all by *Emlyn*, and also demi-figures of Prophets in pulpits, some original, some by *Emlyn*. In the spandrels of the desk fronts are e.g. Doubting Thomas, the Ascension, Pentecost, and (in three scenes) the Last Judgement.

Among the misericords are a gatehouse and a mermaid. –
N stalls from W to E. On the poppy-heads are along the upper
row scenes from Christ's Passion ending with the Crucifixion
and along the lower row the continuation to Emmaus (not all
in the correct chronological order). The small Prophets here
are all by *Emlyn*. Among the scenes on the desk fronts are
many animals and grotesques, e.g. a lizard, two snails, a sala-
mander, and a scene with the fox, a monkey as a doctor, and a
cat and a rabbit pouring something into the fox's mouth, then
(E block) an army camp, a cow and a boar, a cat and a squirrel,
a bull playing a lute, the Fifth Trumpet (from *Revelation*), a
ship, a fox and an ape, St John Baptist and the Lamb etc., and,
at the E end, *Emlyn*'s entertaining George III and Queen
Charlotte at a Thanksgiving in St Paul's on the occasion of the
king's recovery in 1789, first driving to St Paul's in a coach,
then the ceremony inside the cathedral. The misericords of the
N stalls have e.g. Samson and the Lion, an eaglet, griffins, an
Amphisbaena, a dog chasing rabbits, an owl mobbed, and
(lower rank) men in armour, a Wild Man, a friar, an antelope,
an elephant and castle.

Now the S return stalls. On the poppy-heads again Edward
III and St George, all by *Emlyn*, the small Prophets again
largely original (including David and Moses) and a few by
Emlyn. On the desk fronts the Annunciation (Sovereign's
Desk), Visitation, Magi, Circumcision, Crucifixion, Resurrection, Women at the Sepulchre, and Harrowing of Hell. The
misericord of the Sovereign's Desk is iconographically unique:
the Meeting at Picquigny between Edward IV and Louis XI.
Then a gatehouse. The S stalls (W to E) have partly the rarely
told story of St George, partly scenes from the life of the
Virgin and the Last Judgement. They are all original and the
most worthwhile pieces, though the figures are stocky and
the telling is naïve. One thought of contemporary stalls in
Germany such as those at Ulm fixes the level of aesthetic value
at Windsor firmly. Among the prophets here are probably
(upper row) Isaiah and Jeremiah. The desk fronts have e.g. the
Coronation of the Virgin, the Journey to Emmaus, and the
stories in the two side spandrels (these three by *Emlyn*),
the Nativity and the Visitation, then (E block) stories of the
martyrdom of a mother and child (Cyriacus and Julitta?) and
at the E end the Attempt on King George III's Life in 1786
(two tympana and four spandrels). Of the S side misericords
the following may be singled out: a jester with bagpipes, two

dogs, two wyverns, two wrestlers, two lizards, two dragons, four dogs, Wild Man, cockatrice, unicorn, apes and grapes, rose bushes, and (lower row) three monks and a fox, monkeys, 'Who sups with the devil . . . ', three groups from the Dance of Death, the pelican, pedlar and apes, two men gambling and quarrelling, two boys at a game.

THE GARTER STALL PLATES.* The seven hundred plates form a 'heraldic storehouse of the highest artistic excellence', unequalled in Europe, wrote St John Hope. In accordance with a statute of the Order of the Garter the plates have been placed on the backs of the knights' stalls, originally at death, but, from at least 1489 onwards, within a year of installation. They are of copper or brass, with gilded or silvered surfaces on which the arms of the knights have been richly enamelled or painted. The earliest is that of Ralph, Lord Bassett (s side, Stall 13), erected c.1390 in a stall in the original chapel, and transferred with some ninety other plates to the new choir about 1483. The finest plates are probably those dating from the c 15, and, notably, a group of twenty-seven erected c.1421 which are cut out to the shape of the heraldic design; of these, the plates of Hugh Stafford, Lord Bourchier (N 19), Sir Sanchet Dabrichecourt and William Lord Latimer (both s 25) are superb examples. The plates of the first half of the c 17, although large in size and somewhat florid in design, are finely engraved; those of Charles I as Prince of Wales (s 3), Count Palatine of the Rhine (s 5), and King Gustavus Adolphus II of Sweden (s 3) are typical. During the c 17 enamel was replaced by paint, and except to heraldic specialists, the later painted plates are of very much less appeal. A revival of enamelling in 1908 symbolized a return in some degree to earlier standards, as has the occasional use in recent years of the cut-out shape. The plates of Earl Baldwin (s 27) and of Sir Winston Churchill (N 23) are, for instance, a marked improvement on those of such of their predecessors as Benjamin Disraeli, Earl of Beaconsfield (N 25), and the third Marquess of Salisbury (s 18).‡

LECTERN. Early c16; of brass, with two desks. A mighty piece, probably Netherlandish.

* This account was kindly contributed by Mr Maurice Bond, and I am extremely grateful to him for it.

‡ The eighty-seven surviving plates of before 1485 were splendidly reproduced by Hope in his *Stall Plates of the Knights of the Garter* (1901); and a complete list is provided by E. H. Fellowes in *Knights of the Garter* (St George's Chapel Monograph, 1939, with supplement, 1963).

16b   EAST AMBULATORY. DOOR to Henry III's former chapel,
C13, with extremely elegant ironwork, much more spaciously
done than usual. The ironwork is signed: *Gilebertus.* – Stone
SCREEN like that of a chantry chapel to hide the access to a
staircase. Probably by *Brakspear.* – SPIRAL STAIR by *Brakspear*, very successful. – MONUMENTS. Theodore Randue
† 1723. Excellent; of the reredos type; no effigy, no figures,
hardly any ornament. – Col. Brudenell † 1768, pretty tablet. –
Robert C. Parke † 1815. By *Humphrey Hopper.* Small group
of the dying officer, his horse, and a helping soldier.

NORTH CHANCEL AISLE. FONT. Fragment of a Purbeck
marble font of the time of Henry III. It was round and had
heads at the angles. One remains, and some flat stiff-leaf.
– DOOR. With outstanding ironwork, a rose and a square
piece round the keyhole. – STAINED GLASS. By *Willement*;
mostly heraldic. – MONUMENTS. Edward IV. Standing wall-
monument, made in 1789 by *Emlyn.* Gothick, with large brass
lettering. – Earl Harcourt † 1830. White statue by *Sievier*,
1832. Relief scenes l. and r. on the high base. – Chantry Chapel
of Lord Hastings † 1483, the chantry established in 1503.
Stone screen ; inside PAINTINGS of the story of St Stephen;
provincial. On the w and e walls niches with canopies and angel
friezes. Lierne-vault with star shapes. – Sir John Elley † 1839.
Big white block with bust by *R. Trentanova* of Rome, 1815.
– Dean Gerald Wellesley † 1882. By *J. E. Boehm*, 1883–4.
White marble; recumbent effigy.

SOUTH CHANCEL AISLE. LINCOLN CHANTRY. This was
originally Master John Schorne's Chapel (*see* above). The iron
GRILLE is C15 work. – MONUMENTS. Edward Earl of Lincoln
28b   † 1585. Alabaster. High tomb-chest. Two recumbent effigies,
he on a half-rolled-up straw mat. Children kneeling against
the tomb-chest. Also helm and gauntlets of alabaster. Achievement against the w wall.* – King Edward VII *see* Chancel.
– Henry VI. Black slab to commemorate the place where the
king was laid to rest after his coffin had been transferred from
Chertsey Abbey in 1484. His HELMET above. – The HELMET
of Charles Brandon a little further w. – ALMSBOX. Of iron,
with letters H in black letter. H stands no doubt for Henry,
and this remarkable box was in all probability made to receive
offerings at Henry VI's tomb. – OXENBRIDGE CHANTRY.
Canon Oxenbridge died in 1522. The chantry is much like the

* Above this chapel two upper rooms with HEADS and HELMS of some of
the Garter canopies.

earlier Hastings Chantry, and it ought to be noted that there is not a sign of the Italian Renaissance yet, except in the PAINTINGS, dated 1522, which are in the Antwerp style of c.1520. – PAINTINGS. Four large panels of standing Kings. Part of Bishop King's Chantry, c.1495. – MONUMENT to the Duchess of Gloucester, 1859, signed not only by *W. Theed* but also by *Sir G. G. Scott* as designer. Tomb-chest of several marbles, polished, inlaid brass cross. Above four snow-white reliefs in the quatrefoil shapes of Ghiberti's Baptistery doors.

BISHOP KING'S CHAPEL. Bishop King of Bath and Wells, † 1503, was a Canon of Windsor. However, that is not enough of an explanation of why he alone should have been allowed a chapel so visibly sticking out of a perfectly uniform chapel. The King Chapel was built in 1492–6. The tomb is in the open arch between chapel and aisle. Interesting wall decoration of mottos and patterning, very harshly done, without any arch, curve, cusp, or foil. – STAINED GLASS. Heraldic panels; C15. – On the floor three BRASSES. Canopy of William Magge, first warden of the College, 1380. – The other two brasses of the 1630s.

CROSSING. ORGAN GALLERY. A handsome 'veranda-screen'. Designed by *Henry Emlyn* and made of *Coade* stone in 1790–2. Horace Walpole called it 'airy and harmonious'.

NORTH TRANSEPT (Rutland Chapel). Large Perp stone SCREEN. – MONUMENTS. Lord Roos † 1513 and wife. Grand alabaster monument with recumbent effigies, about as good as any made of that material at that time in England. Against the tomb-chest mourning knights one side, mourning ladies the other, and angels holding shields. All in the shallow ogee-headed recesses which are found so frequently in the alabaster monuments of the early C16. – Brass to Canon Honywoode † 1523. A plaque with the kneeling dean presented by St Katherine to the Virgin. – Copper-gilt plaque to the Duchess of Exeter and her husband. He died in 1483, she in 1476. Two kneeling figures and the Trinity over. – Charles Okes † 1860. Tablet with a most remarkably geometricized ship.

SOUTH TRANSEPT (Bray Chapel). Large Perp stone SCREEN. It has the Bray rebus, a hemp-bray, in the frieze. The same in the N transept screen, since, as has been said, Sir Reginald Bray was responsible for more than his chapel. – MONUMENTS. Frame of Robbia coloured fayence. It must date from the early 1520s, but its context is not recorded. The nearest to it are of course *Giovanni da Majano*'s roundels at

Hampton Court, and they date from 1521. Giovanni is indeed the most likely author of this frame. – Sir William Fitzwilliams † 1551. The typical Purbeck marble tomb of the early c16 with pendant (ogee-headed) arches. Ornamented angle colonnettes. A pretty device is the way in which the tomb-chest is detached from the canopy. – Sir Richard Wortley † 1603. Alabaster tablet set in the Robbia frame. – Bishop Giles Tomson † 1612. Also alabaster. Frontal demi-figure with a formidably Assyrian beard. He was indeed 'moribus gravis'. In a shell niche. – Bishop Brideoake † 1678. Semi-reclining effigy, white, between black columns. Large, wide-open segmental pediment. A large vase of curiously organic shape in it. Signed by *William Byrd* of Oxford. – Prince Christian Victor of Schleswig Holstein. By *Emil Fuchs*, 1902. Père Lachaise rather than England. Large, white angel with a sword. – In the centre the Prince Imperial, son of Napoleon III, † 1879. By *Boehm*. Recumbent effigy, white on a white sarcophagus. Long French inscription.

21a & b   NAVE. STAINED GLASS. W window, with sixty-five figures. the majority of them largely original early c16 work, a rare and impressive survival.

NORTH AISLE. FONT. Of wood, mid c17. Foot with four sirens, stem a short column, cover with thin garlands along the edges. A curiously inexpensive, undemonstrative piece for St George's Chapel. One would like to know its story. – MONUMENTS. King Leopold of Belgium. By *Boehm*, 1878. White statue. Lively face. – King George V and Queen Mary. 1937 by *Sir William Reid Dick*. The effigies of marble, very unlively and yet not monumental. The design of the monument by *Lutyens*.

32   NORTH WEST (Urswick) CHAPEL. Iron GRILLE of c.1510–20. – Princess Charlotte † 1817. By *Matthew Cotes Wyatt*. If proof were needed that the Romantic decades could combine the sensational with the chaste – here it is. A snow-white scene acted by life-size figures. Below, the princess dead on a ledge covered entirely by a heavy sheet from under which only the fingers of one hand hang down. To the l. and r. four mourning women, all completely hidden by their mantles. Above, the princess ascending to heaven, one breast bare, and two angels l. and r., one holding the still-born baby, the other crossing his arms. All this takes place in front of a stone tomb, the entrance to which is scarcely visible because of a large white curtain. The monument is perhaps the most complete state-

ment of one ideal of funerary sculpture of the early C19. The effects are very strong, but the whiteness and the emotionless faces that are seen make it safe in the church. The folds also are disturbed only in a few places. – PAINTINGS. Two very good panels of bishops of c.1500. Influenced by Goes? – STAINED GLASS. Behind the monument. Large figures, strong colours; probably early C19.

SOUTH AISLE. FONT. Designed by *J. L. Pearson* and made in 1888.

SOUTH WEST (Beaufort) CHAPEL. Iron GRILLE of c.1510–20. By *Jan van den Einde* of Malines. – SCULPTURE. Small Spanish C13 Virgin. – MONUMENT. Earl of Worcester † 1526. Alabaster. Two recumbent effigies. An angel stands stiffly at their heads. His feet rest against a goat, but about them also two little bedesmen. – STAINED GLASS. Largely by *Willement*, probably c.1845–50.

VESTRY. PAINTING. Large, dramatic Last Supper by *Benjamin West*. – Large numbers of TILES, some possibly of Chertsey, others of Penn make, 1355, from the Aerary.

PLATE.* Secular Dish with rose in the centre, gilt, 1548; pair of Flagons, 1576 and 1583; pair of Chalices and Covers, 1612 and 1616; Chalice, 1612; pair of large Flagons with St George, 1660; three large gilt Basons with Christ blessing a child, Christ washing St Peter's feet, and the Last Supper, all 1661. Also of 1661 two large gilt Patens; another Paten; two Flagons; pair of large Chalices, gilt, 1667; also a pair of Candlesticks of c.1660 and a pair of larger Candlesticks of c.1694 (by *A. Nelme*).

LOWER WARD

HORSESHOE CLOISTER, W of the chapel. It is not a cloister in the usual sense of the word, as it is open towards the chapel. The horseshoe shape is in fact unique. It was built in 1478–81 as houses for the Priest Vicars, who sang the services as predecessors of the present Minor Canons. It is timber-framed with brick-nogging and prominent ogee-shaped diagonal braces. Each vicar had a separate house. There are altogether twenty-one of them. The houses have a newel stair by the entrance and the chimney in the outer back wall. In front of the houses runs the cloister walk. It has depressed-ogee-headed openings. Nearly everything that meets the eye is

* One volume of the *Historical Monographs* already referred to is E. A. Jones: *The Plate of St George's Chapel* (1939).

Scott's of 1871. Behind the Horseshoe Cloister to the NW is Henry III's CURFEW TOWER, finished off by *Salvin* in 1863 in a Carcassonne way. Inside a splendidly strong rib-vault: one quadripartite bay and a six-ribbed apse, as it were, with seven deep pointed-tunnel-vaulted niches in the thick walls. From here a SALLYPORT exit to the town in the thickness of the wall. Many steps; pointed tunnel-vault.

Behind the Horseshoe Cloister to the N the CHAPTER LIBRARY, once the HALL OF THE VICARS, provided in 1415–16, a large room with an open timber roof. The tie-beams are original. The chimneypiece has Denton's rebus, i.e. probably came from Denton's Commons, a range built in 1520 and demolished in 1859.

In the gap between the Horseshoe and the chapel appears MERBECK, as they now call it. It was probably a canon's house, and is like a manor-house. Hall-house type, though of the projecting solar and office wings much is Victorian. Timber-framing and brick-nogging. The hall has a four-light window with transom and uncusped lights and a fine roof with collar-beams, arched braces, and wind-braces. Chimneypiece with a big hood and a curious, rather bleak frieze. The l. extension of the house has a bold overhang.

To the r. of Merbeck an irregular early C18 brick house and then a memorable stone patch with one N window of the Great Hall of the C12, reconstructed by Henry III. Segment-headed arch and stepped inner arch. During the reconstruction of the house behind this wall in 1965, beneath the internal C17 and C18 plaster walls, extensive medieval work was discovered. The house in fact comprises the block of domestic royal chambers, dating from the C12 and C13, which stood between the Great Hall and the castle wall. On the first floor immediately above the cliff is the main chamber, perhaps as reconstructed *c.*1225; stone walls, fireplace, fragmentary wall paintings, including an upper layer of C15 plainsong music. On the second floor, set in a later wall, a tall cylindrical chimney, C12 or early C13, one of very few surviving, with later C13 scissor-beam roof trusses alongside. These discoveries are important in that little survives elsewhere in the castle of pre-Edward III date, and very little in the country at large of the fabric of Henry III's royal lodgings. To the E an interesting canon's house of 1660. Brick with giant pilasters. Even the Ionic capitals are of brick. It is very characteristic of the mid C17. These houses were canons' residences.

Another one, Georgian, stands across facing W. This has a hipped roof and forms the W end of the Canons' Cloister, on which *see* below.

Back to the chapel and looking S the range of the Military Knights already referred to. At its E end is **Henry III's TOWER**, remarkable because its two high upper windows with their round arches and transom-like balustrade represent the one survival of *Hugh May*'s work for Charles II, a compromise externally between classical and medieval. He started work in 1675; for this is the date of the warrant to pull down what was to be replaced.*

The area E of St George's Chapel is particularly interesting. Here once more the epochs mix. There is a Perp doorway immediately E of St George's Chapel, and this ought to be taken. It leads into a passage with a panelled segmental vault. The blank arches in the W wall correspond to the three arches of entry to **HENRY III's CHAPEL** which were noticed in the E ambulatory of St George's Chapel. They probably led into a galilee, and the chapel itself followed E of it. It has in the past been suggested that the wall in question was the actual W wall of the chapel and the wall opposite did not originally exist. This is disproved by the wall **PAINTING** of a head the style of which is clearly Henry III. The quality is outstanding. Further evidence for the chapel itself is the **CLOISTER** to its N, a cloister which is now of the time of Edward III. The chronology must be carefully watched. Of Henry III's time the sumptuous doorway from the cloister to the passage into the galilee just mentioned. Stiff-leaf capitals, richly moulded arch. Also of his time the equally rich blank arcading to the E of this dooway, i.e. along the S wall of the cloister-walk. The cloister arches themselves with rather heavy Perp tracery belong to the work of Edward III in connexion with the Order of the Garter. At the corners piers with canopied niches. Edward III's work started in 1350, but already in 1344 he had erected the mysterious **ROUND TABLE** of wood, 200 ft in diameter. If only we knew where to look for it and what it was like. The mason was William of Ramsey (of the St Paul's chapter house), the carpenter William of Hurley. Altogether Edward III spent on Windsor the fabulous sum of £50,000. Henry III a hundred years before had spent *c.* £15,000.

The most interesting surviving job of Edward III's years is the **PORCH** from the W into the cloister. It is singularly unre- 4b

* *See* also State Apartments, p. 288.

stored and a prime example of the transition from Dec to
Perp. Wall panelling still with ogee-headed and ogee-footed
quatrefoils. Charming outer door-surrounds, blank cusped
and subcusped and again with occasional ogees. Two bays of
ingenious lierne-vaulting with the basic diagonal and ridge-
ribs interrupted by lozenges as if they opened and closed
scissor-wise. This porch has a S doorway which now leads into
the vestry and would originally have led on to the galilee of
Henry III's Chapel. The S side of this doorway, now inside
the vestry, was originally cusped, and the arch has a frieze of
small quatrefoils. The remaining features of Edward III's in
the cloister are doorways with hood-moulds on pretty bracket-
like stops.

In the cloister S walk a wall PAINTING of a royal head. It
must be of c.1270 and is of the very highest quality. – MONU-
MENT. In the cloister W walk Ann Aldworth † 1695. Cartouche with bust at the top and three putto-heads.

Above the W cloister walk is the original LIBRARY, now
divided into the Chapter Room and the Chapter Clerk's
Office. The Office has a C15 ceiling with bosses, the original
Treasury or AERARY (1353–5), the Muniment Room, lying
above Edward III's porch, a typical mid C14 rib-vault with
diagonal and ridge-ribs only and hollow-chamfered ribs.
Plain big bosses – all solid and no frills. – Good medieval
TILES here.

From the N cloister walk a passage leads to the CLOISTER of
1353 with the houses for the canons and the vicars of the
College (see below). It is a long narrow cloister with a timber
arcading towards the centre. The arches have disappeared.
Scott, in crossing the cloister by a middle passage, reconstructed them. The residences along the N side are built against
Henry II's wall and into Henry II's Winchester Tower. From
the terrace here the HUNDRED STEPS lead down into the town
by way of a C19 barbican at bottom level.

The cloister E walk borders on what was Edward III's
GARTER CHAPTER HOUSE of 1350–2. This is now the ground
floor of the DEANERY. Its upper wall, flint and brick, appears
above the cloister. The upper wall dates from the time of
Dean Wren, Sir Christopher's father. One C14 side window is
still in good order. It is Perp, of four lights with one transom
and a quatrefoil frieze at the foot. Between the chapter house
and the Chapel of Henry III is a VESTRY with a tierceron-
star-vault. Walls with blank cusped and subcusped arches.

Henry III's Chapel was replaced by the present ALBERT MEMORIAL CHAPEL. But when was this done ? St John Hope dated it all *temp.* Henry VII, though he had to admit that no records survive. Mr Harvey recently has made out a good case for *temp.* Edward III. His intention was to provide a chapel for his two new foundations of 1348: the college of secular canons, consisting of Dean, 12 Canons, 13 Priest Vicars, 4 Clerks, 6 Choristers, and 26 Poor Knights,* and the Order of the Garter, consisting of the Sovereign and 25 Knights Companion. The remodelling (or rebuilding) of the chapel took place in 1350–4.‡ Another argument in favour of Edward's time is the polygonal apse, which fits the c14 better than the c15 – see e.g. Lichfield or the Greyfriars at New Winchelsea. The four-centred arches of the windows are in contrast to the arches of St George's Chapel, and their tracery is more akin to that of Edward's chapter house than to any of St George's. Henry VII may still have gone over it when he decided to make it a grand chantry chapel for Henry VI following on E of St George's Chapel. It is aisleless and has four-light windows with two transoms, and pretty pierced battlements. The doorway by which we entered this whole area is probably Henry VII. Four centred-arch, thin continuous mouldings. A second doorway leads into the chapel proper. Above the former a transparent repetition of the four-light windows of the chapel with the sky looking through. The chapel has a lierne-vault, with two long, straight ribs, parallel to the ridge-rib, but also simpler than in St George's. The chapel was unfinished when Henry VII died. Cardinal Wolsey, Canon of Windsor, with his knack for doing things grandly and showily, took the chapel over and finished it in 1514. He wanted it for his own monument, which he ordered in the new Renaissance style from *Benedetto da Rovezzano* in 1524 and which is now in the crypt of St Paul's. After his death Henry VIII held on to the chapel, as he held on to Hampton Court, and had the tomb converted for his own use, but he was ultimately buried in St George's Chapel, and so this chapel fell into disuse and decay. The sarcophagus was left lying about, and the candlesticks (*see* above) were sold. Charles II for a time thought of replacing it by a chapel to his

* Actually, however there were never more than three Poor Knights before the mid c16.

‡ The original REREDOS of Nottingham alabaster was so big that eight horses had to pull it.

martyred father, and *Wren* designed a domed rotunda in 1678. In 1810 George III had a vault made beneath it as the tomb house for his family. He intended to make the chapel the Garter Chapter House.

The first look into the chapel is one of amazement. This is not Henry VII, it is a Victorian shrine, and Queen Victoria did indeed convert it into an Albert Memorial. The original impression can no longer be obtained. The room is now dominated by *Gilbert*'s masterpiece, and it is impossible to overlook it. If one succeeds, then it will be seen that the chapel as remodelled in 1863–73 and redecorated by *Baron H. de Trinqueti* of Conflans was restrained as well as rich. Round the walls below the windows runs a band of large stories told in etched marble (i.e. really line drawings like the cartoons for paintings) and separated from one another by white marble reliefs. Below is a dado of coloured marbles. The etched marble executed by *Jules Destréez* is classical in style in a sense which is familiar from mid C19 France and Germany but not England. To the l. and r. of the entrance standing angels; in the tympanum Entombment. The vault is decorated by *Salviati* mosaic. – REREDOS. Marble, with Christ rising, and two angels; good. By *Sir G. G. Scott*; the sculpture by *Trinqueti*. – STAINED GLASS. By *Clayton & Bell*. – MONUMENTS. Duke of Clarence † 1892. By *Alfred Gilbert*. The Duke was the son of the Prince of Wales. Gilbert was summoned to Sandringham and commissioned. The Prince, future Edward VII, apparently approved of this exceedingly daring, radically novel monument. It was all but complete in 1898. Then, however, Gilbert's procrastination got worse, his troubles mounted, he was declared bankrupt in 1901, moved to Bruges, and did not return to London till 1926. It was only after that date that he made the five missing statuettes (St Hubert, St Nicholas, St Catherine of Siena, St Etheldreda, St Catherine of Egypt). The monument has the recumbent bronze effigy on a high marble sarcophagus. A large upright bronze angel holds a crown above the Duke's head. The fabulous thing is the grille around the monument. The ornament as well as the small figures are totally post-period-imitation – the nearest England ever got to Continental Art Nouveau. The iconographical daring is as great as the aesthetic originality. Iconographically a Tree of Jesse is meant. – To the E Cenotaph to Prince Albert. By *Trinqueti*. White recumbent effigy, two angels kneeling by his head. Figures on the tomb-chest as well. They are largish

33

angels at the corners, and allegories of Justice, Truth, Love, and Charity. – To the W Duke of Albany † 1884. Also white, but generally simpler. By *Sir J. E. Boehm.*

Past the apse of the chapel one sees on the l. again the DEANERY, with a courtyard open to the S and having on its W side the C14 chapter house (*see* above) and on the E side work of *c.*1500. The courtyard represents part of the line of the DITCH between Lower Ward and Middle Ward.

MIDDLE WARD

One enters between early C19 ranges and has at once the Round Tower in front.

ROUND TOWER. It stands on an artificial mound and was originally surrounded by its own ditch, of which something remains on the S side. The tower is of the type known as a shell keep, that is a high, circular or nearly circular wall (102 by 95 ft) with only lightly constructed buildings inside. This wall is in its lower parts of the time of Henry II, but the top 33 ft are by *Wyatville,* put on to counteract the effects of the heightening of the S and E ranges of the Upper Ward and of many towers. The main interest of the interior lies in the timber-framed building erected by Edward III in 1354–61 inside the shell. The principal floor has C19 two-light windows with two-centred arches and a transom. There are small straight-headed windows of two lights below, and these look original. To some of the upper windows corresponds the hall inside, with an open timber roof. On the level below are some sturdy timber posts. The staircase with vertically symmetrical dumb-bell type balusters and the details of the ring corridor at the upper landing seem to belong to the remodelling by *Hugh May* for Charles II.

The Round Tower can be reached in two ways. If, on approaching from the Lower Ward, one forks r., one finds oneself in a dramatic *Wyatville* passage between walls and then in front of a *Wyatville* range across from which a closed corridor ascends the mound.

If instead one forks l., one passes the small MAGAZINE TOWER of 1857 and a gateway to the NORTH TERRACE. This, which allows an inspection of the N side of the castle, dates from the 1570s and is one of the few contributions to the castle of Queen Elizabeth I. The Norman Gateway is the entry to the Upper Ward.

The NORMAN GATEWAY is not Norman. It dates from 1359,
except for the l. one of the big round towers, which is by
Wyatville. The centre part is of brown stone and has machicolations. The entry arch has the characteristic sunk-quadrant
mouldings and a groove for the portcullis. Two-bay vault inside with diagonal and ridge-ribs.

On emerging from the gateway, the irregular buildings to
the s finish in the corridor and staircase up the mound to the
Round Tower. Parts of the group are mid C14, one part is late
C15, the rest being Wyatville's.

The range on the N side is more telling. It is the one now
used by the ROYAL LIBRARY. It consists of two parts. The
higher, r. part is the earlier. This dates from 1497. It is of three
widely spaced bays and three storeys. The side bays each have
one oriel window high up. The centre is a much larger oriel
window of complex plan: oblong with canted corners, and in
the middle a further canted projection. This liking for projections of unusual plan is expressed also on the outer side of the
range, where the w end is an oriel of a triangular plan with a
point in the middle and convex lobes l. and r. A fashion for
such oriels ensued and is principally represented by Henry
VII's Chapel in Westminster Abbey. The range w of this is
dated 1583. It is lower, and has to the s three canted oriel
windows, to the N a nearly symmetrical front also with oriels,
the middle one attached to a big square projection.

As one moves on E, one has in front the w end of the N
range of the Upper Ward, the range with the State Apartments.
Turning s, out of the irregular and comparatively small court
in which one has been standing, one reaches the Quadrangle.
This is a very large oblong courtyard, about 375 by 230 ft.
Although the buildings around are of divers dates, the early
C19 has impressed its stamp upon them indelibly. There is
little to distinguish between what *James Wyatt* did for George
III from 1796 and what his nephew *Sir Jeffry Wyatville* did
from 1820 to 1830 for George IV, except that Wyatt used
Portland stone for his windows, Wyatville for all his dressings
a brown stone. Wyatt was made Surveyor General after
Chambers's death in 1796 and finished work at Windsor when
George III moved in in 1804. The king was insane from 1810
to his death in 1820. Wyatville began in 1820. It is said that
Wyatville's work alone cost over one million pounds.

What characterizes all the work of the first third of the C19 is a curious and unmistakable unison of contrived variety with yet maintained uniformity. A lively skyline of battlements and towers, an interruption every so often of the walls by entrance features of several shapes and – especially on the E front – by bay windows and oriel windows is not enough. The long straight walls towards the quadrangle between the various features remain, and their even fenestration provides an un-medieval, really Georgian, rhythm, as does the stone walling, made to appear more even than it is.

In detail the ranges round the quadrangle consist of the following. The NORTH RANGE is much wider than the other two. It had ever since Henry II represented the principal living quarters of the castle. The width allowed for inner courts, of which one is now filled in by *Salvin*'s Grand Stair-case, a second and larger one by the Waterloo Chamber. A third still exists S of the Kitchen. The walls of the Waterloo Chamber, the walling S of it towards the quadrangle, and much walling N of it is in fact still Norman, but there are no features left to show it. The medieval Great Hall was along the S front of this range.

The SW part of the N range, looking S, W of the Porte Cochère, and looking W is of the time of Edward IV, even if the windows are *Wyatt*'s. The NW range of rooms facing the North Terrace, and there four storeys high, is what remains of Charles II's remodelling of 1678 etc. Evidence of these latter dates will be found inside. The Porte Cochère is of course *Wyatville*'s (date 1827), as are the Visitors' (or Equerries') Entrance in the NE corner and the Sovereign's Entrance in the SE corner. Wyatville also added, for convenience's sake, the long corridor along the inner sides of the E and S ranges. He heightened these two ranges to provide more acceptable servants' quarters, but kept the heightening recessed behind the line of the corridors so as to preserve the dominance of the N range. Most of the main windows of the N range are of a standard two-light type, but above the Porte Cochère are four-light windows to S, W, and E, and towards the N terrace, above the entrance into the range, is a large five-light window. On this side the polygonal Brunswick Tower at the NE corner is entirely *Wyatville*'s. It is connected with the bay with the five-light window by another corridor of Wyatville's. The SE corner tower, called Queen's Tower, is a *Hugh May* addition or alteration, as a string course shows. In front of the whole E front is the SUNK GARDEN, made by *Wyatville*, with along its

N side the former ORANGERY, also *Wyatville*'s, and remorselessly Perp in its glazed openings. In the sunk garden a splendid stone VASE with the Judgement of Paris by *E. Pearce*, c.1680–90. The principal accent of the S front of the S range is George IV's Gateway (foundation stone 1824), a state exit towards the Long Walk, which looks of spectacular length from here. The gateway is *Wyatville*'s, though its E tower is in fact of Edward III's time. The W end of the range, a strong round tower, called Edward III's Tower, however, is entirely C13 work. Broadly speaking, what the S and E ranges represent is Norman outer walls against which originally there were no buildings or wooden buildings and then a thin range of building of the time of Edward III. It is in front of this that Wyatville made his additions.*

The quadrangle is permanently surveyed by the equestrian MONUMENT of Charles II at its W end. This is of 1679, bronze, and stands on a high stone base. On the base reliefs by *Grinling Gibbons*, garlands, coats of arms, etc. The statue was carved in wood by a German and then cast by *Josias Ibach*, also a German. In the inscription he adds to his name 'Stada Bramensis 1679 FVDIT'. This probably means Stade, not too far away from Bremen.‡

THE STATE APARTMENTS

The State Apartments are entered from the North Terrace by a *Wyatville* doorway leading to a long Wyatville cross-VESTIBULE, divided by slim imitation Perp piers into a nave and aisles, and vaulted. The vestibule ends to the S in the grand porte cochère. Turning E from here (not open to the public) one is in a long two-naved C14 undercroft with octagonal piers and single-chamfered ribs. The continuation of this is a room with single-chamfered wall shafts and single-chamfered ribs, also probably C14. To its N is a vaulted corridor with hollow-chamfered ribs. A little way to the N of this is the monumental KITCHEN, dated 1828 and about 70 by 30 ft in size. Its walls are *temp.* Charles II and it runs through two storeys. The open timber roof and lantern lighting of course are *Wyatville*'s. The

---

* Are the two tall windows in the Clarence Tower facing W two more surviving of *May*'s work? Their proportions are like those in Henry III's Tower in the Lower Ward (*see* p. 281).

‡ At Stade, as the Municipal Archivist, Dr Wirtgen, kindly informs me, there was indeed an organ maker Nicolaus Ibecchius of Marburg, *floruit* c.1640–50.

public turns W from the S end of the vestibule, along another two-naved C14 undercroft, identical with the former, and then N into *Salvin*'s GRAND STAIRCASE, made in 1866. It fills the former open Brick Court and is in the Early Dec style, has a large lantern, and is somewhat arid. The vault of the GRAND VESTIBULE adjoining it to the E on the upper floor is by *Wyatt* and much more lively. Fans and a lantern. This was the staircase hall before Salvin's. Against its N wall under a wooden canopy is a seated figure of Queen Victoria by *Boehm*; 1871. The walls of the room are actually C14 work, i.e. Edward III had at least three if not four ranges round Brick Court.

It is advisable to turn from the staircase first N; for here is the first of the three surviving rooms of the rebuilding in 1677–8 by Charles II. It is the KINGS' DINING ROOM (former State Ante-Room). The ceiling is by *Verrio* and represents a Banquet of the Gods. Like all Verrio's work it lacks sparkle, let alone brio. The wood-carving is by *Gibbons* and *Henry Phillips* and, needless to say, done superbly. Phillips since 1661 had been the King's Master Carver in wood, whereas Gibbons became Master Sculptor to the King in 1684. The room is square with a W and an E alcove. These have skylights, probably of Salvin's time; for before he built the staircase, there was of course enough light from Brick Court. The room has a later C18 chimneypiece of white marble with coupled Tuscan columns.

To the E and facing N follows the KING'S DRAWING ROOM (former Rubens Room). Here and in the following rooms all that remains of Charles II's time is the top cornice. The ceiling is *Wyatville*'s. Now W, along the N side. One more room here has a later C18 chimneypiece. The *Wyatville* ceilings are very instructively post-Georgian, even if some are of George IV's reign (as George IV's Brighton Pavilion is post-Georgian). But those of the King's Dressing Room, the King's Closet, and the Queen's Drawing Room (former Picture Gallery) are in fact William IV's, with dates 1833 and 1834. The ceilings are still in geometrical panels on the Georgian system, but garlands tend to be thicker and looser, branches lusher, leaves more naturalistic.

In an irregularly octagonal CABINET, E of the Queen's Drawing Room and joining it to the King's Dining Room, are *Gibbons* coats of arms and oval panels with heads in relief. They are re-set. From the Queen's Drawing Room W one could enter the ROYAL LIBRARY (not open to the public). The

first and largest room has the date 1834 in the plasterwork. w
of this is QUEEN ELIZABETH'S GALLERY of 1583 with a rich
broad banded plaster ceiling, said to be a copy of the original
one. If that is so, it would be a very early case of broad bands
instead of thin ribs. Original, however, the splendid chimneypiece of stone, wth tapering pillars with strapwork l. and r. of
the opening and columns, pilasters, and niches in the overmantel.

The QUEEN'S BALLROOM (former Van Dyck Room) is s of
the Queen's Drawing Room and faces w. Though the room
was remodelled by *Wyatt*, the ceiling is of the *Wyatville*
period. The chandeliers are English and were ordered in 1804.
Back now to the s side to see the other surviving rooms of the
Charles II period: the QUEEN'S AUDIENCE CHAMBER and
the QUEEN'S PRESENCE CHAMBER. The ceiling by *Verrio* of
the first represents Queen Catherine of Braganza in a chariot
drawn by swans to the Temple of Virtue, that of the second,
much darker one, represents the queen under a canopy spread
by Time and surrounded by Virtues. The carvings are again
by *Gibbons* and *Phillips*. Both rooms have good late C18
chimneypieces. That in the Presence Chamber was brought
from Buckingham Palace by William IV and is by *Bacon*,
dated 1789. It has extremely elegant long corbels l. and r. of
the opening, and on the mantelshelf a clock with two semi-
reclining figures.

E of the Presence Chamber and s of the Grand Vestibule is
the GUARD ROOM, including the deep square projection above
the porte cochère, and E of the Guard Room ST GEORGE'S
HALL. The s wall of this – minus of course the features and
especially the windows – is *temp.* Edward III, the N wall
partly that and partly Norman. The Norman part was outer
wall towards the courtyard, where now the Waterloo Chamber
is. St George's Hall is 185 ft long. Before Wyatville it was two
rooms. The w half was *Hugh May*'s glorious CHAPEL of
1684–6, the most Baroque interior of England, it has been
said. It was swept away by Wyatville in 1829. The low-
pitched timber roof is in fact of plaster. At the E end is a
canopy for the throne, a gallery, and wood panelling. No-one
would call it very festive. One realizes this particularly force-
fully as one proceeds into the GRAND RECEPTION ROOM, N
of St George's Hall; for here *Wyatville* for once went Rococo,
and though the detailing is all somewhat riotous, the effect is
certainly gay. w of this room is the GARTER THRONE ROOM,

facing N and with Norman N and S walls. The details, and particularly the ceiling, are Wyatville's, but the plentiful carved panels and foliage hangings are *Gibbons*'s and come from Hugh May's chapel. W of the Throne Room and past the Ante-Throne Room one would again be in the King's Drawing Room.

Finally, between the Throne Room and St George's Hall, lit only from above, as it was built by *Wyatville* in the place of an open court, the WATERLOO CHAMBER. Its date is 1830, but it was re-decorated by *Blore* in 1861. It was built to hang *Sir Thomas Lawrence*'s portraits of some of those who helped to defeat Napoleon. The room is vast, but it tends to be gloomy and would be more so if it were not for the splendid chandeliers. The lantern lighting is interesting, with its curiously nautical raking profile. Again *Gibbons* panels and foliage hangings are re-used.

THE EAST AND SOUTH RANGES

These are not open to the public.

In the E range the most interesting room is the DOMESTIC CHAPEL, E of St George's Hall and N of the Visitors' (or Equerries') Entrance. It is by *Blore* and was made in 1842. The sanctuary was enlarged and the octagonal lantern made in 1852. The result is a curious indeterminate shape, with the sanctuary to the N. Gothic wood panelling. – SCULPTURE. A very fine terracotta group of the 1870s by *Dalou*: an angel and children, the latter being Queen Victoria's grand-children. – Along the E front of the E range runs a number of State Rooms, the most impressive being the GREEN DRAWING ROOM (carpet by *Grüner*) and the CRIMSON DRAWING ROOM with its excellently crisp decoration, especially of the doors, which came from the Regent's Carlton House. Both 55 these drawing rooms are *Wyatville*'s. The Gothic furniture in the STATE DINING ROOM may be part of that designed by *Pugin* in 1827 for *Morel* the decorators, when Pugin was only fifteen years old. Other furniture in this series of rooms was also originally at Carlton House. W of the rooms runs Wyatville's corridor, to end at the SE corner of the quadrangle by the SOVEREIGN'S ENTRANCE and the odd-shaped staircase behind it. This leads to the most private flat of the royal family, which is in the SE corner of the castle. Some rooms here and in the adjoining guest suites and guest rooms of the S range on to Edward III's Tower have been refurnished very recently by *Sir Hugh Casson*. Also in the s range is the QUEEN'S AUDIENCE CHAMBER. This dates from 1860–1.*

THE MEWS

The Royal Mews or stables are visually part of the town rather than the castle. They extend along and E of St Alban's Street and were built in a gothicizing but on the whole sensibly utilitarian way by *Blore* in 1839–42. The RIDING SCHOOL has two-light windows with Y-tracery. The largest entrance is by a gateway at the s end opposite the post office. To the same group belongs BURFORD HOUSE, originally built by the Duke of St Albans for Nell Gwynn, but so thoroughly blored that not a single feature of the house as illustrated by Kip can be recognized.

THE PARK

Windsor Forest in the Middle Ages was a vast expanse of woods and heath extending from Reading to Chertsey and from Guildford into Buckinghamshire. Such wood and heath land could be called a park; for a park in the Middle Ages was simply enclosed or reserved hunting country. Park became what we mean by it only in the course of the C17 and even more the C18. At Windsor the distinction of the park into Home Park and Great Park is an arbitrary one. The difference is really only that the Home Park is closed to the public,‡ whereas large parts of the Great Park are accessible, even if few of the buildings.

Home Park

From the castle the predominant feature is, and even more was before the tree disaster, the LONG WALK. This is three miles long and was made in 1685 and planted with elm trees. Unfortunately they had to be felled in 1945. The trees now are planes and chestnuts, and a final decision on what thinning out will be best is to be made later. Its *point-de-vue* is the equestrian statue of George III which belongs to Great Park.

In the Home Park the buildings are as follows.

* The PLATE of Windsor Castle – as against St George's Chapel – cannot here even be summarized. Readers must be referred to E. Alfred Jones: *The Gold and Silver of Windsor Castle*, 1911, a sumptuous folio with 103 plates and a complete, amply annotated list.

‡ Except for the meadows N of the Datchet road.

FROGMORE HOUSE. Out of an early C18 house which had seven bays and two or already two and a half storeys *Wyatt* in 1792 made the present house for Queen Charlotte. The lower wings are also initially Wyatt's, and so is the veranda or arcade towards the garden. This has seven bays, now glazed, and Tuscan columns. The wings were enlarged early in the C19 by big bow-fronted pavilions and the porte cochère on the entrance side, of two pairs of columns, was possibly also made then. Inside, there is a handsome staircase starting in one arm and returning in two. It has a wrought-iron balustrade. Also there is a pretty room decorated by *Mary Moser* with flower 53 garlands on walls and ceiling. On the first floor a gallery runs from front to back. This is decorated in a rather crude Pompeian manner, perhaps by *Princess Elizabeth*, one of George III's daughters. Close to the house are the STABLES, with two towers with cupolas, framing the archway.

The beautiful grounds of Frogmore House were probably devised by *Sir Uvedale Price*, the great amateur–expert of the Picturesque. His father was Vice Chamberlain to the Queen. There is a lake, and there is a GOTHIC TEMPLE by *Wyatt*, really a small pavilion with attachments designed in a ruinous state. The windows are Perp. The interior is Early Victorian, with niches and a panelled ceiling. Also in the grounds the TEA HOUSE, High Victorian probably, two cottages set at r. angles with central Tudor brick chimneys and surrounded by wooden verandas.

NW of Frogmore House is FROGMORE COTTAGE, plain, two-storeyed, early C19, and behind this an INDIAN KIOSK taken by Earl Canning in 1858 from the Kaiserbajh at Lucknow.

W of Frogmore House are the two mausolea which have changed the character of that part of the park so decisively.

MAUSOLEUM OF THE DUCHESS OF KENT. 1861 by *A. Jenkins Humbert*, the architect of Sandringham. Begun during the lifetime of the Duchess. Domed rotunda with rusticated substructure and above detached columns of pink granite with bronze bases and capitals. Copper-covered dome. The detail is French rather than English. The interior is by *Grüner* (see below). Walls with heraldic painting on scarlet ground and blue glass above with stars. The STATUE of the Duchess is by the younger *William Theed*.

ROYAL MAUSOLEUM, i.e. mausoleum of Prince Albert and Queen Victoria. 1862–71 by *A. J. Humbert* and Professor *Grüner* of Dresden, Prince Albert's favourite specialist in

decoration. Grüner also did the initial sketch for the whole
building. The building cost £200,000. It is externally in the
Romanesque style, i.e. with *Rundbogen*, and in plan a Greek
cross with low convex ambulatories in the re-entrant angles,
which results inside in an octagon with four arms.* The whole
is crowned by a dome. The centrality is mitigated by an E
portico of three arches. In front of this two life-size bronze
STATUES of Angels, one with a sword, the other with a
trumpet. They are by *Georg Howaldt* of Brunswick. The outer
GATES and the inner DOOR, the former bronze, the latter brass,
were designed by *Grüner* and are of outstanding workmanship
(*Potter & Sons*).

The style of the interior is a rich Italian High Renaissance,
deliberately Raphaelesque, and for this style, less at home in
England than in Germany, the mausoleum is a key monument.
In Germany the style was handled most skilfully by
Semper in Dresden, and the interior of the mausoleum was
indeed designed by *Grüner*, who lived in Dresden, had
published a book on Italian fresco decoration in 1844,
and had started a Raphael corpus with Prince Albert in 1853.‡
Tunnel-vaulted arms, giant pilasters for the main piers, niches
with large statues between them, painted Evangelists in the
spandrels above. The STATUES are by *Heinrich Bäumer*
(David), *Hermann Hultzsch* (Isaiah), *Gustav Kuntz* (Daniel),
Friedrich Rentsch (Solomon), all of Dresden. Rentsch's is the
most classical. The others turned out more Baroque. The
Evangelists were painted by *Nicola Consoni*. In the dome below
the tripartite windows oval medallions painted by *Pfänder*
from Consoni's designs. The gilded ribs rest on papier-maché
angels by *Hultzsch*. The STAINED GLASS in the mausoleum is
by *Ion Pace*, and a replacement of *c.*1909. The large PAINT-
INGS in the four chapels or cross arms are again by *Consoni*,
after Raphael compositions. On the vaults of the chapels more
painting: by *Julius Frank* and *Pfänder*, again Raphaelesque.
The pretty relief medallions in the spandrels of the arches are
the work of *Pietro Galli*, who also did the excellent RELIEF of
the Deposition on the altar frontal. In the centre is the
MONUMENT to the Queen and the Prince Consort, 1864–8,
two white marble effigies by *Baron Marochetti*, high up on a

* Mr Winslow Ames tells me of the Coburg Mausoleum at Coburg, an
octagon with wings built in 1846 and seen by Queen Victoria in 1860.

‡ Passavanti's *Raphael* had come out in 1839, confirming and spreading
the cult of Raphael in Germany.

big tomb-chest, with four large kneeling bronze angels at the corners of the tomb-chest. In the l. and r. transepts MONUMENTS to Princess Alice Grand Duchess of Hesse and her child by *Boehm*, 1878–9, and to the Duke of Kent, Queen Victoria's father, also by *Boehm*, 1874. White marble effigies. The group of Princess Alice and the child, both asleep, is on the pattern of Chantrey's popular Sleeping Children. – Also a white STATUE of the Emperor Frederick III † 1888, by *Boehm*, and a white group of Victoria and Albert in Anglo-Saxon costume by the younger *Theed*, 1867. She looks admiringly up to him.

CROSS to Lady Augusta Stanley † 1876 of blue granite in the style of the Anglian crosses. The cross is directly in front of the Duchess of Kent's mausoleum.

To the SSW of Frogmore House is SHAW FARM, Italianate in the Osborne way and utilitarian. The two LODGES S of it are by *Wyatville*. Of much greater interest and appeal is Prince Albert's DAIRY of 1858. Nobody will be enthusiastic about its exterior, but the colourful fayence (*Minton's*) interior has so much charm, with its panels of putti and its medallions of children of the royal couple. The interior design and probably some of the execution is by *John Thomas*, Albert's favourite sculptor. By him personally very probably the fountains with herons carrying a shell on which is a human figure carrying a smaller shell. The dairy belongs to Prince Albert's HOME FARM, which has an eminently typical but unattractive tower. The buildings, according to the *Ill. L. News*, were designed by *Mr G. A. Dean*, 'the well known agricultural architect and land agent'. Opposite the Home Farm is the AVIARY, with bargeboarded gables.

ADELAIDE LODGE, ⅓ m. NE, is the only surviving part of the original ROYAL LODGE, built for the Regent by *Nash*. It is picturesquely bargeboarded and was re-erected here in 1831. For Royal Lodge otherwise, *see* below.

PARK STREET GATES and other HOME PARK LODGES. Tudor, by *Wyatville*, yellow brick and stone.

Great Park

Windsor Great Park is still 4,800 acres in size, as against Richmond Park, the largest London Park, which has only just over 2,000. Hyde Park even at the time of Henry VIII had less than 700.

The Long Walk ends at the EQUESTRIAN STATUE of George III

known as the Copper Horse. This is by *Westmacott*. The statue was made in 1824–30 and with its granite base stands over 25 ft high. Westmacott received £18,712 for the statue. The figure in studied disarray. An equally straight walk, nearly as long and, to the N, with a steady view of the Round Tower, leads from QUEEN ANNE'S GATE (the lodge is of stone and has bargeboards)* at the S end of King's Road to Ascot. This is called QUEEN ANNE'S RIDE and goes through between THE VILLAGE and Prince Albert's WORK-SHOPS. The workshops are sound utilitarian brick structures, by *Teulon*, 1858–61. The village is by *S. Tatchell*, of the 1930s, in the garden-suburb style. From here the public road, the King's Road, can be reached in three ways, two ending in LODGES which were built in 1952 and 1960 (*R. Tatchell*). By the Ranger's Gate is RANGER'S LODGE, a simple white Regency house. The third way out is further S, by SANDPIT GATE, Gothic, stuccoed, embattled, with a turret, and all rather square, and then past FOREST LODGE, a larger Georgian brick house of nine bays, the side thirds two-storeyed, the centre a half-storey higher. On the ground floor in the centre and the centres of the wings Venetian windows. The higher middle part of the house has giant pilasters. FOREST GATE is the place where the public road is finally reached. This is of the same type as Sandpit Gate. Beyond the public road to the NW two more buildings belonging to the Great Park, the FLEMISH FARM, an insignificant building of Prince Albert's years, and CRANBOURNE TOWER, all that is left of Charles II's Cranbourne Lodge, a high, polygonal Late Georgian brick tower with a yet higher stair-turret and pointed windows. On the ground floor a handsome room with a polygonal lierne-vault of plaster and the date 1808.

But the centre of Great Park is the other side of the Copper Horse, not W, like Queen Anne's Ride, but E. It is here that the precinct of ROYAL LODGE lies. This is entered by two neo-Georgian LODGES by *Tatchell*, grand and chaste. They form a group with three cottages each side of the entrance. The Royal Lodge itself is a large, pink-washed, rather institutional build-ing with a three-storeyed centre and two-storeyed wings and some minimum Early-Victorian-looking Tudor detail trying

* N of the gate, i.e. strictly outside the park, are Estate COTTAGES of 1853, red and blue brick with gables, and most probably by *Teulon* (*see* in the text a little further on). Yet further N a group of between-the-wars COTTAGES, nicely composed, with a squat tower.

to be in harmony with the one surviving feature of the 1820s, *Wyatville*'s Dining Room (now drawing room), originally added to Nash's cottage orné (*see* above: Adelaide Lodge). This has five windows with ogee tops and Perp tracery. The garden was remodelled by *G. A. Jellicoe* in 1932-5. In the garden a COTTAGE, about half real size, built and furnished entirely for Queen Elizabeth II as a child. Door, one little bay l., one r., thatched roof.

Also in the gounds of Royal Lodge the CHAPEL by *Teulon*, 1863-6. It has a nave and a chancel, a lower S transept, and a S aisle whose windows have odd cross-gables. High open kingpost roof inside, round piers with typically High Victorian leaf capitals, complicated timbering of the aisle roof. – STAINED GLASS. In the E window 1863. – W and one N window by *Kempe*, 1902 and 1905. – EMBROIDERY. Florentine Frontal assigned to the C15. Presented by Queen Mary, George V's queen.

S of Royal Lodge is CUMBERLAND LODGE (University of London), built at the time of Charles II and inhabited in the mid C18 by the Duke of Cumberland of Culloden fame and Ranger of Windsor Park. Of the original building very little, if anything, remains. The house was damaged by fire in 1811, restored by *Wyatville*, much enlarged in 1870 by *Salvin*, and again remodelled in the C20. On the far side are Gothick details. Long STABLES with cupola. In axis with the turreted Gothick side of the house, some ¾ m. away, is the OBELISK commemorating Culloden. Close to this axis, a little off to the E, ALMSHOUSES of *c.*1950.

A little W of Cumberland Lodge the ROYAL SCHOOL, a one-storeyed village school, symmetrical, of brick, with pretty, fancy glazing bars. It was established in 1845.

Further away, S of Cumberland Lodge and rather pathetically on its own, the stiff EQUESTRIAN STATUE of Prince Albert, given by the women of England. It is by *Boehm*, 1887-90.

This leaves two important parts of Great Park which lie by the A30 and S of it: Virginia Water and Fort Belvedere.*

VIRGINIA WATER is a large, eminently picturesque, many-fingered lake made for the Duke of Cumberland about 1750 and enlarged later in the C18. It is about 120 acres in size. It was planned by *Thomas Sandby*, who also arranged for the CASCADE close to the Wheatsheaf Hotel. A little further W are

---

* They are actually in Surrey.

52b the RUINS, i.e. columns from Lepcis Magna presented to the
Prince Regent in 1816, intended for the portico of the British
Museum, but finally re-erected at Virginia Water in 1826. The
red brick bridge of the Ascot road cuts most unhappily through
the remains. The pine trees on the other hand do them good.

Near the NE tip of Virginia Water a TOTEM POLE from
British Columbia was re-erected in 1958 to mark the centenary
of that province. It is 100 ft high.

FORT BELVEDERE started life as a triangular tower called Shrub
Hill Tower some time before 1757. The angles had polygonal
turrets. It was built for the Duke of Cumberland. The architect was *Isaac Ware*. The triangular shape which was later
imitated by other such towers was chosen here, it is said, to
give views of Windsor Castle, St Paul's, and the Hogsback,
which at that time was still the s boundary of Windsor Park.
In 1827–9 *Wyatville* extended this tower into a castellated,
picturesquely irregular residence. The prominent main tower
is a heightening of Wyatville's too. In the two original turrets
which are not taken up by the staircase are still plaster ceilings
of *c.*1750. The hexagonal centre room has recently received a
new domed ceiling.

(CLOCK CASE, E of the road to Egham. A square tower of brick
on an eminence. It is said to have been built by the Duke of
Cumberland for an observatory, and there is a letter of 1812 of
which Mr R. Mackworth Young kindly sent me a copy, stating
that it is part 'of the Old Gate Way of Whitehall which stood
at the entrance of the narrow part of Parliament Street', i.e. the
King Street Gate, *temp.* Henry VIII.)

THE TOWN

CHURCHES

ST JOHN BAPTIST, High Street. 1820–2 by *Charles Hollis*, under
the supervision of *Wyatville*. The chancel was rebuilt and enlarged by a polygonal apse in 1869–73 in the Dec style by
Teulon. The church is of brown stone and in its proportions
and details typical of 1820. W tower with oversized pinnacles.
Two vestibules l. and r., as if aisles were embracing the
tower. They are straight-topped and embattled. Windows of
many shapes and types, rather arbitrary, even if one forgets
those altered by Teulon. The interior has preserved its three
galleries and its slender iron piers. Iron also the roof, with its
traceried spandrels. – CHANCEL DECORATION. *Salviati*

mosaic. – SCREEN. High wooden screen, designed by *Sir Arthur Blomfield*, 1898. – RAILINGS to the s chapel. By *Grinling Gibbons* himself, made for the chapel at Windsor Castle. Balusters and three openwork panels. Two of them have pelicans, the third foliage. The balusters are vertically symmetrical and have leaves round the bulbs. They probably were part of the communion rail. Gibbons was paid for work in the King's Chapel in 1680–2. – PAINTING. Last Supper by *Francis de Cleyn*, a German from the Baltic who came to England in 1623 and died in 1658 (w gallery). – STAINED GLASS. Early C20. No artists seem to be recorded. – PLATE. Silver-gilt Chalice, 1573; Chalice, 1629; two silver-gilt Flagons, 1635; silver-gilt Paten, 1637; silver-gilt Almsdish, 1732; two Chalices, 1777. – MONUMENTS. Edward Jobson † 1605. Small tablet with kneeling figures (s aisle). – Richard Braham † 1618. By *Edward Marshall*. Angels and allegorical figures in the Mannerist style (N vestibule). – Rebecca Southcot † 1642. Demi-figure, not quite frontal, in a scrolly surround (N vestibule). – Mrs Nazareth Pagett † 1666. By *Marshall*. Black columns, black inscription. At the top two busts, at the foot engraved skull with wings (main vestibule). – Hartgill Baron † 1673. Garlands of books l. and r. 'Predella' with a heart and two owls. He was secretary to Prince Rupert. – John Hounslef † 1722. Coarse cartouche still in the C17 tradition (N vestibule). – Dr Hale † 1728. Reredos tablet. No figures (s vestibule). – Sir Thomas Reeve † 1735. By *Peter Scheemakers*. Standing monument. Two busts before an obelisk. Two putti l. and r. (N vestibule). – Topham Foot † 1712. Reredos and a weak bust. By *P. Scheemakers*, i.e. between *c*.1730 and *c*.1780. – Thomas Scourfield † 1765. With a totally asymmetrical Rococo cartouche at the foot (w wall). – Elizabeth Grope. By *T. Sharp*, 1832. Mourning woman over a sarcophagus (s aisle).

ST AGNES, Spital, Winkfield Road. 1874. Brick, lancets, a curious plan, with a short nave and a prominent s transept with E aisle. – FONT. Norman, drum-shaped. Intersecting arches and stylized long leaves hanging down under them.

ALL SAINTS, Dedworth Road, *see* Dedworth, p. 126.

ALL SAINTS, Frances Road. 1862–4 by *Sir Arthur Blomfield*, and a typically early work of his: inspired by Butterfield but just that much smoother. Red brick and blue-brick bands. No tower. Pointed-trefoiled lancets and plate tracery. Big plate-tracery w window. Big Geometrical E window. Spacious interior without tension. Round piers with fancy shaft-rings. Red, yellow, and blue brick walls. Large clerestory.

ST ANDREW, Barry Avenue, the parish church of Clewer. The village, as described on p. 304, has been nearly submerged by Windsor, but the church and the graveyard have preserved their village character. Flint, with a very short w tower with shingled broach spire. The ground floor has Norman windows, and inside there is indeed prominent Norman work: the arch from the s aisle E, unmoulded, and perhaps the original chancel arch and the s arcade of round piers with square abaci and flat leaf capitals including waterleaf. That dates this work. The tower arch has similar capitals, but the pointed arch may not be in its original state. The N arcade is by *Woodyer* (*see* p. 305); 1858. Most of the exterior is also his, though the church is in fact medieval almost entirely. – FONT. Norman, tub-shaped. Arches with elementary leaves in the spandrels. Flat zigzag frieze at the top. – REREDOS. Sculpture of Christ in Majesty and Saints. Designed also by *Woodyer*. – Tall wooden SCREEN. Victorian. – BENCH ENDS. Two with poppy-heads, very bare (nave W). – STAINED GLASS. By *Kempe*, s aisle, 1902. – PLATE. Silver-gilt Flagon, 1626. – MONUMENTS. In the churchyard Quarter-Master Edward Adams, 1819. With a military still life, including an evidently live horse. – Earl Harcourt † 1830. By *Sievier*. Excellent Grecian tablet. Snakes l. and r. The foliage elements are just getting richer and more florid. – Canon T. T. Carter † 1901. Miniature bronze relief with recumbent effigy and the piers of the canopy quite detached in front of it. By *W. Bainbridge Reynolds*.

ST EDWARD (R.C.), Alma Road. 1867–8 by *C. A. Buckler*. The estimate was for £4,000 (GS). Of ragstone. Large, but without a tower. Late Geometrical tracery. High clerestoried interior.

ST STEPHEN, Vansittart Road. 1874 by *Woodyer*. Very plain. Yellow brick, no tower. Low aisle windows. They and the clerestory windows have the motif of detached shafts or piers inside in front of the windows. – REREDOS. Large and impressive, with Christ upright below a crocketed gable and between coupled shafts with rings.

HOLY TRINITY. 1842–4 by *Blore*. In the middle of a square, in the isolation the C19 liked. A big, clumsy yellow-brick job. W tower with spire, embraced. Wide interior with galleries set between the quatrefoil arcade piers. They carry four-centred arches. Small clerestory. Transepts.

CONGREGATIONAL CHURCH, William Street. 1832 by *Jesse Hollis* (BC). A fine, proud chapel, still undisturbed classical. Yellow brick, three bays with a three-bay pediment. Tuscan porch. Arched upper windows.

BAPTIST CHAPEL, Victoria Street. 1839. Equally proud and equally classical, but quite different. Stuccoed. Giant Ionic pilasters, tall arched windows, frieze with symmetrical palm fronds. Pediment.

PUBLIC BUILDINGS

TOWN HALL (or Guildhall), High Street. Designed *c.*1687 by *Sir Thomas Fitch.* The execution after his death in 1689 supervised by *Wren.* Completed in 1690. Cost £2,000. Brick and stone dressings. Three by six bays. The ground floor open as usual. Tuscan columns carrying a straight entablature on the long W side, semi-elliptical arches on the N and S show sides. On these sides the upper floor has pilasters, four of them, but the angle ones not at the angles, where quoins seem to have arrived first. Wren would not have done that. In the centre of the N side in a niche Queen Anne and the date 1707, in the centre of the S side Prince George of Denmark and the date 1713. This statue was given by Christopher, Sir Christopher's son. Inside the open ground floor also Tuscan columns. They don't touch the ceiling, an anomaly explained by legend as the sign of Wren's secret insistence on knowing more about the security of structure than the council who insisted on the columns. The upper floor all altered.* The E part of the town hall was added *c.*1830 on the site of the Shambles.

GENERAL POST OFFICE, see p. 303.

EAST BERKSHIRE COLLEGE OF FURTHER EDUCATION, Claremont Road. By *Bridgwater, Shepheard & Epstein,* 1954–*c.*66. A satisfactory design, modern, and placed well in its surroundings.

ST GEORGE'S SCHOOL, Datchet Road. 1803.‡ Yellow brick, long front, with two three-bay pedimented pavilions and an eleven-bay centre with a colonnade and a top lantern. The angle pavilions have arched windows set in blank arches.

EDWARD VII HOSPITAL, St Leonard's Road. 1909 by *A. W. West.* Two-storeyed centre with a mansard-tile roof. Three-bay pediment and cupola. The curious arched window above the pediment is a sign-manual of the Edwardian decade.

* REGALIA. Small Cup, 1627; silver-gilt Mace and Cup, 1660; Mayor's Chain and Badge given in 1820 and enlarged in 1830.

‡ This is the choir school of St George's Chapel.

COMBERMERE BARRACKS. The Guard Room, Museum, H Q Offices, Naafi Shop, and Junior Ranks and Sergeants' Messes are by the War Office Architects' Department (*Sir Donald Gibson*, architect in charge *D. Wager*), 1960–4.

SOUTHERN REGION STATION. By *Sir William Tite*, 1850. Red brick, Tudor, with blue brick diapers and patterns, including 1851, V R, P A. At the far end of the platform access to the Royal Waiting Room, a bijou of a few rooms with a turret and spirelet. Windows Tudor with arched lights. The main room has a bay window, canted and ending in a point, i.e. imitated from Henry VII's Chapel at Westminster Abbey, and inside a ribbed ceiling with a pendant.

PERAMBULATION

The town of Windsor certainly started and grew on the doorstep of the castle. The area of town hall and parish church is minute, about a quarter of the area of the castle. As one leaves Henry VIII's Gateway one is in CASTLE HILL. The big Georgian stone house opposite with the later Gothic porch is no preparation for that small area, nor is the Early Victorian shop of Nos 10–11. But then CHURCH STREET and Market Street branch off it, and they give the true picture of size and scale. In Church Street a delightful mixture of things, ending in the Early Victorian front of the SHIP HOTEL across, in Church Lane. Nos 4, 5, 6 are late C17. No. 6 has a square timber-framed bay resting on big carved brackets. No. 7 is timber-framed. The house at the corner of CHURCH LANE has a roughcast early C18 front and round the corner a timber overhang. This has one thin buttress-shaft with bracket, a sign of pre-Renaissance origin. Opposite the MASONIC HALL, formerly Free School, built in 1725–6. It is of brick, in the Late-Wren–Hawksmoor style, see especially the short side elevation to St Alban's Street. There is here a pediment right across and above it two chimneys connected by an arch. To Church Lane the house has seven bays and segment-headed windows. Doorway with pediment on brackets and narrow arched windows l. and r. Above an arched window instead of the doorway and niches instead of the windows. At the corner of Church Lane and Market Street the former GUILDHALL OF HOLY TRINITY, built in 1518, and now the THREE TUNS.

From Church Lane to the town hall and past it to the N. Next to it huddles a tiny one-bay house, datable apparently to *c.*1718.

Now down to the river by THAMES STREET. The walk starts with the WHITE HART HOTEL of 1890, lifted straight out of Kensington.* Four storeys and an angle turret. Then some early c18 houses, especially Nos 18–20, made inconspicuous by their shop-front. By the bend on the castle side Messrs COURAGE'S offices, yellow brick, seven bays, two and a half storeys, three-bay pediment, doorway with Tuscan columns and pediment, all reasonable and serviceable. To its r. the MONUMENT to Prince Christian Victor of Schleswig-Holstein † 1900. Standing bronze figure by *W. Goscombe John*, 1903, in an aedicule. Lower down on the same side, at the corner of Datchet Road, the MONUMENT to George V, 'first sovereign of the House of Windsor', low, broad, restrained, and a little too demonstratively monumental. Centre the crown on a blocky base. L. and r. wide, shallow basins. 1936 by *Lutyens*.

Opposite the SOUTH WESTERN HOTEL, c17, with three gables and an oversailing upper floor. Finally, shortly before the bridge, on the other side, the OLD HOUSE HOTEL, late c17, recessed, with two differing wings. The centre is of seven bays and only one and a half storeys, with a pedimented three-bay projection and a pedimented porch on Tuscan columns. *Wren* is supposed to have lived here (when ?).

Back to the town hall and now in the opposite direction along the HIGH STREET. Again the occasional Early Georgian brick house, then the CASTLE HOTEL with a handsome early c19 cast-iron blacony. No. 13 is curious, with the large upper studio-like windows and the cast-iron balconies of about 1840. Then a very fine late c18 front with four stucco reliefs of putti representing the four seasons. No. 4 again has good early c19 railings. Opposite a bigger and prouder Victorian group: the WESTMINSTER BANK, of stone, Latish Classical, by *Cronk Blomfield*, 1910, then a house of 1886 in the Kensington Queen Anne, and the gabled Tudor POST OFFICE of 1885–7 (by the *Office of Works*).

The continuation of High Street is PARK STREET, a very complete Georgian street, thanks partly to Georgian imitation. But Nos 12–16 deserve notice, three-storeyed, stuccoed, with angle pavilions with giant attached columns and centre with arched windows and a continuation to the r. in a rounded corner to Sheet Street. Also noteworthy Nos 23–24, late c18, opposite, with a pair of doorways with alternatingly blocked

* The architect apparently was *R. Robson* (*Builder*, 23 November 1889). I owe this information to Mr Spain.

pilasters, arched windows on the top floor, and a parapet. The best group, especially in terms of doorways, is right at the end on the r.

SHEET STREET is dominantly Victorian and culminates in the ROYAL ALBERT INSTITUTE, 1879–81 by *Bacon & Ingress Bell*. Tudor Gothic; red brick and stone. In VICTORIA STREET, round the corner just a little: THE LIMES, three-bay stucco with giant Ionic angle pilasters, early C19, the WINDSOR ALMSHOUSES of 1862, yellow and red brick, Gothic, with steep gables and dormers, and No. 67, High Victorian Gothic but dated 1888. Victoria Street continues w as Clarence Road, from which branches CLARENCE CRESCENT, a neat piece of planned development by *William Bedborough*, c.1845. Two-storeyed houses with angle pilasters, elegant iron balconettes, and pillared porches, a large communal garden across the road completing the layout.

After this detour we must return once more into Sheet Street, where HADLEIGH HOUSE now re-establishes the Georgian lead. The house lies back from the street. It belongs to the later C18 and has five bays and two and a half storeys, a doorway with Adamish Ionic columns and a pediment, and good wrought-iron garden gates. Opposite the WINDSOR MOTOR COMPANY, good and recent (by *Challen & Floyd*), timber and glass. Again opposite, a yellow-brick Early Victorian terrace, called YORK PLACE (Nos 51 etc),* and so into KINGS ROAD, where more such terraces. Nos 39–63 are called BRUNSWICK TERRACE and so must be earlier, c.1795–1800.‡ Also they are red brick exposed. Three storeys and basement. First-floor verandas. Nice houses opposite too; white: especially the ROYAL ADELAIDE HOTEL, fag-end of classical, with tripartite windows bending round corners. ADELAIDE TERRACE, dated 1831,§ is stuccoed, eighteen bays long, with a four-bay pediment on two plus two pilasters, quite an acceptable compromise. Yet further out EDINBURGH GARDENS, new housing by *Edward Whiteley*, and QUEEN'S TERRACE, fiercely Jacobean, red and blue brick and shaped gables. By *Teulon*, exhibited at the Royal Academy in 1849.

That leaves only one outer stretch – in what used to be the village of Clewer. From St Andrew, the Clewer parish church,

---

* The Rev. Basil Clarke has found out that this is by *Robert Tebbott*, who died in 1850.

‡ George III married Caroline of Brunswick in 1795.

§ Adelaide had become queen in 1830.

s there is first at the N end the OLD MILL HOUSE in Mill Lane. Red brick, Late Georgian, the windows in giant blank arches. Then, amid the recent crop of suburban houses, type 1930s and type 1950s, THE LIMES, timber-framed, with a brick front of six bays but the timbering with brick infilling visible towards the church. After that the YOUTH HOSTEL, 1707, four bays, brick, with a very good wrought-iron garden gate.

Further s, in HATCH LANE, to conclude with, the HOUSE OF MERCY, by *Woodyer*.* Begun by him in 1853 and continued to his death. He never charged a fee. The material, needless to say, is brick, the style that joyless Gothic which for schools, hospitals, and convents was almost a matter of course. The original chapel of 1857 is small and has as its only enrichment an E window with Geometrical tracery. The present chapel dates from 1881 and is astonishingly grand and lavish. Nave and aisles of five bays with very high round piers. Ornate chancel with apse. Lively and original patterning of red and black brick and stone in the chancel. The high vault looks proud but is of canvas. – High SCREEN. – Large carved stone REREDOS and REREDOS of the s aisle. – STAINED GLASS by *Hardman*. – MONUMENTS to the foundress Harriet Monsell † 1883, a large brass on the chancel floor, and to Canon T. T. Carter, rector of Clewer and the first warden, † 1901, a recumbent alabaster effigy under a canopy. Designed by *Bodley*. Canon Carter's brick house opposite, like a very large rectory, is to be demolished. – An extension by *Woodyer*, built in 1873, runs N from the NE angle of the original quadrangle, an extension of 1874, also by *Woodyer*, continues the original street front to the s. Large extensions of 1926 by *Cecil Hare* lie s and SE of the latter.

WINKFIELD

9070

ST MARY. An interesting and confusing church. The brick sw tower is of 1629. The windows also all of brick. Their motifs are worth remembering (cf. Ruscombe). This tower was built inside a church of c.1300 of which a few windows survive. The walls of the church are of a dark brown conglomerate, except that the brickwork of the tower extends a little further N along the W wall. Whatever happened inside these conglomerate walls is obliterated by the fact that about 1592 the area was divided in two by a row of octagonal wooden columns

* Now called Convent of St John Baptist.

carrying longitudinal arched braces instead of arches. Whether the c14 church had already been two-naved cannot be said. The twin arrangement did not interest nor worry *G. E. Street* when in 1858 he rebuilt the chancel so that it looks tripartite into the bipartite nave. The lavish chancel decoration is by *Woodyer*. The TILES and Botticelli quotations are signed E. I. and dated 1890.* – FONT. Octagonal, richly carved, and entirely High Victorian. It is by *Bentley* and dates from 1863. – PULPIT. Handsome and simple; given in 1707. – High Victorian iron SCREEN with high candlesticks. – STAINED GLASS. In the s chapel s by *Kempe*, 1883. – s chapel E, the foiled window by *Moberley* (*Powell's*), 1860. – MONUMENTS. Thomas Montague † 1630. Brass plate, showing him three-quarter figure distributing alms (by the pulpit). – Many tablets, e.g. Thomas Wise, master mason to King Charles the Second, † 1685. – An entertaining comparison is Sir Thomas Theophilus Metcalfe † 1822 and Lord Metcalfe † 1846, the first Gothic, the second Grecian, but both by *Bedford*.

At WINKFIELD STREET, ½ m. NW, two good houses. NEWINGTON HOUSE is late c18, three-bay front, widely spaced, parapet with two urns. Four oval paterae between ground floor and first floor. A little further NE KNIGHT'S HALL, timber-framed with brick infilling, with original c16 (or c15 ?) timber roof.

About 1¼ m. E of these WINKFIELD PLACE, facing Windsor Forest. Five bays, two and a half storeys, porch with pediment on Tuscan columns.

1 m. NW from here, i.e. about 1½ m. N of the church, NEW LODGE by *Talbot Bury*, 1858 (BC). Symmetrical Gothic façade with three gables but with an asymmetrically placed enormous tower. Gothic interior features.

1¾ m. NW of the church CRUCHFIELD HOUSE, c18, with an early Victorian classical façade of seven bays and three storeys. The first-floor windows all with pediments. Rusticated angle pilasters.

Then s of the church first ASCOT PLACE, 1 m. SE. For this *see* Ascot, p. 70. At the sw corner of the estate KEEPER'S COTTAGE, timber-framed with brick infilling; c15.

WINNERSH *see* SINDLESHAM

---

* The Rev. Basil Clarke tells me that the tiles were designed by *Woodyer* and painted by *Mrs Daubeny*, wife of the Vicar.

WINTERBOURNE   *4070*

ST JAMES. Tower of blue and red brick, dated 1759. Plain arched openings. Battlements. The N chapel is C18 too. It was built in 1712. The chancel now looks all the work of a Mr *Hudson*, who restored it in 1895. The rest of the church is by *Hugall*, 1854, but a few old parts were re-used: notably a lancet window in the chancel S wall and the chancel E window, which is early C14 (cusped intersecting tracery but with ogee-headed lights).

WINTERBOURNE HOUSE. Later Georgian, of red brick. Recessed centre with a porch of two pairs of Tuscan columns. The projecting wings carry pediments. Behind, some older timber-framing.

BUSSOCK WOOD (now Phillip's Hill House), 1¼ m. ENE. By *Mervyn Macartney*, 1907. Red brick, William and Mary style, large.

HOP CASTLE, 1¼ m. NNW. A Georgian hunting lodge, and the most delectable of follies. Built of rough, whole flints with plenty of bones. The centre of the house is an octagon. This is covered by a roof of ogee outline. To its l. and r. lower wings with urns at the corners. In them are just two small rooms. Behind the octagon the entrance hall. Its walls and those of the staircase into the basement are covered with pebbles and shells – grotto-fashion. The octagon has small niches in its sides.

WOKEFIELD PARK *see* STRATFIELD MORTIMER

WOKINGHAM   *8060*

ALL SAINTS. A Victorian church externally, if it were not for the fact that the W tower and the clerestory are of dark brown conglomerate. But all the details are of *Woodyer*'s restoration of 1864–6. Even a Norman S doorway is provided, it is said, on the strength of a few surviving stones. But inside the arcades of five bays are medieval. The pier bases are Norman, the round piers themselves may be C13 in their lower parts, but they were lengthened when the clerestory was built. Their present details of capitals and moulded arches point to *c*.1400. – FONT. Octagonal, Perp, the underside of the bowl with intertwined tree branches. – STAINED GLASS. E window by *Hardman*. – PLATE. Set of 1729. – MONUMENTS. Elizabethan brass plate with kneeling couple in an architectural surround with a guilloche frieze in the pediment. – Edward Colton † 1682. By *Woodruff*. Two black columns, open scrolly pediment, no figures. – Humphrey Cantrel. Late C17. With pretty putto heads and putti.

ST PAUL, Reading Road. 1862–4 by *Woodyer*, a prosperous High Victorian, 'West-end' church. The building was given by John Walter of Bear Wood. Rock-faced stone. NE porch steeple with spire, bristling with pinnacles on the buttresses. The tracery of the tower is C13 plate tracery. The rest is a free, not very attractive Dec. The aisles were added in 1874. The arcades have quatrefoil piers with thin shafts in the diagonals and naturalistic leaf capitals, fern, geranium, etc. The clerestory has an original arrangement of rere-arches on detached shafts. In the chancel N is different from S. On the S side e.g. a very odd, very low clerestory. – FONT. A very original piece, eight-lobed, and with a decoration of freely growing water-lilies with intricately intertwined stalks. It is one of the not so infrequent cases of the High Victorian anticipating the Art Nouveau. – STAINED GLASS. Mostly by *Hardman*.

ST SEBASTIAN, *see* Heathland.

TOWN HALL. Gothic, by *Poulton & Woodman*, 1860. Red brick with blue brick and stone dressings. Flèche. The front to the N is fairly consistent, with its row of gables. The E side is irregular. To the S, i.e. the Market Place, a curious composition of a single-storey semicircle flanked by two windowless blocks.

PERAMBULATION. The town hall is roughly triangular, as it stands on an island in the MARKET PLACE which is also roughly triangular. No houses of great interest, the best on the E side Nos 21 and its neighbour, the former red, of five bays, with a pretty doorway with set-in Doric columns, the latter white with tripartite windows. S of these, in DENMARK STREET, on the same side, just one timber-framed house with oversailing upper floors, oriels, and gables; C17 probably. To the N, i.e. the church, one can go by two streets, PEACH STREET, with one group of C17 cottages with overhangs, or ROSE STREET, which is more rewarding. It is long and fairly wide and starts with a high C18 brick house of three bays facing up northward and ending with a white one of three bays facing downward. In between only minor things, but one group of timber-framed C16 and C17 cottages ought to be preserved. The whole area is decaying and will evidently be redeveloped. At the N end Rose Street narrows, and the approach to the church is visually very successful. At the very end on the W side a corner house, timber-framed, with the timbers visible to Wiltshire Road, tile-hung to Rose Street.

The best houses are W of the Market Place in Broad Street and Shute End. BROAD STREET is as wide as a market place. On the N side the YOUTH EMPLOYMENT OFFICE, red brick, Late Georgian, with five bays plus two projecting ones. On the S side BARCLAYS BANK, the most ambitious house of Wokingham, late C18. Five bays plus low one-bay wings. The centre bay has the doorway with Tuscan columns, a lunette window above, and a top pediment. Again on the N side OXFORD HOUSE, early C18, four bays, with a good shell-hood, and COLBOURN HOUSE, five bays, Later Georgian. At the corner of RECTORY ROAD the POLICE STATION with its Tudor details and the characteristic and quite original tower. Strongly battered buttresses, Baroque doorcase, spire with concave outline. It is of 1904, by *Joseph Morris*, County Surveyor from 1872 to 1905, and very similar to the police station of Maidenhead. The end of Broad Street is TUDOR HOUSE, C16, pretty and much restored. Timber-framed. Two symmetrical gables. On along SHUTE END. The N side is called THE TERRACE, because it lies higher up than the S side. The bank of grass is visually very effective. The bigger houses, however, are on the S side. No. 6 and No. 8 are two good pieces, 6 lower, with panelled parapet, 8 of three storeys with a doorway with pediment on pilasters. Of the several nice Georgian houses on the terrace side Nos 29–31 deserves a mention. It is a pair, with the two doors under one segmental arch.

Much ought to be picked up at Wokingham outside the area of the old centre. Going in a circle clockwise from N to N the start is ASHRIDGE FARM, ⅝ m. N of the church. Gabled, C17, timber-framed. Fine central chimney of four stacks with star-shaped tops.

In BRACKNELL ROAD, i.e. E of the centre, ST CRISPIN'S SCHOOL, the first built by the Ministry of Education's own team of researchers into rational school building (*David Medd, Mary Crowley*) under the direction of *S. A. W. Johnson Marshall*. The school was built in 1950–3. The work was inspired by that of the Hertfordshire Architect's Department. The school is of light steel construction, the components to modular sizes. A free group rising from one to four storeys. In the four-storey block are class rooms above the entrance hall and library. To the r. the dining hall, and then in the higher cross-wings gym and hall. To the l. a looser grouping of low crafts-rooms and labs. By the side of the main entrance PAINTINGS by *Fred Millett* on the composition slabs, including a modular girl.

At HOLME GREEN, 1½ m. SE, LOCK'S HOUSE, Early Georgian, of five bays, blue headers and red dressings, segment-headed windows, hipped roof with pedimented dormers, doorway with pediment on fluted Doric pilasters, and HOLME GRANGE, an extremely good design of *Norman Shaw*'s of 1883. It is of the Home Counties brick-and-tile-hanging type, but the picture of the entrance front with its gables and dormers of different sizes and directions and the off-centre porch must be seen to be appreciated. To the garden the centre is a big chimney-breast, and this is followed by a transomed bay window set at a corner so that the narrow side is parallel with the chimney.

1 m. SSW is the LUCAS HOSPITAL, the best building of Wokingham without any doubt. It was built in 1665 and is
44 very progressive for that date. Brick. Long front with two projecting wings. Two storeys, the windows wood-mullioned. In the centre a steep three-bay pediment with a coat of arms in a cartouche and cornucopias. Small cupola. The wings end with large arched windows. The r. one contains the chapel, the l. the hall. In the CHAPEL wooden chancel arch of reredos type with a large open segmental pediment. – COMMUNION RAIL. Of dumb-bell type. – STAINED GLASS. In the E window grand coat of arms, yellow, white, some blue.

63 W of the Hospital LUCKLEY, by *Sir Ernest Newton*, 1907. Inspired by the Elizabethan E-type of façade, but in the long, low, stretched-out façade, the proportion of bare wall to window, the porch with its segmental hood on Ionic columns, and the circular window to its r. entirely free, and unmistakably early C20.

In MOLLY MILLARS LANE, ¾ m. SW, new factories, the best A. JOHNSON & CO. by *Yorke, Rosenberg & Mardall*, a fine, clean Miesian job. Steel frame and blue brick without windows for the production area, steel frame and white brick, stretchers only, for the office area. The fenestration here is arbitrary, a compliment to 1960 *v.* the Mies tradition. Good also the inquiry pavilion at the entrance to REDYNE LTD, by *J. G. Fryman*. Circular core with four arms coming out diagonally. The rest is a glass box, set under it.

⅞ m. W the HOSPITAL, the former WORKHOUSE, built in 1850, red brick, minimum Tudor.

MILL CLOSE, Emmbrook. Flats of three storeys in rows. 1960 etc. by *G. V. Hives & Sons*.

GLEBELANDS, in Glebelands Road, off Rectory Road (*see* Police, above), is, like Luckley, by *Sir Ernest Newton*. It is of 1897, also Tudor, also E-shaped, but only just on its way out from historicism, e.g. by the simplified door-hood. The centre towards the garden is a typically Newtonian polygonal bay window with a chequer pattern.

The TITHE BARN HOTEL of 1904, near by, is a telling contrast: the conventional *v.* the unusual and progressive affluent house of the turn of the century. Half-timbered.

WOODLANDS ST MARY 3070

ST MARY. 1851 by *T. Talbot Bury*, with SW turret carrying a spire.

INHOLMES, ⅞ m. S. 1905–7 by *Leonard Stokes*. Sizeable, and in a correct neo-Georgian.

ROOKS NEST, ¾ m. NW. Early C17. E-shaped façade. Flint, but the central porch of brick. Round to the r. big brick chimney. The details all over-restored.

WOODLEY AND SANDFORD 7070

ST JOHN EVANGELIST. 1873 by *Woodyer*. Flint; E.E. With new Reading housing everywhere around. Nave, chancel, and N aisle. S porch in the westernmost bay of the nave with a towering two-tier bellcote turned S. This is the one remarkable feature outside. The remarkable feature inside is the tall, tripartite, somewhat bleak stone SCREEN.

CONGREGATIONAL CHURCH, ½ m. S. Minute, Gothic, with low spire; stuccoed. 1834.

SCHOOL, Howth Drive. By *R. Sheppard, Robson & Partners*. A good, clear design.

SANDFORD MILL, 1½ m. ESE. A very pretty group of white weatherboarded mill and separate miller's house in the trees.

GEORGE INN, by the Loddon Bridge, on the Reading–Wokingham road. Handsome, three-bay, Late Georgian brick house with tripartite windows.

WOOLHAMPTON 5060

ST PETER. 1861 by *John Johnson*. Bellcote with spire on a flint stump. E.E. details, very gross inside, especially the chancel and the two-bay arcade to the low transepts. Fancy timber porch. – FONT. Evidently part of the rebuilding. – STAINED GLASS. W window by *Willement*, 1861. – PLATE. Set of 1813.

RECTORY, ¼ m. NW. Tower-like Early Georgian house of three bays, basement, principal floor, half-storey, three-bay pediment, attic, and hipped roof. Blue brick with red dressings. The blue brick all headers.

The present village is not by the church but along the Bath road. On the S side a nice mixture of houses, including a timber-framed one with overhang and a five-bay Georgian one. Also a Gothic DRINKING FOUNTAIN of 1897.

Up the hill to the church past KENNET ORLEIGH on the E, THE COURT on the W, both by *Mervyn Macartney* c.1910–15, the former symmetrical neo-Tudor with touches of the neo-William-and-Mary, the latter neo-William-and-Mary. Then WOOLHAMPTON HOUSE. (The S wing mid Georgian, the W part older, with a Georgian front and a later top storey, to the E Georgian and Victorian. In 1848 *Vulliamy* worked at Woolhampton House.)

DOUAI ABBEY. English Benedictines went to Paris after the Suppression and moved on to Douai after the French Revolution. From here they went back to England in 1903 and took over the Catholic Diocesan College founded in 1838. The CHAPEL of that school still exists. It dates from 1848 and is by *G. J. Wigley*, a humble building of nave and chancel, but with a rich REREDOS by *Gabriel Pippet*. – The altar itself is by *Sebastian Pugin Powell*, 1912–13. – SCULPTURE. Virgin and Child, demi-figure, stone. In an Italian Baroque style. – STAINED GLASS. The still pictorial Crucifixion in the E window no doubt of c.1849. Most of the glass in the chapel looks French.

E of the chapel a block of 1884–6 (top floor 1910), continued to the S in 1888 and on a large scale (with the gatehouse and the entrance tower) in 1893–5. This latter enlargement is by *F. A. Walters*. The long extensions of the original buildings towards the new church are by *Pugin Powell* and date from 1914 and 1922. Of 1935–6 the E extensions *by J. D. Kendall*.

The ABBEY CHURCH is by *J. Arnold Crush* and was begun in 1928. Most of the nave has not yet been built. Tall start of the nave, with clerestory, lower apsed chancel. All brick, but very white stone inside. The interior more conventional than the exterior, but neither of great architectural interest. Dec style.

Recently (1963) *Frederick Gibberd* has been commissioned

to design a lower nave and a complete abbey l. and r. of the church. The foundation stone was laid in 1964.

WOOLLEY PARK *see* BRIGHTWALTON

WOOLSTONE

ALL SAINTS. Nave, chancel, s transept, bellcote. Late Norman N doorway, waterleaf capitals, hood-mould on beasts' heads. Small lancets N and S. One N window early C14 with nicely cusped Y-tracery. The s transept s window is late C13, of two lights with pointed-trefoiled heads and a trefoiled circle. In the chancel N wall two Dec windows. Inside, the chancel arch (two slight chamfers) looks early C13, the s transept arch goes with the s window. – FONT. Of lead. Circular, with strange, rather bleak and disorderly patterns; C14 probably. – CHAN-DELIER. Brass, with one tier of arms. – PLATE. Cover Paten, 1581.

SE of the church a Georgian HOUSE of six bays with hipped roof.

DISC BARROW, on Woolstone Down. The barrow has a central mound 25 ft in diameter and 1½ ft high, standing on a platform 50 ft in diameter. It is surrounded by a ditch and external bank. 200 yds N is a bowl barrow 21 ft in diameter and 3 ft high. A second bowl barrow, 2 ft high, lies 180 yds to the NW.

MOUND, just below Uffington Camp, on the Woolstone–Uffington border. This very large circular mound is probably the motte of a MOTTE AND BAILEY CASTLE.

WOOTTON

ST PETER. Nave and chancel and recent timber bell-turret. Mostly Perp, but the E window Dec. – TILES. A number displayed on one wall of the porch. They are probably of the C14. – CHANDELIER. Brass, apparently C18. – STAINED GLASS. E window by *Kempe*, with his wheatsheaf, *c.*1900. – PLATE. Paten with the Vernicle, *c.*1500. – Chalice, Flagon, Almsdish of 1786.

BOARS HILL, the villa suburb of Oxford, belongs to Wootton. The villas are embedded in green, much as in Surrey.

RIPON HALL. Gothic. Built in the 1890s for the then President of Trinity College, Oxford. Enlarged for Lord Berkeley in 1902–4 (tower, hall). The recent shingle-hung addition by *M. & D. Dove*, 1963–4.

WYTHAM

ALL SAINTS. The entrance to the churchyard is by a small doorway from Cumnor Place. It is Perp with a two-centred arch, but has an inscription in Roman letters. The church was rebuilt in 1811–12 by Lord Abingdon, using materials from Cumnor Place. Nave and chancel, unbuttressed w tower. On the N side one late C14 window. On the s side Dec windows. Chancel E Dec as well. These four windows again come from Cumnor. They are all four of two lights with usual flowing patterns. One has a wheel of four mouchettes. The nave roof on good corbels including a bagpiper. – COMMUNION RAIL. C18. – STAINED GLASS. Old bits (C15) nave N. – Chancel s foreign roundels, etc. Chancel E Adoration of the Shepherds, C18. – PLATE. Cup, 1594; Paten on foot, 1693; Flagon, 1709; Paten on foot, 1722. – BRASS. Robert de Wytham † 1406 and wife. Fragmentary; originally c. 30 in. long.

WYTHAM ABBEY. Originally built in the early C16 with two courtyards. One of them is now covered over and contains the main staircase. Though the house looks generally the result of the remodelling of 1809–10 by *Thomas Cundy* (BC), there is plenty left of the early C16, especially on the w side. The embattled oriel window is certainly in order. It establishes the motif of straight-headed windows with arched lights. Such windows also occur on the E side, the climax of which is the gateway tower. Straight-sided pointed arch with continuous mouldings and two separate oriels over. A polygonal turret behind. The s side is not original. Rumour has it that Cundy's front was taken down and rebuilt c. 1870. The porch is of c. 1925. The whole, whatever the dates, is picturesquely irregular.

YATTENDON

ST PETER AND ST PAUL. Of the building of c. 1450 of which a former inscription reported the nave roof remains, with tie-beams, collar-beams on arched braces, and two tiers of wind-braces. The rest appears entirely Victorian. The short shingled broach spire e.g. is of 1896. – PULPIT. Jacobean, with the usual blank arches and plenty of arabesque. – Two BENCH ENDS with linenfold panelling. – STAINED GLASS. In the chancel N by *Powell*, 1874, designed by *Burrow*. – PLATE. Paten of 1713; Chalice of 1722. – MONUMENT. John Harris † 1743. Tablet with an oval still life of death and eternity.

w of the church two good Georgian houses, THE GRANGE and the MANOR HOUSE, the former of 1785, the latter with an outer stair to the pilaster-framed door. A little further w the former READING ROOM, given and designed in 1878 by *Alfred Waterhouse*, Lord of the Manor. By him also the WELL HOUSE, now bus-shelter, 1876. Waterhouse himself lived at Yattendon Court, where his new mansion was begun in 1878. This, however, was demolished in 1926 and replaced. Also by *Waterhouse* the SCHOOL of 1891.

Of Georgian houses two more deserve a glance, both E of the church: the RECTORY, of five bays, with a curious doorway, where a kind of apron, as they are used in early c18 houses below the window-sills, appears as a tympanum. E of this THE MALTHOUSE, a roughcast three-bay cottage with Gothic glazing bars.

GLOSSARY

ABACUS: flat slab on the top of a capital (q.v.).

ABUTMENT: solid masonry placed to resist the lateral pressure of a vault.

ACANTHUS: plant with thick fleshy and scalloped leaves used as part of the decoration of a Corinthian capital (q.v.) and in some types of leaf carving.

ACHIEVEMENT OF ARMS: in heraldry, a complete display of armorial bearings.

ACROTERION: foliage-carved block on the end or top of a classical pediment.

ADDORSED: two human figures, animals, or birds, etc., placed symmetrically so that they turn their backs to each other.

AEDICULE, AEDICULA: framing of a window or door by columns and a pediment (q.v.).

AFFRONTED: two human figures, animals, or birds, etc., placed symmetrically so that they face each other.

AGGER: Latin term for the built-up foundations of Roman roads; also sometimes applied to the banks of hill-forts or other earthworks.

AMBULATORY: semicircular or polygonal aisle enclosing an apse (q.v.).

ANNULET: see Shaft-ring.

ANSE DE PANIER: see Arch, Basket.

ANTEPENDIUM: covering of the front of an altar, usually by textiles or metalwork.

ANTIS, IN: see Portico.

APSE: vaulted semicircular or polygonal end of a chancel or a chapel.

ARABESQUE: light and fanciful surface decoration using combinations of flowing lines, tendrils, etc., interspersed with vases, animals, etc.

ARCADE: range of arches supported on piers or columns, free-standing: or, BLIND ARCADE, the same attached to a wall.

ARCH: round-headed, i.e. semicircular; pointed, i.e. consisting of two curves, each drawn from one centre, and meeting in a point at the top; segmental, i.e. in the form of a segment;

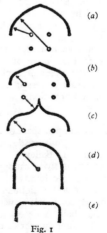

Fig. 1

pointed; four-centred (a Late Medieval form), see Fig. 1(a); Tudor (also a Late Medieval form), *see* Fig. 1(*b*); Ogee (introduced c.1300 and specially popular in the C14), *see* Fig. 1(*c*); Stilted, *see* Fig. 1(*d*); Basket, with lintel connected to the jambs by concave quadrant curves, *see* Fig. 1(*e*) for one example; Diaphragm, a transverse arch with solid spandrels carrying not a vault but a principal beam of a timber roof.

ARCHITRAVE: lowest of the three main parts of the entablature (q.v.) of an order (q.v.) (*see* Fig. 12).

ARCHIVOLT: under-surface of an arch (also called Soffit).

ARRIS: sharp edge at the meeting of two surfaces.

ASHLAR: masonry of large blocks wrought to even faces and square edges.

ATLANTES: male counterparts of caryatids (q.v.).

ATRIUM: inner court of a Roman house, also open court in front of a church.

ATTACHED: *see* Engaged.

ATTIC: topmost storey of a house, if distance from floor to ceiling is less than in the others.

AUMBRY: recess or cupboard to hold sacred vessels for Mass and Communion.

BAILEY: open space or court of a stone-built castle; *see* also Motte-and-Bailey.

BALDACCHINO: canopy supported on columns.

BALLFLOWER: globular flower of three petals enclosing a small ball. A decoration used in the first quarter of the C14.

BALUSTER: small pillar or column of fanciful outline.

BALUSTRADE: series of balusters supporting a handrail or coping (q.v.).

BARBICAN: outwork defending the entrance to a castle.

BARGEBOARDS: projecting decorated boards placed against the incline of the gable of a building and hiding the horizontal roof timbers.

BARROW: *see* Bell, Bowl, Disc, Long, *and* Pond Barrow.

BASILICA: in medieval architecture an aisled church with a clerestory.

BASKET ARCH: *see* Arch (Fig. 1e).

BASTION: projection at the angle of a fortification.

BATTER: inclined face of a wall.

BATTLEMENT: parapet with a series of indentations or embrasures with raised portions or merlons between (also called Crenellation).

BAYS: internal compartments of a building; each divided from the other not by solid walls but by divisions only marked in the side walls (columns, pilasters, etc.) or the ceiling (beams, etc.). Also external divisions of a building by fenestration.

BAY-WINDOW: angular or curved projection of a house front with ample fenestration. If curved, also called bow-window: if on an upper floor only, also called oriel or oriel window.

BEAKER FOLK: Late New Stone Age warrior invaders from the Continent who buried their dead in round barrows and introduced the first metal tools and weapons to Britain.

BEAKHEAD: Norman ornamental motif consisting of a row of bird or beast heads with beaks biting usually into a roll moulding.

BELFRY: turret on a roof to hang bells in.

BELGAE: Aristocratic warrior bands who settled in Britain in two main waves in the C I B.C. In Britain their culture is termed Iron Age C.

BELL BARROW: Early Bronze Age round barrow in which the mound is separated from its encircling ditch by a flat platform or berm (q.v.).

BELLCOTE: framework on a roof to hang bells from.

BERM: level area separating ditch from bank on a hill-fort or barrow.

BILLET FRIEZE: Norman ornamental motif made up of short raised rectangles placed at regular intervals.

BIVALLATE: Of a hill-fort: defended by two concentric banks and ditches.

BLOCK CAPITAL: Romanesque capital cut from a cube by hav-

Fig. 2

ing the lower angles rounded off to the circular shaft below (also called Cushion Capital) (Fig. 2).

BOND, ENGLISH or FLEMISH: see Brickwork.

BOSS: knob or projection usually placed to cover the intersection of ribs in a vault.

BOWL BARROW: round barrow surrounded by a quarry ditch. Introduced in Late Neolithic

times, the form continued until the Saxon period.

BOW-WINDOW: see Bay-Window.

BOX: A small country house, e.g. a shooting box. A convenient term to describe a compact minor dwelling, e.g. a rectory.

BOX PEW: pew with a high wooden enclosure.

BRACES: see Roof.

BRACKET: small supporting piece of stone, etc., to carry a projecting horizontal.

BRESSUMER: beam in a timber-framed building to support the, usually projecting, superstructure.

BRICKWORK: *Header:* brick laid so that the end only appears on the face of the wall. *Stretcher:* brick laid so that the side only appears on the face of the wall. *English Bond:* method of laying bricks so that alternate courses or layers on the face of the wall are composed of headers or stretchers only (Fig. 3*a*). *Flemish Bond:* method of laying

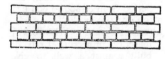

(a)

(b)

Fig. 3

bricks so that alternate headers and stretchers appear in each course on the face of the wall (Fig. 3*b*).

BROACH: see Spire.

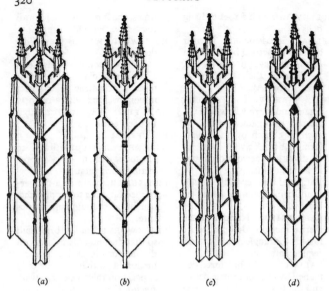

(a)   (b)   (c)   (d)

Fig. 4

BROKEN PEDIMENT: *see* Pediment.

BRONZE AGE: In Britain, the period from *c.*1800 to 600 B.C.

BUCRANIUM: ox skull.

BUTTRESS: mass of brickwork or masonry projecting from or built against a wall to give additional strength. *Angle Buttresses:* two meeting at an angle of 90° at the angle of a building (Fig. 4*a*). *Clasping Buttress:* one which encases the angle (Fig. 4*d*). *Diagonal Buttress:* one placed against the right angle formed by two walls, and more or less equiangular with both (Fig. 4*b*). *Flying Buttress:* arch or half arch transmitting the thrust of a vault or roof from the upper part of a wall to an outer support or buttress. *Setback Buttress:* angle buttress set slightly back from the angle (Fig. 4*c*).

CABLE MOULDING: Norman moulding imitating a twisted cord.

CAIRN: a mound of stones usually covering a burial.

CAMBER: slight rise or upward curve of an otherwise horizontal structure.

CAMPANILE: isolated bell tower.

CANOPY: projection or hood over an altar, pulpit, niche, statue, etc.

CAP: in a windmill the crowning feature.

CAPITAL: head or top part of a column.

CARTOUCHE: tablet with an ornate frame, usually enclosing an inscription.

CARYATID: whole female figure supporting an entablature or other similar member. *Termini Caryatids:* female busts or demi-figures or three-quarter figures supporting an entablature or other similar member and placed at the top of termini pilasters (q.v.). Cf. Atlantes.

CASTELLATED: decorated with battlements.

CELURE: panelled and adorned part of a wagon-roof above the rood or the altar.

CENSER: vessel for the burning of incense.

CENTERING: wooden framework used in arch and vault construction and removed when the mortar has set.

CHALICE: cup used in the Communion service or at `Mass. *See also* Recusant Chalice.

CHAMBERED TOMB: burial mound of the New Stone Age having a stone-built chamber and entrance passage covered by an earthen barrow or stone cairn. The form was introduced to Britain from the Mediterranean.

CHAMFER: surface made by cutting across the square angle of a stone block, piece of wood, etc., usually at an angle of 45° to the other two surfaces.

CHANCEL: that part of the E end of a church in which the altar is placed, usually applied to the whole continuation of the nave E of the crossing.

CHANCEL ARCH: arch at the W end of the chancel.

CHANTRY CHAPEL: chapel attached to, or inside, a church, endowed for the saying of Masses for the soul of the founder or some other individual.

CHEVET: French term for the E end of a church (chancel, ambulatory, and radiating chapels).

CHEVRON: Norman moulding forming a zigzag.

CHOIR: that part of the church where divine service is sung.

CIBORIUM: a baldacchino.

CINQUEFOIL: *see* Foil.

CIST: stone-lined or slab-built grave. First appears in Late Neolithic times. It continued to be used in the Early Christian period.

CLAPPER BRIDGE: bridge made of large slabs of stone, some built up to make rough piers and other longer ones laid on top to make the roadway.

CLASSIC: here used to mean the moment of highest achievement of a style.

CLASSICAL: here used as the term for Greek and Roman architecture and any subsequent styles inspired by it.

CLERESTORY: upper storey of the nave walls of a church, pierced by windows.

COADE STONE: artificial (cast) stone made in the late C18 and the early C19 by Coade and Sealy in London.

COB: walling material made of mixed clay and straw.

COFFERING: decorating a ceiling with sunk square or polygonal ornamental panels.

COLLAR-BEAM: *see* Roof.

COLONNADE: range of columns.

COLONNETTE: small column.

COLUMNA ROSTRATA: column decorated with carved prows of ships to celebrate a naval victory.

COMPOSITE: *see* Order.

CONSOLE: bracket (q.v.) with a compound curved outline.

COPING: capping or covering to a wall.

CORBEL: block of stone projecting from a wall, supporting some feature on its horizontal top surface.

CORBEL TABLE: series of corbels, occurring just below the roof eaves externally or internally, often seen in Norman buildings.

CORINTHIAN: *see* Order.

CORNICE: in classical architecture the top section of the entablature (q.v.). Also for a projecting decorative feature along the top of a wall, arch, etc.

CORRIDOR VILLA: *see* Villa.

COUNTERSCARP BANK: small bank on the down-hill or outer side of a hill-fort ditch.

COURTYARD VILLA: *see* Villa.

COVE, COVING: concave undersurface in the nature of a hollow moulding but on a larger scale.

COVER PATEN: cover to a Communion cup, suitable for use as a paten or plate for the consecrated bread.

CRADLE ROOF: *see* Wagon roof.

CRENELLATION: *see* Battlement.

CREST, CRESTING: ornamental finish along the top of a screen, etc.

CRINKLE-CRANKLE WALL: undulating wall.

CROCKET, CROCKETING: decorative features placed on the sloping sides of spires, pinnacles, gables, etc., in Gothic architecture, carved in various leaf shapes and placed at regular intervals.

CROCKET CAPITAL: *see* Fig. 5. An Early Gothic form.

CROMLECH: word of Celtic origin still occasionally used of single free-standing stones ascribed to the Neolithic or Bronze Age periods.

Fig. 5

CROSSING: space at the intersection of nave, chancel, and transepts.

CROSS-WINDOWS: windows with one mullion and one transom.

CRUCK: big curved beam supporting both walls and roof of a cottage.

CRYPT: underground room usually below the E end of a church.

CUPOLA: small polygonal or circular domed turret crowning a roof.

CURTAIN WALL: connecting wall between the towers of a castle.

CUSHION CAPITAL: *see* Block Capital.

CUSP: projecting point between the foils in a foiled Gothic arch.

DADO: decorative covering of the lower part of a wall.

DAGGER: tracery motif of the Dec style. It is a lancet shape rounded or pointed at the head, pointed at the foot, and cusped inside (*see* Fig. 6).

Fig. 6

DAIS: raised platform at one end of a room.

DEC ('DECORATED'): historical division of English Gothic architecture covering the period from *c*.1290 to *c*.1350.

DEMI-COLUMNS: columns half sunk into a wall.

DIAPER WORK: surface decoration composed of square or lozenge shapes.

DIAPHRAGM ARCH: *see* Arch.

DISC BARROW: Bronze Age round barrow with inconspicuous central mound surrounded by bank and ditch.

DOGTOOTH: typical E.E. ornament consisting of a series of four-cornered stars placed diagonally and raised pyramidally (Fig. 7).

Fig. 7

DOMICAL VAULT: *see* Vault.

DONJON: *see* Keep.

DORIC: *see* Order.

DORMER (WINDOW): window placed vertically in the sloping plane of a roof.

DRIPSTONE: *see* Hood-mould.

DRUM: circular or polygonal vertical wall of a dome or cupola.

E.E. ('EARLY ENGLISH'): historical division of English Gothic architecture roughly covering the C13.

EASTER SEPULCHRE: recess with tomb-chest, usually in the wall of a chancel, the tomb-chest to receive an effigy of Christ for Easter celebrations.

EAVES: underpart of a sloping roof overhanging a wall.

EAVES CORNICE: cornice below the eaves of a roof.

ECHINUS: Convex or projecting moulding supporting the abacus of a Greek Doric capital, sometimes bearing an egg and dart pattern.

EMBATTLED: *see* Battlement.

EMBRASURE: small opening in the wall or parapet of a fortified building, usually splayed on the inside.

ENCAUSTIC TILES: earthenware glazed and decorated tiles used for paving.

ENGAGED COLUMNS: columns attached to, or partly sunk into, a wall.

ENGLISH BOND: *see* Brickwork.

ENTABLATURE: in classical architecture the whole of the horizontal members above a column (that is architrave, frieze, and cornice) (*see* Fig. 12).

ENTASIS: very slight convex deviation from a straight line; used on Greek columns and sometimes on spires to prevent an optical illusion of concavity.

ENTRESOL: *see* Mezzanine.

EPITAPH: hanging wall monument.

ESCUTCHEON: shield for armorial bearings.

EXEDRA: the apsidal end of a room. *See* Apse.

FAN-VAULT: *see* Vault.

FERETORY: place behind the

high altar where the chief shrine of a church is kept.

FESTOON: carved garland of flowers and fruit suspended at both ends.

FILLET: narrow flat band running down a shaft or along a roll moulding.

FINIAL: top of a canopy, gable, pinnacle.

FLAGON: vessel for the wine used in the Communion service.

FLAMBOYANT: properly the latest phase of French Gothic architecture where the window tracery takes on wavy undulating lines.

FLÈCHE: slender wooden spire on the centre of a roof (also called Spirelet).

FLEMISH BOND: *see* Brickwork.

FLEURON: decorative carved flower or leaf.

FLUSHWORK: decorative use of flint in conjunction with dressed stone so as to form patterns: tracery, initials, etc.

FLUTING: vertical channelling in the shaft of a column.

FLYING BUTTRESS: *see* Buttress.

FOIL: lobe formed by the cusping (q.v.) of a circle or an arch. Trefoil, quatrefoil, cinquefoil, multifoil, express the number of leaf shapes to be seen.

FOLIATED: carved with leaf shapes.

FOSSE: ditch.

FOUR-CENTRED ARCH: *see* Arch.

FRATER: refectory or dining hall of a monastery.

FRESCO: wall painting on wet plaster.

FRIEZE: middle division of a classical entablature (q.v.) (*see* Fig. 12).

FRONTAL: covering for the front of an altar.

GABLE: *Dutch gable:* A gable with curved sides crowned by a pediment, characteristic of c.1630–50 (Fig. 8a). *Shaped gable:* A gable with multi-curved sides characteristic of c.1600–50 (Fig. 8b).

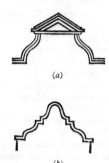

(a)

(b)

Fig. 8

GADROONED: enriched with a series of convex ridges, the opposite of fluting.

GALILEE: chapel or vestibule usually at the W end of a church enclosing the porch. Also called Narthex (q.v.).

GALLERY: in church architecture upper storey above an aisle, opened in arches to the nave. Also called Tribune and often erroneously Triforium (q.v.).

GALLERY GRAVE: chambered tomb (q.v.) in which there is little or no differentiation between the entrance passage and the actual burial chamber(s).

GARDEROBE: lavatory or privy in a medieval building.

GARGOYLE: water spout projecting from the parapet of a wall or tower; carved into a human or animal shape.

GAZEBO: lookout tower or raised

summer house in a picturesque garden.

'GEOMETRICAL': *see* Tracery.

'GIBBS SURROUND': of a doorway or window. An C18 motif consisting of a surround with alternating larger and smaller blocks of stone, quoin-wise, or intermittent large blocks, sometimes with a narrow raised band connecting them up the verticals and along the face of the arch (Fig. 9).

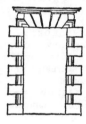

Fig. 9

GROIN: sharp edge at the meeting of two cells of a cross-vault.

GROIN-VAULT: *see* Vault.

GROTESQUE: fanciful ornamental decoration: *see* also Arabesque.

HAGIOSCOPE: *see* Squint.

HALF-TIMBERING: *see* Timber-Framing.

HALL CHURCH: church in which nave and aisles are of equal height or approximately so.

HAMMERBEAM: *see* Roof.

HANAP: large metal cup, generally made for domestic use, standing on an elaborate base and stem; with a very ornate cover frequently crowned with a little steeple.

HEADERS: *see* Brickwork.

HERRINGBONE WORK: brick, stone, or tile construction where the component blocks are laid diagonally instead of flat. Alternate courses lie in opposing directions to make a zigzag pattern up the face of the wall.

HEXASTYLE: having six detached columns.

HILL-FORT: Iron Age earthwork enclosed by a ditch and bank system; in the later part of the period the defences multiplied in size and complexity. They vary from about an acre to over 30 acres in area, and are usually built with careful regard to natural elevations or promontories.

HIPPED ROOF: *see* Roof.

HOOD-MOULD: projecting moulding above an arch or a lintel to throw off water (also called Dripstone or Label).

ICONOGRAPHY: the science of the subject matter of works of the visual arts.

IMPOST: bracket in a wall, usually formed of mouldings, on which the ends of an arch rest.

INDENT: shape chiselled out in a stone slab to receive a brass.

INGLENOOK: bench or seat built in beside a fireplace, sometimes covered by the chimneybreast, occasionally lit by small windows on each side of the fire.

INTERCOLUMNIATION: the space between columns.

IONIC: *see* Order (Fig. 12).

IRON AGE: in Britain the period from *c.*600 B.C. to the coming of the Romans. The term is also used for those un-Romanized native communities which survived until the Saxon incursions.

JAMB: straight side of an archway, doorway, or window.

KEEL MOULDING: moulding whose outline is in section like that of the keel of a ship.

KEEP: massive tower of a Norman castle.

KEYSTONE: middle stone in an arch or a rib-vault.

KING-POST: see Roof (Fig. 14).

KNEELER: horizontal decorative projection at the base of a gable.

KNOP: a knob-like thickening in the stem of a chalice.

LABEL: see Hood-mould.

LABEL STOP: ornamental boss at the end of a hood-mould (q.v.).

LACED WINDOWS: windows pulled visually together by strips, usually in brick of a different colour, which continue vertically the lines of the vertical parts of the window surrounds. The motif is typical of c. 1720.

LANCET WINDOW: slender pointed-arched window.

LANTERN: in architecture, a small circular or polygonal turret with windows all round crowning a roof (see Cupola) or a dome.

LANTERN CROSS: churchyard cross with lantern-shaped top usually with sculptured representations on the sides of the top.

LEAN-TO ROOF: roof with one slope only, built against a higher wall.

LESENE or PILASTER STRIP: pilaster without base or capital.

LIERNE: see Vault (Fig. 21).

LINENFOLD: Tudor panelling ornamented with a conventional representation of a piece of linen laid in vertical folds. The piece is repeated in each panel.

LINTEL: horizontal beam or stone bridging an opening.

LOGGIA: recessed colonnade (q.v.).

LONG AND SHORT WORK: Saxon quoins (q.v.) consisting of stones placed with the long sides alternately upright and horizontal.

LONG BARROW: unchambered Neolithic communal burial mound, wedge-shaped in plan, with the burial and occasional other structures massed at the broader end, from which the mound itself tapers in height; quarry ditches flank the mound.

LOUVRE: opening, often with lantern (q.v.) over, in the roof of a room to let the smoke from a central hearth escape.

LOWER PALAEOLITHIC: see Palaeolithic.

LOZENGE: diamond shape.

LUCARNE: small opening to let light in.

LUNETTE: tympanum (q.v.) or semicircular opening.

LYCH GATE: wooden gate structure with a roof and open sides placed at the entrance to a churchyard to provide space for the reception of a coffin. The word lych is Saxon and means a corpse.

LYNCHET: long terraced strip of soil accumulating on the downward side of prehistoric and medieval fields due to soil creep from continuous ploughing along the contours.

MACHICOLATION: projecting gallery on brackets constructed on the outside of castle towers or walls. The gallery has holes in the floor to drop missiles through.

MAJOLICA: ornamented glazed earthenware.

MANSARD: *see* Roof.

MATHEMATICAL TILES: Small facing tiles the size of brick headers, applied to timber-framed walls to make them appear brick-built.

MEGALITHIC TOMB: stone-built burial chamber of the New Stone Age covered by an earth or stone mound. The form was introduced to Britain from the Mediterranean area.

MERLON: *see* Battlement.

MESOLITHIC: 'Middle Stone' Age; the post-glacial period of hunting and fishing communities dating in Britain from *c.* 8000 B.C. to the arrival of Neolithic communities, with which they must have considerably overlapped.

METOPE: in classical architecture of the Doric order (q.v.) the space in the frieze between the triglyphs (Fig. 12).

MEZZANINE: low storey placed between two higher ones.

MISERERE: *see* Misericord.

MISERICORD: bracket placed on the underside of a hinged choir stall seat which, when turned up, provided the occupant of the seat with a support during long periods of standing (also called Miserere).

MODILLION: small bracket of which large numbers (modillion frieze) are often placed below a cornice (q.v.) in classical architecture.

MOTTE: steep mound forming the main feature of C11 and C12 castles.

MOTTE-AND-BAILEY: post-Roman and Norman defence system consisting of an earthen mound (the motte) topped with a wooden tower eccentrically placed within a bailey (q.v.), with enclosure ditch and palisade, and with the rare addition of an internal bank.

MOUCHETTE: tracery motif in curvilinear tracery, a curved dagger (q.v.), specially popular in the early C14 (Fig. 10).

Fig. 10

MULLIONS: vertical posts or uprights dividing a window into 'lights'.

MULTIVALLATE: Of a hill-fort: defended by three or more concentric banks and ditches.

MUNTIN: post as a rule moulded and part of a screen.

NAIL-HEAD: E.E. ornamental motif, consisting of small pyramids regularly repeated (Fig. 11).

Fig. 11

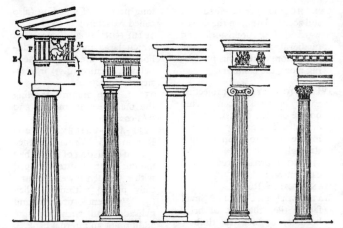

Fig. 12. Orders of Columns (Greek Doric, Roman Doric, Tuscan Doric, Ionic, Corinthian) E, Entablature; C, Cornice; F, Frieze; A, Architrave; M, Metope; T, Triglyph.

NARTHEX: enclosed vestibule or covered porch at the main entrance to a church (*see* Galilee).

NEOLITHIC: 'New Stone' Age, dating in Britain from the appearance from the Continent of the first settled farming communities *c.* 3500 B.C. until the introduction of the Bronze Age.

NEWEL: central post in a circular or winding staircase; also the principal post when a flight of stairs meets a landing.

NOOK-SHAFT: shaft set in the angle of a pier or respond or wall, or the angle of the jamb of a window or doorway.

NUTMEG MOULDING: consisting of a chain of tiny triangles placed obliquely.

OBELISK: lofty pillar of square section tapering at the top and ending pyramidally.

OGEE: *see* Arch (Fig. 1c).

ORATORY: small private chapel in a house.

ORDER: (1) *of a doorway or window:* series of concentric steps receding towards the opening; (2) *in classical architecture:* column with base, shaft, capital, and entablature (q.v.) according to one of the following styles: Greek Doric, Roman Doric, Tuscan Doric, Ionic, Corinthian, Composite. The established details are very elaborate, and some specialist architectural work should be consulted for further guidance (*see* Fig. 12).

ORIEL: *see* Bay-Window.

OVERHANG: projection of the upper storey of a house.

OVERSAILING COURSES: series of stone or brick courses, each one projecting beyond the one below it.

OVOLO: convex moulding.

PALAEOLITHIC: 'Old Stone' Age; the first period of human culture, commencing in the

Ice Age and immediately prior to the Mesolithic; the Lower Palaeolithic is the older phase, the Upper Palaeolithic the later.

PALIMPSEST: (1) *of a brass:* where a metal plate has been re-used by turning over and engraving on the back; (2) *of a wall painting:* where one overlaps and partly obscures an earlier one.

PALLADIAN: architecture following the ideas and principles of Andrea Palladio, 1518–80.

PANTILE: tile of curved S-shaped section.

PARAPET: low wall placed to protect any spot where there is a sudden drop, for example on a bridge, quay, hillside, housetop, etc.

PARGETTING: plaster work with patterns and ornaments either in relief or engraved on it.

PARVIS: term wrongly applied to a room over a church porch. These rooms were often used as a schoolroom or as a store room.

PATEN: plate to hold the bread at Communion or Mass.

PATERA: small flat circular or oval ornament in classical architecture.

PEDIMENT: low-pitched gable used in classical, Renaissance, and neo-classical architecture above a portico and above doors, windows, etc. It may be straight-sided or curved segmentally. *Broken Pediment:* one where the centre portion of the base is left open. *Open Pediment:* one where the centre portion of the sloping sides is left out.

PENDANT: boss (q.v.) elongated so that it seems to hang down.

PENDENTIF: concave triangular spandrel used to lead from the angle of two walls to the base of a circular dome. It is constructed as part of the hemisphere over a diameter the size of the diagonal of the basic square (Fig. 13).

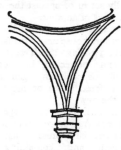

Fig. 13

PERP (PERPENDICULAR): historical division of English Gothic architecture covering the period from c.1335–50 to c.1530.

PIANO NOBILE: principal storey of a house with the reception rooms; usually the first floor.

PIAZZA: open space surrounded by buildings; in C17 and C18 England sometimes used to mean a long colonnade or loggia.

PIER: strong, solid support, frequently square in section or of composite section (compound pier).

PIETRA DURA: ornamental or scenic inlay by means of thin slabs of stone.

PILASTER: shallow pier attached to a wall. *Termini Pilasters:* pilasters with sides tapering downwards.

PILLAR PISCINA: free-standing piscina on a pillar.

PINNACLE: ornamental form crowning a spire, tower, buttress, etc., usually of steep pyramidal, conical, or some similar shape.

PISCINA: basin for washing the Communion or Mass vessels, provided with a drain. Generally set in or against the wall to the s of an altar.

PLAISANCE: summer-house, pleasure house near a mansion.

PLATE TRACERY: see Tracery.

PLINTH: projecting base of a wall or column, generally chamfered (q.v.) or moulded at the top.

POND BARROW: rare type of Bronze Age barrow consisting of a circular depression, usually paved, and containing a number of cremation burials.

POPPYHEAD: ornament of leaf and flower type used to decorate the tops of bench- or stall-ends.

PORTCULLIS: gate constructed to rise and fall in vertical grooves; used in gateways of castles.

PORTE COCHÈRE: porch large enough to admit wheeled vehicles.

PORTICO: centre-piece of a house or a church with classical detached or attached columns and a pediment. A portico is called *prostyle* or *in antis* according to whether it projects from or recedes into a building. In a portico *in antis* the columns range with the side walls.

POSTERN: small gateway at the back of a building.

PREDELLA: in an altarpiece the horizontal strip below the main representation, often used for a number of subsidiary representations in a row.

PRESBYTERY: the part of the church lying E of the choir. It is the part where the altar is placed.

PRINCIPAL: see Roof (Fig. 14).

PRIORY: monastic house whose head is a prior or prioress, not an abbot or abbess.

PROSTYLE: with free-standing columns in a row.

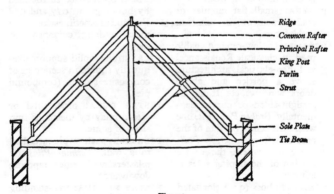

Fig. 14

PULPITUM: stone screen in a major church provided to shut off the choir from the nave and also as a backing for the return choir stalls.

PULVINATED FRIEZE: frieze with a bold convex moulding.

PURLIN: see Roof (Figs. 14, 15).

PUTHOLE or PUTLOCK HOLE: putlocks are the short horizontal timbers on which during construction the boards of scaffolding rest. Putholes or putlock holes are the holes in the wall for putlocks, which often are not filled in after construction is complete.

PUTTO: small naked boy.

QUADRANGLE: inner courtyard in a large building.

QUARRY: in stained-glass work, a small diamond- or square-shaped piece of glass set diagonally.

QUATREFOIL: see Foil.

QUEEN-POSTS: see Roof (Fig. 15).

QUOINS: dressed stones at the angles of a building. Sometimes all the stones are of the same size; more often they are alternately large and small.

RADIATING CHAPELS: chapels projecting radially from an ambulatory or an apse.

RAFTER: see Roof.

RAMPART: stone wall or wall of earth surrounding a castle, fortress, or fortified city.

RAMPART-WALK: path along the inner face of a rampart.

REBATE: continuous rectangular notch cut on an edge.

REBUS: pun, a play on words. The literal translation and illustration of a name for artistic and heraldic purposes (Belton = bell, tun).

RECUSANT CHALICE: chalice made after the Reformation and before Catholic Emancipation for Roman Catholic use.

REEDING: decoration with parallel convex mouldings touching one another.

REFECTORY: dining hall; see Frater.

RENDERING: plastering of an outer wall.

REPOUSSÉ: decoration of metal work by relief designs, formed by beating the metal from the back.

REREDOS: structure behind and above an altar.

RESPOND: half-pier bonded into a wall and carrying one end of an arch.

RETABLE: altarpiece, a picture or piece of carving, standing behind and attached to an altar.

RETICULATION: see Tracery (Fig. 20e).

REVEAL: that part of a jamb (q.v.) which lies between the glass or door and the outer surface of the wall.

RIB-VAULT: see Vault.

ROCOCO: latest phase of the Baroque style, current in most Continental countries between c.1720 and c.1760.

ROLL MOULDING: moulding of semicircular or more than semicircular section.

ROMANESQUE: that style in architecture which was current in the C11 and C12 and preceded the Gothic style (in England often called Norman). (Some scholars extend the use of the term Romanesque back to the C10 or C9.)

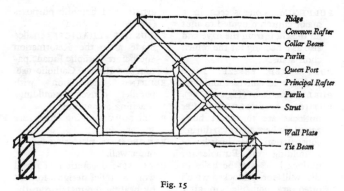

Ridge
Common Rafter
Collar Beam
Purlin
Queen Post
Principal Rafter
Purlin
Strut
Wall Plate
Tie Beam

Fig. 15

ROMANO-BRITISH: A somewhat vague term applied to the period and cultural features of Britain affected by the Roman occupation of the C1–5 A.D.

ROOD: cross or crucifix.

ROOD LOFT: singing gallery on the top of the rood screen, often supported by a coving.

ROOD SCREEN: *see* Screen.

ROOD STAIRS: stairs to give access to the rood loft.

ROOF: *Single-framed:* if consisting entirely of transverse members (such as rafters with or without braces, collars, tie-beams, king-posts or queen-posts, etc.) not tied together longitudinally. *Double-framed:* if longitudinal members (such as a ridge beam and purlins) are employed. As a rule in such cases the rafters are divided into stronger principals and weaker subsidiary rafters. *Hipped:* roof with sloped instead of vertical ends. *Mansard:* roof with a double slope, the

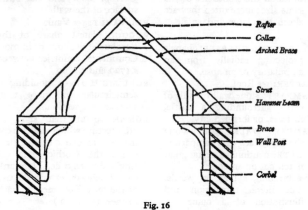

Rafter
Collar
Arched Brace
Strut
Hammer Beam
Brace
Wall Post
Corbel

Fig. 16

lower slope being larger and steeper than the upper. *Saddleback:* tower roof shaped like an ordinary gabled timber roof. The following members have special names: *Rafter:* roof-timber sloping up from the wall plate to the ridge. *Principal:* principal rafter, usually corresponding to the main bay divisions of the nave or chancel below. *Wall Plate:* timber laid longitudinally on the top of a wall. *Purlin:* longitudinal member laid parallel with wall plate and ridge beam some way up the slope of the roof. *Tie-beam:* beam connecting the two slopes of a roof across at its foot, usually at the height of the wall plate, to prevent the roof from spreading. *Collarbeam:* tie-beam applied higher up the slope of the roof. *Strut:* upright timber connecting the tie-beam with the rafter above it. *King-post:* upright timber connecting a tie-beam and collar-beam with the ridge beam. *Queen-posts:* two struts placed symmetrically on a tie-beam or collar-beam. *Braces:* inclined timbers inserted to strengthen others. Usually braces connect a collar-beam with the rafters below or a tie-beam with the wall below. Braces can be straight or curved (also called arched). *Hammerbeam:* beam projecting at right angles, usually from the top of a wall, to carry arched braces or struts and arched braces. (*See* Figs. 14, 15, 16.)

ROSE WINDOW (or WHEEL WINDOW): circular window with patterned tracery arranged to radiate from the centre.

ROTUNDA: building circular in plan.

RUBBLE: building stones, not square or hewn, nor laid in regular courses.

RUSTICATION: *rock-faced* if the surfaces of large blocks of ashlar stone are left rough like rock; *smooth* if the ashlar blocks are smooth and separated by V-joints; *banded* if the separation by V-joints applies only to the horizontals.

S

SADDLEBACK: *see* Roof.

SALTIRE CROSS: equal-limbed cross placed diagonally.

SANCTUARY: (1) area around the main altar of a church (*see* Presbytery); (2) sacred site consisting of wood or stone uprights enclosed by a circular bank and ditch. Beginning in the Neolithic, they were elaborated in the succeeding Bronze Age. The best known examples are Stonehenge and Avebury.

SARCOPHAGUS: elaborately carved coffin.

SCAGLIOLA: material composed of cement and colouring matter to imitate marble.

SCALLOPED CAPITAL: development of the block capital (q.v.) in which the single semi-circular surface is elaborated into a series of truncated cones (Fig. 17).

Fig. 17

SCARP: artificial cutting away of the ground to form a steep slope.

SCREEN: *Parclose screen:* screen separating a chapel from the rest of a church. *Rood screen:* screen below the rood (q.v.), usually at the W end of a chancel.

SCREENS PASSAGE: passage between the entrances to kitchen, buttery, etc., and the screen behind which lies the hall of a medieval house.

SEDILIA: seats for the priests (usually three) on the S side of the chancel of a church.

SEGMENTAL ARCH: *see* Arch.

SET-OFF: *see* Weathering.

SEXPARTITE: *see* Vault.

SGRAFFITO: pattern incised into plaster so as to expose a dark surface underneath.

SHAFT-RING: motif of the C12 and C13 consisting of a ring round a circular pier or a shaft attached to a pier.

SHEILA-NA-GIG: fertility figure, usually with legs wide open.

SILL: lower horizontal part of the frame of a window.

SLATEHANGING: the covering of walls by overlapping rows of slates, on a timber substructure.

SOFFIT: underside of an arch, lintel, etc.

SOLAR: upper living-room of a medieval house.

SOPRAPORTE: painting above the door of a room, usual in the C17 and C18.

SOUNDING BOARD: horizontal board or canopy over a pulpit. Also called Tester.

SPANDREL: triangular surface between one side of an arch, the horizontal drawn from its apex, and the vertical drawn from its springer; also the surface between two arches.

SPERE-TRUSS: roof truss on two free-standing posts to mask the division between screens passage and hall. The screen itself, where a spere-truss exists, was originally movable.

SPIRE: tall pyramidal or conical pointed erection often built on top of a tower, turret, etc. *Broach Spire:* a broach is a sloping half-pyramid of masonry or wood introduced at the base of each of the four oblique faces of a tapering octagonal spire with the object of effecting the transition from the square to the octagon. The *splayed foot spire* is a variation of the broach form found principally in the south-eastern counties. In this form the four cardinal faces are splayed out near their base, to cover the corners, while the oblique (or intermediate) faces taper away to a point. *Needle Spire:* thin spire rising from the centre of a tower roof, well inside the parapet.

SPIRELET: *see* Flèche.

SPLAY: chamfer, usually of the jamb of a window.

SPRINGING: level at which an arch rises from its supports.

SQUINCH: arch or system of concentric arches thrown across the angle between two walls to support a superstructure, for example a dome (Fig. 18).

SQUINT: a hole cut in a wall or through a pier to allow a view of the main altar of a church from places whence it could not otherwise be seen (also called Hagioscope).

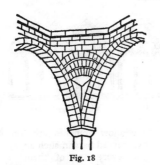

Fig. 18

STALL: carved seat, one of a row, made of wood or stone.

STAUNCHION: upright iron or steel member.

STEEPLE: the tower of a church together with a spire, cupola, etc.

STIFF-LEAF: E.E. type of foliage of many-lobed shapes (Fig. 19).

Fig. 19

STILTED: see Arch.

STOREY-POSTS: the principal posts of a timber-framed wall.

STOUP: vessel for the reception of holy water, usually placed near a door.

STRAINER ARCH: arch inserted across a room to prevent the walls from leaning.

STRAPWORK: C16 decoration consisting of interlaced bands, and forms similar to fretwork or cut and bent leather.

STRETCHER: see Brickwork.

STRING COURSE: projecting horizontal band or moulding set in the surface of a wall.

STRUT: see Roof.

STUCCO: plaster work.

STUDS: the subsidiary vertical timber members of a timber-framed wall.

SWAG: festoon formed by a carved piece of cloth suspended from both ends.

TABERNACLE: richly ornamented niche or free-standing canopy. Usually contains the Holy Sacrament.

TARSIA: inlay in various woods.

TAZZA: shallow bowl on a foot.

TERMINAL FIGURES (TERMS, TERMINI): upper part of a human figure growing out of a pier, pilaster, etc., which tapers towards the base. See also Caryatid, Pilaster.

TERRACOTTA: burnt clay, unglazed.

TESSELLATED PAVEMENT: mosaic flooring, particularly Roman, consisting of small 'tesserae' or cubes of glass, stone, or brick.

TESSERAE: see Tessellated Pavement.

TESTER: see Sounding Board.

TETRASTYLE: having four detached columns.

THREE-DECKER PULPIT: pulpit with Clerk's Stall below and Reading Desk below the Clerk's Stall.

TIE-BEAM: see Roof (Figs. 14, 15).

TIERCERON: see Vault (Fig. 21).

TILEHANGING: see Slatehanging.

TIMBER-FRAMING: method of construction where walls are built of timber framework with the spaces filled in by plaster

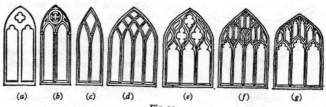

or brickwork. Sometimes the timber is covered over with plaster or boarding laid horizontally.

TOMB-CHEST: chest-shaped stone coffin, the most usual medieval form of funeral monument.

TOUCH: soft black marble quarried near Tournai.

TOURELLE: turret corbelled out from the wall.

TRACERY: intersecting ribwork in the upper part of a window, or used decoratively in blank arches, on vaults, etc. *Plate tracery: see* Fig. 20(a). Early form of tracery where decoratively shaped openings are cut through the solid stone infilling in a window head. *Bar tracery:* a form introduced into England *c.*1250. Intersecting ribwork made up of slender shafts, continuing the lines of the mullions of windows up to a decorative mesh in the head of the window. *Geometrical tracery: see* Fig. 20(b). Tracery characteristic of *c.* 1250–1310 consisting chiefly of circles or foiled circles. *Y-tracery: see* Fig. 20(c). Tracery consisting of a mullion which branches into two forming a Y shape; typical of *c.* 1300. *Intersecting tracery: see* Fig. 20(d). Tracery in which each mullion of

a window branches out into two curved bars in such a way that every one of them is drawn with the same radius from a different centre. The result is that every light of the window is a lancet and every two, three, four, etc., lights together form a pointed arch. This treatment also is typical of *c.* 1300. *Reticulated tracery: see* Fig. 20(e). Tracery typical of the early C14 consisting entirely of circles drawn at top and bottom into ogee shapes so that a net-like appearance results. *Panel tracery: see* Fig. 20(f) and (g). Perp tracery, which is formed of upright straight-sided panels above lights of a window.

TRANSEPT: transverse portion of a cross-shaped church.

TRANSOM: horizontal bar across the openings of a window.

TRANSVERSE ARCH: *see* Vault.

TRIBUNE: *see* Gallery.

TRICIPUT, SIGNUM TRICIPUT: sign of the Trinity expressed by three faces belonging to one head.

TRIFORIUM: arcaded wall passage or blank arcading facing the nave at the height of the aisle roof and below the clerestory (q.v.) windows. (*See* Gallery.)

TRIGLYPHS: blocks with vertical

grooves separating the metopes (q.v.) in the Doric frieze (Fig. 12).

TROPHY: sculptured group of arms or armour, used as a memorial of victory.

TRUMEAU: stone mullion (q.v.) supporting the tympanum (q.v.) of a wide doorway.

TUMULUS: see Barrow.

TURRET: very small tower, round or polygonal in plan.

TUSCAN: see Order.

TYMPANUM: space between the lintel of a doorway and the arch above it.

UNDERCROFT: vaulted room, sometimes underground, below a church or chapel.

UNIVALLATE: of a hill-fort: defended by a single bank and ditch.

UPPER PALAEOLITHIC: see Palaeolithic.

VAULT: *Barrel-vault:* see Tunnel-vault. *Cross-vault:* see Groin-vault. *Domical vault:* square or polygonal dome rising direct on a square or polygonal bay, the curved surfaces separated by groins (q.v.). *Fan-vault:* late medieval vault where all ribs springing from one springer are of the same length, the same distance from the next, and the same curvature. *Groin-vault* or *Cross-vault:* vault of two tunnel-vaults of identical shape intersecting each other at r. angles. Chiefly Norman and Renaissance. *Lierne:* tertiary rib, that is, rib which does not spring either from one of the main springers or from the central

boss. Introduced in the C14, continues to the C16. *Quadripartite vault:* one wherein one bay of vaulting is divided into four parts. *Rib-vault:* vault with diagonal ribs projecting along the groins. *Ridge-rib:* rib along the longitudinal or transverse ridge of a vault. Introduced in the early C13. *Sexpartite vault:* one wherein one bay of quadripartite vaulting is divided into two parts transversely so that each bay of vaulting has six parts. *Tierceron:* secondary rib, that is, rib which issues from one of the main springers or the central boss and leads to a place on a ridge-rib. Introduced in the early C13. *Transverse arch:* arch separating one bay of a vault from the next. *Tunnel-vault* or *Barrel-vault:* vault of semicircular or pointed section. Chiefly Norman and Renaissance. (*See* Fig. 21.)

VAULTING SHAFT: vertical member leading to the springer of a vault.

VENETIAN WINDOW: window with three openings, the central one arched and wider than the outside ones. Current in England chiefly in the C17–18.

VERANDA: open gallery or balcony with a roof on light, usually metal, supports.

VESICA: oval with pointed head and foot.

VESTIBULE: anteroom or entrance hall.

VILLA: (1) according to Gwilt (1842) 'a country house for the residence of opulent persons'; (2) Romano-British country houses cum farms, to which the description given in (1)

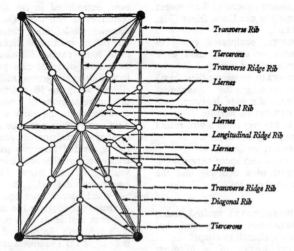

Transverse Rib
Tiercerons
Transverse Ridge Rib
Liernes
Diagonal Rib
Liernes
Longitudinal Ridge Rib
Liernes
Liernes
Transverse Ridge Rib
Diagonal Rib
Tiercerons

Fig. 21

more or less applies. They developed with the growth of urbanization. The basic type is the simple corridor pattern with rooms opening off a single passage; the next stage is the addition of wings. The courtyard villa fills a square plan with subsidiary buildings and an enclosure wall with a gate facing the main corridor block.

VITRIFIED: made similar to glass.

VITRUVIAN OPENING: A door or window which diminishes towards the top, as advocated by Vitruvius, bk. IV, chapter VI.

VOLUTE: spiral scroll, one of the component parts of an Ionic column (*see* Order).

VOUSSOIR: wedge-shaped stone used in arch construction.

WAGON ROOF: roof in which by closely set rafters with arched braces the appearance of the inside of a canvas tilt over a wagon is achieved. Wagon roofs can be panelled or plastered (ceiled) or left uncovered.

WAINSCOT: timber lining to walls.

WALL PLATE: *see* Roof.

WATERLEAF: leaf shape used in later C12 capitals. The waterleaf is a broad, unribbed, tapering leaf curving up towards the angle of the abacus and turned in at the top (Fig. 22).

Fig. 22

WEALDEN HOUSE: timber-framed house with the hall in the centre and wings projecting only slightly and only on the jutting upper floor. The roof, however, runs through without a break between wings and hall, and the eaves of the hall part are therefore exceptionally deep. They are supported by diagonal, usually curved, braces starting from the short inner sides of the overhanging wings and rising parallel with the front wall of the hall towards the centre of the eaves.

WEATHERBOARDING: overlapping horizontal boards, covering a timber-framed wall.

WEATHERING: sloped horizontal surface on sills, buttresses, etc., to throw off water.

WEEPERS: small figures placed in niches along the sides of some medieval tombs (also called Mourners).

WHEEL WINDOW: *see* Rose Window.

INDEX OF PLATES

INDEX OF ARTISTS

INDEX OF PLACES

ADDENDA
(AUGUST 1965)

pp. 55 and 147 [Abingdon, The Chequer, and Great Coxwell barn.] In their excellent paper in *Medieval Archaeology*, vol. 8, 1964, Messrs J. M. Fletcher and P. S. Spokes discuss crown-post roofs, i.e. roofs in which the kingpost is replaced by, as it were, a kingpost truncated at the level of the collar-beam. Some of their findings could already be incorporated in the text, but in addition attention must be drawn to the Abingdon Chequer (p. 55), whose roofing is of *c.* 1340, and to the explanation of the grandeur of the Great Coxwell barn (p. 147) by the fact of Great Coxwell Manor belonging to the Cistercian Abbey of Beaulieu in Hampshire.

The following additions were very generously communicated to me by Mr Paul Thompson, who is working on a Butterfield biography.

p. 68 [Ascot Priory.] Mr Thompson gives the date of the chapel as 1885.

p. 75 [Avington.] The church was restored by *Butterfield* in 1847, and he also designed at the same time the former RECTORY opposite the church.

p. 84 [Beech Hill.] The PARSONAGE is by *Butterfield* too.

p. 166 [Letcombe Bassett.] SCHOOL. By *Butterfield*. *c.* 1860.

p. 214 [Shaw.] SHAW–CUM–DONNINGTON SCHOOL. 1875 by *Butterfield*; master's house 1883.

p. 254 [Wantage, King Alfred Grammar School.] The back buildings are by *Butterfield*, 1872.